A. J. H. Duganne

Camps and prisons

Twenty months in the Department of the Gulf

A. J. H. Duganne

Camps and prisons
Twenty months in the Department of the Gulf

ISBN/EAN: 9783744748964

Printed in Europe, USA, Canada, Australia, Japan

Cover: Foto ©ninafisch / pixelio.de

More available books at **www.hansebooks.com**

Camps and Prisons.

TWENTY MONTHS

IN THE

DEPARTMENT OF THE GULF.

BY

A. J. H. DUGANNE,

AUTHOR OF "A HISTORY OF GOVERNMENTS;" "FOOTPRINTS OF HEROISM;" "WAR
IN EUROPE;" "A COMPREHENSIVE SUMMARY OF HISTORY;" ETC. ETC.

SECOND EDITION.

NEW YORK:
J. P. ROBENS, PUBLISHER,
37 PARK ROW.
1865.

INDEX OF CHAPTERS.

INTRODUCTION.

The Writing and Publication of the following work result from a promise made by the Author to his comrades in exile as prisoners-of-war, to imbody certain interesting occurrences of CAMP and PRISON life, in a form which might recall mutual experiences and friendship. A review of leading incidents and affairs in the DEPARTMENT OF THE GULF,—during 1863-'4 — becomes necessarily interwoven with the narrative. Personal statements and actual observations have alone furnished material for the book.

TWENTY MONTHS

IN THE

DEPARTMENT OF THE GULF.

CHAPTER I.

SEA AND LAND.

STORM and cold drift, with clouds of midnight, into
far-away fog-banks of Labrador. Our good ship skims
over Southern waves, and leaps before the "trades,"
for her haven in wide-rolling Mississippi. So, lying
languid on quarter-deck, in golden sunshine, I dreamily
remember long hours of state-room torture, endured
while sea-sickness crouched upon my breast like the
nightmare, and I would have bartered untold galleons
of treasure, and fleets of golden-fleeced argosies, for a
single gulp of greenwood air and a couch on terra
firma. Now, thanks be to smoother seas, and a balmy
foretaste of Southland, I feel neither burning nausea
nor blinding vertigo, and can look down upon silver-
winged nautili, and watch the polychrome scales of
dolphins and quick-flashing fins of flying-fish, with serene self-consciousness of "getting on nicely," as our
surgeon saith.

So, then, over these gleaming waters, from day-spring
till starlight, we look placidly into ever-receding hori-
zons of cloudless azure. Some of us while the hours
with books, and others tramp the deck, or lounge upon

the quarter, or haply doze through dream-land, from
eight bells to dinner-time, and " so to bed," as ancient
Pepys hath it. In good time, at morning watches,
" Uncle John," my color-captain, dog-ears *Les Miserables*, and (not .in good time) his cabin-comrade, Captain T., blows bugle-blasts that make *les miserables*
of all of us. Meantime, perhaps, my burly chaplain
spreads his ample base upon a corner of my wolf-robe
carpet, and anon comes Captain McL., of " Massachusetts Fourth," brainful of mathematic lore, to start
conjecture as to the latitude of pirate Semmes and his
ubiquitous Alabama. Suddenly " Sail ho ! " startles us
into animation ; and the shrouds get presently black
and blue with eruption of Sambos and sailors, crowding and chattering, while bunks and berths give up
their sleepers to share the new sensation. " Two
things," said Fanny Osgood :

> " Two things break the monotony
>   Of an Atlantic trip ;
>   Sometimes, alas ! we ship a sea,
>   And sometimes—*see a ship !* "

But our nautical cousin turns out to be some harmless merchantman, and no terrible " 290 " this time ;
whereupon, "Uncle John" and his lieutenant, " the
Buffer," proceed to light their meerschaums, and the
captains of hundreds, and their brave subalterns in
command of squads and detachments, and all gallant
adjutants, quartermasters, commissaries, and convalescents, take heart of grace, and descend to mess-
tables, whence smell of savory sea-meâts ariseth aroma-
tically.

Long since, on starboard quarter, we saw the crest
of Abaco Island sinking behind sun-tinted wave-comb-

ings, and looked back upon the "Hole in the Wall," bathed in ruddy glory, like painted oriel of some ocean cathedral. We are racing now, at twelve knots, with bountiful trade-wind stiffening our piles of canvas, till the ship rides on even keel, and her topsails are poised like sea-gulls. Thus, buoyantly, till land looms hazily over our bows, and the Floridas fling out their sand-tretches to greet us; and so, south-westerly, through far-flashing gulf waters, till beaches and bars lie low before us, and we furl sails, at night, by the Pass à l'Outre, with turbid waves surrounding, and beyond, through sunset mist, a glimpse of that Great River, which the old Algonquin tongue called MISI-SEPE.

This storm-beaten pilot, who climbs over our wea-ther-bow from a frail shallop, that is wind-and-wave harried, like himself, might tell us concerning livelier times than this around the river-mouths; might talk to us of fleets that used to cluster at these water-gates, with freights of "gorgeous merchandry" from all the isles and continents. But he waits in vain, this " an-cient mariner," for aught save transports nowadays, with stores of shot and shell, and "villainous saltpetre," and that other war-material described as "rank and file." He piloted iron-gloved Butler over yonder bar-riers, some nine months since, and can tell us, if he likes, how Farragut ran the gauntlet of rebel forts, and gave back our starry flag to the arms of the Father of Waters.

But there is no call for pilot-yarns anent this brave old Viking, Flag-officer Farragut. He writes his auto-graph in "curve-lines of beauty," graven by shells and cannon-balls on rebel strongholds. Stout-hearted cham-pion of wooden walls, with honest, sailor-like scorn for all new "contraptions" of iron-clad rams and turreted monsters! So, hereabouts, marshalling his old-fashioned mortar-fleet, under hard-hitting Porter, and flinging some hasty armor of chain-cable over the oaken sides of his war-vessels, he pipes all hands to quarters, at three o'clock in the morning, dashes, with full head of steam on, right into the teeth of rebel forts, and gun boats, and rams, and fire-rafts, and floating batteries and all infernal machines of torpedoes and destructives and, at noon, looks back on forts dismantled, rams, gunboats, and batteries sunk or captured, and the old flag streaming over all, to fly henceforth while flows the Mississippi.

This was the style, nine months ago, in which bluff Farragut and Porter escorted Cyclopean Butler to his seat of government, the queenly Crescent City. No pilots waited clamorously on that fire-eating feat of passing Scylla and Charybdis in the shape of Castles Jackson and St. Philip. No tariff of port-charges, or rates of pilotage, at so much gold per tonnage, could have passed the Stars and Stripes beyond those frowning batteries; but little recked Farragut of iron-clad embargo while his keels could cleave deep water. Therefore, flung he his ships, catapult-like, at the rebel barbacan, and swept this Mississippi channel, as Van Tromp, the Dutchman, swept a British one, with besom at his mast-head. And therefore, also, our valiant leader, General Banks, under whose notable banner myself and comrades float this day at the Passes, has found it not so difficult to follow whither single-eyed Butler led nine months ago. No hostile batteries now hold angry parley with a Union fleet, and indubitably it is pleasanter to hear blank cartridges exploded in one's honor than to breast a point-blank shot intended for one's diaphragm. So, I felicitate the successor of

General Butler, that case and shrapnel are no longer used in Jackson and St. Philip guns, to greet a coming Major-General.

Morning breaks over wide lagoons and far-extending marshes. Presently, lashed fast to hoarse-puffing steam-tug, our good ship leaves Pass à l'Outre, and glides by muddy channel-mouths, till the Balize appears ; and thereafter we thump heavily over shallows and run forefoot into sand-bars, whence, being dragged away bodily by double tug-power, we at last slide safely into deeper streams, and thence past wave-washed beach and watery waste of sea-grass, and anon beneath the fortress-guns, and further up between rich banks of black alluvium, and, still further, dropping anchor under perfumed walls of orange-groves, beyond which shimmer roofs of palace mansions lapped in green plantations. So, haply, through vernal day and night, inbreathing sweets of myrtle leaf and rare magnolia bloom, till "English Turn" is reached, and we pass the battle-stone that marks where Andrew Jackson won his laurel-wreath.

It was a rare game of Southern "bluff" that gave this river-bend the name of "English Turn," so saith our ancient pilot. When Iberville, or his brave *frère* Bienville, or some other notable vassal of *le Grand Monarque*, first sailed down this mighty river from far-away wilds of northern "Acadie," it was only to meet a fleet of British war-vessels laboring up the channel, and already within an imminent league or two of a little French encampment just located near the site of what is now New-Orleans.

"Turn back !" shouted our Gallic explorer, hailing from his shallop-deck.

"Wherefore shall I turn back ?" demanded the bluff

English commander, who had been the first European to toil from the Passes up thus far, and who, of course, deemed the country discovered for his British sovereign.

"Because," answered the crafty Frenchman, who had never been below this point at all, "because His Most Christian Majesty, Louis XIV., hath prior suzerainty here, by right of discovery, and hath, moreover, divers fortresses above and inland to defend his right and ownership!"

"Say you so, Monsieur Frenchman?" quoth the Briton, quite non-plussed by such bold rejoinder; "then must I needs turn back, since our nations be at peace, and yours hath the prior claim of colony!"

And so, this simple Englishman turned back, with all his caravels, through the river-channels which he had been the first to sound, and our shrewd Iberville kept his shallop and his camping-ground, and presently thereafter founded, just above, the town of New-Orleans. Thus, by a "bluff" game, were the British sent adrift, and this river-bend, where Gaul and Saxon met, has been known from that day to this as "Englishman's" or "English Turn."

And now, a century and a half since those French brothers, Iberville and Bienville, planted their Crescent City in a curve of the Great River, and only half a century since Andrew Jackson levelled his rifles on British lines, and saved this Crescent City from spoliation, we range our war-ships and transports, our squadrons and batteries, to fight once more the immemorial battle that the free must ever wage with despotism. Sleep calmly in thy Hermitage tomb, thou loyal-souled Old Hickory! Be sure that the conflict will still go on, as if thou wert here, as of old, to lead it. . . .

And the end will be that which Eden witnessed when
Lucifer measured his might with Michael, and the
Archangel's

> " ———— griding sword with discontinuous wound
> Passed through him."

For it is all in vain, this rebel strife of evil against
good; night warring sunshine; slavery fronting freedom. Our treason that hath sowed the wind, will reap,
ere long, the whirlwind. Satan stood awhile, we read,

> " Like Teneriffe or Atlas, unremoved ;"

but soon the season came when he and his infernal
host, constrained by wrath Divine, fell " subjugated "
back, till at the last,

> " Headlong themselves they threw,
> Down from the verge of heaven."

In the glow of sunrise, with aroma of tropical foliage
ascending, incense-like, from river-banks, we glide quietly past this slumbering empress city of the South. No
longer sitteth she girdled with fleets of ships and gilded steamers, as of yore; her lap of levées piled and
overrun with cotton-bales, and sugar-hogsheads, and
all immense and varied stores, tribute of half a continent, brought incessantly from distant interiors,
through bays and bayous, and by rivers and lakes, and
upon highways and railroads, and in wains and flat-
boats, and on cars and rafts, to fall at the feet of a
royal commerce which commanded all the world.
Drunken with wealth, at length, yet selfish with greed,
and insensate with jealous hatred of the North, her
benefactress, she cast her lot with treason, and " said
unto evil, Be thou my good !" Therefore, this peaceful morn, New-Orleans lies safe, but stricken, on the
bosom of her great nursing-mother, the Mississippi.

The flag which was once her pride and her protection, protects her still; but alas! she hath now no pride in it. In her arrogance, she betrayed that banner, and it is now the sign of her abasement. So she sits in her ashes and sackcloth, for a space, till anon these mighty waters shall be stirred above her, and this river of her sustenance will bring back to her bosom the offerings of other years—the freights of white-fleeced wealth, the treasures of corn and of honey, whereon she waxed fat in her prime, ere the evil days fell upon her. Will she profit by the past? Will she take warning from the present?

Thus musing, pacing with folded arms the quarter-deck, or leaning over taffrail, I behold the panorama of war-ships and gunboats and painted river-craft, and the far-between piles of bales and barrels on the levée, and the still city-streets, and the fields and plantations above, abandoned and desolate, unrolling gradually before me, till, at length, the mate's shrill treble rouses me from reverie, and I hear the sailors at the chains, and a sudden grinding of iron that tells of the anchor-fall.

"This is Carrollton," observes my adjutant. "Are the men to disembark, sir?"

"I shall go ashore and report. We will await orders before landing the men."

Dull and desperately muddy is this Carrollton, though, I am told, there are fine plantations still extant in the neighborhood. A railroad track of seven miles connects the town with New-Orleans. Here are camps and depots; and above, toward Lake Ponchartrain, some fortifications of increasing strength. A fine highway, called the Shell Road, intersects the village, and we new-comers are ordered to encamp on fields which border it. Meantime "the windows of heaven are opened" abruptly, and rain descends like a deluge. So, under "adverse circumstances," as even Mark Tapley himself might consider them, we disembark from transport, and go into camp jollily.

Now ensue great strife of tent-pitching in mud-sloughs and on overflowed bottom-lands; deep floundering of mules and commissary-wagons; swift goings to and fro of quartermaster and sergeants; terrible objurgations of truculent teamsters; curses, not low, of company caterers, over drenched "hard-tack" and ruined rations, with no fires to cook them withal. But at last, night-shadows fall; "tattoo" is beaten, and somnolizing "taps" resolves our motley crowd into sheltered soldiers. At ten o'clock, no biped walks outside the tents save rubber-blanketed sentinels, marching their lonesome rounds through wet and darkness.

Sunrise, or the hour for sunrise, sees me stirring, seeking a more eligible site for permanent encampment. Here we are all afloat, and likely to remain so, if these pluvial skies continue over us. Beyond our lines I see a cavalry-camp, with horses picketed in pools and puddles. At our rear, the Massachusetts Fourth lies, somewhat fenced from freshet by the higher ground it occupies. Just past the Shell Road, I discern a camp of "regulars," the men in ragged garb, and worn by recent hardships. They are the remnant of our gallant border troops, sold out to Texan prisons by a traitor, Twiggs, two years ago, and just released by cartel from their long captivity. So much for Carrollton camps seen through water-spouts. Positively, also, there is no prospect of our discovering a better camping-ground in all these flat lands; so I must even

compound with necessity, and accept matters as they
are till the rain ceases.

I retrace my steps after long search along the Shell
Road, past the dreary cemeteries, with their gloomy
cypresses, heavy and weeping; past the cities of the
dead, with mausolea of marble and masonry, rising tier
on tier, wherein are packed away the relics of mortality;
palace-houses for rich dead, high above swampy soil,
and safe from diluvial desecration; trenches and holes
for poor dead, below the watery surfaces. As in life,
so in death! Wealth to the high places—poverty to
the low ones!

CHAPTER II.

THE CRESCENT CITY.

CREOLES, contrabands, coquettes, coffee-distillers. Of truth, chaos seems come again in this mart of all marts, the French market of New-Orleans. I am elbowed by turbanned and bandannaed "aunties," of ebony aspects; ogled by coal-eyed demoiselles in silk aprons, and leered at by copper-colored *cuisiniers*, in cotton night-caps. I stumble over multitudinous egg-baskets, skirmish among itinerant orange-girls, tangle myself in labyrinths of nosegay venders.

Thus explorative and perambulant, through stalls and over crossings, and around impassable *trottoirs*, this blessed Sunday morning of February, eighteen hundred and sixty-three, I scan with wondering eyes, these human hives, and mentally ejaculate:

Is this an American city?

Peradventure not! Assuredly this market-place is of no narrow, autochthonic type, but polyglot, cosmopolitan, and carnival-like with.

> "Jews,
> Turks, Tartars, Yankee Doodles, and Hindoos."

Or, if Turk and Hindoo be wanting, and Tartars represented only by shrewish fish-wives, there is no lack, I aver, of as motley and outlandish moulds of humanity as ever wore turban in Stamboul, caftan in Ispahan, or sugar-loaf tile by the ghauts of Ganges.

And here, clustering, chattering, chaffering; here, light-thoughted, mobile, effervescent; the French and demi-French, the Creole, the Octoroon, the Quarteroon,

the Mulatto, and the sable-skinned, meet and jostle one
another, as they have met and jostled any and every
day during seven or eight-score years, since New-
Orleans knew market-places. Here bubble into noticeable upper-light the real undercurrents of Crescent
City alienism from Anglo-Saxon characteristics. Here
congregate mercurial natures, perennially antagonistic
to all plodding habitudes of Northern life — to all
gauge and plumb-line methodism of existence. Shrewd,
doubtless, these people, in their business ways—verita-
ble *bourgeoisie* in trade instincts ; but, nevertheless,
more given to stock and cotton-gambling than to
downright labor of merchandising, whereby our North-
men grapple fortune whether she will or no. Some
time in the future, when the lessons of this war shall
have been conned over wisely, there will be mixing of
Northern phlegm with subtle fluids of more tropical
mind and matter, and thereafter, doubtless, much
noteworthy vitality and strength developed in Southern trade as well as temperament. Till then, New-
Orleans, like her Gallic market, must remain *sui generis*.

Diverging, finally, from choked-up passages of traffic, and extricating myself from coils of muslin-capped
"bonnes," and paper-capped "epiciers," and endless
knots of Cubans, Mexicans, Nicaraguans, Peruvians,
Brazilians, Frenchmen, Spaniards, Irish, Dutch, and
Africans—all jabbering, eating, drinking, smoking, and
bargain-making—I cross the street, and drop presently
into the silence and solitude of Jackson Square, with
its fresh foliage inviting to shade, and its cool turf
tempting to repose. And here, with ancient recollec-
tions rising, like ghosts around me, I may muse awhile,
unheedful of the din and clatter of market-places, unmindful of restless crowds shut out from me by walls
of fragrant greenery.

This massive monument before me, with equestrian Jackson reining his prancing war-horse on its capitals, and that brave legend underneath, which stern Old Hickory's life exemplified—

"The Union—it must and shall be preserved!"

How effigy and inscription both rebuke the shallow Treason and Rebellion that are crouching even now beneath this war-steed's hoofs! But yonder French market cares less about Jackson than about Third Bonaparte; possibly ready, this morning, to toss caps for Napoleon "Protector," as it did, one year ago, for Davis "President."

This Jackson Square was the *Place d'Armes* of the *ancien regime*, sacred to reminiscences of Gallic chivalry. The antique cathedral still overlooks it, flanked by prison and court-house; and the bell that rang its founder's knell still tolls, each seventh-day sunset-hour— so I have heard—to call the priest below to offer mass for his poor soul who built it. Peace to his ashes!

Here, on river-banks were fought *impromptu* duels, melodramatically, with music and by moonlight. Here were trod stately minuets, in hoops and farthingales; and here were danced boleros, with tambour and bandolin. Here landed martial youths from France—adventurers in quest of fame or fortune, dreamers of El Dorados, seekers for Golden Fleeces. The ancient *noblesse* of those splendid courts which blazed around Fourteenth and Fifteenth Louis, were wont to send their scions to these shores, where they might pass novitiate of arms, in wars against the Indian kings and werowances. Rude fields of knight-errantry were here, in olden days, when Choctaws, Chickasaws, sun-worshipping Natchez, and other red-skinned rangers of the wild, disputed, step by step, the white man's usurpations.

This venerable pile overlooking me—Cathedral of Saint Louis—and this *Place d'Armes* wherein I meditate—what stories they might tell of *fêtes* and gay assemblages, and grand processions, in the hundred years gone by since New-Orleans was sold or given away by France to Spain.   This mighty river, also, making crescent-curve within its yielding banks; how might it speak of Ponce de Leon, seeking elixir of life, and of brave De Soto, finding draught of death; and of stout La Salle, sailing down from his Fort of " Broken Heart," and claiming all these lands and lordships, from Niagara to the Mexic Gulf, as realms and sovereignties of Louis the Magnificent.

Then came the brothers—Iberville, Bienville ; opening the eighteenth century with empire-founding on this crescent-curve, and wearing out their lives, and dying, at the last, heart-broken, like their predecessors, in the strife with iron destiny.

Then Crozat waved his golden sceptre over the Atlantic, and would fain have mined for crown-jewels, and strewn them over thrones, and made his only child a queen to walk on them; poor Crozat, merchant-prince, who dreamed of rearing up an empire in the Louisianian wilds that should be peer of France its mother; ruined Crozat, who received the whole broad land by royal grant, and poured his treasures out like water, for its nourishment, till it brought him misery, as his recompense.

Then rose John Law, the indomitable Law, the very necromancer of all golden sleight-of-hand and sudden fortune; his glittering image of Finance, with feet of clay, bedded in Mississippi banks !   To him was given

the ruined Crozat's fief of territory; to him a royal
bank charter; to him the grand monopoly of a trading
company, with power to swallow up and dominate all
other companies in France! Then loomed up in the
eyes of men that giant bubble, that immense, unreal,
but dazzling will-o'-the-wisp, the Mississippi Scheme,
that promised to make every stockholder a Crœsus, and
to enrich the whole soil of France with auriferous
alluvion from swamps of Louisiana.

Truly, our Father of Waters hath had strange
foster-children in his day and generation! There is no
lack of romance in the history of those years when
Louisiana was a *protégé* of princes. Some time hereafter, when rebellion shall have been mellowed down to
the amber atmosphere of legendary lore, those ancient
chronicles of Mississippi realms will be delved for as
classic myths. Then, possibly, the wars of France, and
Spain, and Britain, with the old Algonquin races, for
this slime of bogs and bayous, will be harped upon by
thirtieth century Homers, and embalmed in ballads that
shall smell of nineteenth century mummy-dust.

Whether this *place d'armes* may then be bulwark-
ed in by cotton-burdened levee; whether the sable
helots that have toiled in field and ground in mill,
to build up Crescent City grandeur, shall have stand-
ing-room as men where now they cower as slaves;
whether, at last, the gold of freedom, fused in alembic
of battle-fire, and tried by subtile test of martyr-blood,
shall shimmer, thrice-refined, before the face of nations—may be, or may be not, a Sphynx-riddle, to exercise our skill at present-day divination. But, O Gali-
leo! the world moves! The Mississippi flows to the
Gulf — the Gulf-stream cleaves its ocean path; and
neither stream nor river can return again one single

atom of the dirt, the *débris* of a thousand banks washed in their watery courses. So flow the rivers and the ocean-streams of human progress, laving lands, and climes, and continents, and washing, mining, wearing off great banks of wrong, that nevermore can be brought back, while roll the waves of time!

I walk, pensively, from Jackson Square, pausing a moment at the gate, to glance at gliding figures of devout French Catholics, that disappear within the dusky portals of the old cathedral opposite — some maiden hurrying to early mass; some sinner to confession; some feeble grandame hobbling on her cane; some mother sprinkling little ones from font of holy water in the porch. Along the pavement, then, beneath the eaves of antique houses, I pursue my walk; perhaps with inward marvelling at the open shops, so novel to our Northern eyes; *boutiques* of jewellers, with flashing *bijouterie* piled behind plate-glass, and *magazins* of costly stuffs, for eyes of female sinners wending church-wise, and *entrépôts* of fancy wares and tinsel gewgaws; all displayed beneath the Sabbath sun, to tell a Yankee stranger that he sees New-Orleans.

I ask myself whether the influx of Northern soldiers and society fresh from healthful restraints and thoughtful of " steady habits," may not speedily have influence on these looser customs of a demi-foreign city. I am answered by clatter of horse-hoofs and rattle of carriage-wheels, as a *cortege* of gay-uniformed staff-officers in saddle, and of light-robed *demi-monde* in cabriolets, whirls round the corner, and away — to Shell Road racing, and, anon, to Sunday orgie at Lake Pontchartrain! I speculate not much, therefore, on good examples brought with shoulder-straps.

General Butler, in the past, I hear, was charged

with many sins by rebels and their parasites. I doubt, however, if that democratic chief did ever entertain such masques of gold-foil folly as now revolve around our two-starred (I had almost written ill-starred) new commander. Such dazzling double coils of gilt cord and red tape! such cyclopædic volumes of the art of war off duty! I think this Gulf Department must have store of "rule or ruin" in its future, if headquarters and its soldier-civic purlieus be prognostic of events. I fancy this Crescent City may, ere long, be a paradise for paymasters who, on majors' stipend, shall get rich betimes; and that quartermasters here, on captains' pay, shall win their Golden Fleeces easier than Jason did.

Meantime, the Sabbath wears; and St. Charles's Rotunda, prodigal of tinselled and close-buttoned uniforms, and atmosphered with light tobacco-clouds, looks down on jaunt of pleasure-crowds, and opens doors to welcome all who pay. Hotel and city — true coquettes of fortune! Both beckon and embrace the Northern stranger, while both are rebel at the heart.

But, thanks to Northern souls and arms, this great Rotunda is no more a slave-mart! Yon castaway block of stone, that once was pedestal for human statuary sold to highest bidders, will never bear its sable shame again. The padlock and the chain, the scourge, and yoke, and handcuff, and this idol-block, whereunto souls and bodies of a wretched race were sacrificed — thank heaven! they lie as rubbish now, cast out, with racks, and torture-wheels, and "questions" of the past, to be accursed for ever!

CHAPTER III.

ORDERED TO LAFOURCHE.

AN orderly dashes up to my tent, with missive from Headquarters. "You will report immediately to General Emory."

I sally out at once, and lose myself in darkness of boggy fields and foot-paths lately submerged by the rain-deluge. Nevertheless, accomplishing the distance between the General's quarters and my own, I present myself before him with due alacrity. He is a stern-looking man, middle-aged, who in his youth, doubtless, was handsome. Engaged with an Adjutant, inditing orders and dispatches, he looks up as I enter, nods, and points to a chair.

General Emory has a good record of past service before the war. He directed a military reconnoissance in Missouri and California, publishing a graphic volume of Notes thereon, some sixteen years ago; and his official reports to Government on the Gold Regions, and as historian of the Mexican Boundary Commission, are of interest and value in a literary point of view. So, waiting here for orders, I regard the physiognomy of my General sympathetically, both as soldier and author.

Camp gossip gives General Emory a reputation for rigor in discipline—painting him as a rough and gruff, bashaw-sort of commander; but I fail to notice any traits of martinetism in his serious lineaments. Curiously, however, an anecdote told by our volunteer "boys" about the General crosses my mind at this moment.

They had been demolishing fences, as usual, these brave boys, gathering firewood for coffee-boiling; and, as usual, likewise, those innocent sufferers, the "se-cesh" planters, had complained to the General of their grievances; whereat a special order issued from head-quarters. It recited the enormity of "depredations," the necessity of "inflexible discipline," the duty of officers and men to respect the "rights of property." It concluded by restricting all wood-foraging in future to the "top-rails of fences."

The boys found those top-rails very readily, we may imagine. In fact, to quote their own vernacular, they "couldn't find any thing else but top-rails."

"At what hour can your regiment march to-morrow morning, Colonel?" asks General Emory abruptly; whereat I collect myself, and reply pertinently:

"At nine o'clock, sir!"

"Very well! I admire your promptness, sir! How many do you report for duty?"

"Seven hundred, sir."

"I shall send you where 'Yellow Jack' may have a chance at them."

"We shall be prepared to do our duty, sir, wher-ever we go."

"I hope so! I have no doubt, sir! You will strike your tents and be ready to march as early as possible to-morrow morning, with two days' rations, sir." . . . A pause.

"Any other orders, General?"

"You will get them in the morning. Good-night, sir." (Giving his hand.) "God bless you!"

So saying, the General dismissed me, and I returned

to camp from a first visit to headquarters, and a first interview with General Emory. Next morning, in a dispatch by him to General Banks at New-Orleans, my command was noticed for prompt and satisfactory response to orders.

Great bustle of preparation that night among officers and men of the regiment; much use of "strange oaths," I fear, in connection with mud, rain, and damaged rations. Morning and nine o'clock come duly, but no orders yet. I dispatch my Adjutant to report at headquarters our readiness to march. Presently thereafter, Colonel N—— arrives at camp from the city, bringing orders for immediate inspection, preparatory to the making out of pay-rolls; a welcome intimation to the men of long-deferred disbursements. We hasten the ceremony, and get through famously; so that "high twelve" sees us ready for the road; whereon, rejoicingly, we bid good-by to Carrollton, and presently depart, carrying much of its saffron soil away with us, on boots and breeches.

Not off yet, however. Slow-dragging wagons, on miry roads, with much loading and unloading of regimental baggage, tents, ammunition, and the like *impedimenta*, protract time wearisomely, till it is dusk before our transport casts off cable from the shore, and steams, with freight of soldiers, down the Mississippi. Algiers is our landing-place, there to reëmbark on cars for interior destination; and, after tribulation at depot, and great clamor for absent railway agent, who at length appears, sleepy and snappish, we stow ourselves miserably in freight-boxes, inch-deep with mud and molasses-drippings, and thereafter are lumbered away by a husky locomotive on special train of New-Orleans and Opelousas Railroad.

Algiers is opposite the Crescent City; and this rail-road, having eastern terminus here, must describe nearly a westerly, or perhaps south-westerly, course, to its other teminus, at Brashear City, on the shore of Berwick Bay; now the outpost of our military occu-pation westward. General Weitzel, with about four thousand Americans, holds Brashear City, fort, and camps; while opposite, at Berwick City, rebel batter-ies are planted, with an unknown force of Louisianians, Texans, Arizonians, who maintain the Teche and At-takapas country, from Berwick Bay to Red River. .This Opelousas Railroad is at present a misnomer, whatever it may promise in the hereafter of Southern stock-jobbing. Positive drubbing of rebels, and much provost-governing of Franco-Yankee parishes, must be accomplished, before Union arms and arts shall reclaim that garden of Louisiana which lies between the lakes and wealthy Opelousas.

Leaving Algiers, and its closely-settled neighbor-hoods, we steam through leagues of fertile country, marked by rich plantation-lands, some desolate and weed-grown, others thriving still, with goodly surety for the future. We traverse parishes Jefferson, St. Charles, and Lafourche, stopping at stations guarded by blue-coated infantry from staid Connecticut, whose bayonets gleam at every bridge and platform. Here, between Raceland and Bayou des Allemandes, the guerrillas attacked a train, some seven months since, killing and wounding several brave Vermonters. It is to foil the plots of bridge-burners and raiders from the rebel parishes above, that constant vigilance is neces-sary on this Opelousas Railroad line. Whether such meagre squads as we have passed thus far, could be of much account against a rebel foray, may, at least, be doubted. Scarce one thousand men, attenuated over eighty miles of rail, could hardly hold their ground against a stout attack from rebels " to the manor born," who know each inch of vantage.

Suddenly a halt, and then a slow advancing over bridge-timbers. We have reached our depot of destination ; and I look out of car-window on broad expanse of bayou-water, hemmed by levee-banks, or either side of which are lower grounds, here cultivated, there a swamp or thicket. Near the railroad track are clumps of negro-huts, the homes of " contrabands," whose dark irruption presently fills up door and window-frames, and overflows upon the fields and levee. Here, by the station, are dilapidated warehouses, a tenantless hotel, once " fashionable," and, perhaps, a half-score straggling domiciles, fronting the bayou-bank. A quiet, dull, deserted-looking place, despite the transient animation of a train-arrival. But here is to be our camping-ground, and I hasten to reconnoitre.

It is the railroad crossing at Bayou Lafourche, where, dumped from cars, amid litter of tents, deal-boards, commissary chests, and boxes filled with ball-and-powder stuff, my moiety of the regiment, called " Ironsides," remains to guard the bridge and its approaches. Not unsupported, as it seems, however ; for just below the levee-banks are lines of tents, and the head-quarters-flag of Colonel H———'s regiment flaps yonder at an ample house-porch.

Lafourche Bayou is one of those broad arms of the Mississippi, which stretch out from its giant breast, be tween the Red River and lower lakes. Effluent near the " ville " of Donaldson, and taking in its course three other " villes," Napoleon, Labadie, and Thibodeaux, it strikes this railroad-bridge a mile below the last-

named town, and thence flows south and easterly, till
it debouches through Mississippi delta and is lost in
the mighty Gulf of Mexico. Hard by its outlet, lies
Barataria Bay, where pirate folk of old — La Fitte
and others " o' that ilk "—were wont to rendezvous.
Numberless are the secret coves, and hidden creeks,
and intricate islet channels which fringe the gulf shores
near these bayou-mouths ; and, indeed, such haunts for
water gentry are patent to this coast, from Mississippi
Passes to the Sabine bars that shift on Texas shallows.
" There be land-rats and water-rats—water-thieves and
land-thieves "—on all these bottoms and lagoons, in
spite of our blockading squadrons ; and, if "contraband " tales be not all apocryphal, there are cotton-
bales enough smuggled between Mobile and Galveston
to purchase stores and ordnance for the whole rebel
Confederacy.

In peace times, Bayou Lafourche was gay and Galli-
can with pleasure-steamers and watering-houses. Then
Thibodeaux, the parish seat, was a *distingué* town,
holding its head up among rural districts ; and its
wealthy creole residents and planters hereabouts could
sip their *café* and claret like " grands seigneurs," as
they aspired to be. But, " Helas ! " as Monsieur says,
with a shoulder-shrug, " la guerre ! on a changé tout
cela ! "

Very true, my dear Planters ! This war has played
the mischief with all your luxurious security ; but you
have yourselves to thank for the change, and must
needs make the best of it. That, at least, is the verdict
of my cook George, yellow in epidermis and African
in descent, who has lately emancipated himself from
some Lafourche " owner," and is quite satisfied with
his portion of the war-changes.

Half a century ago, this Lafourche country promised comfort and competence to a hundred thousand white men, who, settling here, with skill and toil, might build up homes for free-born families. But speculat. ing Capital came also to this treasury of cotton and sugar; and thereafter the curse of "adding field to field" laid grasp upon the future. So, up to our war-advent, the soil had been monopolized and swayed by Landlordism, with its huge estates and negro-swarms, while ignoble "free labor" yielded acre after acre, and foot by foot, till it is now crowded back into the swamp-bottoms, squalid and ague-stricken.

In their day, the planters of Lafourche have lived like nabobs. None dashed it with a higher head or freer hand in St. Charles's rotunda or *salons* of New-Orleans than the cotton or sugar lord of this favored district. None lost or won his golden *rouleaux* at faro, or sported his blooded horse-flesh at Metairie courses, or squandered his thousands on wine and women in the metropolis, with more *abandon* than your creole planter from the rich Lafourche, who counted his slaves by hundreds, and his income by tens of thousands. This purple-and-fine-linen-clad gentleman has come to grief since rebellion days, and of his cash, cotton, and "contrabands"—"helas!"— "the places that knew them know them no longer!"

Nevertheless, there be notable landmarks left of the style in which this princely planter flourished. You white-wooled patriarch of ebon hue, whose rheumy eyes are watching me, might tell brave tales of "Ole Mauss' Charles" and "Young Mauss' Henry" in the olden time. And yonder white-walled mansion down the bayou, bosomed in a grove of dark-green figs and myrtles, and bright-gleaming oranges, and clambered over by a maze of hyacinths and sweet geraniums, and hedged with white japonicas, magnolia-clumps, and trellised jonquils, kissing a dried-up fountain; if its walls could speak—this lonely house—what secrets of luxurious Southern life might I be master of!

But the old drivelling slave, and the palatial dwelling which his life-long labor helped to build, are alike abandoned by their rebel owners. The maëlstrom of secession—dread agency of Nemesis for myriad crimes and follies in the past — has gulfed the barons of this haughty Southland, and their serfs alone remain to point out mouldering roof-trees of the ruined " masters."

I leap into saddle and gallop about the grounds of this "Johnson place." The flowers are choking under grasp of rank weeds. The rare fruit withers on unpruned limbs. The garden-walks are tangled, and a garden-roller, in my path, is overrun with wild honeysuckles. Grass grows stirrup-high on the once beautiful lawn.

Out over the fields, with slackened bridle, I pursue the plantation-road, passing through miles of rotting cane, decadence of ungathered crops. I reach the negro-quarter, with its compact hamlet, and pass the mill and sugar-houses, with their ponderous machinery, vats, and *bagasse* troughs. It is all *bagasse* now; all refuse and rubbish of the past.

An aged black is sunning himself at a hut-door, and rises, with a polite bow, as I draw rein before him.

"What is your name, Uncle?" (All old negro men are "uncles" in this country.)

"Antoine, sah."

"Do you belong to this place, Antoine?"

"Yes, sah—I stops har! me an' de ole Aunty."

" Did you live long with Mr. Johnson? "

" Yes, mauss'—shore I did ! I lib'd har with Mauss' Johnsing—dat was 'fore he run'd away, sah; 'fore de missis run'd away, sah!' "

" How old are you, Uncle? "

" Dunno zackly, mauss." I'ze a berry old nigger — shore! "

" How many of your people are living here? "

" 'Clare I dunno zackly, sah! Dar's a heap o' ole darkies t'oder side de cane, sah!' "

I ride on, past the sheds and out-buildings. Doors are swinging from jambs; roofs are falling in. Through broken window of the sugar-house I see huge vats, half filled with molasses—thousands of gallons—soured and crusted with dust. A plough, nearly buried in sand, is climbed over by tough grass, like the garden-roller which I noticed near the "great house." All things smell of neglect.

Another gray-wooled negro approaches. He holds his hat in hand, discovering a wide forehead, strongly marked features, intelligent eyes. I inquire his name, and learn that he is known as "Uncle Phil;" that he is a plantation-preacher; that he was formerly a slave and overseer's assistant on the Johnson estate.

" You must know all about the place then, Uncle Phil? "

" Yes, sah!" (Uncle Phil speaks good English, with but little twang of negro *patois*.) " I've lived in this Lafourche country sixty years, sah. It was a grand country for rich white people, sah! "

" You were an old servant of Colonel Johnson, I suppose."

" I was one of his SLAVES, sah!" rejoined Uncle Phil in an impressive tone, as he looked up at me.

"Was the Colonel a good master, Uncle Phil?"

"As far as slavery let him be, sah!" answered the old negro in his self-possessed way, that seemed to assert a conscious but suppressed power in the speaker. I began to get interested in my colloquist, and, beckoning a woolly-pated urchin from one of the cabin-doors, threw the bridle of my horse to him, while I dismounted beside Uncle Phil.

"You are so well acquainted with the plantation," I said, "it would gratify me to walk about with you."

Uncle Phil touched his weather-stained palmetto hat, and led the way through stacks of out-houses, from saw-mill to sugar-mill, displaying to my interested gaze the troughs, the coolers, vacuum-pans, and mighty iron kettles, the reservoir of syrup, piles of hogsheads, damp with mould, the broken cane-wagons, the shattered "carrier" that once bore its saccharine freight from field to engine-house.

"You understand this business well, Uncle Phil," I remarked, while listening to the negro's brief and lucid explanations of the complicated sugar-working process.

"I was sugar-maker here for many a year, sah," answered Uncle Phil.

"You could carry on a sugar-plantation yourself," I suggested.

"I think so," responded the old man, quickly; "at least, so far as sugar-making goes; I understand *that*, sah."

I looked about me over wildernesses of weeds and parasitic plants that were invading the Johnson estate strangling its former life of bloom and fruitage. I surveyed the lonesome negro-quarters, the dismantled enginery, the fast-decaying sugar-mill. I recalled the fact, that thousands of such broad plantations, with their wealth of soil and means of facile labor, were, like this one, given over to destruction; while the toiling people who had made them Edens of productiveness, were cast out on the highways or compelled, like Uncle Phil, to eke out bare existence on the scanty promise of a stunted corn-crop.

I hazarded another conjecture: that Uncle Phil might manage a hundred of his fellow-laborers without using whip or stocks; and that he could, peradventure, make as much sugar with them as his quondam owner did in "flush times" of Lafourche parish.

The negro turned, and steadily met my glance. "I think, sah," he replied, "that a hundred MEN might do as much as a hundred SLAVES!"

"You suppose, then, that emancipated slaves could carry on the labors of these plantations now lying idle?"

"Give us the chance, sah!" cried Uncle Phil, with sudden sparkle of eye and lifting of voice. "Give us the opportunity to do what we *can* do, and do it for *ourselves*, sah, and you'll know that free work is better than chained work! All we ask, sah—all I want for my people, sah—is to be rid for ever of—MASTERISM!"

It is impossible to convey by words the singular expression, the peculiar meaning, mingling scorn and hatred, which that one word, "masterism," seemed to bear, as uttered by this negro sugar-maker. For myself, I realized that a volume of abolition speeches might have less of pith and power.

And here I opportunely recollect that Lafourche parish is one of the "excepted" districts of Louisiana, wherein "slavery" is still extant and recognized by Presidential proclamation; so that Uncle Phil would still be slave of Colonel Johnson, should that gentle refugee return and make his peace with our forgiving Government.

Emerging from the ruined sugar-mill, I pass the negro-huts again. A score of feeble and decrepit blacks look out at door and window. They regard me timidly, but smile and nod at Uncle Phil with obvious deference. He is their preacher, their leader, their advocate, poor souls! who have no advocate or friend beside, in the great world of war and diplomacy.

And here, in spite of plausible plea of conciliating planter interests — spite of kid-glove fingering of slavery-issues, whereby the Louisiana of General Butler is to be made the Louisiana of General Banks — I think I see in Uncle Phil, and such as he, the real *sub-strata* of an honest governmental policy. I discern the "*juste milieu*," whereby these great estates, abandoned by their traitor owners, might be saved at once from greedy camp-followers and from perjured agents of their late proprietors. I imagine each broad plantation, with its vast machinery, confided to the hands which earned and paid for all the wide improvements. I fancy a "sugar-maker" like Uncle Phil still watching over every reservoir, and—backed by wise authority, assisted by selected men of science and of honesty—producing wealth for Government—large profits to the power that breaks his chain and gives him manhood in exchange for slavery. I see a grand militia, armed and drilled upon these green savannas; no longer chattel-souls, but conscious of their strength and numbers, marching to the cane and cotton-fields by tap of drum, and guarding bridge or railway line with ready rifles, and with surer knowledge of the ground than ever can be gained by Northern regiments.

But, this is day-dreaming! Who will lift up these Uncle Phils to independent toil while speculators hover, like so many vultures, in our army's rear? Who will drill these negroes into semi-military laborers on their old plantations, and make of them an "army of occupation" for the soil which white men shall redeem from Treason's despotism? I must suppress these fancies, lest I be accused of treason likewise—treason against the policy of "conciliating planters."

CHAPTER IV.

LAFOURCHE CROSSING.

CAMPED at Lafourche Crossing, I begin to look about me. Colonel H——, of Twenty-third Connecticut Volunteers, being senior field-officer of the troops guarding this line of railway, acts as Brigadier-General of the two regiments. He occupies a snug mansion, deserted by absconding rebel owners, and the tents of a couple of his companies are pitched around him. The Colonel is an active, efficient commander, comprehending his position and the people hereabouts, and placing as much faith in "professed" Unionism as the actions of those professing entitle them to command. He has a lively contempt—wherein I confess to share very heartily—for provost-marshals who hunt runaway negroes, for camp-followers who lease plantations, and for quartermasters who set up sutler-tents.

This New-Orleans and Opelousas Railroad—conducted under governmental auspices, superintended by a Federal field-officer, inspected at divers points by captains and lieutenants, who demand your passports, and watched by pickets and sentinels, who "present arms" at the bridge-crossings—is an expensive public luxury in these times of non-production in freights and of free travel in soldier-clothes. Its eighty miles of well-constructed track connect Algiers with all the back plantations, and in peaceful days they drained a country rich in generous harvests, and mobile with busy traffic. Thibodeauxville, the shire-town of Lafourche, was growing visibly before the war; and even this dull "Crossing" was a famous summering-place, where steamboats, plying from Baton Rouge and New-Orleans, were wont to fly their gay bunting, and where sporting gentry came to eat buffalo-fish and drink Burgundy, while alligators splashed the mud beneath their window-sills.

Two miles upon the road to Thibodeaux, I ride past broken gateways, despoiled shrubberies, and dismantled outbuildings of an estate that was once a sumptuous residence, owned by the traitor, General Bragg. Both northerly and southerly from my camp are many noble country-seats falling to decay; their owners exiles in their native land, wielding the rebel's sword, as generals, colonels, majors, in confederate armies, while their families crave shelter in some district safer than their own from "Yankee vandalism." Misled and miserable people! their folly bears with it a fitting retribution. Betraying the government which protected them, they dared not trust their families behind; and so, abandoning both home and country, they invited strangers to their hearths and plunderers to their possessions. Yet, notably, I have more respect for these self-exiled zealots in a wretched cause than for a class of time-servers who, by the easy mouthing of a "loyal oath," have kept their fine plantations unmolested; more politic knaves, who, when secession flourished, were foremost of the herd that swore by "Southern rights," and vowed eternal hatred to the "tyrant North." Heartily do I despise, as I do most religiously distrust, such double traitors, who so loosely wear their sheep-skin of allegiance that the wolf snarls out beneath it as they crouch. But all these "oath-bound" patriots are to be "conciliated" by the kid-gloved scheme of mild manipulation now in favor with our Gulf authorities. These " Union men " are all to be " attracted " back by sugar-gilt upon the pill of Federal government. Unworthy policy, and doomed to be a failure ! The rebel viper must be grasped in iron gauntlet, and its sting extracted by a resolute hand, or burnt out, if it be necessary, by fiery caustic. These renegades, who buy impunity by an oath, are either true or false to the Union. If they swear truly, they certainly require no new " conciliation," since the government is of their choice. If they be not the loyal men they seem, but traitors who have sworn a lie, let them abide by it ; and if they will not, let them suffer for their double treachery.

My quarters at Lafourche are in the old hotel ; a ventilated building, whereof no door hath complement of hinges, and no window-frame can boast a tally of its panes. But there are separate rooms—some dozen ; and in each the wood-work of a once pretentious bedstead ; so that myself and staff have shelter and retirement.

Rearward of this palatial pile, the camp of my " command " extends triangularly upon a plot of meadow, skirted by a little " collect " of the bayou oozings, just below the railroad grade. Beside this sluggish sluice the " boys " have ranged their tents, built cookhouses, and reared a flag-staff, whence the Stars and Stripes wave gallantly. Intrusive water-moccasins, and other serpents of the Southern slime, are rather troublesome to bed and board as yet ; but soldiers soon get snake-skin belts thereby, and speculate already on prospective boots of alligator-hide, contingent on the visit of some " cayman " from the neighboring swamps.

Our surgeon, careful and discreet, selects betimes his

regimental hospital, locating it beyond the camp-lines, in that fine old mansion of the Johnson family. This Colonel Johnson, I am told, is nephew of the famous "Richard M.," who "killed Tecumseh," as the ballad says. He is in service of the rebel government, and upon his "place" are only left those few poor negroes —driftwood, like old "Uncle Phil"—who have survived their master's awful shipwreck.

Other human fragments lie in limits of Lafourche, however—*débris* of the old-time "masterism;" scattered or huddled here about the "Crossing." Their rude huts near the track, that shelter scores of women, children, and disabled men, are likewise marked, like shops of pawnbrokers, with dumb mementoes of a ruined "upper class." Old damask-covered sofas, brocatelle chairs, and rosewood bedsteads, tarnished now and broken; cracked vases, fragments of rich glass and China wares; torn linens and bedraggled silks, that once adorned the mistresses, now mocking misery in the hovels of their slaves. All shreds like these, of former luxury, may now be scanned and pondered over in this negro camp beside the railroad crossing. Men, women, urchins, huts, rags, wretchedness—the dust-heap of a worn-out "caste system" that never more will rise to rule again.

Orders arrive from General Weitzel to detail a company of my command for "provost-duty" in the parish of Lafourche; and so I send to Thibodeaux that "free companion," Captain H——, with valiant Dutch Lieutenant K——, to quarter on plantations in true provost fashion. Sundry scruples have I, nevertheless; because this brave *garçon* H—— bears reputation of truculent "abolitionism," and I fear some outburst of his liberty-loving spirit may clash with shrewd "conciliation" plans of our chief General.   But here a skeptical staff-officer wags his head and smiles at my anxiety.

"Colonel," he says, "you think our free-tongued Captain may be too outspoken for these slave-lords on plantations."

"I apprehend his Northern principles and bold opinions on the slave-question may cause some rash explosion."

"My dear Colonel," quoth the staff-officer, laying hand upon my arm, "just wait a bit.   Before the week runs out, our abolition Captain will be hand-in-glove with slave-owners, and as tender-toned upon the 'divine institution' as the smuggest doughface of a Northern pulpit."

"You cannot mean that the Captain will abandon his avowed hatred of slavery!"

"Wait, Colonel, and let time answer.   If a provost-captain can be made from an abolitionist, I'll wager that a tolerable pro-slavery man can be made from the provost-captain."

And it turns out so.   My courteous Captain presently takes unto himself pleasant relationships with much-abused planters, and with widowed proprietresses of elegant mansions and sugar estates, and with ladies whose husbands and brothers are rebel generals, colonels, and the like; whereafter all awkward Northern prejudices concerning Southern institutions are gracefully waived in deference to that "good society" into which our provost-captain is post-prandially inducted, and the quondam "abolitionist" becomes *votre tres humble serviteur* to all the creole barons and baronesses who choose to smile on him.

I do not overdraw the sketch, O freedom-loving friends of mine who read these pages!   The entire system of provost-marshal rule, with its detailed regiments and companies, its plantation-guards, its rebel passports and protections, not to speak of vile abuses, covering tyranny, and theft, and frauds, and traitorous collusions, has been fruitful of the worst results wherever exercised in unrestricted scope. And of what restrictive power are written, sometimes verbal, orders, over officers whose very office must be more or less an irresponsible one, based as it is on military absolutism, and liable to be wielded for the personal ends of him who holds its brief but potent tenure of authority?

Here comes to me from Thibodeaux—from provost-marshal of the parish, ranking first lieutenant of some regiment, wherefrom he is " detailed on special duty "— here comes, I say, an order to deliver up a negro man or woman, servant of a captain in my regiment. The bearer of this order is a creole planter, very red in face and fierce of speech, who vows that he will have his slave by provost-marshal dictate and authority, whether I will or not. Behind him march two blue-clad soldiers, with the number of my regiment upon their caps, but acting now as provost-guards, and sent by one of my own captains, acting now as provost-officer, to " enforce " this order for delivery of a negro to the person who has claimed him as a slave.

"I vill have my slave," says the creole planter. " General Banks makes one grand arrangement — one Labor Contract — wiz ze plantaire! I sall keep my slaves, and ze yankee officier must return zem to myself—when zey run avay; when zey hide in ze federal camp! I comprehend it ver' well! I vill have my garçon—my slave, Colonel!"

"Very well," I reply to this excited gentleman, " what have I to do with all this ? "

"Ah! truly! you sall have me search of your camp! I sall find my slave and take him. Come wiz me, guard!"

"Not so fast, sir. I cannot allow civilians to pass within my camp-lines."

"Eh, well! Zen you sall command ze soldier to bring out my runaway."

"Pardon me, sir, I am prohibited by law of Congress from returning any fugitive slave to servitude."

"Zen you sall permit ze provost-guard to go in ze camp, to seize ze *mechant*, ze culprit."

"I am forbidden by General Orders to allow any violence to be used in reclaiming a runaway."

"But, *begar!* how sall I get back my slave, Colonel?"

"Sir, I am forbidden by Special Orders to oppose any obstacle to the return of a runaway. If you can induce your servant to go with you, of his own will, I shall interpose no objection. But there must be no violence used, you understand."

"*Milles tonnerres!* Colonel! you vill tell me one—two—three—several things! How can I see my garçon if I sall not enter ze camp? How sall I induce him to go back wizout ze handcuff? How sall I make arrestation wizout ze guard to put zis *maudit*, zis rascal, in ze stocks? How sall I make him not run away any more wizout ze flogging? Now you tell me, Colonel, no violence! Vhat you mean, sare, eh?"

"I have nothing to do with your domestic affairs, sir. My duty is to guard this railroad, and to meet the enemy as a soldier."

"But, *mon dieu*, Colonel, I sall regard zis Labor Contract wiz ze General Banks like one grand swindle

of ze plantaire! I sall make complaint! I sall pro-
test—vhat you call repudiate—zis Labor Contract!"

My irascible creole takes his leave, and the provost-
guards go back to their captain. After a few days,
I receive notice that a complaint has been made at
headquarters. General Weitzel writes to Colonel
H——, and Colonel H—— writes to Colonel N——,
and Colonel N—— writes to me; requiring explanation and defence. I transmit, thereupon, a communication to General Weitzel, wherein I assume my position
to be that of a soldier and not a hunter of runaway
negroes. I express my readiness to obey all lawful
authority, but claim that a special act of Congress
makes it a penal offence for any military officer to return a fugitive slave to bondage. I adduce, likewise,
certain orders of General Bowen, Provost-Marshal
General, prohibiting the use of violence in the arrest
of alleged runaways. Finally, I ask for General
Weitzel's opinion regarding my position, and soon after receive an indorsement of it, under that gallant
General's order.

But provost-authority, as exercised by venal or pre-
sumptuous military subordinates, is continually asserting new prerogatives. Here, one morning, comes
a planter from Thibodeaux, and with him a man in
civilian's clothes, to identify a laborer in the quartermaster's department, who is claimed as a runaway plant-
ation-slave. The negro walks into the highway, feeling
quite secure, because he sees no provost-guard, with
musket, ready to arrest him; but suddenly the pretended citizen throws off his coat, and shows a jacket,
marked with sergeant's stripes. Then pulling out a
pair of handcuffs, with his left hand, while his right
displays a pistol levelled at the negro's head, he bids

the shivering "contraband" to jump into a wagon standing near. I hear a yelling from the negro-camp, and in another moment, Colonel H——, of Twenty-third Connecticut, makes hasty rush across the bridge, leaps down upon the provost-sergeant, and with voice and arm uplifted, flings him from his nearly-captured prize. A chorus of exulting exclamations breaks from sable throats, and is echoed by the shouts of sympathizing soldiers on the bridge; while Monsieur Planter and his provost-guard "decoy" retreat to their close wagon, into which they hoped to drag the hapless "fugitive."

These visits of planters, provost-soldiers, or negro-hunting scouts, are of daily occurrence, and their strategies to snare the runaways are numerous. Occasionally a more high-handed measure is attempted. The levee breaks away, near Thibodeaux, and a call for laborers to stop the dangerous "crevasse," is made upon this post. Our quartermasters, at the "crossing" are invoked, to send their able-bodied "hands" without delay; so I direct a detail to be forwarded at once to the "crevasse." Meantime, the parish road becomes impassable, and planters rush about, complaining that their lands will all be devastated. At length a force of several hundred negroes grapples with the danger, and it speedily disappears. In four-and-twenty hours, the levee-banks are sound again. But it is now the turn of quartermasters to complain. Their laborers are missing, and reports arrive concerning squads of blacks, inveigled, kidnapped, and detained by planters, under provost-marshal's orders; while more squads are sent to jail, accused of anti-labor-contract contumacy. Here is another coil to disentangle. Provost-authority backs itself on General Banks, and points to orders based on his agreement with the planters; whereby every negro found upon plantations after date is held to have indorsed his owner's contract, and is henceforth bound to labor for a certain pittance, and forbidden to leave, on penalty of re-delivery to his master. So, then, these crafty provost-men and planters—taking swift advantage of the presence of their quondam slaves, repairing a "crevasse,"—have pounced upon the helpless blacks, and driven them within the boundary of "plantations." And now the cry of quartermasters for laborers, and the wail of "contrabands" thus kidnapped, unite their comment on the Labor Policy of General Banks; a policy which, though it be well intended, neither satisfies the planter nor protects the negro; which practically enforces thraldom worse than former slavery; which robs our army and our government of thousands who might win and keep the rebel country by their own stout hands; and which can never end in aught but profit to the speculating hordes that swarm about this Gulf Department, like voracious sharks upon the track of fever-ships.

CHAPTER V.

THIBODEAUX AND TERREBONNE.

I RIDE along the banked-up margin of Lafourche Bayou, by acres of abandoned plantations, through miles and leagues of ruined corn, and cane, and cotton fields. Some of the lands are still "squatted" over by ebony representatives of squandered wealth; gaunt effigies of wasted substance; gnarled limbs and roots of the great bohan-upas that has brooded over all this clime, and bred beneath it slimy coils of treason and rebellion. They are left, these victims of the Past and the Present. God help them! What shall be their Future?

Last night a pair of worn-out "man-machines" crept near our camp-fires—male and female octogenarians, waifs on the sable sea that beats incessantly upon the shores of Freedom. The man, with mumbling jaws, rehearsed his story. How he saw the sunshine first in Maryland; was "sold into" Kentucky; sent to field-work in his fifteenth year; hoed corn till thirty; meantime fathering some seven children; sold again to Louisiana, with his "wife"—their children being dispersed through all the South; then "worked" on cotton fields; thereafter in the "cane," till fifty summers more rolled by; and then—a Northern bugle sounded through the old slave's soul, and he became a "contraband," or "fugitive," or "vagrant," as our General's "labor-contract" might describe him. Twice seized, and twice remanded to his " owner ;" twice flogged, and once more flying from his bondage—at length, last night, he fell within these lines. I do not think that provost-men can take this couple without " violence."

These " short and simple annals of the poor " are better than statistics. I want no stronger witness of the bald injustice of all servile labor than the contrast of a master dwelling in his palace and the servant in his hut; one reaping riches faster than his lavish hand can squander it; the other drudging hopelessly from birth to death, with all his toil appropriated by an " owner," and with even the offspring of his loins " sold off " to swell that owner's hoards. This wretched slave of eighty winters—this withered pair who passed the hours of night in bathing mutual lash-wounds by the light of camp-fires—have little notion of political economy, and never heard of Adam Smith, or Malthus, or Ricardo; but the " male " can tell you that, for fifty years, he never was presented with a solitary sixpence by his wealthy master, nor received a single suit of clothing, summer or winter, for his toiling body. His master understood " economy," and had read *De Bow*, perhaps; and so he made the slave's " affections " pay per centage, like his limbs, exacting, as the condition of the husband being allowed to see his wife, who lived upon a near plantation, that the wife should clothe her husband; which she did for half a century. How admirably were the interests of neighboring planters here combined! The owner of the " male " reduced his chattel's yearly " cost " to just the " bacon rations ;" while the master of the " female " counted all the children of his slave as so much thrift; and " thrift is blessing, when men steal it not," said Shylock to Bassanio.

But now these old slaves look after me, from camp, with faith that I can keep them in their new estate of freedom! Their rheumy eyes already burn with the strange light of emancipation. O Liberty! incomprehensible, divine abstraction! I think it might lift even these worn-out "men-machines" high up among humanities.

I draw bridle in Thibodeaux, at headquarters of my politic captain of the provost-guard. No simple tent of line-officer, fronting his company-street, but a gentleman's costly mansion, shaded by fragrant trees, with lawn and garden shrubbery, and "grounds," and out-buildings, and stables for the "stud," which must be kept at call for provost-captain's service. Dismounting, stirrup held and bridle tended by a brace of unctuous "contrabands," I enter the spacious hall, and thence upon a drawing-room, where lolls one mild lieutenant on silk-cushioned sofa, and another thrums piano-forte, while their orderly mixes claret-punch in cut-glass goblets. The captain is on duty at the Court-house, where he occupies the Judge's bench, dispensing summary law on helpless sons of Ham, but listening graciously to "special pleading" of soft-spoken dowagers who "claim protection for their property." Meantime, the "provost-guard," a company of brave men, who enlisted for the battle-field, are quartered here and there upon plantations, to awe the blacks and hold them closely to the "labor-contract;" to protect the "planter's interests," by hunting straggling recusants, and generally to act as "overseers" in pay of Federal treasury. How speedily the soldier sinks into the satellite; how soon the guard becomes a jailer; how certainly the life of ease and indolence de-

moralizes and undisciplines the man, let army-lists determine

Thibodeaux has its nunnery and schools for Catholic
young ladies, and its sable-cassocked priests, like any
" ville" in France. I meet a singular procession near
the church—a *cortége* of some twenty mounted men,
escorting solemnly an open wagon, on which is borne a
little coffin, decked with flowers. They go to bury
some *petite enfant* in oven-tomb ; and as I turn off,
by the road to Terrebonne, I pass the cemetery—a
weed-grown space, with brickwork graves, like tables,
built above ground. Here are multiplied, in layers and
shelves, those mouldering masonry inclosures that contain the dust of generations. The soil of Lower Louisiana is no soil for catacombs. We walk above no caves
and find no grottoes in these bottom-lands ; we mine
no tertiary veins of lead or iron, quarry not for coal or
marble—all the riches here is mud, alluvion of lakes
and bayous fed by fertilizing Mississippi—the Nile of
all our South-west Egypt, which was a house of bondage, likewise, for its laborers.

Headquarters of the One Hundred and Seventy-
sixth are at Terrebonne Railroad crossing, which I
reach by horseback ride of four miles from Lafourche
via Thibodeaux. The distance by the track is three
miles, through a belt of woods and swamps, allowing
laterally not even a bridle-path. Here Colonel N——
has pitched, picturesquely, his camp, beside the railway
grade, its rear abutting on the shrubberied grounds of
an extensive sugar-grower of the past. I find the
Colonel in his tent, with Adjutant, engaged in ponderous correspondence on that never-ending theme, the
rights of planters. Here, in the regimental letter-book,

already have accumulated teeming folios full of ques
tions for the future, between capital and labor, bond
and free. I have more faith in war-guns than in law
canons for the ultimate adjudication of these knotty
problems.

Colonel N—— and myself mount horses for a trot below the camp, upon the road to Houma. Three miles
from the railroad is a large plantation, once inhabited
by Major Potts, a brother of the Rev. Dr. Potts, or
controversial fame. The Major, it is said, possessed
the finest library in the State, outside of New-Orleans,
and left it, with his broad domain—house, furniture,
crops, stock, and "people"—all to be the spoil of
squatters, provost-marshals, soldiers, and camp-followers. The negroes tell us how the books were scattered, mutilated, and consumed as fuel, long ago. A
solitary volume of *Hyperion*—blue and gold—was
found by Colônel N—— in a deserted chamber—the
last sad relic of that splendid private library.

A "company canal," now nearly dry and choked
with weeds, extends from Thibodeaux to Bayous Black
and Blue, and once sufficed as channel for the country
trade in Terrebonne; large flat-boats, piled with cotton-
bales and sugar-hogsheads, penetrating what seem now
but narrow ditches by the highway. The town of
Houma, twelve miles from the railroad, was quite an
entrepôt of inland commerce; and the bayou banks
and lake-shores of this parish were, at one time, lively
with the transit of deep-laden wains. This whole allu-
vial country is a planter's paradise. No richer lands
are found upon the continent than are embraced within
the water-belts of Louisiana.

The town of Houma—once a seat of aborigines, who

left their name to it—was noted, some months since, as
the theatre of a cowardly massacre, by ambushed rebels,
of some wounded Union soldiers, who were being
transported in a wagon through the district. The victims were thrown into a trench dug in the public
street of Houma. But iron-handed General Butler
speedily avenged them. He sent the gallant Colonel
Keith, with men and guns, to cleanse this nest of traitors. Keith compelled the Houma citizens to disinter
our murdered soldiers, and re-bury them in coffins and in
graves made by their own reluctant hands. He then
took measures of retaliation; burned the houses, su-
gar-mills, crops, and machinery of rebel sympathizers;
hunted the guerrillas through woods and swamps, and
levelled Houma jail to dust with battering-rams. Then,
hoisting our "old flag" upon the court-house, he demanded that the planters thereabout should pay the
charges of his expedition; then drove away some hundred head of confiscated cattle, and left Houma to re-
cover at her leisure. So much for Butler's notable
lex talionis.

We ride back, past decaying messuages, alight at
camp, to drink a dish of coffee, and then, remounting,
take the road to Thibodeaux, where the Colonel and
myself propose to pass the evening at our provost-
captain's quarters; for I had caught a glimpse of books
in that snug homestead of an exiled rebel, and desired
to spend a leisure hour with them. Arrived and seated, while our steeds are duly cared for, we get presently engrossed by teeming *portefeuilles* of engravings,
crayon sketches, and *etudes*, that lie upon the par
lor-table. Afterwards the library key is brought, and

we are ushered to a pleasant side-room, lined with book-cases well stored with goodly volumes.

Here is another revelation of secession folly and " midsummer madness." This is the private library of Squire Bush, a lawyer and a prominent States rights man of Lafourche. Surrounded here by every comfort, blessed with wealth, and more than commonly endowed with intellect; a wife and blooming family around his board; this man became a leader of the wretched horde who clamored for disunion. I apprehend ambition was his failing—that sin whereby the angels fell. I can recall his name, as noted somewhat in Know-Nothing annals; and doubt not that the " bubble reputation " lured on this husband, sire, and citizen, to stake his all upon the dice of revolution. So this night a Northern stranger moralizes amid the ruins of his household treasures, and the Yankee provost-soldiers stretch their legs upon his hearth-stone, unmindful of the lares and penates that should guard it. These shelves of tomes in divers tongues; these desks, and maps, and globes, and study-lamps; these red-taped rolls of manuscript, and pigeon-holes of pamphlets, journal clippings, club reports, and half-writ speeches; all the *opima spolia* of a busy mental life, are left at last to alien scrutiny—abandoned to the forfeiture that tracks their owner's hopes and happiness hereafter.

I grow melancholy over these relics of a peaceful past; I wax indignant with the thought that all this ruin was a suicidal act. What grievance drove the lawyer of Lafourche to treason and rebellion? What tyranny assailed his quiet home, that he should cast its comforts to the winds of civil strife? No chattel

could escape from all these labyrinths of swamps and
bayous; no abolitionist might penetrate these parishes, remote from Northern borders.   Why, then,
must Lawyer Bush play Catiline to his country?

I solve this problem at a later period of my Southern residence.   I learn some time hereafter not to base
this rebel movement on a negro issue only.   I gain,
with new experiences, an insight to the real cause that
underlies all seeming motives of the South in measur-
ing her strength against a government upheld by equal
rights.

Meanwhile, here sit we, hostile strangers from the
North, amidst the dusty lumber of a Southern home.
The family portraits rest against the wall, backs turned
upon us.

I handle many a duplicate of favorite authors in my
own home library.   Here stand, in line, battalia of
books, which show the classic taste of their collector.
The British Poets muster, rank on rank, some ninety
strong; the British Essayists beneath; and here are
Dickens, Irving, Cooper, Bulwer, Thackeray; with
hundreds, rank and file, of literary yeomen; and brave
historians—Bancroft, Alison, Guizot, Thiers, Lamar-
tine, Macaulay, Prescott, Motley, Michelet, and costly
books of plates; and Lamennais, Chateaubriand,
Rochefoucault; with seventy volumes of Voltaire, and
twenty of Jéan Jacques Rousseau, and . . .

I am alone among the living-dead, oblivious of the
dead-alive, who feebly, in this age of feebleness, essay
to wrestle with great truths, in cabinet or camp, kid-
gloved and shod with silk.   I fain would linger in the
company of stalwart souls that smile out of these
book-cases.   I think I could lock door and curtain

casement, sitting down amid these ancient friends of mine, forgetful of all outside drums and bugle-calls. How wiser had it been for Lawyer Bush, if he had barred his gates and ears against the treason that encompassed him, and remained "at home," amid his books and family, unmeddling with Rebellion's "perilous stuff." But he would not; and so it is that strangers tread his halls, while he must be an exile from them. So it is that I, like him, quit home and quiet study for the camp and hostile action. The sin and folly of this rebel, and of such as he, have sundered households over all our land.

This lawyer's reference-books, dust-covered, fill capacious wall-shelves, and are piled on floor and furniture in an office which he occupied on Thibodeaux main street. In all their multiplex authorities, all their precedents, commentaries, and annotations, he found, it seems, not one small text to warn him of the penalties of treason. Peradventure, this man had been a better patriot with less of law and learning. Assuredly, he might be a happier husband and father to-day, in this peaceful mansion of his, with beloved faces round the hearth-stone, and his old flag of stars waving above the roof-tree.

CHAPTER VI.

TIGERVILLE.

BRIGADIER-GENERAL WEITZEL stops one day at the Crossing, whispers into the ear of Colonel H—— that rebels are reported to be moving on the upper waters of Lafourche Bayou, and enjoins upon him to be vigilant here about the railroad ; whereat great preparation on our part ensues. We double guard, set extra pickets, station lookouts for the night. Some weeks ago, we underwent a midnight panic, when nocturnal wanderers in the shape of runaway horses " drove our pickets in," and divers rounds of cartridges were burnt, to imminent peril of all " stragglers." I have my own doubts now concerning the propinquity of rebels, but nevertheless take all precautions, and await developments, on my soldier's pallet, lapped in dreams of home and happiness.

" An hour passed on—the Turk awoke ! " It is no marvel that he did so, if half a dozen voices rang in his ears, at once, as they do in mine; announcing foemen " thick as leaves in Vallambrosa." I buckle on my sword and sally out, to find the camp aroused and under arms. Our quartermaster, very deaf, is listening nervously for a charge of rebel cavalry, while he supplies ammunition from one door and distributes whiskey rations at another. Shots rapidly follow one another from surrounding darkness, and gallant subalterns cry, Steady, boys, steady," and white-faced fellows circulate reports of "killed, wounded, and missing." Meantime, I light a cigar, and despatch "George" on horseback to Thibodeaux, to learn if provost-guard be still extant, and another messenger to Terrebonne, by rail and hand-car, to report the "alarm" to Colonel N——. I get my men in line upon the bridge and levee, ex-change a joke or two with others skeptical of danger as myself, and so the night wears on, and morning comes, and every body, glum and weary, goes to bed or breakfast, conscious of a quite unnecessary "scare."

Such incidents, diversified by out-post visiting, oc-casional scouting on the bayou roads, impromptu slave-hunts, with a week or two of court-martials, whereat I sit in solemn dignity as president, to try some tipsy sentinel or poaching picket—such is service at the Crossing, melancholy and monotonous.

At length, an order for removal. Guard-duty is to be divided on the road; my regiment to form a line of posts from Terrebonne to the front, at Brashear City; the Twenty-third Connecticut to hold all stations from Lafourche to Algiers terminus. I go to Tigerville.

To Tigerville: a quiet, slumberous place, at conflu-ence of two sluggish bayous. Near the station-house, by railroad track, the section superintendent — for-merly a steamboat captain—pleased himself, some time before the war, in modelling a dwelling after pattern of the river-craft he used to navigate. A stack of buildings longitudinal, with bows, and stern, and mid-ships like a steamer; with masts and flag-staffs, tower-ing over cabin-parlor, caboose-kitchen, and forecastle-cow-house; snug, unique, and pretty as a picture. Here the bluff proprietor drank his Bourbon like a lord; a staunch upholder of the Union, save when, now and then, " inspiring, bold John Barleycorn " put words into his mouth which sounded strangely like secession sympathy. Some said this worthy skipper's steam-boat-house not only owned two flag-staffs, but possessed two flags to hoist upon them, as occasion might demand. However this might be, no bunting flew from them but Stars and Stripes while I abode in Tigerville.

I pitched my little camp upon a narrow cross-road leading from the railway to a freight-house on the bayou margin. Near this, the barred-up shutters of a single-storied, many-windowed building seemed to indicate the shell of what was once a warehouse; but it proved to be a billiard-room, with table, balls, cues, chalk, and tally-board intact and tempting; whereupon my juniors quickly fixed their quarters in proximity, and an ivory tiraillade soon scared the rats away.

A wooden cot, or cabin of the " poor-white " style with room for bed and board, hard by the camp, be-came headquarters, where I stretched a mattress, and arranged mosquito-net. " George " ensconced himself in kitchen out-building, " John " made his dormitory in a closet at the rear of mine, and so my new establish-ment was complete.

The town of Tigerville was once, I learn, a busy set-tlement, with prosperous traffic gliding over its bayous, and radiating from the iron track which passes through its meadows. Two rustic bridges span the water-courses and the village straggling on each side of them. Left of the railroad, and between it and the swamps, the bayous and plantations lie. A signboard on the Tigerville Hotel — now tenanted by sable squatters—indicates the public road to Houma, east-ward, and to Brashear City, in a westerly direction.

Upon the right hand of the railway, there are open fields hemmed in by grand old woods, through which, with many windings, the road to Chickahoula, Terrebonne, and Thibodeaux conducts. From Thibodeaux, by the Chickahoula highway, or by a more circuitous route, *via* Terrebonne and Houma road, all travel from Lafourche once found its way to Tigerville, and so to Berwick Bay and the Attakapas country. The railroad superseded bayou roads, of course, for purposes of transportation, to New-Orleans and the bay; but these old highways, following the water-lines, with swamps, and forests, and broad belts of rich plantations as their background, are indispensable for interpenetration of the fertile parishes which stretch to the Mississippi "coast," and thence trend downward toward its seaward passes.

A stone's throw from my quarters, rises an Indian mound; one of the "high-places" where aborigines worshipped or made mausolea for their dead. It towers above the roofs of manor-houses, and looks down upon the negro-hovels like a mountain in the dead level of surrounding marsh and swamp. Traditions claim this country as the hunting-ground of Choctaws. An old confederacy of red tribes once possessed the lower Mississippi lands, beginning with the Houmas, near our present "coast," and numbering many clans whose very names are now forgotten. These nations built their forts from Bayou Bœuff to Red River, ranging across the Teche and Atchafalaya, and through all the beautiful Attakapas. They waged fierce war against the French for nearly a century before their remnants, broken and disheartened, migrated to wildernesses far beyond the Mississippi, and were ultimately lost amid the predatory hordes which rove around the bases of Sierra Madre.

I am speedily exploring the surroundings of Tigerville. Cool hours of morning, before ten o'clock, and evening, before sunset, are allotted to a ride through neighboring plantations. Mid-day heats forbid all outdoor locomotion, and at twilight rise the fogs and swamp malaria, laden with seeds of typhus and ague. A canter of ten minutes bears me to Bronson's mansion, long since abandoned by its owners in fee-simple— months ago denuded of its furniture by provost-marshal's confiscation. A robust negro swings the courtyard gate wide open, and a dozen sooty urchins scamper round my horse hoofs as I cross the lawn. The house is empty, doors and windows closed. Some old house-servants occupy the back-buildings, and are raising vegetables in the kitchen-garden, as of yore. They have retained a few remains of former household comforts in their keeping, white counterpanes and "quality" mosquito-nets, and pieces of choice china-ware.

Across a bridge, upon the opposite bayou-bank, are negro-quarters, and the sugar-buildings, with their rusting heaps of fine machinery. The slaves of this estate are mostly dwelling hereabouts, and working up the land "on shares." Left destitute by their owners, who abandoned every thing and fled before the march of our victorious expedition under Weitzel, these negro field-hands organized themselves in a rude "labor-phalanx," chose a leader, and took up the cultivation of their old domain, where "Massa Bronson" left it. They have now at least a moiety under cultivation, and expect to make a "right smart crap." The chosen "overseer"—a thoughtful-featured colored man, called

"Jim," rehearses all his hopes and fears to me. His "sociates" are "right smart" and "willing to work," and only want a "chance," but "Mauss Bronson, when he run'd away to Tuckapaw, didn't leave no stock on de place, an dar's a oveseer o' ole mauss staid yer, an' *he's* a'gin de black people workin' de place, unless dey give de craps to *him*."

"But how do you work the place, if you have no stock, Jim?"

"I'ze gwine to tell you 'bout de stock, Cunnil. Dar wasn't no critters on de place—mauss tuk 'em all away; but de Linkin sogers 'lowed us tree hosses, and we skeer'd up some old mules in de swamps out yer. Den we sot about gittin' a crap, but it's mighty hard work, Cunnil, kase de ole white overseer am a'gin de black people."

"But your master has run away, Jim. Government now owns this plantation. Your old overseer has no authority here."

"D-dar's de diffikil, Cunnil. De ole overseer's got all de pigs and de yerlin's, an' he sez de provost-sogers put him yer, to carry on de place, so dat we isn't no 'count whatsomdever."

I begin to have an adequate idea of the difficulties attending this "free labor experiment" organized by negro Jim and his comrades. Subsequently I ascertain all the points of their case.

These contrabands, it seems, cast on their own resources through the treason and secession of their master, met together and deliberated in true democratic spirit on their situation. The result was, that they "organized" for daily labor in the cultivation of a large plantation. They had no capital but their toil-hardened

hands. They begged some "stock" of passing soldiers, and a sympathizing cavalry captain gave them
three unserviceable horses. To these they added several venerable mules reclaimed from wanderings in the
swamp. Thus aided, they essayed to carry on the
"government plantation;" when an overseer, their former driver under "ownership," stepped in with new
authority derived from high permission of a provost-
marshal, sub-lieutenant of some regiment he had not
seen since it was ordered into service. Betimes, our
too-ambitious laborers of "African descent" discover
that their owner's representative is still their "master,"
ordering tasks, appropriating hogs and kine and chickens, and asserting generally his domination, as of
yore.

Here, then, a brace of "overseers," the white and
black; no great encouragement to present work, and
promising small future compensation to the workers.

For my own part, I sympathize with Jim and his
stout phalanx; but beyond this I am powerless. The
provost-marshals sway plantations, and are regnant
in all labor-contracts. Possibly, if I were martial arbi-
ter of all this parish, or of this broad belt beside the
railway, I might have a voice in "organization." I
would say to Jim, one day, that he could guard this
road at Tigerville as well as I can. I would bid my
commissary serve out rations to the man, and to his
negro comrades, men like him. My quartermaster
should supply them all with good substantial clothing,
for their quondam owner has bequeathed them only
rags. My ordnance officer should give them hoes,
carts, digging implements, and—muskets and cartridge-
boxes. So then, black-skinned overseer, called "Jim"

or any other name, with " gang," or " squad," or " company " of " organized laborers," WELL-ARMED, might constitute a portion of as good militia as this Opelousas road requires, for " home defence." I do not think the presence of their wives and children on plantations, worked and guarded by these men, would make them less efficient. I do not think a just or generous share in all the products of their toil would make them less desirous of protecting this fine country from the assaults of rebels. I dare surmise that these abandoned cane and cotton-fields would thrive as well beneath the willing hands of black-skinned soldiers, armed with rifles and supplied with ploughs, as ever they could thrive under reluctant toil of black-skinned Helots, with no interest in the land they cultivate. What says my overseer Jim upon the question?

" Yes, Cunnil, we is mighty sharp to l'arn—de black people is."

" Jim! how many black men are there in Tigerville, as strong and able-bodied as you are? "

" Reckon dar's a heap, Cunn'l. Mebbe dar's two hundred on Mauss Knight's place, an' de Hopkins place, and dis yer place whar we is, Cunn'l."

" Very well, Jim, supposing those two hundred men could learn to load and fire, like my soldiers, and were to have guns and powder a-plenty, and I should say to them, You shall have half of all the crops you raise on the plantations you work ; but you must watch this railroad, as my men do, and keep the rebels from burning bridges. Do you think you could do it, Jim?"

I wait for an answer, while the negro seems to ponder thoughtfully. Presently he appears to comprehend my entire meaning, for a big tear slowly gathers in his eyes, and his voice quivers, as he speaks.

"Cunn'l," says overseer Jim, "I'ze a poor black man! We is all berry poor and berry low, kase we was in slavery all our born days; but de good Lord 'lightens de black man's mind, ebber since de Linkum sogers come, and ———"

He brushed his coarse sleeve across his wet eyes, and stopped abruptly.

"Well, Jim!"

"Cunn'l, I'ze ready an' willin' to take de gun an' de sword, an' fight for de good cause. We.is all ready an' willin'; we pray to de Lord for a chance. "

"Jim, there are nearly two thousand of your people in Terrebonne parish, all strong men; do you think, if you were well armed, you could keep the Tuckapaw rebels from coming back and making slaves of you again?"

"Dunno, Cunn'l, de Lord only knows dat. But I'ze shore o' dis yer thing, Cunn'l, we'se all gwine to jes' die in our tracks 'fore dey make us slaves any more. De battle is not to de strong, Cunn'l; but gib us a. chance, an' we is cl'ar for you, Cunn'l. De black people is mighty sharp to l'arn."

I leave my overseer Jim on Bronson's place, and trot on toward the Hopkins mansion, to reach which I cross the bayou on a highway bridge, and, turning past a massive sugar-mill, ride in upon a spacious square, with well-built cottage-houses fronting on two sides. These are the negro-quarters — quite a little village; a picket-fence, with carriage gateway, separates the square from a capacious lawn, on which the "great house" stands; a handsome structure of the Southern style, with broad piazza and a pleasant show of breeze-inviting casements. Here is more "abandonment." The lower rooms are void of furniture; and an "overseer" steps out to tell me so, and to inform me that he represents the "property." A few cadaverous negro children and a wrinkled yellow woman are the only representatives of "labor" that I see about the premises. A few weeks subsequent to this, my first inspection of the Hopkins place, a tall adventurer from Tennessee obtains it, on a lease, from Government, and sets in to make a sugar fortune. The situation of this Hopkins place is very eligible for a speculation of the kind. Its works are close upon the bayou, which here broadens, flowing toward the Bœuff. A railroad platform is within a quarter-mile of it, and the highway deflects around its sugar-fields. The rebel Hopkins must have been a prosperous man ; and yet so bitter was he in his treason, that, as gossip says, he reared a gallows on his grounds, to hang the "abolitionists." His influence, doubtless, caused more moderate men, like Bronson and some others of his neighbors, to espouse the rebel cause, and, in an evil hour, desert their fine estates and happy homes. So Tigerville plantations lie around these bayou-waters in "admired disorder," tempting speculation from afar. Already do the needy hangers-on at New-Orleans begin to snuff prospective wealth without necessity of personal work. Before the year runs out, there will be "masters" in profusion for these tenantless mansions. What should deter our enterprising sutlers, and "resigning" officers from easy ventures in the sugar business ? "Security" is easily obtained, while Government contracts to furnish mules, and men to "stock" the lands, and even advances "salaries " for the patriotic gentlemen who hope to make their fortunes in the business.

And all the while, that great black human Force, whose life-long strength has been expended, for a hundred years, in servile toil, is reckoned in the "labor-contracts" only as the "stock," whose service is to multiply the gains of capital. No sound, humanitarian plan for lifting up this "stock" to manhood; no provisions for a future self-respecting peasantry, whose souls and bodies now are in our hands, as clay, to mould them as we will; no statesmanlike attempt to solve the mighty labor-problem of our nation's future; none of these grand questions are involved in "labor-contracts" and "plantation-leases." This is the day of provost-marshals and omnipotent staff-officers in unexceptionable styles of undress uniform. God help our country if no MEN come up, to take the place of girls and boys in office!

CHAPTER VII.

SPORTING IN A BAYOU.

THROUGH the morning hours, I have been exploring the mysteries of a Louisiana morass; penetrating regions of green gloom, gliding into cavernous wilds of filamentous vegetation. Seated in a canoe of primitive fashion, the hollow of a log, that packs my sides and limbs in coffin-like snugness, I have ascended miles from camp, under ghostly cypress limbs, and through slimy mould of rank confervæ.

Balancing in my "dug-out," I paddle slowly down the sluggish bayou. A summer sun rides near its zenith, but only straggling beams of heat can penetrate the over-spreading cypress boughs. The temperature is of delici-ous coolness; for shadows lie all day upon these hidden waters. Profound quiet broods over *marais* and forest, sometimes for hours, save when the flutter of a bird awak-ing from its noontide dream, or the occasional plash of an alligator slipping off the bank, makes momentary rip-ples on the stillness. The grey Spanish moss droops mo-tionless in long festoons, or coils fantastically over pen-dent foliage, shrouding all the life beneath with sombre cerements. Fire-blasted cedar trunks, grim and pallid, look out like ghosts at intervals, uplifting spectral limbs. Small breaks of sunshine tell of openings in the timber, whence come gleams of emerald turf and glimpses of in-terior landscape; lovely bits of light and shade, chequer-ed by wild vines, trellised over ancient oaks; deep nooks of greenery and labyrinths of leafy arches, curtained with a gauze of purple haze; and slumbering pools, bridged over by the cones of cypress bolls.

An alligator's shining crest appears above the water, scarcely two boat-lengths ahead of me. The reptile swims so noiselessly that no one could detect its presence by the ear. I level my revolver and send a bullet at his wake. The missile strikes, but glances from the monster's scaly hide as if deflected by steel armor. In a moment all the bayou is alive with saurian fugitives, startled by my shot. They show their gleaming vertebræ here, there, and all about me. A black, corrugated head has risen close behind my crazy "dug-out." I take quick aim at it, internally shuddering at the prospect of a sudden capsize into this "certain convocation" of wide-jawed "swamp-angels." Whizz goes the bullet, and I plainly see it penetrate the alligator's fore leg, at the articulation of the shoulder. He sinks like a log. Meantime a score of ugly shapes have reached the bayou margins; some are crawling over the muddy sedges to gain their "paths" to the remoter swamp. These paths or trails are well defined, and might be followed, were it worth the while to wade through slimy morasses. I empty my remaining barrels at the nearest marks, and paddle toward a cypress clump, to take an observation from some point that looks like vantage ground. But here my flat keel "grounds" upon a ten-foot alligator that has wedged his long proboscis between roots and bolls. My "dug-out" oversets, as the monster flaps his huge tail, backing into deep water, and I have a single moment left me, to spring upon a log imbedded near the shore. Here, with useless paddle and discharged revolver, I remain a cast-away, my "dug-out" half submerged, pushed off some twenty yards by the retreating alligator.

I find myself in awkward straits. I mentally repent

my recent "troubling of the waters." The log which
gives me foothold sways like a Mississippi "sawyer." It
is fast at one end, but beyond that end some twenty feet
of morass separate it from *terra firma*. The cypress
clump is only a little islet near the bayou edge, with
sedgy mire between it and the banks. It behooves me
to extricate myself, if possible, from immediate peril of
a plunge, neck-deep or lower, into Louisiana subsoil.

My saurians have vanished, and the bayou is lonesome
as before. Its leaden drapery of swamp moss; its wilderness of motionless leaves; its unbroken shadows and
unrippled waters; all are lapsed into the lethargy of
noon. I might stand shouting on this shaky log till midnight, with no other answer to my voice than muffled
echoes of the shrouded woods.

Steadying myself with the paddle, I shift one foot and
cautiously essay to plant it on a cypress boll. These
curious vegetative freaks, the bolls, grow clustered at the
foot of cypress trunks, emerging from the watery ooze in
conical shafts, shaped much like minie cartridges. It is
said that engineers have found them useful as foundation
piles, in road-making through swamps. However this
may be, I vouch for one thing from my own experience—
that to cross a bridge of cypress bolls in military jack-
boots is no trifling effort of pedestrianism. Hindoo
theurgy has a causeway narrow as a sabre-edge, for souls
to walk over hereafter. I venture to declare that cypress
bolls make causeways as precarious for bodily feet to lo-
comote. I shiver to recall the slips and slides, the shakes
and quakes, the knee-bows and back-crookings which this
journey over slimy cypress cones exacted of me ere I
reached a segment of the tree base that afforded solid
standing. Hardly was the feat accomplished ere I heard
a rustle overhead, and realized, to my horror, that I had

enemies to contend with, worse than alligators or the mud that breeds them.

I had gained a ridge of spongy soil clinging about the cypress roots. The gnarled trunk was thick with aged moss, which I grasped with my right hand, while my left held by the paddle, as a staff. The rustling startled me, and, glancing up, I spied the variegated body of a large snake coiled about the tree, not ten feet above me. And, looking down, I saw, so nearly in my path that a footstep forward would have trodden on it, another serpent, lying in convolutions, and apparently asleep, upon the dank green turf. A glance sufficed to tell me that it was a moccasin-snake.

I do not like to recollect the sickening feeling that for a moment came over me, as I noticed the two reptiles with what seemed a single eye-shot. I have a horror of the serpent tribe, and would rather face a battery than a rattle-snake. But here was no retreat. I could not re-trace my steps upon the cypress-cones. To jump into that gloomy bayou, and, perhaps, be presently entangled in the horrible subaqueous vegetation over which I had paddled my "dug-out," or to encounter, at the miry bottom, objects of I knew not what impurity and venom, seemed no pleasanter alternative. I had no weapon but the paddle. I could not strike one snake, even the sleeping one, without causing the other to attack; and yet I could not pass around the tree, upon that spongy ridge, unless I over-stepped the moccasin. And I knew not whether this cypress-clump, with its base of mossy peat, might not be peopled by a colony of serpents. I had heard of snake-dens in these bogs; of breeding coverts, where the copperhead, hooded-adder, and moccasin mingled their horrid progenies.

The time consumed while I stood motionless, supported

by my paddle and the tree, was very brief, scarce computable; yet in that instant these and many other thoughts gleamed through my mind. The sudden danger, promptings to escape it, and regrets at having provoked it, were reflected simultaneously with thoughts of home and consciousness of present surroundings. The bayou solitude, its shadow and its quietude; the thickly-woven green fronds, upon the water; the heavy grey moss on the trees; and, more distinct than other things, the snakes coiled over head and at my feet—were pencilled by a single mental flash. Drawing my paddle from the water, with a cautious hand, I released my hold upon the mossy cypress-trunk, and raised one foot to step across the snake before me. At this crisis something caused the other one to uncoil suddenly, and in an instant I beheld its glistening head and forked tongue thrust downward, while its eyes burned with a light like living emeralds. I felt a horrible attraction to return their gaze. I thought of stories that I had often scoffed at; tales of fascinated birds and children. I thought of Eve's temptation, and of Coleridge and the Lady Geraldine, and almost fancied, that those luminous eyes were set under a female forehead, and the snaky coils beneath were silken folds of a lady's garments, wrought in gold and opalesque embroidery. This spell, if spell it could be called, was quickly broken, as I marked the serpent's tail abruptly flung around a limb above me, and its crest curved angrily over a coil of spiral rings. Involuntarily I shrank from the threatened spring, and, as I did so, the snake suddenly depressed its body, darted out its head uneasily to and fro, then glided to a higher limb, and disappeared amid the maze of leaves and moss. Another second, and I heard a loud, clear voice, breaking the stillness, like a silver trumpet.

"De cane is in de sugar-biler—
    O de goold an' silver, massa!
Dar's a dollar comin' Christmas;
    O de goold an' silver, massa!'"

Plash, plash! a pair of paddles timed the musical refrain; and close beside my sunken "dug-out" I saw another canoe glide noiselessly across the stream, propelled
by an old negro, who was singing a plantation song. I
hailed him lustily, and bade him take me from the cypress
clump.

The son of Ham was dwarfish, thin, and dried as any
herring, and I doubt if there was skill or harmony in his
minstrelsy; but I never felt such pleasure in the voice
of Mario or Sontag as I did in hearing that grotesque
boatman. Hardly had his paddle struck the cypress-bolls,
when I stepped toward his skiff.

"De gracious! massa Cunn'l, is you dar? Lef' dat yer
cypress hole mity quick, sah! Dar's snakes out yer! Dar's
mocassins yerabouts, mass' Cunn'l!"

I took my seat in the skiff as steadily as was possible,
stretching my legs out, with a sigh of relief. Then, telling the negro to remain quiet a moment, I proceeded to
re-load the revolver, which I had placed in its belt-case.
I levelled and discharged one barrel at the moss-grown
boughs that concealed the larger serpent. I fired another
at the tree-base, where reposed the moccasin.

"Dar's snakes yer, sartin, mass' Cunn'l!" said the
negro; "dat's de cypress hole whar all de sarpints
come from. Hope some ob dem's done killed by de Linkum bullets, sah!"

A notable response to the darkey's remark was ob-
servable in the cypress clump and its surroundings.
The spongy peat about the central trunk, and all the
mass of tangled undergrowth which hemmed the water-
surface, appeared at once in motion. Overhead, both moss

and foliage were agitated, as if shaken by a breeze. A hissing, spiteful and prolonged, pierced through the mazy vegetation. I fired four charges more, in quick succession, at the cypress hole.

"Dem sarpints done skeered, if dey isn't hit, mass' Cunn'l!" cried the old negro, encouragingly, as he paddled his skiff away from the horrible locality. I did not tell him how "done skeered" I had been myself, a little while before, but listened quietly to his encomiums on my courage in exploring snake-haunts.

"If dey'm one sarpint in dat cypress hole," said the citizen of African descent, "dey'm sartin shore tree or four million. I seed dem sunnin' darselves, sah, berry often, when de bayou's done dry, out yer by de bolls. Dar's a ole gum tree toder side de cypress, whar dar's more'n forty million!"

I made some allowance for Uncle Bill's arithmetical mistakes; but assented to the main fact, that there were "some snaix," as well as alligators, in that bayou. Uncle Bill earned a dollar, and I am quite sure that I realised the value of it in my reptile experience.

CHAPTER VIII.

AFRICAN DESCENT.

THE sun sets. I have discussed the evening rations, and am sitting in my quarters, enveloped with smoke-clouds. My servant George kindles fire upon an iron shovel, in the doorway, thereby blinding human optics, in order to expel mosquitoes, that loom up in customary twilight cohorts. Mosquitoes, in this land of swamps, are not like our feeble insectorial phlebotomists of Long Branch or Cape May. In Louisiana they are the Mamelukes of flying tribes, charging at cavalry bugle-calls, and slinging dart and javelin with unerring skill into targets of epidermis. "Soon as the evening shades prevail," their sting is legion and their buzz abominable. In camp, our only refuge, outside of mosquito-netting, is in the pungent smell and dense fume of dry and fibrous road-manure. Formerly, the people hid from sun-down to "sun-up," under canopies and within walls of gauze; not nets for beds only, but pendent, likewise, over tea-tables, and closely circumscribing chairs and sofas. Thus girt in by bars transparent, one may tolerate these sultry summer evenings; but to be exposed, under assault of countless and ubiquitous tormentors, is what no man with a cuticle not quite rhinocerine could endure without becoming frantic.

"Some cullud gen'l'men desires to speak to you, sah!" says George; emerging from his cloud-compelling incantations.

I nod permission, and the "colored gentlemen" presently introduce themselves, with much shuffling at door-sill; five negroes from neighboring estates; all manifestly gotten up for the occasion. Their cotton shirts are immaculately clean, the collars of great size. Their Kentucky jeans, of many patches, are glossy with recent soapsuds.

"Good ebenin', Cunn'l!—Is ye in, Cunn'l?" inquires the spokesman, showing flashing rows of ivory, as he ducks his head. "Cunn'l, we'm's a delegation ob—ob—"

"Ah, indeed! What can I do for you?"

"We r'esents de cullud popylashin, which am libin' yer abouts, Cunn'l? We'se done heerd ob de prok'lashin, Cunn'l!"

"Oh! you have heard of the proclamation!"

"Yis, yis, Cunn'l—de day ob fas' an' pray, sot apart. We'se all cl'ar Unum people, Cunn'l, but las' y'ar we's all 'bleeged to keep de day ob fas' an' pray fur Jeff's'n Davis, whe'r'o'no; now dis y'ar, we's gwine to keep de Lord's fas' day fur de Unum, 'cordn' to Mauss' Linkum's pro'lemashin, Cunn'l!"

"How did you know about the proclamation?"

"De Linkum sojers down in camps yer, tole us 'bout it, Cunn'l; an' we done heerd one Linkum ossifer readin' it out ob de paper to dat yaller gen'l'man what cooks for you, Cunn'l!"

"Very well, my loyal friends; I see nothing to prevent your keeping fast-day, if you desire."

"Dar's anudder suckumstance, Cunn'l, which we'm gwine to ax you a favor fur de cullud popylashin; 'kase we'm a delegashin 'pinted fur dat same. You see, Cunn'l, we's got no house ob de Lord whar cullud pussons can 'semble; dar's no place fur to pray to de Lord, 'cept de cane an' de swamp; an' dar's a Lord's house ober de bayou, Cunn'l, shot up all de time, 'kase Secesh owns it, an' Secesh an't gwine to wush'p, 'kase dey'm 'bleeged to pray for Mass' Linkum an' de ole Unum."

"So the 'Secesh' own that little church over the bayou?" I inquired.

"Yes, Cunn'l, sartin'; 'kase dat yer church was 'rected fur de maussas an' missys roun'bout yer! I tell you de troof, Cunn'l, dey nebber let pore brack slabe gwo in dar, 'cep' fur to scrub de flure; an' now de dure am close', an' dey nebber gwos dar demselves, 'kase mos' all de maussas an' missys done run'd away to Tuckapaw."

"The church is never used now, you say?"

"Sartin' not, Cunn'l. Dat ar' bressed Lord's house, nebber h'ar de voice ob pray an' praise any more dar."

"Well, go home to your people, and tell them they shall have the church on fast day, and on Sabbath days also, if they promise to keep the building in good order."

"De Lord bress ye, Cunn'l! you'm berry kind to us, an' we's nebber gwine to forget yer!"

"I shall attend church with you, on fast-day, my friends!"

"De good Lord bress ye, Cunn'l! We'm oberjoyed to h'ar you say dat. Now, we's gwine to fas' an' pray, an' hab a joyful time in de Lord."

Betimes, on fast-day, Tigerville appears alive with peripatetic black people. Much tribulation and suppressed bile in planterdom; muttered maledictions, I fear, on galleries of great houses; scowls and evil glances under broad-brimmed hats of loungers on railroad platforms—all signs like these betoken under-currents of uneasiness in our small body politic. There is reason. Such shocking innovation on past conservatism as the opening of a meeting-house to negro worshipers, was well calculated to disturb the equilibrium of any parish town in Louisiana. But here, on Terrebonne territory; from old French times the bosom-soil of slaveholding oligarchies; here, where the chattel-caste has been lashed, chained, branded, yoked in iron-toothed collars, filleted with steel-spiked garlands, shod with shackle-bars; burned, starved, hanged, drowned, and buried alive; in such a paradise of bondage as this parish used to be; what cruel revolutions must have forced the way to such an outrage as is now contemplated—the worshiping of God by negroes, under roof-tree of a church, pursuant to "Yankee proclamation."

But the blacks themselves are troubled very little with the chagrin of their quondam lords. This "Lincoln Fast-Day," breaking over moss-hung swamp-forests, finds few workers on plantation grounds, within a half-score miles of Tigerville. Black loyalty asserts itself, militant against "masterism" and reckless of "labor contracts," for this day, at least. The sable pilgrims to our unpretending wooden temple, on the bank of Bayou Black, are no solemn-faced sinners, sackclothed and ashy, creeping along with unboiled peas in their boots. Clean-shirted, shining, jubilant, they come; in pairs and squads; young Toms and Jacks, with dusky Phillises and Dinahs; buskined and barefoot; capped, 'kerchiefed, and palm-hatted; hooped, ruffled, furbelowed, rainbow-hued; a "Vanity Fair" of holiday negrodom, arrayed in smiles, grins, grimaces, and serio-comic dignity.

I don my uniform; forgetting not chapeau and silken sash; gird sword upon me; and attend, for the first time in life, a negro church service. The scene is picturesque.

A small but pretty edifice, whitewalled and ornamented with green blinds, retires a little from the bayou-road in cloistral seclusion. Its open windows are surrounded by groups of negroes, decked with the gayest treasures of their simple wardrobes. Beyond, are oven-tombs, receptacles of prostrate frames that once were clothed with flesh and moved erect within these temple precincts. The mausolea are half-hidden under rank luxuriance of grasses, weeds, and clambering vines. Small clumps of violets and strawberry blooms are sprouting at their bases; green fans of dwarf palmettos, stiff and spinous, grow, hedge-like, round them. A background of dense foliage—oaks and gum trees, heavy with moss—thickens into the semi-circling cypress-swamp; and far back stretch wildernesses of unbroken morass, widening ever, until swallowed up by sea-side marshes.

The church is crowded; doors and casements choked with joyous black people. It is an epoch in their lives, this liberty to preach and pray, within church-walls, quite independent of an overseer. I sympathize with their blameless demonstrations; for I have heard of the thorny paths wherein many walked, in years gone by, to life beyond the grave; of scourgings, chains, and pillories for black confessors of Immanuel's name, who met in cypress-swamps and canebrakes, to exchange their lowly testament of Christian faith. I know that many of these poor worshipers belonged to masters who denied them even one day of rest in seven; that most of them were once forbidden to meet for purposes of worship, lest that ever-present phantom, Insurrection, might arise between them and the owners of their souls and bodies. It is no marvel to me, then, this great "joy in de Lord," overflowing from humble hearts. The day of Fast is day of Jubilee for them; Feast of Purim, whereby they commemorate a Great Deliverance of their Race.

Now arises, at the sacred desk, a patriarch of the plantations, bald and wrinkled, but bright-eyed. He has never learned to read the Word of God, but from his memory of Scripture texts collected during a septuagint of years,

> "He wales a portion, with judicious care,
> And 'Let us worship God!' he says, with solemn air."

I should fail to render, even with phonographic pen, the fervid language, much less the earnest manner, of this dusky preacher, holding forth to his fellows, with · "spontaneous, rushing, native force." No rounded periods, no flourishes of rhetoric, no well-culled flowers of diction, challenge admiration; but the utterance of feeling, clothed in rudest words, is often more impressive than all grace of oratory. He dwells upon the sufferings of his people, their years of degradation, their martyrdom to servile toil. He counts their manifold wrongs, and calls to mind their timid hopes, glimmering like swamp-lights across the dark pathways of past endurance; their feeble midnight longings, wherewith they evermore yearned toward "sun-up;" their struggling faith in the coming Dayspring, which was to "c'lar 'way all de fogs from de ma'shes," and "p'int de way out ob Slabery's swamp, to de green field ob Liberty!"

"Bress de Lord for his mercy, brudd'rin!" shouts the old man. "O, gib t'anks to de good Lord! Dis mighty Deliberance is done come yer at last; an' de paff ob de poo' slabe am made straight; an' we'm marchin' out ob de wilderness! De Lord bress dese Yankee sojers! May de angel ob de Lord march 'long side ob dem, with His flamin' sword! O poo' culled brudd'rin' an' sistern! nebber turn you' back on de Linkum sojers! Run an' do all de errands fur dem; gib dem to shar' whatsomeb-ber you'm got fur to eat an' to drink; nuss dem when dey'm done sick! pray fur dem ebbery day an' night, my poo' brudd'rin and sistern! After all, you isn't able to pay half ob de debt you'm owin' dem! Oh! you'm got a

debt owin' to dese Yankee sojers all you' libes. Dey is
done fotched de blessin's ob liberty to you an' to me, poo'
darkeys! I is willin' to wu'k fur dem! I is willin' to
nuss dem! I is wantin' to pray to de Lord, all de time,
dat he will stan' by de Yankees and gib dem de victory.
I is willin' to die fur dese sojers yer! Bress de Lord,
we'm all willin' an' ready to lie down an' die fur Ab'm
Linkum an' his sojers, dat gib us our bressed freedom to
wush'p in dis yer house ob de Lord, after we'm wu'k'd
in de house of bondage all our days an' y'ars befo'!'"

Who could depict the energy and expression that accompanied this exhortation? Perspiration trickled from
the preacher's every pore; large drops beaded his swârt
forehead, glittering like a nimbus. His withered arms
were flung out wildly; he bent his attenuated frame over
the desk, as if to reach bodily and enclasp his hearers.
Our soldiers, gathering outside the doors, were evidently
much affected by the vehemence and sincerity wherewith
divine protection was invoked for them. I write the
preacher's words; but I cannot more than indicate the
chorus attending every effective pause; a curious mono-
toned vocal symphony, which, like some long-drawn con-
gregational "Amen!" responded in a sort of humming
chant. The rhythmic melody of this low refrain of
mingling voices cannot be realized without a hearing of
it. It is not so much an audible syllablizing, as a suppressed hum, like inward singing.

PREACHER. Brudd'rin' an' sistern! we'm gwine to
praise de Lord for 'mancipation!

CONGREGATION. Bress de Lord fur 'mancipation!—
U-m-m-m-O-m-m-m-O!

PREACHER. We'm gwine to cross de Jordan, marchin'
troo de Land ob Canaan!

CONGREGATION. Troo de Land ob Canaan. U-m-m-m-O-m-m-m-O!

PREACHER. Oh! we'm happy dis yer day! Oh! we'm joyful! May de Lord bress dis ossifer dat gib us de church fur wush'p in! De Lord strengthen dat man's hand, an' stan' by 'm in de day ob battle, an' nebber, nebber leabe go ob him! 'Kase he'm de poo' brack man's friend, may de Lord bress 'm fur 't! May de Lord bress 'm an' stan' by 'm!

CONG. De Lord bress 'm, and stan' by 'm! U-m-m-m-O-m-m-m-O!

PREACHER. Sing a new song onto de Lord! Bress Ab'm-Linkum! Bress de Unum sojers! Bress de Yankee people! Glory, brudd'rin'! glory, sistern! Glory to de Lord ob Deliberance! Oh! glory hallelujah!

CONG. Glory, glory, hallelujah! U-m-m-m O-m-m-m-O!

And so the strange ritual of these blacks went on; and the church, so long disused, so long without a preacher or a prayer, was thus reconsecrated to the God of Freedom. I doubt if worship arose from any altar in our land, that day, more fresh and single-hearted than these orisons of lowly Christians, who were creeping out of darkness and dolor toward the sunrise of a future that shall know no bondage.

The opening of this tabernacle to negro worshippers did not please some score of property-holders, who esteemed themselves the "public" of our small community; but Sabbath-days in Tigerville were observed, thereafter, in spite of this futile jealousy. Meantime, my little camp began to have a history in plantation circles, and to be looked upon by the poor people as a kind of City of Refuge, for the oppressed among them. Many were the appeals whereof I presently found myself called upon to be the umpire; multitudinous the questions I was expected to arbitrate. Possessing no administrative authority beyond the pickets of my post, I could do nothing in a hundred cases where much good ought to be done, and much evil might be prevented under competent jurisdiction. There is no limit to the influence of white officials over these docile blacks, where once the latter's confidence and respect are gained. The common cant of harsh or prejudiced men, that "negroes are worth nothing without the whip," is merely an excuse for ignorance or tyranny I have the word of masters, who formerly owned and worked their hundreds, that the slaves accomplished quite as much where neither lash nor manacle was used, as where these were the only means of discipline. Our laborers of the south require not "mastering," but "conducting" As a race, they are industrious, quick witted, and faithful, where they feel themselves protected. Exceptions to this rule are not more noticeable in black-skinned peasantry than in white.

An old man comes to me, one morning, mounted on a decent pony. He has his tale to tell. His "missus," whom he had served for half a century, "got skeered" when General Weitzel's forces marched through Terrebonne parish, and she proposed a "labor-contract" to her nearly-superannuated bondman. There being no use for him at home, he was allowed to "hire out" to a neighboring planter, on condition that a portion of his earnings should be appropriated for the clothing of his wife and children, who were to remain in service with the "missus." "Ole missus drawed a writin'", said this simple black, "an' tole me fur to make my mark agin it—"

"But how did you know what the writing was, uncle?"

"Ole missus say its all right fur me an' my ole ooman, sah. Ole missus say she dunno whedder de yankees

gwine to make de cullud people 'mancipate, or whedder
we's to 'tay whar we is—She say, she 'fraid we's gwine to
be sot free, an' I'se berry ole niggah, so I's better go hire
out wi' Dutch massa, an' s'port myself, 'kase times is hard."

"You agreed to that, uncle !"

"Yes, sah! I t'ought I mought 'arn sometin' fur de pore
chil'n—so I'se glad, massa, fur to do mos' ennyt'ing ole
missus tell me. Den I 'gree wi' de Dutch, up dar on
Houma road, fur six dollar a mont'. I'se wu'k faithful,
sah, summer an' winter, de good Lord knows dat; an'
I'se done 'arn'd sebenty tree dollar, 'sides draw'n' seben
dollar fur de chil'n. Den ole missus come, an' try fur
ter git all de money, 'kase she say she make 'noder 'gree-
ment wi' Dutch massa. She say he done 'bleege to gib her
all de wage, 'kase de niggers not 'mancipate in Tarbonne."

"Where is the writing you signed?"

"I gib dat ar' writin' to my ole ooman fur safekeep,
an' de missus done took it back ag'in, sah! Ole missus
say dat writin' no 'count, 'kase de yankee gineral gwine
to lef' all de massas an' missys hab de slaves back ag'in,
jes' like ole times 'fore de war."

I begin to see through the difficulties under which this
"person of African descent" is laboring. His politic
mistress, anticipating the worthlessness of property in
slaves, had shrewdly bound her septuagenarian chattel
to an agreement whereby she could keep his wife and
grandchildren in her service at the old laborer's expense;
but being subsequently assured that no immediate emancipation was to be apprehended in Terrebonne parish, she
repudiated this "labor contract," and claimed the earnings
of her too-confiding servant.

Next day, a sallow white man, assuming to represent
the mistress of my client, arrived at camp, intent on "ex-
tradition." He laid claim also to the old man's pony,

averring that the animal was stolen. I called up the fugitive, for cross-examination; but his previous story remained uncontradicted. It was, moreover, acknowledged on the part of "the prosecution," that the pony had been given, while a sickly colt, to the negro, by his "young massa," now an officer in the Confederate service. "Young mass' reckon'd de colt 'ud die; but I jes' nuss'd it, an' 'tended it, an' de pore leetle cretur' done got well; 'kase I buy 'm de doctor stuff wi' my own money, what I done 'arn'd mysef, sah? I wu'k'd for dat colt, an' I wu'k'd fur de chil'n; an' dat ar' leetle hoss was gib me by young mass'—an' dar nebber was nobody on de place dat did n't know de pony 's my pony! De Lord b'ar me witness, sah, fur de troof what I say, sah."

So asseverates the "contraband." But as "a negro has no rights which a white man is bound to respect," my sallow-faced caucasian claimant continues to assert property in both man and beast, and presently blusters about provost-marshal authority, threatening thereunto to appeal; whereat I call a sergeant, of somewhat *decided* abolition sentiment, and quietly abandon the case into his hands; the result whereof appears, next day, in the addition of a new negro cook to one of our messes, and the purchase from that cook of a handsome pony by one of my officers. Meantime, the "disputed wages" remain in trust of "Dutch massa," to await ultimate developments of our conciliation policy.

My servant John, a sable valet, brought from home with me, presents himself one day, with aspect of deep import. John is intelligent, and has improved some opportunities of instruction. He is big now, with an educational project. He would establish a school. He will give lessons in spelling and reading to plantation children. He is confident of his ability to teach all he knows himself.

I inquire into the matter, and find that John has received liberal offers from heads of families. A class of twenty scholars is promised, and each colored father is to contribute the sum of ten cents weekly for teacher's salary and expenses. Will I give permission? John thinks he can do "a heap of good." He has collected a dozen spelling books, besides some copies of Soldiers' Hymns.

"Where did you obtain the spellers, John?"

"O, sir, a good many colored ladies on the plantations saved up all the spelling-books their young masters used to study."

"But they could not read them, John, and were forbidden to learn."

"Yes, sir—but you know, they 'spected to learn sometime, sir! They say they always 'spected us Yankees would come along, some day, and learn 'em to read—so, you see, Colonel, they saved up all the spellin'-books and bibles they came across, sir!"

"Go, and try your skill at teaching, John! I have no objection."

A few days after this, in passing by a ruinous warehouse, near the freight-depot, I hear a hum of voices through an open door-way. John has his school in session. He sits in glossy dignity, with a white paper shirt collar stiffening his ebony neck; a book in one hand, and a rod in the other. Under his vigilant eyes two rows of seats extend; occupied by sooty urchins, woolly locked and barefooted, of every tender age, from three year-olds to youths and maidens in their teens. All wear a serious air. Responsibility rests upon each laboring brow. These children of the bondman race, with ragged spelling-books; this sable teacher, but a child in years

himself; those toil-marked sires and mothers, bowing in
yonder fields, beneath a midday southern sun, to carn the
pittance that shall win their little ones a glimpse into
the realms of knowledge which have made the white men
kings and masters of this earth;—all have their mute
significance for me! To doubt that Providence is opening up a better future for the American Helot, is to
doubt that Providence exists.

From the summit of an Indian mound, within a stone's
throw of my camp, I overlook the rail-track, curving out
from eastern woods and winding into western morasses.
White tents, in two rows, with a street between, are
flanking the station. From a tall flag-pole, our banner
of stars is shining in Louisiana sunshine. Sentries are
posted on the bridge, at intervals along the rail, and on
the edge of yonder timber belt, wherefrom the Chickahoula road debouches on these Tigerville plantations. A
hundred of my men are at skirmish drill, between this
mound base and the road, and I hear the ring of Captain
Cutter's orders—"Rally by fours! Take intervals!" No
other sound disturbs the heavy stillness of a sultry day.
All things seem as sluggish as the bayou, covered with
its green slime of vegetation. Planter K— nods in his
arm-chair on a balcony of the dwelling-house just underneath me, and planter K—'s score of black-skinned field-
hands are bending backs in surrounding sugar furrows,
while a yellow "mistress of his halls and heart" sits in
the porch shade, gorgeously arrayed in gown of red and
saffron turban. This favorite queens it shrewdly over
old man K—, so gossip prates; and our soldier boys,
who often witness loud "intestine broils" between these
"high contracting partners," are accustomed to make comments far more apt than elegant. This planter's human

chattels had their private revolution only a few months since, when Weitzel marched through Tigerville. Some glimmer of "northern light" had penetrated that osseus opacity which Pritchard builds about the negro *pia mater;* and these rogues began to preach, in their rude way, the democratic heresy that "all men are, and of right ought to be, free and independent." The apparition of Yankee bayonets in Lafourche and Terrebonne soon brought about a "strike," and presently a "compromise," whereby woolly-headed Labor made pact with panic-stricken Ownership, agreeing to serve as formerly, on promise of a fractional share in the proceeds of the crop. It was a bold experiment on the part of negro proletarians; but I dare prophesy that "masterism" will gladly compromise with "chattelism" whenever challenged in a similar spirit. Shut up these vassals and their lords together in a populous slave district, and let "non-intervention" be proclaimed by all the outside world, and I venture to predict that Ownership will soon "negotiate" for its very toleration on the soil. Black diplomacy, supported by black courage, and enlightened by contact with bayonets that have learned to think, might settle all "labor contracts" on a sounder basis than our General's conciliation scheme. Nevertheless, I fear, under present auspices, that "ole man K—" will get the whip-handle in his grasp again, unless timely measures, such as strong-handed Butler knew how to inaugurate, shall once more dominate the labor question. Here comes to me Lucy, one-armed "griffe" girl, with dismal story of a night's experience.

"Ole mauss' tole me to mind de birds in de corn-field, 'kase he sez he got no use for me in de house. Den ole mauss' lick me, 'kase I isn't able to hol' de hoe wi' dis yer lef' arm. Den I hollered, an' old mauss' done put me in de 'tocks all las' night."

"How did you lose your arm, Lucy?"

"Done broke dis yer arm in de mill, sah. Ole mauss' hired me out yer to wu'k, an' de bones was all done mashed in de 'sheenry. Den ole mauss' got tousan' dollar damage fur dis yer arm I done lost off. After dat he cuss me, an' sez I aint wuff nuffin' no more, 'cept to mind de birds in de corn."

"Well, Lucy, it is not hard work to watch the birds. You can do that, certainly."

"Ole mauss' druv me out in de rain, an' tole me hoe corn, or I gits nuffin' to eat; an' den I try to hol' de hoe-handle in dis yer arm, an' de hoe done slip down. Ole mauss' seed it dar, an' he cuss me for foolin', an' lick me till de blood run; and I done got de rheumatiz, sah, 'kase de rain come down on de 'tocks."

"But your master has no right to put you in the stocks, Lucy."

"Ole mauss' carpenter, Joe, done fixed up de 'tocks. He sawed, 'om out ob gum plank."

"Well, Lucy, go back and tell your master that I say he must let you alone. He must neither flog you nor put you in the stocks. And you, Lucy, must mind the birds as well as you can. Sergeant D——, go with this woman, and say to Mr. K—— that I allow no stocks or whipping-posts."

Sergeant D—— takes the "griffe" in charge, conveying her, with my message, to planter K——; whereat that Southern patriarch waxes warm, and denies that stocks have been erected on his place. As for whipping, he claims to hold authority from a provost-marshal, to flog his slaves whenever they are refractory, and threatens to appeal to this high official for an endorsement of his right. So reports Sergeant D——:

"Mr. K—— says that the Provost Marshal has authorized him to chastise his slaves, and if they venture to resist, to send for him, and he will see it done."

"And you found no stocks on the grounds, Sergeant?"

"Old man K—— denied they were there, sir; but I looked around and found the institution."

"Report that fact to the officer of the day, Sergeant."

"If you please, sir——" Sergeant D——, formerly a lawyer, and always the gentleman in his manners, makes a military salute, and looks at me with a smile.

"Well, sir."

"Thought it would save trouble, sir; cut the stocks down, myself."

A humorous eye-twinkle accompanies this speech of the non-commissioned officer. I compress my lips. "You exceeded your orders, Sergeant," I remark. "Report what you have done to the officer of the day."

Sergeant D—— goes out, with no very deep conscious-ness of having offended his commander through stock operations. Stout fellow! the present is not his first iconoclastic experiment with Southern idols and fetiches; for his New England hatred of oppression has more than once made him the champion of maltreated humanity in our camp neighborhoods.

My orderly now reports himself at the rear, presenting a newly-arrived fugitive from "service or labor." It is a fine-looking type of the field slave—sable-hued, stalwart, and full-eyed. His arm hangs in a sling, and his broad, naked breast and massive throat, his sable *torso* gleaming under a tattered shirt, are models of statuesque contour. There is something of self-reliant energy in the aspect of this man; in the curved upper lip and steady eye; in the firm though respectful repose of his attitude.

"Colonel," says my orderly, "this poor fellow ran away

from his old man, and got a ball put through the shoulder. He stopped at Lafourche hospital, and Dr. Willetts took the lead out. I've given him some old clothes of mine, and if you've no objection, he can help around the stable, sir."

"What is your name, my boy?" I inquire of the "contraband."

"Toussaint, sah," replies the black, with a French accent.

Toussaint! The name recalls a chronicle of the man's race—a history whereof, haply, this poor fugitive is utterly ignorant, but which dwells in books and traditions among the records of heroism and endurance. My thoughts traverse the tropic waves between these green bayous and Cape Francais, to rest for a moment on that wonderful slave who made himself the leader of three hundred thousand liberated bondmen; that brave negro, of whom his Spanish opponent, the Marquis d'Hermona said: "If an angel descended on earth he could not inhabit a heart apparently more good than that of Toussaint L'Ouverture!" Here, before me, is another Toussaint, courageous and intelligent, strong and patient, who might ask only favorable surroundings to become, likewise, a chief of his enfranchised comrades. There is manifest material in this sable man before me to constitute a hero, give him but heroic opportunity.

I subsequently discover that my Louisiana Toussaint is already a hero, in his way. Slave of an arbitrary master, whose tyrannic behests were cruelly seconded by a brutal overseer, this negro has suffered many stripes and tortures, for espousing the cause of fellow-chattels feebler than himself. He has dared to defy oppression and brave suffering, from the promptings of as generous a spirit as that which nerved his namesake in the Haytien isle. Defending his fellow blacks, he incurred the fear and hatred of those who held his life and limbs at their mercy. After years of endurance, he fled to the swamp. Abandoning his wild life there, because a woman whom he loved remained in bondage, he returned to his master's estate, on the promise of "amnesty for the past." The promise was only kept till a fitting moment appeared for breaking it. The black was ordered to perform some impossible task, and refused. Again the overseer's lash menaced him; but Toussaint's manhood revolted once more. He grappled with the white man, and flung him to the ground, whence he rose foaming with rage. At this juncture, the master galloped up, and, with furious imprecations, ordered the overseer to scourge his rebellious chattel.

"Don't come nigh me!" said Toussaint, quietly, his black eyes kindling with deep resolve.

"Knock him down! brain him!" was the owner's savage command to the overseer; who, whirling his heavy whip, merciless as an ox-goad, sprang forward to execute vengeance.

Toussaint was ready, and met his enemy with a blow that stretched him again upon the earth at the foot of the master, and in presence of half a hundred field hands at work around them. Such an outrage would have invoked death upon the perpetrator on any plantation. The owner drew his revolver, and spurred his horse forward, to make an end of the slave at once. Toussaint awaited the bound, seized his master's steed by the head, and, with main strength, forced him up, and back, throwing horse and rider together, beside the prostrate overseer. The white man had only time to fire a single shot, but that had struck the slave, lodging in his shoulder. Toussaint felt himself wounded, and broke for the woods which skirted the plantation. His master, extricating himself from the stirrups, discharged the remaining barrels of his revolver after the fugitive, but without effect. Toussaint gained the swamp.

All that day, and far into the night, white men, with horses and dogs, were summoned from neighboring estates, to hunt the runaway negro. But Toussaint, wounded as he was, contrived to distance or baffle pursuit, and ten days afterward reported himself at the quarters of our surgeon, near Lafourche Crossing. He had heard of the regiment, and inquired for its commander. He asked for nothing, but to have the bullet extracted from his arm, which was soon done by our skilful surgeon. Then, declining repose, he took a few morsels of food and set out on a fifteen mile march to my camp at Tigerville.

"What do you want to do now, Toussaint?"

"Anything you have to do, sah, till my arm's done cured; after that, work or fight, jes' as you say, sah!"

I reflect, as I look upon this determined fellow, with his massive frame, his alert manner, that a thousand such fighting men would not disgrace good leadership. For the present there is no fighting to be done by blacks; so I turn Toussaint over to the charge of his friend, my orderly. An hour afterwards, I see him swinging a heavy bucket of water with his unhurt arm, while the other hangs in its sling. Again I see him currying a horse, or carrying fuel to the mess-room. "Toussaint," I remark to him, "you must let your wound get well. You must rest!"

"Thank you, sah! but I reck'n it'll git along, sah! I'd rather wu'k, sah, if you please, sah!"

I do not know many white soldiers who would not prefer a furlough under Toussaint's circumstances. Very few, certainly, would report for fatigue duty, with a bullet hole through the shoulder.

Toussaint, black as a Nubian, was blessed in a wife, who might have been a queen of the Amazons. Of majestic figure, with straight, glossy hair, oriental eyes, features regular, and complexion more Indian than Afric, the beloved of my brave freedman had been a quadroon beauty in her day. She might easily attract notice among the slip-shod female followers of our negro servants, and it was not long before I observed her, *tete-a-tete* with Toussaint, on the steps of the kitchen quarters. "She takes up with me," was the black's quaint manner of revealing their conjugal connection, and I congratulated Toussaint upon his taste.

A tropical-natured woman must this have been, in her day of strength and comeliness, upon a Louisiana sugar domain. Her features, now marked by the ridges of smallpox, her expressive eye, whose dilating pupil and tawny iris are rimmed with latent flame, have, in past days, doubtless, been eloquent of feeling and affection, of wrath and passion. She is but a ruder type, however, of a myriad of her race and sex whose blood claims nearer kindred with purer tides; whose attractions, impulses, and aspirations, were moulded to a like fullness with those of the blue-veined dames who bought and sold such beings as mere chattels. This wife of Toussaint is but one of a hundred thousand, perhaps, whose lineaments assimilate with Caucasian traits, but whose unhappy destiny has precluded all other claim to Caucasian sympathy than that which is founded on the transmission of their own vices with those of their masters, to offspring as unhappy as themselves.

The mother of this quadroon was the favorite of her master, and the mother of several of his children. This wife of my freedman has kindred white as any creole lady in Lafourche; a sister, yet a child, beautiful and a slave, who endures the torture of her servile life and the imminence of that fate which has befallen all her sisters, rather than leave her mother, who yet clings with strange affection to her master's fortunes. This mother, once in her anomalous life, was nursing a child at her breast, the offspring of her owner, when that owner's lawful wife became a mother likewise. The fragile mistress either could not or would not give her infant nourishment, and the master called upon his slave to take the mother's place. He took her own child from the wretched woman, locked it in another room, and went his way. The slave-mother was forced to suckle the babe of her mistress, with the cries of her own neglected one ringing in her ears, and she unable to reach or rescue it. Half distracted, she implored the master to permit her to have her own child; but the inhuman white man laughed, and told her that the "brat might die; he could afford to lose it!" The little starveling's cries grew weaker till they ceased in death. The slave-mother suckled her master's white child, while her own perished with hunger.

Does this story seem improbable? I have been convinced of the truth of more unnatural deeds perpetrated on the unoffending and helpless. The wife of Toussaint, and sister of the murdered negro babe, is now at the north, and can tell of darker doings on that plantation where her youth was passed.

Not she alone, but others, witnessed the murder of a young mulatto boy, for his refusal to be witness to a sister's wrongs in the house of his master. The youth, who was a house-boy, fled to the plantation, and asked to be permitted to perform the hard labors of a field hand. His master remanded him to the mansion, whence he again eloped, to take his place among the negro gangs. Then his owner tied him by the wrists to a tree, and flogged him, till his flesh hung in rags—till his limbs were marked with one continuous bloody weal—till fatal wounds had been inflicted on the most delicate organs of his body—and the boy fainted from pain and loss of blood. He was conveyed to his pallet, never to rise again. He lingered till the next morning, when his master approached, and professed to be repentant for having so cruelly abused him. "Massa," murmured the dying slave, "I forgives you; but I'se feared you is too wicked for God ebber to forgive you!"

CHAPTER IX.

BERWICK BAY.

LONG before break of day, one sultry morning in May, I am awakened to receive a special order from Brashear City. The commandant of that post sends word that he expects the rebels; I am invoked to march with reinforcements—all that can be mustered; to take cars at once. A train of contrabands and cattle, from the Teche, in charge of Colonel Chickering, is threatened by a force of Texans, Arizonian Indians, Louisianian guerillas; four thousand strong, the bruit goes. Subsequently, I lose this special order, with plundered papers generally; or it might now recall, in print, the precious panic which inspired it.

Col. Nott, who has been during many weeks lying ill of fever, remains at my quarters, an invalid, attended by nurse and surgeon. I take my leave of him; and, having mustered our effectives, some five hundred men, all full of spirits at the prospect of field-service, we set out cheerily. At ten o'clock A. M.—after taking up detachments on the road, we reach Brashear City, and I report to the commandant. Awaiting orders, I learn that a messenger from Col. Chickering has arrived; that his train is safe; that no immediate attack of rebels is to be apprehended. So, presently, instead of encountering enemies, I find myself invited to meet friends, at Col. Walker's headquarters, where an ample dinner tempts and satisfies our destructive appetites. Thereafter, taking ddle, I cross the Bay in a ferry steamboat, to see the cattle and contraband train, last instalment of spoils, resultant from raid of General Banks through the Teche country, on his way to Port Hudson campaigning. I land on the shore of Berwick City. Here be materials for a Hogarth; life, action, incongruity; a panorama, a kaleidoscope of curious shapes and varied hues. Two thousand beeves, involved in sinuous labyrinth; crowding, leaping, rushing hither and thither, their horny fronts now lifted now depressed, their ceaseless roaring sounding like the wind-lashed sea on a lee shore: three thousand mules, rampant, venting hideous screeches; plunging, rearing, flinging out heels like battering rams: a thousand wagons in coil that seems inextricable, be-ridden by a thousand teamsters in a thousand rages: a din of lowings, bellowing, brayings, threats and maledictions: a Gordian knot of brutes and brutish bipeds, bristling bayonets, brandished whips, artillery mud-locked, cavalry cart-crushed; and, in the whirl of all, in the way of all, overtramped, and driven and cursed by all—the NEGRO!

A spectacle for the ethnologist, a problem for the statesman, a theorem for the Christian: six thousand curly-headed, dusky-skinned, immortal-souled humanities! I know not what ganglionic difference there may be between this crisp-wooled poll before me and my own straight-haired cerebrum; I care not to investigate the mysteries which Nature hides in seed and generation; I only see six thousand men, women and children, lying in mire and dust, after their weary marches; men, giant-thewed, with brawn like steel; mothers, giving suck from sound breasts; light-hearted, bright-eyed youths and docile children; resting here by the waters of Atchafalaya, as another enfranchised slave-race rested, forty centuries ago, on Jordan's banks, after Exodus from Darkness and Bondage.

They are black, these people—these humanities; but the horse I bestride is likewise black, and I see, not far from me, a score of lusty oxen sable-skinned. I do not remark the instincts of white ox or white horse pitting him against his fellow of a darker hide. It is left for Man to learn those loftier prejudices which regard the hue of his poor clay, ere it returns to dust. I know not what gradations of skin-honor could be enforced in a world's congress of ambassadors from every human clan. The etiquette of cuticular priority, with Anglo-Saxon pigment for its high-color mark, might not be tolerated, I think, by a large majority of tribal representatives!

Here, now, six thousand integers of that great sun-scorched race which multiplies in African tropics, are cast up, by a tidal wave of war, upon this jutting promontory of Freedom. They lie, helpless and imploring, on the strand of an enlightened Civilization. And by other war-billows, on other sands and reaches of Liberty, uncounted multitudes, besides these thousands, find themselves this day flung up before the face of Man, and in the sight of God, to challenge a superior race which has, until now, ignored their kindred. Vain is sophistry against the *argumentum ad verecundiam* of these mutely-eloquent waifs of Rebellion, appealing to our large-heartedness, our great-mindedness, as a nation and a people. Unenviable casuist is he who, in the light of that dread hand-writing which is now declaring the doom of Southern oppression, shall attempt to cheat his conscience with the cry of Cain—"Am I my brother's keeper?" The question of the day and generation must be grappled with, or woe to posterity! That question pleads for solution in the myriad anxious eyes peering up to us out of ignorance and slavery, but not less does it plead, could we but recognize it, in the glorified regards. of heroes and martyrs, who look back from heaven to the Freedom for which they suffered.

These children of the fetter, newborn from the throes of a mighty Revolution, are children indeed, upon the threshhold of a new existence. "The world is all before them!" They are hardly recovered yet, from the intoxication of their first sweet draught of freedom. The future in their eyes is rose-colored. There is a degree of novel pleasure for them even in the jeers and blows of brutal teamsters, who must have a customary vulgar fling at "niggers," as they pass. That bright, wonderful presence, LIBERTY, is all around them; and in their rude joy of her, they seem to "walk on thrones." Poor children! manly-limbed and strength-endued, but very infants in experience of life!.... I would to God, that some great, loving Heart could be intrusted with your destiny; that some wide Intellect could inform the sympathies of our nation with your few wants and many capacities! Heaven, I have faith to believe, will, in its own good season, raise up the merciful Avenger of your history. Happy our Republic, if its Rulers shall appreciate, in time, the mutual need of Black and White, to recognize a kindred of interests in our National Future!

The coil of men and brutes, of soldiers and freedmen, of war-munitions and transportation-means, at length evolves its meshes, and Col. Chickering reports his convoy from the Teche country. Thereafter, I am ordered to cross the Bay, with my battalion, and march to a point opposite the upper extremity of Brashear City, protected by the guns of Fort Buchanan. Nightfall finds us encamped on spacious grounds belonging to Dr. R——, an Englishman, who has lived here as a planter many years, and professes neutrality, as between the North and South. He occupies a handsome dwelling-house on the bay shore. His well-fenced lands and substantial sugar-works give evidence of wealth and thrift. Greeting us with friendly salutation in the twilight, he tenders bountiful store of sweet potatoes to the hungry. I ride out, to inspect the vicinage, make points of observation, set guards and pickets, get a personal lodgment and staff-quarters, and thus establish an out-post for Brashear City.

Next day, receiving an order as commander of the 176th Regiment of New York Volunteers, to relieve the commandant of Brashear City, I present the papers to Colonel Walker, who is, by the same despatch, directed to report with his regiment at Port Hudson. Shortly afterward, the senior officer of troops upon the railroad, Colonel Holmes, arrives at Brashear City, from Lafourche. His regiment and commission entitle him to priority of post command, and I report to him as superior officer, in pursuance of supplementary orders from New Orleans.

Day by day, now, the shores of Berwick Bay become gradually relieved of their entangled lines, animal and vegetable. Contrabands and cotton-bales are hurried off upon railway-flats. Shrewd cattle-brokers, after swarming about the quarter-master's doors, drive off their bargains of beeves. Mules are trotted away to army markets or plantations. Carts, chaises, family coaches, saddles, harnesses, debris of Attakapas "confiscation", are invoiced, via rail, to New Orleans auction blocks. The bay-side hospitals, where sick and wounded soldiers have been quartered, give up, day by day, their convalescent occupants. At length, comparative quiet reigns upon the Berwick City water-front. Ferry boats make less frequent crossings. A few stragglers only linger daily upon the strand, where we encountered, a week ago, such troops of black and white. As I ride now, from the ferry-landing to camp, along a mile of road, with scattered houses, mostly vacant, on one side, I seldom meet a wayfarer. Yet some of the abandoned buildings were abodes of ease and elegance two years ago. Below our guarded lines resides a brother of my friends, the L——s of New York; in whose interesting family are two deaf mutes, intelligent and amiable children. Dr. R——'s household is likewise a refined and agreeable one. These resident owners have had opportunities of comparison between the rebel troops and ours; as all this bay-shore was occupied, until about two months since, by forces of the enemy. Surveying one another, *vis-a-vis*, from opposing fronts, of Brashear and Berwick cities, the belligerents were accustomed to exchange artillery compliments almost daily, and many of the buildings hereabout bear marks of shot and shell.

Dr. S—— sets plates for my officers at his hospitable table, but I content myself with a single *dejeuner*, and a chat with Madame P——, well known in former seasons as a patroness of Newport, where she occupied a *cottage ornee*. Still handsome and stately, this widow, with an ample fortune in sugar lands and their concomitant living chattels, dwells luxuriously npon a romantic bend of Bayou Teche, above the town of Franklin, in St. Mary's parish. She professes staunch loyalty to the Union, and assures us that her negroes were so much attached to her that they voluntarily returned to labor after having dispersed to the woods and swamps, or mingled with the advancing army of General Banks. I could easily divine that this sparkling lady might find it for her interest to remain the *chatelaine* of her own castle. With affability and tact, to say nothing of good business knowledge, as her Amazonian weaponry, she would be able, doubtless,

to keep her household gods and goods inviolate under
martial surveillance of both red and white roses. Too
much a clever woman of the world to cry "A plague on
both your houses," she might give smiles as subsidies,
and purchase safeguards by soft words for North and
South alike. Much easier is this, and far more politic,
than the usual abandonment of house and lands to "tender
mercies" of remorseless confiscation boards.

It was on the simple negro servants of pleasant Madame
P—— that sundry graceless scamps of our "grand army"
played divers pranks of knavery. Our forces bivouacked
near her lands, in passing up the Teche; and, shortly after
they had marched away, the lady one day noticed that her
sable handmaids were busied with great washing of garments and bleaching of cotton and fine linen to unwonted
snowiness. Lawns were bestrewn with lawn; every bush
had a rag on it; the hedgerows were festooned with all
fibrous particles of apparel that could be whitened by the
power of alkalies. From morn to night the blacks were
in hot water at wash-tubs. Kitchen tables smoked with
heaps of unmentionable articles, glossy under calender
and smoothing-iron. What could this sudden storm of
cleanliness import? The mistress marvelled, and a confidential tire-woman at length enlightened her.

"You see, missy, we's gwine to hab our white robes all
ready when de messenger come."

"Who is the messenger, Lucille, and why must you
have white robes ready?" queried Madame P——, with
I know not how many visions of Millerite preparations
suggested to her fancy.

"Why, missy, dar am a high ossifer gwine to come yer
to Tuckapaw, from Massa Abe Linkum hissef, missy.
He'm gwine to write de cullud people in de great book."

"What nonsense are you telling me, Lucille?"

"It am rale troo, missy; no mistake dis yer time. We's all done got de stiff-cats."

"Got what, Lucille?"

"Got de stiff-cats, missy, wid Massa Linkum's picter ob hisself on dem. We's shore to git de goold an' silber back, when de high ossifer done come to Tuckapaw."

"Gold and silver back! What do you mean, Lucille?"

"O, missy, you know we's done 'mancipate dis yer minit, but we isn't gwine to leabe Tuckapaw. We is prefer to stay wid our kind missy."

"Well, tell me about the gold and silver, and why you are washing all these clothes, child."

"'Kase it am ordered to be, missy. We's to gwo all 'rayed in white robes, like de lambs, an' 'tan' all togeder out yer by de bayou. Sartin shore, missy, de high ossifer am gwine to come up in de biggest ribber boat, wid all de flags flyin', and we is to holler out rite smart for de Unum——"

"And the gold and silver, Lucille?"

"O, we's gwine to hab all de goold an' silber done paid back agin, and ebery cullud pusson am to git a house an' garden, and dar 'm not gwine to be no more workin' fur oberseers, only jes' fur reg'lar wages—"

"Indeed! But what do you mean by getting your gold and silver back, child?"

"Lor' sakes, missy, I isn't tole you 'bout dat yit; an' I declar' I isn't done showed you de Linkum stiff-cat."

"No, indeed, you have not, Lucille."

"Dar, m'm, de stiff-cat. De Linkum sogers gib us all one, 'fore dey done marched away."

Saying this, the maiden drew from her dusky bosom a scrap of paper. It was creased and discolored, but Madame P—— contrived to decipher the printed contents. It was simply a square of pictured tissue paper,

bearing a lithographed head in one corner, and a soap-
maker's advertisement following—in fact, the common
imitation of a bank certificate, which we often see pasted
on the lid of a fancy soap box or at the end of a match
package.

" Dat yer's de rale picter of Massa Abe Linkum," cried
Lucille, with dancing eyes. " De sogers done gib us all
stiff-cats like dat yer."

" And you gave the soldiers your money for this, Lucille?" queried Madame P——.

" Sartin, missy. De sogers done tell us dat Massa
Linkum want to borry all de goold an' silber in Tuckapaw,
jes' for three mont's, till de high ossifer done come up
de bayou. Den, Lor bress you's dear heart, missy, we is
gwine to hab all our names took down in de book for
Massa Linkum, an' we is gwine to be 'clar'd 'mancipate
for ebber an' ebber. Den we's git back all de goold an'
silber, an' de high ossifer—spec' he must be Massa Linkum's own chile—he gibs all de cullud people de houses
an' de gardens—"

"Well, Lucille, how much money did you all give to
the soldiers ?"

" Done gib dem all our sabin's, missy—all what we
sell de chickens far, an' all we done git fur de moss,
long 'fore de war."

"Lucille, you are a great goose, and neither you nor
your silly people will ever see your money again."

"Lor' bress you heart, missy, we'se got de stiff-cats!"

" Well, child, you have been cheated with your precious ' stiff-cats,' as you call them. I suppose Anne has
one."

" Yes, missy, an' Molly, an' Cassy, an' Phemy, an'
eberybody. We is all s'kure."

But poor Lucille learned, to her great chagrin, and

that of " eberybody," among the simple-minded community, that they were all the " victims of misplaced confi.
dence." Their white robes were never called into requisition, and they waited vainly for the advent of a " high
ossifer" with greetings from "Massa Linkum." The
whole thing was a wicked swindle of the poor blacks by
some vagabond Federal soldiers, who had succeeded in
obtaining upwards of eight hundred dollars in specie.

The outpost established by my regiment, on Berwick
shore, was one which should have been maintained and
strengthened. I here mounted a score of my young men,
daring fellows, who delighted in scouting sorties upon the
road toward Pattersonville. These could have been kept
always advanced, as vedettes, and would have been alert
to discover any indications of hostile approach. During
my brief occupation of this position, several rebel scouts
were brought into camp as prisoners, securing for us
items of intelligence regarding the enemy, which fore-
shadowed his intentions. But " coming events" were not
to be averted through foresight or watchfulness on our
part. In a short time, we received orders to fall back
over the Bay, and pitch our tents at Brashear.

CHAPTER X.

BRASHEAR CITY.

THE administration of military affairs at Brashear City, during three weeks of June, 1863, exhibits, on a small scale, the ruinous results of neglect by superiors and mismanagement by subordinates. Withdrawn from the' outpost on Berwick City shore, my regiment is now encamped at Brashear, about a quarter-mile from the rail-road depot, and on the shore between that point and Fort Buchanan. Behind us extends the camp of the Twenty-Third Connecticut Volunteers. On either side are other camps, occupied variously by cavalry squads, convalescents representing every regiment in the Department, and straggling soldiers, assumed to be detached for all sorts of purposes. In round numbers, there are probably a thousand privates, more or less able to do duty, who, under nominal supervision of surgeons or sergeants, pass their days in lounging and card-playing, without organization, drill, or duty. Probably, a hundred camp-followers and civilians might be added to the number of this idle population. For defence of the place, there are six companies of the One Hundred and Seventy sixth New York Infantry, under my command, as Lieutenant-Colonel; the Colonel being confined to his quarters by sickness; two companies of the same regiment, acting as garrison of Fort Buchanan; several companies of the Twenty-Third Connecticut Infantry; a detachment of the 21st Indiana Artillery, commanded by Captain Noblett,

and a few squads of cavalry and infantry, detailed for
provost duty, or in charge of government property; an
effective sum total of perhaps six hundred rank and file.
This is my computation of the force, at the time our occupation of the Berwick shore is discontinued. At this
date, Col. Walker has just been relieved by Col. Holmes;
and within a very few days subsequently, Col. Holmes
being attacked by fever, the command of Brashear City
devolves on the Lieut. Colonel of the Twenty-Third Connecticut Volunteers.

Here we begin to snuff a breeze of danger. Previous
to our recrossing the bay, my scouts, as has been mentioned, captured several rebel stragglers, through whom we
gained intelligence of a Confederate force concentrating
on the Teche. Now we hear daily rumors of their presence and increasing numbers between Pattersonville
and Franklin. At daybreak, one morning, I receive
abrupt orders to report my regiment at the steamboat
wharf. The boys jump into line with alacrity, and
"double-quick" to the spot. There I encounter the post
commandant, looking very perplexed and flurried. He
orders a crossing to Berwick City; presently counter-
mands the order; again commands the regiment to em-
bark; finally directs a retreat to camp and breakfast.
In a few hours afterwards, our brass field pieces at the
depot begin to play upon the Berwick shore. Somebody
has asserted that rebel cavalry are dodging in Berwick
woods. A score of shells must be sent over the water,
by way of Yankee cards.

The coming night develops general nervousness in
and around post head-quarters. Quartermaster at the depot
sneers about pusillanimity. Officers in knots gossip concerning telegrams, said to be despatched every hour to
New Orleans, asking for aid and comfort. Distrust of

head-quarters competence shows itself among rank and file, as well as officers.

Presently, another official panic sends us, at double-quick, to the steamboat wharf again. This time, we cross the ferry. I leave Major Morgans at Berwick City, in command of detachments from our own and the Connecticut regiment, and then, placing a howitzer on another ferry-boat, steam up the bay, and drop some shells into an old sugar-house, to dislodge an imaginary force of lurking rebels. Maj. Morgans patiently holds his ground, with a brass piece commanding the road, till I reinforce him, after supper, with whiskey rations for our arid troops. Thereafter, with Surgeon Willets, very daring and quite skeptical regarding proximity of foemen, I ride to the "front"; gallop a couple of miles over a moonlit road, outside the pickets, and return unscarred to the ferry. Infantry and artillery then get home to camp again.

Shortly after this midnight campaign, our lieutenant-colonel-in-chief begs Gen. Emory to relieve him of that military nightmare which oppresses him in the shape of his post-command. Accordingly, General Emory, without apparently troubling himself to inquire concerning the real necessities of Brashear City, deputes a Napoleonic young lieutenant-colonel, who has been doing display duty at New Orleans during the season, to take command of our beleagured outpost. Subsequently, I learn particulars: how, when a fortieth or fiftieth telegram had reached Headquarters of the Defences of New Orleans, the General had remarked:

"This commandant at Brashear seems uneasy. He is determined to resign, and asks me to send somebody to relieve him. I know of nobody here."

This is said in presence of a young *attache*, lately provost-marshal at Thibodeaux; one Lieutenant Kingsley;

who opportunely interposes, with the suggestion : "General, here's Lieut.-Col. Stickney, of my regiment, the Forty-7.-2*Massachusetts. He is doing nothing."

"Well, let Stickney go !"

So Lieut.-Colonel Stickney is relieved from the duty of attending public school festivals, in full dress, with the band of his regiment ; and, presently, he comes down to assume command of the Bay and its surroundings. Reporting at his quarters, I encounter a pragmatic young gentleman, of apparently feminine nerves, who starts at the fall of a book, entreats me to remain up all night with him, and thereupon, forgetting the request, lies down for a nap on the sofa. Meantime, he has signalized his military genius by ordering my regiment, under command of the major, to go and keep guard at the railroad depot till morning.

A new military broom now begins to sweep. Vigilance and discipline cavort under double check-rein.

Lieut.-Col. Stickney blooms into Acting Brigadier Stickney, and appoints our quondam provost-marshal Kingsley his aid-de-camp. Adjutant Whiting, of Twenty-Third Connecticut, rises to post-adjutant's dignity, therewith getting sleepless days and nights in prospect. Now begins the reign of real military excellence at last ; nine months martinetism on dress-parade. Our post-commandant becomes ubiquitous ; riding on a black steed to my tent, at tattoo, to order the extinguishing of a lantern, lest rebels at Berwick City should take it for a target ; gallopping on a white courser to the fort, with orders for the gunners to look well to their pieces. Post-orders indeed multiply hourly. Now, a squad of twelve men must report at head-quarters ; now a company ; now a lieutenant and twenty ; presently the regiment is summoned to duty. I am directed to have a drum at my

pillow, for instant beating of the long roll; to cause the
men to keep awake all night; to make them "sleep on
their arms." No light must appear in camp; no gun
be discharged, however foul. My men are "exercised"
day and night; marching to railroad depots, or dumped
at stations, to fight mosquitos in darkness. Drilling gets
chronic under a midsummer sun; expeditions, with the
gunboat and ferry steamers, make sorties to the bay
shores and river-mouths; descents are ordered on Berwick City; a place which might be held, with three companies of infantry, a couple of howitzers, and a mud fort,
against the whole rebel army. Bombardment of this
tenantless town, and the lonely shore above it, goes on
incessantly. A bunch of pendent moss can hardly stir
in the breeze, on that Berwick side, but straightway
Fort Buchanan launches its thunders, and our shore batteries pound at it. Occasionally a rebel spurs his mustang through the woods, or leisurely draws bridle on the
beach road. Brashear City then becomes ludicrously
militant. Cannons blaze, musketry rattles, convalescents rush to the "front," with tobacco pipes in their
mouths. A hundred missiles shower around the rebel,
who dodges them easily, and rides off, laughing at us.

Meantime, what is done to make Brashear City defen-
sible, should a rebel assault be indeed threatened?
Fort Buchanan, commanding the Bay and the Atchafalaya
mouths, with heavy siege guns, is yet entirely open to a
rear attack. No line of earthworks, not even a rifle-pit,
stockade, or block-house, defends the city from approaches
by the railroad or the belt of woods that intervenes between us and the labyrinth of lakes, accessible at any
time by a rebel force from above. Pickets are thrown
out nightly some mile or less behind the fort; and a gun-
boat, patrolling the bay, is supposed to take occasional

cognizance of the water approaches from that direction. Beyond this, Brashear City is entirely exposed to surprise from its back country.   .

But, here are a thousand, more or less, experienced, serviceable stragglers; convalescents waiting to be ordered to their regiments. These men, drawing daily rations, and consuming them, are lying useless about their camps. Why are they not placed under efficient officers, organized into companies, supplied with arms and ammunition from the mass of stores that have accumulated here? These men are nearly all veterans. Brigade them with our regiments, and we shall have a force of two thousand men at Brashear City and the railroad stations. Add to these, two thousand negroes, who can be mustered in twenty-four hours, to dig and fortify the approaches to this post; and who shall say that Brashear City is in danger?

I think General Emory, before experimenting with an important outpost through a post-commandant who wears out the energies of our few organized companies by extra duty, should have come here and examined matters for himself. Had he done so, we might now be occupying days and nights more usefully than in making Quixotic forays on the railroad line.

But our acting brigadier is chief, and on him must devolve responsibility. So, when a captain and lieutenant of my regiment venture to suggest an organization of our loose forces—and get themselves snubbed, for their pains—I have no more to do about the administration of military affairs than simply to obey orders.

But, finding myself rudely reprimanded, one morning, on account of a certain number of pieces being foul at guard-mounting in my regiment, I remark to the post-commandant, that he might have ordered my officer of the guard to report to me.

"You are to blame, sir—you!" exclaims the acting brigadier, fulminating from his saddle, on my devoted head, as I sit at breakfast, in front of my tent.

"I beg pardon, sir. According to regulation, I inspected every piece in - the regiment, no longer ago than last Sunday. The muskets that are dirty must belong to the pickets which were out, sir."

"It is your fault, sir! Consider yourself under arrest, sir!"

"Consider myself under arrest?"

"Yes, sir!"

"Very well, sir!" I reply, saluting. And my superior officer (by virtue of a month's priority of date in commission) rides off, at a gallop. I finish my breakfast and wait for the post-adjutant, or some other officer, to come and demand my sword; but nobody appears.

Towards evening, I walk over to Col. Nott's quarters, a house near one of the flanks. The Colonel is convalescing from his late illness, but yet too feeble for duty. I relate to him the last exploit of our acting-brigadier, in placing me under arrest. To Col. Nott the affair appears ridiculous. "Did he take your sword?"

"No, sir; nor has he sent for it."

"It looks like a joke," remarks the Colonel, laughing. But I assure him it is no joke; and we presently conclude that I had better return to my tent, lest the post-commander should order me into close confinement.

Next day, another vital expedition is ordered up the river in steamers, and on the Berwick shore. It achieves a sight of several rebels, and makes display of skirmishing; with the loss of one man of my regiment, who shoots himself, accidentally, on board the steamer. Our war-worn soldiers return at dusk, and are ordered to "sleep on their arms." Next morning, another expedition is re-

ported on the tapis ; but the men are allowed a little
needed rest. Just before sunset, as I sit at my tent en-
trance, Col. Stickney rides up to me, with a salute.

"Col. Duganne! you will consider yourself released
from arrest after dress-parade, this evening !"

"Very well, sir !" I reply, saluting.

The acting-brigadier turns his horse's head. Then,
with a smile—

"But those guns were very dirty, Colonel !"

"You might have ordered the officer of the guard to
report that fact to me, sir."

Col. Stickney smiles faintly.

"You will report for duty to-morrow morning, Colonel."

"I fear, I shall not be able, sir !" I reply. During
the day, I had been attacked with a prevailing disorder.

"Very well; as soon as you are able !" rejoins the
post-commandant, and rides off. It is the last I see of
our Acting Brigadier General. I hear, subsequently, that
he behaves with courage and discretion at Lafourche
Crossing, where, with my regiment, under its brave
Major, and some companies of the Connecticut volunteers,
he succeeds in repulsing a rebel force of two thousand
cavalry. The quality of gallantry redeems many errors
that arise from inexperience ; and it may be, that Lieut.
Col. Stickney, under other circumstances, might have accomplished more than he did at Brashear City. But I
cannot reject the conclusion, to which every one conver-
sant with our military administration during the month
of June, must arrive, that, had the time mis-spent, in
daily and nightly forays, been properly devoted to organization and defence, there would have been another
ending to this campaign than the disgraceful capture of
Brashear City and its railroad line to New Orleans.

CHAPTER XI.

REBELS IN THE REAR.

I HEAR myself called at midnight, on the nineteenth of July, and recognize Major Morgans' voice at my cot-side. He has just received an order from Col. Stickney, to march with our regiment to the railroad. My stout Major is wearied out by late exertions, and would gladly have a respite. He inquires if I can take command, but I have not yet reported for duty. Both of us suppose that this nocturnal expedition, like all previous ones, will bring up at some rail road station, or, perhaps, get no farther than Brashear depot. "I shall report in the morning," I remark; "and then you may have a rest, Major!" Unfortunate alternative for me! Major Morgans goes off, with our men, to fight the battle of Lafourche Crossing; I remain, to march in another direction, toward the dreary goal of a Texan prison.

Early next morning, I ride to headquarters, expecting to find Col. Stickney, and report to him. He has gone, with the troops, and left Major Anthony in command of the post. With Major Anthony I have no acquaintance, but learn that he is a cavalry officer, sojourning temporarily at Brashear City. I ride in various directions, endeavoring to meet him, without success.

Meantime, a train of cars loaded with stores, which, pursuant to orders from Col. Stickney, had followed him at a later hour, returns with alarming intelligence. The communication with Lafourche is cut off. A rebel force,

of cavalry and artillery, occupies Terrebonne station.
Lieut. Lyons, of my regiment, posted in a small stockade
at that point, has been made a prisoner.

Presently, I encounter Major Anthony. "Major! I
learn that you are in command of the post. I am senior
officer here, but not having been able to report for duty
before Col. Stickney left, I suppose I cannot relieve you
without orders."

"I wish you could, Colonel," replies the Major. "Col.
Stickney, it is likely, left me in command because you
had not yet reported."

"Well, Major," I rejoin; "we need not differ, on the
point of rank. I will, if you please, go to Bayou Bœuff,
which has now become the front, and make dispositions
to receive the enemy."

"I shall be glad if you will do so, Colonel. I can give
you an infantry company, to add to the force at Bayou
Bœuff!"

"If you will give orders to collect some thirty or forty
of the horses that are ranging on the commons, I will try
to muster riders, and make a cavalry squadron, for duty
at the front."

"I will attend to that at once," answers the Major;
"and have the horses reported at your quarters."

I ride back to camp, and begin to look about for cavalry
recruits. Most of my young adventurers (and the "Ironsides" regiment can boast a goodly proportion of youthful
and dashing braves) are with the main body, under Col.
Stickney. Of the remaining rank and file, a majority have
been on picket for three days, and I see no prospect of
relieving them. A few, beaten out, and some really sick,
are in camp. Out of these, I muster fifteen, ready to take
saddle for scouting duty. Captain Coe, though on the
sick-list, volunteers to lead them.

Blunders and delays regarding the horses, prevent us from getting off. Mayor Anthony fails to organize the promised infantry company. The day wanes, and nothing is done toward organizing convalescents or strengthening our defences.

Here, then, is the condition of Brashear City. Left, during months, without personal supervision by those charged with the responsibility of defending New Orleans, this outpost is, at last, cut off from its base. While in daily expectation of an enemy in front of the fortifications, we find ourselves suddenly menaced from the rear. All the country above Berwick Bay is actively hostile. The approaches to our railroad lines, wrested from rebel occupation by hard fighting two months ago, when General Banks marched, via. the Attakapas district, to Port Hudson, have lapsed into the possession of our enemies. Forced back behind the water front of Brashear, and attempting to occupy, with less than one thousand effective men, the whole railroad between this point and Algiers, we now find our small force split in twain by an invading army of rebels.

A month has been wasted in useless daily explorations of the bay shores; in bootless expeditions, by night, upon the railroad. Our convalescents, many of them veterans, have been allowed to shirk the simplest duty, instead of being brigaded and drilled for defence. Aimless and desultory, the military operations, during weeks past, have left us at last in a condition which invites attack by an alert and well-informed foe.

The camp of my regiment is located about midway between the depot and Fort Buchanan. Separated from our front by the bay's breadth only, Berwick City lies completely under range of our batteries. At a point opposite our ferry wharf, stand a few large vacant buildings, used as hospitals while we held that side of the water. Along the Berwick front, likewise, are several detached dwelling houses and other structures, some tenanted, but the greater number without occupants. On our own shore, in front of the camps, which are pitched thickly for the space of half a mile, along the roads, are posted three field pieces, guarded by reliefs of infantry. A line of sentinels and pickets is thrown along the water-road to points beyond the fort.

Such is the military condition of Brashear City, on the evening of the day when Lieut.-Col. Stickney, leaving his post, takes with him all our effective infantry. Two companies of the 176th N. Y. Volunteers, supporting the Indiana batteries at Fort Buchanan, together with straggling squads of my own and the Connecticut regiment, detailed as provost-guards, or on picket duty, constitute the defensive establishment of this important outpost of New Orleans, while its late commandant finds himself at Lafourche Crossing, thirty miles distant, cut off from his base by a rebel force, several thousand strong, which has struck the railroad station three miles in his rear.

A fitting interlude of the child's play, whereby a month has been frittered in sham sorties, which might have been vitally employed in local organization; a fitting interlude, between past folly and the retribution that is to come, transpires, this night, in the burning of Berwick City.

Of course, we have been battering that forsaken locality, as a diurnal recreation, since our evacuation of it. I know not how many tons of ammunition have blazed against the stupidly-silent place during thirty days past; but it has seemed a customary relaxation for the controllers of government shot and shell, to drop those gentle missiles on Berwick whenever the whim seized them. I am hardly prepared, however, for a wanton firing of the lonely town; and trust that no one is prior to it but the naval hero, commanding our solitary gunboat. He it is who distinguishes himself by this vandal deed. Three days hence, he will perform another exploit, in shamefully abandoning Brashear City at the very outset of rebel assault upon it.

War is revolting, even in its best aspect. Stripped of plumed helmet and glittering armor, Bellona appears in no very charming light, as a truculent woman; and the soldier in rags and filth becomes no hero to the eyes of romance. Grand and beautiful is patriotism struggling against foreign invasion; and liberty breasting tyranny is sublime, whether clothed in peasant homespun or arrayed in knightly panoply. But divest war of all abstract merits, and it is resolved at once into craft and violence. Coarse strength and sharp cunning achieve victory; the heaviest artillery decides conquest; the richest exchequer assures possession.

Nevertheless, no one doubts that war, like thunder and lightning, freshets and tornadoes, may have necessity, utility, and beneficence. The end, though not always justifying, will often be found to excuse the means; and it is not to be denied that radical diseases call for radical treatment, in politics as well as therapeutics. Thus, we accept our present national conflict as the result of a political, perhaps a moral, exigency, requiring medical interposition of the heroic school, to save national life. We recognize design brooding over the chaos of our troubles, and anticipate renewed order, to be evoked out of elementary disintegration.

The "inexorable logic of events" overrides qualmishness in military men; nevertheless, I deprecate all acts, which, like the firing of Berwick City, and kindred abuses of power, can be justified by no necessity.

I am seated under an oak, before my tent. The evening is dark, and no lights are allowed in camp. Suddenly, a bright light shoots up from Berwick shore, and I have hardly time to walk from my quarters, past a half-dozen company streets, to the flank, when a blaze, wide and fierce, as if of an hour's duration, appears upon the water front opposite.

Berwick City is on fire. From wall to roof, from garden-fence to out-building, from hedge-row to orchard trees, a devastating flame sweeps along the shore road. Broader and higher the blaze grows momently, throwing its baleful glow on the waters of the bay, and up against the back-ground of forest and clouded sky. I never saw a conflagration spread more rapidly or more devouringly than this. The fiery tongues dart from casements, doors, and eaves, licking up the dry woodwork, like stubble. Roofs, corridors, galleries, are ignited, and the red element extends and mounts, right and left, in lurid wings.

Augmenting in volume till midnight, it is not until near morning that the fire becomes exhausted, for lack of materials to feed upon. The wooden buildings which served us for hospitals and warehouses, with many dwellings and detached edifices, are consumed—leaving the lower portion of Berwick City a blackened waste.

CHAPTER XII.

SABBATH AT LAFOURCHE.

THE rebels choose favorable seasons for their adventurous descents. General Banks, with the main strength of his department, is encamped before Port Hudson. He has made repeated assaults on its stout defenses, with no results but the decimation of " forlorn hopes." Thousands of his gallant men have perished, by disease more than from wounds. Meantime, the enemy rallying immediately on the track of our late Federal raid, have repossessed themselves of the back country, from Vermillion and Teche bayous, to Atchafalaya and Mississippi rivers. They pour down from the Texan border; they swarm on western banks of the Father of Waters.

Thus it occurs, that, on the eventful Saturday which Col. Stickney selected for his expedition to Lafourche Crossing, a rebel force of about three thousand cavalry comes charging down the upper waters of this very Lafourche. Dispatched by Louisianian General Mouton, under command of Col. Major—West Point graduate in Confederate service—a raid of wild riders dashes down the bayou banks, discomfits a handful of Americans at Plaquemine, scours through Napoleon and Labadie, and swoops upon a brace of feeble companies at Thibodeaux. The astonished Federals stay not for compliments, but make good use of horse legs, mule legs, and legs generally, to cover the four mile road, between Thibodeaux and La-

fourche Crossing, in the shortest running time on record
except the run from Bull Run. A race indeed—along
that narrow bayou road, with double-barrelled shot-guns
and border rifles cracking like champagne corks ; our
fugitives lassoed by twos and threes, till half a hundred
or more find themselves turned to the right-about toward
Thibodeaux· jail. Six hundred rebel horsemen, riding
and yelling like Cumanches, pursue our flying provost-
marshals, dispersed plantation guards, and suddenly-re-
lieved pickets, almost to the mouths of Lafourche batteries. A discharge of twelve and thirty-two pound guns
turns them back, but only to meet and merge in Major's
main body, which, to the number of two thousand, rapidly
brings up their rear. For an hour or two, they deploy and
reconnoitre, in the manner of Arabs, and then take cover
in the dense woods and close plantation-fields which border Lafourche bayou.

Not wholly idle, however, are these half-starved and
half-naked Bedouins. Thibodeaux boasts several groce-
ries and a few sutler shops. Thibodeaux harbors numbers of rebel sympathizers, on fine estates and in suburban
chateaux. Thibodeaux " secesh" damsels are pretty and
numerous, and its orchards luxuriant and tempting.
Thibodeaux counts hundreds of negroes, male and female, easy to "gobble," and of clear money value. So
the rebels break over that quiet " ville," with most charming varieties of looseness. While dashing cavalry officers
lend gold-braided arms to interesting plantation widows
and their dark-eyed creole daughters, just out of the con-
vent day-school; while improvised provost-marshal men
take note of captured "Yanks," and consign them to underground cells of the stone prison ; while scouts and
patrols whip in reluctant darkies to new masters; the
rank and file of raiders begin to solace themselves for

long abstinence, by the discussion of fat beeves, United
States brand flour, real "Lincoln" coffee, and (that prize
of all prizes for rebels) United States commissary whiskey.   Canteens, bottles, flasks, and gourds are quickly
filled and replenished; pint-dipperfuls are lost in rebel
gullets, till half the force get staggering drunk, and the
other half wait for a chance to be.

Confederate commanders rule their ragged cohorts
with iron authority, but are careless concerning discipline, so long as no immediate attack is apprehended.
Manifestly the rebel officers know with what small numbers they have to deal, and that Col. Stickney, who con-
trols some five hundred Federals at Lafourche Crossing,
will not be likely to trust them from the shelter of his
railroad-grading defences.   The capture of Thibodeaux,
they know, commands two roads diverging from it, to the
two crossings at Lafourche and Terrebonne ; these roads
describing a scalene triangle, with the railroad for its
hypotheneuse.   A small circular earthwork, stockaded
and ditched around by our New York boys, at Terrebonne Crossing, contains a company of less than thirty
men, left there to defend it.   Col. Major, after chasing
the Federals from Thibodeaux to Lafourche by one leg of
the triangle, sends a troop of his screeching butternuts
to attack Terrebonne by the other leg.   Headlong they
gallop towards our stockade, and hoist a white flag,
Lieut. Lyons goes out to parley.   A demand for surrender is made.   Lyons replies that the stockade was
not built for that purpose; whereupon a revolver is
drawn upon him, and a big oath or two.   At this juncture, up steams a train from Lafourche, bringing orders
from Col. Stickney to evacuate, which our stockade-men
obey, *en masse*, escaping to the cars.   In another moment
a whistle shrieks, the engine is reversed, and away

speeds the train for Lafourche again. Our young commander, Lieut. Lyons, is left on the ground, with a white flag above, and the rebels advancing to capture him.

"You are my prisoner, sir! Go with me, or I'll blow you brains out!" cries a rebel officer, presenting his revolver at Lieut. Lyons. At the same time, his mounted followers charge up the railroad track, fire off their pistols and shot-guns at the retreating steam-engine, and then draw bridles, to vent maledictions upon "Yankee treachery." So, my unlucky sous-officer of the "Ironsides" is compelled to see his brave company receding towards safety, while his own feet must measure the road to Thibodeaux jail, and thereafter march painfully to a Texan prison-pen.

During Saturday night, the rebel camp at Thibodeaux presents a scene of hilarious triumph. Commissary and sutlers' stores are without money or price, and whiskey rations call for no quartermasters' vouchers. The "bonny blue flag" gets bluer than ever; for at least a dozen barrels of "red eye" are mixed with the grey-backed clay of rebellion, till every "sans-culotte" of them can lay claim to a "brick in his hat."

Sabbath is not religiously kept in Thibodeaux parish next day. There are more stores to ransack, niggers to "lick," Yankee prisoners to bedevil, and the whiskey jollification continues. Scouting parties, scouring the roads, at full gallop, and clattering over bayou bridges like wild huntsmen; yells that make the owls hoot at midday in Bayou Blue swamp woods; cheers for Jeff. Davis, and a choral refrain about capturing New Orleans to the tune of "Dixie;" with such little dalliances as eating, smoking, and drinking whiskey, make up the order of rebel discipline in and about the captured "ville," while down Lafourche bayou sweeps cavalry in twos and

fours, making sudden onsets on Federal pickets, and
wheeling in and out of our lines, for pure mischief and
bravado.

The rebel commander, however, means more than menace to the Yankees. Towards sunset he begins to bestir
himself. Bugles sound along his lines, ragged cavaliers
take loving swigs at whiskey cans, and swing themselves
into saddle; and before dusk the entire force, consisting
of Major's, Phillips' and Pyron's regiments, with additions from Mouton's creole levy sets off from Thibodeaux
for a dash at Lafourche Crossing, to carry the bridge at
once, and bag five hundred "Yanks" by supper-time.
Such a roaring, leaping, riotous set never galloped before
to a battle-field. Every man is more or less intoxicated,
and some so drunk that, if they were not Texans and
born riders, they could never keep their saddles. The
afternoon was showery, and as this motley array gallops
down the bayou banks, a terrible thunderstorm breaks
over head, discharging torrents of sheeted rain. I never
saw the water come down in greater volume than it did
that day on the Opelousas Railroad line—flooding the
fields, raising the water courses, making roads like lakes,
and bridle-paths impassable. Major and his rebel horde
seem to exult in the elemental war above them. They
charge down the road, and up against the embankment
behind which our American batteries are posted, with
resolution worthy of a better cause than treason. Perhaps they anticipate an easy victory; perchance they expect to send our five hundred Yankees flying like chaff
before their mustang ponies. Never were traitors more
suddenly brought to a realizing sense, however. Their
columns are permitted to gallop within a hundred yards
of our position, when, from the big thirty-two, and the
three twelve-pounder howitzers, leaps out a withering

fire of grape and canister, flanked by steady volleys from our infantry, who stand up to the work like veterans. Then it is that our "Ironsides" major gives an example of coolness inspiring to his men. Discarding all instructions of Casey, as to firing by file in line of battle, the gallant Morgans sings his orders out as if at musket drill. "Men," he had whispered, while the enemy were yet at a distance, "you know my voice. Now don't fire a gun till I give the order. Recollect, men!" And when the rebel front comes nigh, and the word is passed to our cannoneers, and grape and canister hurtle over the levee, both sides can hear—rebels no less than Federals—a loud, clear voice above the din of strife: "Ready! aim! fire! Rear rank, ready! aim! fire! Front rank, ready! aim! fire! Rear rank——"

And our brave boys stand up to the drill as if at dress-inspection. They bite off cartridges, and load, and ram down, and half-face to a ready, and take aim, and—their deadly fire tells the rest of the story; till rebel horsemen reel, and their steeds, with loose bridles, break before the Yankee hurricane. That voice, giving orders like a drill-master; those volleys, regular as rifle practice; surely, no nine months' discipline is here, our enemies say; and they tell us afterwards that they thought our troops were "regulars," so cool did they show themselves under a Texan charge, with all its yells and aboriginal devilry.

But, though recoiling from the deathful greeting which met their first charge, the rebels are soon rallied by their officers. Forming a second line of battle, they advance again, with headlong determination, stopping not for grape or canister; resolved to ride down both our guns and gunners. But that ringing order peals again—"Rear rank, ready! aim! fire!"—and again leap out the responsive volleys from our infantry lines. A score of saddles

are emptied, a score of horses careering confusedly while
yet forty yards from our batteries. They retreat, in dis-
ordered ranks. Voices of officers, sounding out of the
melee, vainly urge them to the fiery parapet. The second
charge rolls back repulsed. Our American soldiers have
breathing time again.

Colonel Major little expected such an obstacle. His
march from the Sabine had thus far been a mere pleasure
excursion; but Lafourche Crossing shows a lion in his
path. Here are two or three thousand Texan "invinci-
bles" flying back from a mud bank, like so many Mexican
"greasers." Scores of these dare-devil cavalry lie dead
or dying under the levee, within a hundred feet of the
Yankee lines. Those batteries must be carried at all
hazard. West Point Major forms his line for a third
charge.

More swigs at whiskey cans; a sounding of bugles; a
quick, sharp order, "Charge!" from centre to flanks; and
the rebels are riding on again. This, indeed, is a
desperate onset, almost achieving victory. Rowels are
driven into the horses; a fierce war-whoop rings from
front to rear, and the charging squadrons bear down like
thunder-clouds, with a lurid flame from the muzzles of
their guns marking the line of advance. Well for our
brave men that, under previous charges, they stood up
to their drill exercise so coolly. Again listening for
Morgans' trumpet voice, the gallant New York and Connecticut boys remain steady, like veterans, while our
artillerymen sight their cannon against the black, advancing masses that come sweeping through torrents of rain.
Up the embankment this time; up to the cannon mouths;
yes! over howitzers and into infantry ranks, the rebels
sweep like a tornado. They drive back gunners and mus-
keteers, they leap from their saddles, closing upon our

bayonets, bestriding our field-pieces with yells of triumph.
But the Americans answer with an American hurrah,
and when that ceases, the steady emphasis of Morgans'
tone is heard—"Rear rank! ready! aim! fire!" A terrible
volley and a fierce charge of our infantry repulse the foe a
third time, strewing his dead upon the bayou road, as
thick as falling leaves in November. In vain the Texan
chiefs dash hither and thither; in vain they roar commands till their throats grow hoarse. The rebel spirit
is broken, for the day, and even whiskey cannot bring
them to time again. They scatter to the roadside, disperse,
and rally in close order, and then, turning bridles for
Thibodeaux, are lost in the shades of advancing night.
One desperado only lingers where the rebels pierced our
lines. Maddened by alcohol, he charged upon a howitzer,
and sprang from his saddle, at its muzzle. Here, unable
to keep his legs, he falls forward on the gun, clasping it
with both arms, and yelling, with an oath, "Surrender,
Yank! this piece is mine!"

"Take it!" replies the Yankee gunner, with a sword-
thrust that pierces the rebel's midriff.

This ends Texan "charging" on Lafourche Crossing.
A hundred dead rebels are left upon the field, and the
sum of their wounded reaches double that number.

CHAPTER XIII.

BAYOU BŒUFF.

SABBATH morning brings flying rumors from all quarters. We hear of fighting, at Lafourche and Thibodeaux; of rebel advances on the railroad line. In the afternoon, Lieut. Robens, of my regiment, Deputy Provost Marshal, stationed at Tigerville, reports at camp. From him, I glean several items of intelligence respecting the condition of affairs upon the railroad line. As far back as Thursday last, this young officer received hints concerning the rebel advance, which he communicated to the Provost General by letter. A person, who represented himself as a Union fugitive from Alexandria, brought news that "Dick Taylor" was moving down the Teche, with fifteen thousand men; and that his main object was the recapture of New Orleans. On Friday, a negro woman sought protection from a mistress, who had cruelly whipped her, while her master, standing by, boasted that his friends would soon drive the Yankees from Terrebonne, when he should be able to take the "airs out of his niggers" once more. On Saturday, the negroes crowded into Tigerville, bringing exaggerated accounts of rebel forces, and more credible statements regarding the sympathy with which their appearance was greeted by treacherous white men who had pretended to support our cause. My poor black loyalists at Tigerville are eager to make a stand. They demand arms, declaring that they will fight to the death, rather than return to bondage.

Capt. Bailey, Deputy Provost Marshal at Houma, arrives at Brashear, this Sabbath day, reporting rebels to be in large numbers on the road between Houma and Tigerville. A locomotive reconnoissance, upon the railroad, returns toward evening, with information that rebel horsemen were encountered near Chickahoula. During the afternoon, a violent thunder storm breaks over Brashear; and pluvial showers descend upon our camps. Toward dusk, having mustered my small force, I take cars for Bayou Bœuff, leaving the horses to follow by the wagon road. Steaming through rain and darkness, we reach the front, and disembark in mud and water. This dreary and drenched camp at Bayou Bœuff offers scant shelter. I find a single company of my regiment, under Lieutenant Kirby ; some thirty effectives ; bivouacked beneath protecting eaves of a decaying sugar-house roof. The ground about them is shared by a detachment of the Twenty-First Indiana Siege Artillery, under Lieut. Sherfy, who, with Lieut. Kirby's men, lately garrisoned Fort Chene, a harbor fortification some miles below Brashear City. These combined commands had received orders from Col. Stickney, to evacuate the fort, destroy its defences, and report, with its heavy pieces, three in number, at Bayou Bœuff. Accordingly, they are here, and I dig my way, through yellow mire, to their flank, where Lieut. Kirby contrives to seat me in a dry corner of his narrow quarters. Therefrom, after hearing some reports, I seek lodging in a neighboring hut, and sleep the sleep of weariness, till morning.

Monday opens a day of activity. Receiving reports and property accounts from Captain Sanford, of the Twenty-Third Connecticut Volunteers, who, with three companies of his regiment, has occupied the post, I assume command, and prepare to get our defensive *materiel* in

working condition. Much to my surprise, on inspection
of the siege-pieces, I find them planted on the Brashear
side of Bayou Bœuff; a weak position, if assaulted by
any force capable of flanking movements. Slight earthworks have been thrown up, on the levee, and a cannon is
mounted near the bridgehead, on one side of the railroad
track, in line with two others, which command half a mile
or more of the opposite shore and highway approaches
from Tigerville. A signal tower, erected by. General
Weitzel, for observation of the surrounding country, has
been demolished, as I learn, under the same sagacious
orders which caused Fort Chene to be abandoned and its
cannon brought to this place. Is this another manifestation of that military genius which denuded Brashear City
of effectives, and left the Opelousas railroad to be severed by a sudden dash of rebels into Terrebonne?

I mentally ask this question; but have no time to
speculate further. This railroad crossing, at Bayou
Bœuff, is now the point to be defended, and it only remains for me to make the best of defensive facilities.
The land is low on both sides of the railroad; only on
the levee banks, or on the track, can our artillery obtain
a proper range. I order one siege-piece to be elevated
to a position on the grade; but my judgment convinces
me that we are on the wrong side of the bridge, for an
effective defence of this post.

The rebels are known to be in force at Terrebonne,
twenty miles distant by the rail, and their advance may
be looked for hourly. Could I have time to erect a line
of earthworks, at the other bridge-end, to stretch from
the bayou-bank to the timber which crosses the roads, we
might hold the Bœuff against an enemy with hopes of success; for our flanks would be difficult to molest, unless
approached by heavier artillery. A fort, of earth and

cypress logs, upon the other bank, well-victualled and supplied with ammunition, would be better still, and with it I could keep the enemy at bay effectually.

Such are my reflections in surveying the position; but there is no time for "change of base," with rebels in a half day's march of us. To learn the ground, and comprehend its approaches, becomes my first concern, and I lose no time in mustering a dozen of my hard-riding "Ironsides" boys, to go "on scout" and gather information.

Noontime arrives, and with it a locomotive, in charge of Lieut. Stevenson, of my regiment, dispatched for a "reconnoissance" upon the railroad. It carries a twelve-pound howitzer, mounted on a freight-car, fenced by planks and timber buttresses; with sharp-shooters behind, to pick off rebel pickets, should they show themselves. Our Brashear gun-boat now steams up, and fastens to the bridge, and her valorous captain counsels me to pull that structure down, to keep the rebel cavalry from charging over it. I decline the loan of his hawser for such purpose, however, and only make use of the war vessel, to send on her some dozen sick men to our Brashear hospital. So the gunboat steams off again, and in an hour or more the reconnoitring train comes back, with all its armament and sharp-shooters intact and bloodless.

Nevertheless, this rail road battery has visited Terrebonne, and the howitzer has discoursed with rebel artillery. Our iron-horse vedettes made a dash through Tigerville and Chickahoula, and then bore on, with locomotive at the rear, until they neared the open fields of Terrebonne, where Winder's rich plantation skirts one side of the rail road, and Tanner's sugar-grounds hem in the other. Here they saw rebels tearing up rails, and rebels burrowing in earthworks, and rebel cavalry cavorting over neighboring roads and meadows. So, they

stopped, and bowled a shell upon the enemy; whereat a
rebel battery opened on them; and thus, satisfied with *reconnoissance*, and exchanging one or two more shots with
rebeldom, they reversed the engine just in time to escape
a dash of cavalry, and are here safely to report the result
of a railroad excursion. So much I learn through the
reconnoissance, that the enemy had not yet left Terrebonne, and I mentally resolve on breaking ground for a
fort on the opposite levee. It is evident, that the rebels
are in force at Thibodeaux, and not to be doubted, that
they will soon advance upon the Bœuff. But could time
be left me, to throw up defences, on the eastern bridgehead, so that roads and plateaus, leading to the railway,
might be thus commanded, while musketry and howitzer
prevent attempts at crossing from the lakes, or the upper
bayou—I have confidence in my ability to hold the
Bœuff, until our Brashear garrison can be relieved by
way of the Gulf.

Thus encouraged, I at once send out a squad as pickets,
on a hand-car, with orders to repair to Tigerville, some
twelve miles distant by the highway, and by rail road
seven. They are instructed to organize a horse and foot
patrol of certain blacks, selected from plantations on
their route, and known to me as bold and trusty partisans
of ours. Then, strengthening the pickets near our camp,
and sending scouts to scour the various roads, with orders
to be vigilant, I see the sun set on my first day of command at Bayou Bœuff.

No repose yet, however. I must talk with anxious
citizens, who bring reports of rebel scouts, and claim
protection as good Union men; and I must question wide-
mouthed contrabands from Bayou Black estates, who
"seed a rebel" here and there, behind a hundred bushes.
Primary care of all, I must dispatch a messenger to work

his way through rebel lines, and reach Lafourche; for there, perhaps, are "acting-brigadier" Stickney, and my regiment; and there, in that case, is the telegraph still safe, connecting with head-quarters at New Orleans. So I pen a hasty note, reporting my position, and forthwith provide a saddled horse for Sergeant Lewis, who volunteers to ride, walk, crawl, or swim his way to our lines at Lafourche Crossing. "Heaven speed my messenger!" I mentally pray, as he rides away though the twilight. He can make thirty miles to night, on the road toward Houma, and to-morrow he may take the swamp, and so pass from Bayou Blue to Lafourche, unnoticed.

Lieut. Kirby has pitched a tent for me to-day, and my cook George ought to be getting supper, but has not yet returned from Brashear, whither he went, this morning, for our rations. Toussaint, my groom, arrives with the horse, "Black Roman." John remains in camp, at Brashear, with our baggage. So I must accept my lieutenant's coffee and hard bread, or lie down supperless.

I throw myself upon a blanket, but am aroused immediately. A scout brings intelligence of boats seen crossing at Lake Pelourde. It is a movement which may threaten some design on Brashear City. A force from Pelourde might strike the rear of both Bayou Bœuff and Brashear. It is from Brashear that such a force must be reconnoitred or repelled. I look around, for a messenger, and Lieut. Robens, of my regiment, opportunely presents himself. I direct him to mount and ride at once to Brashear, report what I have learned to Major Anthony, and have him take the speediest measures for defence. Presently, I hear the lieutenant gallopping from camp. It is now nine o'clock. He should reach Brashear City between ten and eleven. I lie down again.

From unrefreshing sleep I rise early. It is Tuesday,

the twenty-third day of June, a balmy morning, redolent
of summer sweets.   I hear the wheels of a hand car on
the railroad. It is the Tigerville picket, ordered to report
to me at sunrise.   A steam whistle shrieks from the
woods west of us.   That must be the train from Brashear
City.   Major Anthony promised yesterday that constant commuication should be kept between our camps.
I hope this train brings George, with rations.

But it is a locomotive only; and Conductor "Billy"
reports, that—"The rebels are shelling Brashear."

"Ah! they are at Berwick then! But where are your
cars, sir?"

"I thought I would come and report, sir.   The rebels
are in great force opposite Brashear."

"You had better go back, and couple on the commissary train, if danger be threatened."

The Conductor sprang on his engine.   "I cannot tell
what may have happened," he remarked.   "For fear of
accident, I shall make a signal when I return—two
screams of the steam-whistle, with a pause between
them."

The locomotive rattles away, and I turn, to hear the
report of my railroad picket.   "All right at Tigerville,
Colonel!"

"Have you seen nothing of the enemy, sergeant?"

"No rebels about, Colonel. I had fifty darkeys on
horses and mules, scouting all night, sir. Not a reb to
be seen this side of Chuckahoula."

"Did you leave any of your squad at Tigerville?"

"No, sir! I was ordered to report to camp at sunrise."

"Take another squad—a relief—and go back, for the
day.   I desire you to remain with them, sergeant."

"Yes, sir!" And my sergeant, who like most of the
non-commissioned officers of Co. I, can be trusted for duty

and discipline at all times, goes out to detail the day-picket for Tigerville. In a few minutes, I hear his hand-car rumbling over the rails again.

But the non-arrival of a train, with George and my rations, suggests another *jour maigre*, and I must forage for breakfast presently. Meantime, a cup of coffee—unfailing matinal stimulant in this sultry clime—restores my equipoise. Toussaint saddles "Black Roman," and I ride to the earthworks, musingly. It is a brilliant morning, and the broad bosom of Bayou Bœuff flashes back golden sunshine. I look over the placid landscape; over woods rocking in green luxuriance; over quiet waters laving the levee banks; over peaceful cottages bowered in fragrant orchards. Who would dream that foes are threatening discord and conflict? that black-mouthed cannon are needed here, or that fire shall menace ruin to these homesteads?

The rumble of a hand-car, upon the rail-track, recalls me from reflective mood. Tigerville pickets return, with a report, that rebels in force are within ten and eight miles of this position. Their main body of cavalry is advancing from the Chickahoula road, through Tigerville, and must soon reach Bayou Bœuff. Already, a stream of black fugitives from Terrebonne plantations begins to flow into camp.

It is the twenty-third day of June. At this hour, our comrades at Lafourche Crossing, being reinforced from New Orleans, are marching upon Thibodeaux, to find that place evacuated by Colonel Major and his rebels. But this movement is yet unknown to me; just as the imminent peril of Brashear City remains undisclosed to its late post-commandant.

Imminent peril, indeed! Suddenly, I hear the signal-whistles of Conductor "Billy;" and the crash of a brace of locomotives shakes the track, as they rush into the station. "Billy" springs from the leading engine.

"Colonel! Brashear is captured by the rebels!"

"Captured!"

"They 've got it, sir! Came in from the woods, at our rear! It was a complete surprise, sir!"

"Where is the train of cars you were to bring in?"

"I could not hitch on this engine to it, sir; as the other was between me and the cars?"

"Why did you not "hitch" the other one, then?"

"That was not strong enough to draw the train."

I do not, at this moment, ask the Conductor why he failed to make both locomotives fast to our train of stores, and bring its valuable freight out of the Brashear City depot. Of little account are questions of any sort, at this stage of events; since I have learned the main, disastrous fact, that our base of supplies and safety is now in rebel possession. Cut off and isolated; my feeble post menaced in front and rear; I am now to consider the immediate peril of my own situation.

Very soon I get definite accounts of the morning's occurrences at the Bay. My Quartermaster, Lieut Kimball, reports; bringing wagons containing his own effects, with some regimental property, and a few trunks. Toussaint, George, and John, my servants, arrive next, and presently, numbers of fugitives, soldiers and non-combatants, flock in by highway and railroad. The loss of Brashear is confirmed; and the details thereof take shape under voluble narration of a hundred tongues.

CHAPTER XIV.

REBEL SCHEMES.

GATHERING on the Louisianian borders, from Red River regions above Shreveport, far down to Sabine banks, and, lower still, to the pine-woods and marshes that trend upon waters of the Gulf, the rebel hordes, under various leaders, ranged over prairies and timber bottoms. General "Dick Taylor," son of old "Rough and Ready," commanded the Texan mounted infantry, which, in regiments, "legions," and partisan bands, had crossed the Sabine at Niblett's Bluff, and occupied extensive open tracts lying between the rivers Calcasieu and Atchafalaya. General Mouton, brother to a former governor of Louisiana, collecting all the refugees from New Orleans and lower regions of the Mississippi; all the Creoles and "Cagians" who could be coaxed or conscripted, from bayou-banks and swampish lands; made his rendezvous at Alexandria, and thence co-operated with Taylor's battalions. Both armies, it is true, fell back before the advance of General Banks, when that Federal commander-in-chief made his rapid march from Brashear City up the Teche, ascending to Alexandria, and thence diverging to Port Hudson. But when, I say they fell back, I say all that can be said. They were neither dispersed nor demoralized. Town by town, they contested our progress through the Teche country; abandoning Franklin after a hard-fought battle; evacuating New Iberia after destroying their flotilla and defences; retreating from Alexan-

dria, only when Admiral Porter's guns and mortars had
rendered it untenable. But the numerical damage which
they sustained was slight, and their war-spirit seemed to
wax rather than wane before our advancing stars. No
sooner did General Banks wheel his army Mississippi-
ward, than this war-spirit blazed behind him. Partisans
and guerrillas sprang up on his flanks ubiquitously.
Nomad horsemen hung about and harrassed his wagon-
trains, made sorties on his rear-guard, captured his stragglers, ambushed his scouts. In Lower Louisiana, we saw
them following Col. Chickering's caravan of cattle and
contrabands almost to the guns of Brashear ; and had
they been as enterprising as our escort was actually
feeble, they might have retaken the " spoil," and
" bagged" its custodians. In Upper Louisiana, at the
same time, they were dashing down from the Arkansas
lines, to attack Richmond and Lake Providence ; while
General Banks, re-crossing the Atchafalaya, abandoned
all the lately-captured territory, to find his resources
barely equal to the close investment of Port Hudson.

Such was the aspect of affairs, when General " Dick
Taylor," from his camps between Vermillionville and
Franklin, on the Teche, and General Mouton, from his
headquarters near Opelousas, flung out their advances in
the shape of cavalry and light artillery, under command
of chosen leaders, charged with no less a design than to
open the way for a combined assault on New Orleans.
General Taylor had planned, and General Mouton ordered,
that Col. Major, with his brigade, should cross the Atchafalaya, at Morgan's Ferry, proceed down Bayou Gros
Tete, to Plaquemine, strike off to Bayou Lafourche, and
then descend the banks of that water course to the rear
of Brashear City. We have seen how Major fulfilled his
mission ; when, after burning a half-dozen steamboats at

Plaquemine, and chasing our provost-guards out of Thibodeaux, he charged against stouter stuff at Lafourche Crossing, and fell back with a loss of some hundreds. That was the hour when he should have been followed up by strong reinforcements from New Orleans. That was the moment when a couple of gunboats and another regiment ought to have arrived, by way of sea, to the succor of Brashear City. Why these things were not done, or whether, in reality, there was force enough at New Orleans to have accomplished either, has never transpired through official sources, and, therefore, the good public must remain profoundly ignorant upon the subject. But, if the Crescent City was actually so denuded of strength as to be unable to cover her approaches, or protect her outposts, then it must be concluded that Port Hudson was, at that time, of more importance than New Orleans, and that the former, instead of the latter, had properly absorbed the attention of our generals and their soldiers.

There is no flippancy in this remark; for it cannot be denied, that New Orleans was vitally endangered by the concentration and descent of rebel armies upon its rear and flank ; thus giving to our foes the occupation of a great railway means of transportation, a country able to subsist their largest force, and a population in sympathy with their cause.

While Col. Major was performing his share of the work allotted to subordinate rebel leaders, Gen. "Tom Green," proceeded down the Teche to Pattersonville, and thence started his "musquito fleet" for operations against Brashear City. The "musquito fleet" was a unique armada, consisting of improvised transportation, in the shape of "sugar-coolers," which are long coffin-like wooden boxes, used, as the name implies, on plantations, as receptacles of the syrup during the process of its manufacture into sugar A multitude of these vessels, capable of conveying one or two men, with the addition of such rafts as could be constructed, and a few skiffs, made up the flotilla, whereby some three hundred armed men were enabled to cross the Atchafalaya, navigate Grand Lake, and debouch through Lake Pelourde and Flat Lake, to the rear of Brashear.

Thus matters stood on Monday, the twenty-second of June. The contemplated assault, planned by General Green, is to be made in conjunction with an anticipated advance of Major, with his force, upon the railroad stations still held by our American soldiers. Communication is open, across the back country, between Major and Green; and the latter knows the force and intentions of his coadjutor. Green does not yet know that Major has been repulsed at Lafourche Crossing; nor is he aware that the dashing cavalry-chief has evacuated Thibodeaux, and is hurrying with his ragged riders, from Terrebonne to Chickahoula, believing himself pursued by reinforcements of Federals from New Orleans. Green does not know, and, unfortunately, our troops at Lafourche Crossing, and the commandant at New Orleans, do not know, that Col. Major deems himself cut off from retreat by way of Thibodeaux, and relies solely on the success of an attack on Brashear, to enable him to make his way out of the dangerous trap into which he begins to fear that he has ridden too hastily. Had this fact—for it is a fact—been suspected by Lieut.-Col. Stickney, at Lafourche Crossing, or by my brave Major Morgans, who, about this time, is getting ready for a dash, with our gallant "Ironsides" boys, into Thibodeaux, I am sure they would have profited by the occasion, and lost no time in bringing a few regiments from New Orleans, by rail, to hang

upon the rear of Major and his mustangs. But, they fail
to learn, or to benefit by, the terror of their late assailants,
and, in their turn, as it subsequently appears, become
the victims of a panic, which sends them to the "right-
about," in the direction of Algiers.

· All designs being matured by "Tom Green," for his
project against Brashear, the assault is fixed for daybreak on the morning of Tuesday, twenty-third of June.
Green demands two hundred and fifty volunteers for
secret and hazardous service. Over three hundred
respond, and are placed under command of Major Hunter,
an officer who has seen rough service on the western
frontiers of Texas. Major Hunter comprehends the work
that is expected of him. He is to paddle his "musquito fleet," at dusk of evening, through the chain of
lakes that penetrates behind Brashear City. He is to
land secretly near a previously-reconnoitred point, in the
rear of that timber-belt which makes a back-ground for
Brashear, as Berwick Bay makes its fore-ground. He is
to approach to the edge of that timber, whence he can
overlook the Federal camps and batteries. He will wait
in that position, till Green, from the opposite bay-shore,
shall begin the assault by a bombardment. Then, when
the attention of Yankee officers and men shall be absorbed by the attack in front, Major Hunter is to lead
out his braves from their cover, and, with Texan yells,
dash down upon and capture Brashear City.

How well the crafty rebel commander, "Tom Green,"
advised by numerous spies concerning our weakness, our
disorganization, and our carelessness, adapts his plans
to insure their complete success! Neither Maj. Hunter,
nor any member of his "forlorn hope" has been informed
regarding the feeble condition of Brashear. It is for
them to obey orders, and to essay what they deem

a desperate enterprise. I have the word of many rebels, who were of the number of that "musquito-fleet" force, that they never expected to return alive, unless as paroled prisoners-of-war. Starting in their crazy water-craft, about three hundred strong, at least fifty gave out, either on the lake, or in the toilsome march which followed their debarkation. These were the men and boats reported to me, as having been seen, about sunset, crossing a section of Lake Pelourde, and whose appearance and suspected design, I had, in turn, reported to Major Anthony at Brashear City. From my post, at Bayou Bœuff, there was no means of reaching or opposing them. I knew not, at that time, but that their design was to threaten my own position, by effecting a landing at some point above me, on the Bœuff; I learn, long afterwards, while, a prisoner in Texas, that the original plan of approaches proposed an attack, in conjunction with Major's expected force, first upon my slight defences, and afterwards upon the rear of Brashear.

But whatever may have been the expectations of General Green, it is certain that Major Hunter's men, creeping under darkness, through swamps, up to their belts in mire, for several miles, toward the edge of timber which commanded Brashear City, were not inspired with very sanguine hopes of victory over Yankees. It is positive, moreover, that these rebel raiders, having at last reached, about midnight, a point whence they could look out, over open fields, and spy what appeared to be the encampment of a large army, were suddenly impressed with a panic quite as sensible as that which, about the same time, was urging Col. Major into a gallop from Terrebonne to Chickahoula. Those white tents, stretching along the bay-shore, like a great town of canvass; the fort, at their right, which they knew to be heavily mounted; the silence brooding over all, giving their hearts space to beat audibly against their lean ribs; all combined to make our rebel adventurers feel lonesome and uncomfortable. They had anticipated the hour when "Tom Green" was to fire his signal-guns. They heard no sound of co-operation from the Berwick shore. The dread of being "trapped" took possession of them, and, in spite of Major Hunter's commands and entreaties, they abruptly broke and fled back, through woods and swamps, till they gained once more their "musquito-fleet." There the chagrined commander succeeded in getting them to halt and listen to him. There, as I have been credibly informed, that bold Hunter made use of some tolerably big oaths, in the way of illustrating his harrangue to them. "We may all be shot," he cried, imploring them to re-trace their steps. "Not one of us may get back to the brigade; but, gentlemen, we'd better just fall down in our tracks than go back disgraced, and have old Tom Green tell us so!" All stronger words of the rebel leader, I leave to be imagined; but the result of his speech was, that the "forlorn hope," minus a few stragglers, returned with him, and struck the timber, long after Green's howitzers had begun their barking from the Berwick shore.

CHAPTER XV.

THE CAPTURE OF BRASHEAR CITY.

DAYBREAK on the twenty-third day of July, 1863, was ushered upon Brashear City by the roar of those rebel howitzers which "Tom Green" had promised his "forlorn hope" should announce his presence upon the Berwick shore. Our startled garrison of Fort Buchanan hurried from tents to bomb-proof magazines, and a brisk exchange of shot and shell soon opened the battle in earnest. But little apprehension was felt by the Americans of aught beyond a cannon-bout being intended by the enemy; for it presently become apparent that the assaulting force was not numerically strong, while the calibre of its artillery was much inferior to that of our heavy siege-pieces. No means of transportation appeared at hand, threatening any design to cross Berwick Bay; and such an attempt, indeed, under the range of our cannon and musketry on land, and a flanking fire from the gunboat, would have been hazardous, if not impracticable, to a much larger hostile army.

But, as I have stated previously, the crafty rebels had found means of transportation in another quarter, and were at this hour advancing stealthily on Brashear City through the woods and swamps at its rear. Meanwhile, General Taylor, at his headquarters near Pattersonville, and General Mouton, at Gibbons' Point, opposite Fort Buchanan, were awaiting the success of Green's cannonade, to advance the bulk of their forces toward Berwick

City. General Mouton's immediate strength consisted of two Texan regiments, and an Arizonian battalion, most of them sharp-shooters, who were posted so as to command the Federal fort and direct their fire upon its artillery men. About a mile below, sheltered by woods and by a mound near the shore, "Tom Green" brought his two batteries (Valverde and Nichols) to bear upon the Brashear camps, while his own regiment, the Fifth Texas, and a battalion of Louisiana cavalry under Col. Walker, supported the guns with their small arms.

The first rebel shot was launched at our gunboat, mounting two twelve-pound howitzers, and commanded by a person named Ryder, who, in the words of Admiral Farragut's subsequent report, "is not represented to have been any more vigilant than the rest, and backed down the bay."

That gun-shot was the alarum of our little garrison. In a brief space the grey of morn became illumined by a blaze which leaped from opposing shores of the bay. From the blackened walls of burned buildings at Berwick landing, far up to Gibbons' Point, where a thousand rifles were cracking, the rebel side delivered continuous volleys of bullets and discharges of shot and shells; while, on our part, we were not backward in pouring iron and lead from the fort and lower batteries. The screeching and whistling of various missiles, the barking of single muskets, the rattle of volleys, and the boom of great pieces, soon brought every sleeper out of his bunk or bed, and the water-front of Brashear was speedily alive with defenders. Few showed themselves, indeed, in the range of rebel fire; but there were plenty of " coigns of 'vantage," in the shape of big trees, cook-houses, walls, and embankments; and from behind these points of shelter our brave fellows plied their shots effectually;

till, after two hours' interchange of courtesies between
infantry and artillery of both sides, the rebel fire began
to slacken, and their pieces were more than once driven
from position.

It was at this moment that a yell arose, in the rear; a
mingling of Indian whoop and wolf-howl; the charging-
cry of Major Hunter and his ragged desperadoes, breaking cover from the woods behind our camps; advancing
at double-quick over the open fields that intervened between shore and timber.

Their line of battle was an irregular one; a sort of
involuntary echelon, perhaps the result of unequal marching, perhaps caused by the inequalities of ploughed ground
and stubble which impeded them. But the flanks of
their different companies were separated by wide gaps,
and their ranks were broken in some places by intervals
wide enough for skirmishing. On they came, scarcely
two hundred and fifty men, armed with shot-guns, rifles,
and a few revolvers. One solid company of United States
dragoons could have ridden down and dispersed them
like sheep. One hundred determined infantry-men,
under a resolute commander, meeting them in line of
battle, might have scattered the motley crew by a couple
of well-aimed volleys. Had there been common militia-
organization; had a tithe of the able-bodied idlers of
various camps been thrown upon the flanks of this rebel
rabble, with our howitzers trained upon their front, they
must have bitten the dust, or surrendered, every one of
them, before they could have gained our camp lines.

But the attack meets no sustained resistance. Before
our straggling and unofficered squads can be brought into
any line of defence, the left flank of rebel advance reaches
the cover of an orange grove near the almost vacant tents
of the 176th New York ("Ironsides") and 23d Connecticut

regiments, while its right extends toward Fort Buchanan.
Dashing into the rearmost company streets, they discharge
their pistols into our canvass walls. From the thick
orange-growth they deliver sharp and sudden volleys
of slugs and bullets. An officer of my regiment, Captain
Thomason,·endeavors to rally a small detachment, between
our camp and the one at our rear, now filled with rebels.
He brings them into some order, and fires a brace of
volleys, which have little effect upon the scattered foe.
Col. Nott, rising from his invalid's couch, shows himself
to the men, mounted, and orders them into line, but the
command comes too late for organization. Our brave
fellows, magnifying the numbers of the invaders, and be-
wildered by total lack of preparation and the complete
surprise, begin to drop back, doggedly, firing single
shots, as they seek the shelter of neighboring buildings.
For a few minutes, this sort of skirmishing is kept up;
the rebels, meantime, occupying themselves in ransack-
ing the tents in their possession. Col. Nott calls upon
those nearest to follow, and rides toward the depot, where
the locomotives are fired up, intending to run one to
Bayou Bœuff, and, perhaps, escape from that point, by
means of the gunboat. But his long illness and inactivity
have rendered him feeble, and, on reaching the door of
our hospital, about two hundred yards distant, he falls,
fainting, from his horse. It is a fortunate accident, for
bullets now begin to fly thickly on the road, and a negro
woman is shot in front of the hospital, just as our Colonel
sinks exhausted.

In the meantime, desultory fighting goes on at various
points. Two companies of the " Ironsides" regiment,
garrisoning Fort Buchanan, becoming apprised of an invasion from the timber, get impatient to take part as infantry in the contest. Stout and gallant boys, from Mad-

ison county, they comprehend that, when an enemy is at
hand, some immediate resistance is called for. They
have been working steadily, during two hours, at the
siege-guns, directing all attention to the Berwick shore
foe, and little anticipating a fire in their rear. Now,
aware of the new peril, and conscious of the exposed position of the fort to a land attack, they expect to be led at
once against the rebels. But to whom shall they look
for orders? Captain Noblett, artillery chief, with the
ostensible design of procuring more ammunition, has long
ago mounted his horse and ridden to the depot. At this
moment, just as the rebels show themselves in the
orange grove near our camps, this artillery commander
rolls from his steed, the animal being shot, and makes
the best of his way—not back to his command at Fort
Buchanan—but to the refuge of our hospital. Perhaps
he deems it madness to attempt the running of a two
mile gauntlet of sharp-shooters, in order to rejoin his Indiana battery boys. Very possibly, like other officers, he
comes to the conclusion that "all is lost but honor," and
that "*sauve qui peut*," is the motto for everybody.

Left to his own discretion, Lieutenant Wellington, of
the "Ironsides," tries to make some dispositions for
defence. The large guns of Fort Buchanan, mounted *en
barbette*, are too ponderous to handle, for the purpose of
directing them to the rear. With great exertion, one
piece is dislodged from its position, warped to the rear,
by means of ropes manned by our soldiers, and brought
into range upon the land-side. It is about this juncture
of affairs that Major Anthony appears at the fort, and
begins to take some direction of them. He has galloped
under a shower of bullets from the railroad depot. He
has seen his valiant *confrere*, Captain Noblett, dismounted,
by the fire that left him scathless. He has marked the

rebel force advancing, in its irregular fragments. Now, if he will rally our Madison boys, and the artillery men, at least a hundred in all, perhaps more, he may make a flank movement upon the exultant rebels, and form a nucleus for our scattered squads to rally upon. Lieut. Wellington assures him that his men are ready and eager; that they demand to be led against the enemy. But unfortunately our Major's view of the proper policy is a different one. Very likely, if he saw around him a hundred, or less, of troopers in their saddles, with sabres drawn, and pistols in holsters, our gallant major-commandant of Brashear City would have given the word for a dash upon the rebels, were they double the number opposed to him. But, there are no cavalry at hand; no rough riders to follow his bright sabre and ringing voice. So, Major Anthony adopts the *role* of Fabius rather than that of Marcellus. He orders the heavy gun to be transported out of the fort to a point about half-a-mile lower, upon a road, leading to our camps and the railroad. Here, placed in position, and worked by our willing men, it launches some telling shots against the rebels, who have possession of the camps and are approaching the main street and water front of Brashear.

While these dispositions were made at the upper part of the city, some show of defence continued near the railroad depot. The rebels, swooping down upon our convalescent camps, made short work of the few who ventured opposition. Few indeed were these; for even had the able-bodied of our convalescents been disposed to fight, they had neither arms, ammunition, nor officers to direct them. Two or three lieutenants and sergeants, with small squads, attempted to rally the hundreds who were flying to and fro, seeking cover; but their efforts could not, at such a stage of panic, combine the materials that had been allowed to remain disintegrated during months. Dozens of men were shot down by the rebels unresistingly. In so wild a melée, amid yells and the rattle of musketry, and encompassed by clouds of smoke, the foe could hardly discriminate, even were he desirous of so doing, between the sick and well, the armed and unarmed.

One of our "Ironsides" captains, who has been confined to his quarters by sickness, sallies into the street, and essays to get a body of stragglers into order. He succeeds in bringing ten or fifteen together in line, when a rebel company charges upon them, with the bayonet. Captain Cutter, a cool and bold man, gives the signal to fall back, to secure a better position; but the enemy is close upon them, and a Texan summons him to give up his sword   "I never surrender!" answers Cutter, in his deliberate way; whereupon he is immediately shot through the head, and falls dead; yielding up as gallant a soul as ever made Liberty the goal of ambition.

While these events were transpiring, a stand had been made by Lieut. Stevenson, "of ours," commanding the provost-guard of Brashear City. This brave officer had charge of a twenty-four pounder, which, after doing good service against Green's batteries, over the bay, was wheeled into position for operating against the "surprise party" at our rear. With Lieut. Stevenson, at this post, remained Sergeant Deming, of his company, a young private named Newlan, and two other members of my regiment. These resolute fellows stood to the gun, till, completely environed by foes, they became a target for bullets. Four out of the five, including the lieutenant, were shot down, before their piece was captured.

But such isolated and desperate endeavor; such fragmentary struggles of indignant courage against the fate which no wise foresight had anticipated, and no prudent preparation provided against, could only serve to protract suspense. The first panic of our feeble and disorganized regimental remnants had decided victory in favor of the daring foe. Well must the crafty Green have calculated upon our demoralization and incapacity. Cruel was the neglect, wherever its responsibility may lie, which left our little garrison to meet the brunt of a hostile assault, backed by at least ten thousand rebels, under competent generals.

Flushed with his triumph, achieved at small expense, and promising brilliant results in plunder, Major Hunter presents himself presently before our own Major at the upper batteries. The post-commandant is summoned to surrender Brashear City. It is a superfluous demand, doubtless, on the part of the Texan, since he can see for himself that no further resistance is contemplated; but he asks, furthermore, that our post-commandant shall surrender fleet as well as army; our notable gun-boat, as well as our convalescents and runaways. Major Anthony casts his glance down the bay, and beholds the war-vessel's black smoke streaming backward toward Brashear, as her engines propel her with all speed out of the harbor. He remarks forcibly to the Texan Major, that he wishes the recreant gun-boat could be caught by him, with the wretched poltroon who commands her.

And, after this ebullition of spirit, the preliminaries of peace are adjusted, and the city of Brashear, with its appurtenances, passes once more into rebel possession.

CHAPTER XVI.

TWENTY-FOUR HOURS.

In the homely vernacular of our boys, this June morning, "Brashear City has gone up!" Fugitives continue to pour into my lines. Our Quartermaster, nervous and timid, asks me, a dozen times, if there is no way of retreat; if the gun-boat may not be expected; if I think the Federals at Lafourche can send us succors. Negroes, arriving by the Brashear roads, bring incoherent stories, concerning a massacre by the rebels of many hundreds of the blacks. A report comes that the bay gun-boat has been seen in the Bœuff, and may be expected here during the day. Numberless rumors, regarding the force and designs of our enemies, reach us continually.

I make up my mind to the conviction that an advance of rebels may be apprehended immediately from the bay. I already know what is to be looked for by the approaches from Tigerville; a column of cavalry, with artillery to back it. Here, now, the precarious and indefensible condition of this post becomes yet more apparent. My three siege-pieces and a brass howitzer must not only defend the bridge against enemies on the opposing bayou-bank, but are required to withstand whatever force may be sent from Brashear City against us. I have one outpost only intervening between the bay and my camp. Captain Hopkins, of the Twenty-Third Connecticut Volunteers, is stationed at Bayou Ramos, three miles from the Bœuff, and nearly six miles this side of Brashear

The rebels must cross a bridge at Bayou Ramos. Captain Hopkins may be able to oppose them at that point.

Rapidly reflecting upon our situation, I conceive and as quickly dismiss various plans of defence. There is a narrow water-channel crossing the railway, about two miles below the Bœuff. Woody swamps extend on either side of this "Alligator Bayou," rending it inaccessible save by the railroad or in boats. Could I reach and fortify the bridge-crossing of this bayou, and secure supplies of rations, I might hold the point against any force. Or, with flat boats for transportation, I might retreat up the Bœuff, and there fortify in the swamp. But the lack of means to transport artillery over the rail, or by water, admonishes me that both these schemes are impracticable, in the face of an advancing enemy. Neither have I provisions of food or medical stores. The men of my own regiment here possess scarcely one day's rations. The Connecticut men have a larger supply, but not sufficient for many days, if shared with all, including hundreds of refugees, white and black, now within my lines. Now I appreciate the consequences of leaving our train of cars, loaded with commissary and quartermaster's stores, on the track at Brashear City. Had the locomotives, in their flight, brought off that store train, how amply would I now be furnished with rations and facilities for transportation. With two locomotives at my command, a dozen cars, and sufficient supplies to last through a siege of months, I would have the choice of attempting a dash upon the rail toward Terrebonne, with the hope of cutting my way through to our lines, or I might select some point to fortify, and defy the efforts of rebels to dislodge me. But speculations of this sort are now futile. There are no cars, no supplies, within my reach; and all the flat-boats on the Bœuff, save one, were towed to Brashear, last Monday, by the gun-boat.

I have, then, no adequate means of removal from this indefensible place, and can only hope to make a brief stand against the enemy. On this stand, however, I determine, at once, whatever it may result in; and proceed, thereupon, to make the best dispositions in my power. Dispatching some of my wild-riding boys to neighboring plantations, with orders to impress spades, picks, and log-chains, I proceed to mark out a line of intrenchment on the Brashear side of our little camp. A simple crescent of rifle pits, with obstacles and abattis to flank them, is all that I can hope to interpose against an hourly expected advance from the bay. Two siege-guns commanding the bayou, may remain as they are, and the remaining one is already in position on the rail-road and pointed in the direction of Brashear. Present-ly, amid great shouting, my "Ironsides" boys return, accompanied by a gang of blacks from the plantations, who, with picks and spades, have volunteered for fatigue duty. Ground is broken instantly, and in half an hour, I get a well-defined line of rifle-trenches from flank to flank. Leaving the negro-reliefs to dig, under supervision of a few of our Connecticut sergeants, I set other gangs to cutting down and hauling orange-trees from a grove near by, and dragging such timber, old iron machinery, and other lumber, as can be found around the sugar house, to serve as defensive *impedimenta* for our flanks. The single brass piece I place in our rear, so that it can be readily shifted to either right or left of the rifle-pits. These immediate dispositions made, I take saddle for a reconnoissance of "the situation."

On the wide, open fields, between the opposite bayou-levee and a timber-belt that makes their back-ground, stood a capacious sugar house, once the depot and store-room of an extensive plantation. This building and its surrounding sheds was now filled with army-supplies, officers' trunks, and extra baggage, arms, and military appurtenances of all kinds, that had been stored under their shelter when General Banks moved his army across Berwick Bay, for its march through the Attakapas coun-try. The estimated value of articles here deposited, under orders from Head Quarters, was, at the least, a half million of dollars. It may have been much more; as the trunks, boxes, desks, and such receptacles contained sums of money, watches, jewelry, and other valuables, left behind, for security as well as convenience, by our ad-vancing troops. The regiments to whose members the private property belonged were now at Port Hudson. They had never been enabled to reclaim their extra baggage, and it consequently remained at Bayou Bœuff, or at Algiers, where was another depot of the kind.

I rode to an open door of the sugar-house, dismounted, and entered. A few enlisted men, detached from different regiments to guard the property, were lounging round the purlieus. Bales of clothing, muskets, and revolvers, were piled to the ceilings of the lower rooms. Trunks, marked with the names of various officers and regiments, were collected in ponderous piles. Some of these ap-peared to have been roughly handled; many, doubtless, had been tampered with; for their locks were broken and lids shattered. Several were quite open, their contents exposed, in the shape of fine linen, new dress coats, and luxurious articles generally. I had time only for a cursory glance at the interior, but I could readily see that this sugar-house depot contained most valuable "aid and comfort" for ragged rebels, might they be so fortunate as to secure possession of it.

But such a result I resolved should not be my fault. I did not intend that another prize, in public and private plunder, should be added to the pillage over which rebel capturers were now exulting at Brashear City. From a million to a million and a half dollars worth of rations, tents, ammunition, small arms, artillery, and medical stores, is the estimate made of the prize secured by surprize at Brashear, and I am not willing that another million dollars' worth, or thereabouts, in yet more acceptable supplies, shall be gained through the seizure of this sugar-house. So, with a sigh over the necessary sacrifice, I mentally devote the baggage of brother officers, and all government stores in connection therewith, to the flame of a Federal bonfire. Giving orders at once for the evacuation of the buildings, I mount and ride down the bayou-bank.

Straggling negroes are coming in from different quarters. They report the rebels within three miles of the Bœuff, at a plantation on the lake. I gallop to the doors of negro huts and houses of poor whites upon the bayou borders, giving notice to the inmates that our lines will be drawn in immediately. Some request shelter in my camp; others conclude to "take their chances" with the rebels. I can easily detect the concealed sympathy which many feel for the invaders. Of one fellow I demand a gun which I spy on his premises—a United States musket—and he rather reluctantly yields it.

But, finding myself a mile or more from camp, and suddenly remarking that I have left my revolver behind, I deem it prudent to retrace my course rapidly. A commander "gobbled" by rebel scouts, so far from his men, might add another item to the report of rebel surprises. So, cantering back, loaded with the musket and its cartridge-box, I reach and cross the bridge again.

Work is progressing, under direction of our Connecticut captains and the artillerists.   The rifle-pits are growing deeper, fatigue squads are drawing materials for frail
defenses, and I find the gunners posted at their batteries,
under direction of Lieut. Sherfy, their officer.   I send a
message to Captain Hopkins, who has reported the appearance of a force at his front, on Bayou Ramos.   He
has been called upon to surrender his post to General
Green, and has replied to the Texan chief, that he has
no time to do so.   I direct Captain Hopkins to hold his
ground as long as possible; but if there be danger of the
enemy flanking him, to burn the bridge and fall back to
my lines.

The day wears rapidly.   I am incessantly active; most
of the time in the saddle; now inspecting the rifle-pits,
again overseeing our flank-arrangements, taking note of
everything, without allowing myself opportunity to dwell
upon the darker features of our situation.   When noon
arrives, I give up any hope that the gun-boat will appear.
I see no loop-hole of retreat or escape from the Bœuff,
and console myself simply with the sullen resolution to
make as long resistance as possible, in view of the bare
possibility that assistance may arrive from New Orleans.
If my courier, Sergeant Lewis, shall succeed in gaining
our lines, at Lafourche, there is still a faint hope of
succor from that quarter.   I wish to hold Bayou Bœuff
while a chance of ultimate relief can inspire me.   Such
are my cogitations, while riding up and down, without
food during the entire day, yet wholly unconscious of
hunger, because absorbed by the responsibilities of my
command.   When the rifle-pits are deep enough, I muster
the men, to assign them their positions and commanders.
In yesterday's morning reports, about two hundred and
fifty rank and file were represented to be fit for duty;

but only thirty-seven files now present themselves on the line of the rifle-pits. Are these seventy-two infantry-men the force with which I am to defend Bayou Bœuff? But there are forty artillerists; ten men to each piece; not sufficient for a necessary relief. I direct search for stragglers and skulkers; but this results in a small accession only. Apparently, I have not much numerical strength to back my determination to hold out to extremity.

After assigning stations and immediate commands, I ride to the battery. Lieut. Sherfy stops me, near the large gun which is posted on the track. "Colonel!" he says.—"Here is one of my sergeants, who desires to speak a word to you, sir!"

The sergeant salutes, and approaches. He is a bluff, Saxon-looking man, who has apparently made up his mind to talk bluntly.

"Well, my lad, what do you wish to say to me?"

"Colonel!" responds the gunner, sinking his voice. "I want to ask your liberty to leave!"

"To leave, sir! What do you mean by that?"

"I mean"—in a still lower voice—"I'd like to get away—me and my mates.—You see, Colonel, we were in the secesh service, when Orleans was captured, and we 'listed under the Feds. If the Rebs catch us, sir, all is, they'll hang us!—So we'd like to leave this place, Colonel—"

I look at the man steadily, without speaking, and he proceeds—"You see, sir, of course, we know there's no chance here; it's got to come to surrender—"

I interrupt further parley. "Who told you, sir, that we shall surrender! This place is to be held, sir! You will keep your post, to defend it. If you leave, it will be with a bullet in your back!"

I speak warmly; for the man's apparent lukewarmness is annoying. My earnestness seems to please him, nevertheless; for he steps back to his place by the gun, crying out, with rather an impressive oath—"If it's fight, Colonel, I'll stick by, any way!" A hurrah from the gunner and his comrades cheers me, as I gallop off; but, in spite of this manifestation, I cannot repress the reflection that this poor fellow is fighting with a halter about his neck; that he was morally right in desiring to escape a conflict so hopeless as ours threatens to be, and fraught with such peril to himself personally.

But I have not yet done with my artillery-men. An hour afterwards, a gunner comes to me, as I ride near, with a report that his piece will be unserviceable. An important implement has been lost; a "rimmer," used to increase the calibre or bore, of shells, by making its circumference larger, when necessary, so that a different fuse can be inserted. The man affects to explain that the burning of his shells cannot be graduated, because of the loss of this simple instrument. It is desirable to get a range upon the opposite shore, to cover a battery which the rebels are bringing into position near the Bœuff.

"Do you tell me, that our defence must stop, because you have lost a thing like that, sir?"

"You see, Colonel! we can't——"

"I see that all you need is a common augur, or something of the kind, to make that bore larger! Is there no such tool in camp?"

"We could n't find any, sir!"

I get indignant at the apparent stupidity or indifference of the fellow. Seizing a musket near me, I wrench away the bayonet, and, by a smart blow, break off its glittering point. A tri-edged, augur-sort of instrument remains, which I hand to the gunner, ordering him to test its

utility as a "rimmer." It is inserted in the fuse bore,
and perforates the substance that forms the shells' rim
without difficulty. A "rimmer" is provided, and our
gun rendered serviceable once more.

But I mentally doubt whether the gunners will be as
"serviceable" as their pieces, if such slight difficulties
as this last one can be made the foundation of despondency. It becomes rather problematical to me whether,
with my thirty-seven files in the rifle-pits, and my grumbling artillerists out of it, I can depend on a very resolute
defence of this "Castle Dangerous" of ours.

But evening approaches, and other affairs require attention. The rifle-pits are made; shallow trenches, with
a heap of earth in front, scarcely waist high. Our flanks
are barricaded with old wagons, lumber, and the abattis
of orange trees. We have cleared a large space of the
growing grain in front of our lines, so as to get range for
musket-fire. I now order the demolition of some sheds
in the range of our artillery, and cause fire to be set to
other buildings, which may serve to shelter an advance
of rebels during the night.

Our last piece of fire-works is to be the sugar-house on
the opposite bayou shore. But, before applying our
torch to this structure, I have a word with "Billy" and
the engineers, concerning their locomotives.

The rebels have secured several trains of cars at Brashear City, but no engines. The two in our possession
would be invaluable prizes to them; by aid of which they
might transport their forces and supplies upon the road,
as they advance on New Orleans. These locomotives
must not fall into their hands, in a serviceable condition;
and both conductor and engineers assure me that they
can be destroyed. "It is only necessary," says one, "to
burn out the fire-chest. It will take them a month to

repair them." Another says, "There's a single pin which I can remove, and which cannot be replaced. That will prevent the use of the engine." I have an idea, myself, that the best way to place the locomotives *hors du combat* will be to run them into one another, and then blow them up with gun-powder. But I am satisfied to leave the plan of destruction to our "experts." They only await orders for the work, and these I give them.

Dusk approaches, and I direct that the iron and planks of the bayou bridge shall be removed. The work is commenced, and in a short time a section of rails and several cross-trees are torn up and flung into the Bœuff. The passage of the bridge by cavalry is thus effectually precluded.

I now call a trio of my "Ironsides" youths, and dispatch them to the sugar-house on incendiary business. They cross the bayou in a skiff, and shortly thereafter I get ocular evidence of their work. A cloud of light smoke appears, which gradually darkens, and increases to dense volumes. I hear exclamations running through the camp, as our soldiers discover the vapor and presently catch sight of flames. "The sugar-house is gone up!" "Good bye to Uncle Sam's commissaries!" An officer comes to me, and asks if the burning is accidental, and I assure him that it is not.

About this time, the Connecticut company, under Captain Hopkins, stationed at Bayou Ramos, arrives in my lines, having fallen back, after a brief skirmish with the enemy. General Tom Green is at Bayou Ramos, but as Captain Hopkins fired the bridge before leaving, the rebel advance will be somewhat retarded. They may attack us during the night, however, or at daybreak, to-morrow; and it behooves us to be on the *qui vive*. I proceed, therefore, to post sentinels and pickets, and send scouts toward Bayou Ramos.

There are hundreds of able-bodied negroes in the camp, with their families; a multitude of women and children— refugees from the plantations on both sides of Bayou Bœuff. In making a stand, the blacks can be serviceable; so I muster a few scores, distribute muskets and ammunition to them, and get them speedily in line and under drill. Several enlisted men, of the " Corps d'Afrique," have come in among the fugitives from Brashear, and I select a few of these to act as sergeants.

This nocturnal drill presents a singular spectacle. I have the negroes before me in two ranks, and exercise them in the manual of arms. They are awkward, but eager to learn, and appear to be of good soldier-stuff. I do not find my officers entering cordially into the scheme of arming and drilling negroes; and for this reason I do not commit them to it. I give the black recruits my personal attention, taking the responsibility of consequences. The drill proceeds noiselessly, orders being given with " bated breath." It is dusk evening, and very calm. The sky is somewhat overcast, but we have a lurid illumination from the sugar-house and other buildings on fire. The Bœuff casts back a ruddy reflection of flame, and bright flashes of light quiver on neighboring orange-groves, and make the surrounding fields, and our camp, with its watchful soldiers, distinctly visible Drill concluded, I detail a few of my black volunteers for picket service, and despatch them to the outskirts of camp and verge of surrounding timber, with instructions to lie concealed, keeping strict watch, and should the enemy approach, to bring me a report at once, without alarming the camp.

As evening wears on, the blaze of our burning sugar-house augments in breadth and fury. The dry buildings, the immense piles of tents, with their supports, the quantities of clothing, the trunks, and a mass of other combustibles, combine to furnish fuel for the devouring flame. A roar like low thunder undertones the crackling of burning wood, the explosions of powder, the reports of guns and pistols incessantly discharged by the heat. This conflagration is, indeed, a grand and costly piece of Federal fire-works. Better, however, that the elements regain their constituents, than that rebel hordes find another *commissariat!*

Toward nine o'clock, "Billy," the conductor, his railroad employees, and several citizen refugees, send a committee, to ask permission to make their escape from the camp. These men are convinced that all defence must be abortive, and, as many of them are individually obnoxious to the rebels, they are prudently apprehensive of personal peril should they be captured with the rest. That tall planter, Mr. S——, who has been "running" several government plantations near the Bœuff, during the last year, and who has solved the question of free labor value very effectually, is one of the refugees here. He has already begged to be enrolled as a private in one of our companies, so that he may thus escape scrutiny, and obtain parole as a soldier   But his collossal proportions would render it difficult to conceal his identity, should there be neighboring secessionists about; so Mr. S. unites with "Billy" and the rest, in requesting leave to attempt their escape. I readily grant the permission, as these non-combatants can be of no use to us; and soon after, furnished with a written pass, and stowing themselves in a capacious boat, which they have procured, these men, to' the number of seventeen, set quietly out, through darkness, to descend the Bœuff.

Night darkens; with the fading of flames around us.
The discharges of loaded fire-arms in the sugar-house become less frequent, and at length cease. Silence, utter
and oppressive, falls over camp. I walk out to the rifle-
pits; linger a moment among prostrate forms of sleeping soldiers; peer out through the gloom, across the
bayou and toward the sombre woods hemming us on the
Brashear side; then return, and sit before my tent, absorbed in reflections upon our desperate situation. At
last, weary but yet wakeful, I lie down, to court a brief
repose.

Very brief, indeed, are my slumbers; for at midnight
Captain Coe rushes into my tent. "Colonel! the rebels
are reported in the woods!"

Roused abruptly, I catch but the import of these words;
and, springing from my pallet, with a single exclamation,
"Up!" I hasten to our rifle-pits, and get the men speedily at their stations. The enemy are reported to have
advanced from Bayou Ramos, and to be in force at our
front. They may make an assault at any moment. During two hours we remain in suspense, our infantry resting
on their arms, in the rifle-pits, our batteries double-
shotted and ready to open upon a foe. Long after this, I
learn that it was proposed to General Green to attack us
at this hour. Had the rebels attempted it, they would
have found us prepared for them, and, though they might
have overwhelmed us by force of numbers, the success
would have cost them dear.

But we were not to be molested, and after remaining
in line till two o'clock in the morning, I directed the men
to lie down near the pits and sleep again. I resumed
my own vigils in front of the tent, where I was presently
addressed by Captain Hopkins, the brave officer who had
been compelled to retreat from Bayou Ramos.

"Colonel!" said the Captain, "I would like to speak to you for a moment, if you will excuse me."

"Certainly! I shall be glad to listen to you, Captain."

"It is the opinion of most of our officers and men, sir, that this post cannot be defended without great sacrifice of life, and resistance can be made only for a short time. Would you object to calling the officers together, and hearing their opinions upon the subject?"

"Of course not, Captain! I will call a council of the officers, if they desire it."

"I assure you, sir, that they wish it."

"Very well, Captain! I leave the matter to yourself. You may notify our officers to report at my quarters!"

Captain Hopkins departs on his errand, and in a few minutes the commissioned officers present themselves at my tent. We retire from observation and hearing of the men, to a flank of our barricades, and proceed to discuss "the situation." I state to them, frankly, my view of the difficulties which environ us, and declare that I hold myself ready to be governed by the opinion of the council. After other remarks, I submit the question, as to whether we shall negotiate or fight, to all present, beginning, as in courts-martial, with the youngest in rank.

Lieut. Peck, of the Twenty-Third Connecticut Volunteers, is our junior. He says he will do as his seniors decide, fight or not. All the remaining officers declare for negotiation, considering a defence to be useless; and resistance only calculated to involve a waste of life. My judgment endorses the correctness of this unanimous verdict, although I repine at the necessity which constrains it. It is decided that, if the enemy attack us during the darkness, we shall resist, but that at morning we will consider terms of surrender. This course of action agreed upon, a flag of truce is given in charge of Lieut. Kirby, to display from our post at sunrise.

The council disperses, and I throw myself upon a stool before my quarters. Now, for the first time, do I feel a reaction of my energies. Yesterday, I was from day-break to dusk in the saddle, or occupied in labor, swallowing scarcely a morsel of nourishment, When aroused, at midnight, by the report of a rebel advance, my nervous strength remained intact. But, since the decision of our council of war, I feel every symptom of exhaustion. My faculties are no longer alert, my mind has lost its composure, and my limbs are feeble. The tension of responsibility, which braced my system, is now relaxed, and I feel like casting myself upon the ground to sleep or to weep like a child.

But the die is cast. We have agreed to negotiate, and negotiation can end only in surrender. A tumult of conflicting emotions disturbs me, as I look up to the American flag, which still waves from its staff, over our camp. I almost pray that the rebels may suddenly dash upon us, that we may be spared the bitterness of lowering those beloved colors. I yearn to the "Old Flag," this hour, as to a mother whom I may see no more. God bless the emblem of our "Liberty and Union—one and inseparable!" Its freedom cannot be restricted by our captivity; its giant power will not be impaired by the loss of pygmies such as we are. It will again lead the march of victorious armies over these bayous. It will flame like a meteor on the skirts of flying foes. Perhaps, it may follow us, a messenger of enfranchisement, to the gates of the prison-house to which we must render ourselves. God bless the Old Flag! whatsoever fate shall be ours, who no longer can hope to defend it successfully. God grant that we shall, some time, behold it again, waving over a Restored Union and a Free Republic!

CHAPTER XVII.

CAPTIVITY.

As the dark, slow night-hours wane gradually, I think of the thousand unhappy negroes, men, women, and children, who have sought refuge in this camp. Hard is their fate, to be returned to slavery, after having tasted freedom. The condition and prospective fate of these people embitters for me the pain of surrender.

More then once, I find myself inclined to make a desperate stand, arming blacks and whites, to live or die together. But reflection tells me that the attempt can only end in a massacre of the negroes, perhaps, of my own comrades; and the responsibility of such a result must rest on me, if, reversing the council's decision, I command a conflict which can have no result beyond the sacrifice of life.

But there is one duty I owe to faithful men. My servants must not be left to rebel mercies. John, my valet, came with me from home. George and Toussaint are both attached and zealous followers. I resolve to give them a chance to escape; so, calling them to my tent, I briefly explain matters. George, sanguine creole, is sure he can get through the rebels. Toussaint, brave fellow! hangs his lip. He would like to have a blow at his old oppressors. But, they are all agreed to make the effort to escape capture; and I give each of them a revolver, with good store of ammunition. To John I intrust a message for my wife. Then, wringing the hands of my sable henchmen, and feeling more then one tear drop upon my wrist, I bid them " Good speed," and watch their dusky figures disappearing among surrounding shadows.

The approach of day-break finds me still seated in front of my tent, absorbed in sombre reflections. But there are precautions yet to be taken. Our poor blacks must not be found by the enemy with arms in their hands, as it might jeopardize their lives, in view of Jeff. Davis's recent proclamation, declaring our negro corps and its officers' outlawed from military consideration. I order the recall of our " contraband" pickets, and a muster of their armed comrades. Bringing them into line, they are directed to stack arms, and are then dismissed to their quarters. I adopt this quiet method of disarming the brave fellows, lest they may endanger their own safety and that of my white soldiers by any rash desire to defend themselves. I dismiss likewise several negroes who were placed last night as a guard over supposed spies brought into camp.

The sergeant, whom I dispatched on Monday night, as a courier to our lines at Lafourche Crossing, has returned, without effecting his object. He reports the roads beyond and about Tigerville completely blocked by rebels, to the number of several thousand mounted men, who are advancing on Bayou Bœuff. Day now dawns, and shortly afterwards, I am notified that a flag of truce from General Taylor at Brashear, has appeared, and that the bearer wishes to see the commander of this post. Calling Lieut. Kirby to accompany me, I mount a hand-car, and proceed about a quarter-mile on the railroad, to meet the rebel messenger. We encounter a young man, armed with a rifle, who announces himself to be an officer, and demands the surrender of what he terms "the fort."

Scrutinizing the youth's somewhat dirty and dilapidated appearance, as he stands between a brace of apparent subordinates, not more tattered than himself, I ask whose authority he represents.

"I represent General Taylor, sir!" he replies loftily.

"What is your rank, sir?"

"I am an officer, under General Green's command, sir! I am Captain McNally, sir!"

"But you have nothing about you to distinguish your rank, sir. How am I to know that you are an officer?"

"My honor, sir!" exclaims the young rebel, with a melo-dramatic slap of his breast with the right hand, while the left brings his gun to an emphatic order.

"Well, Captain, I suppose I must take your word for it! And now, as you represent General Taylor, let me ask what terms he proposes to us. I will remark, that I have no desire to sacrifice life in a defence of this post, but, nevertheless, we can give you a good fight here, if we choose to resist."

"It will be useless, sir!" responds the young rebel. "General Green is determined to reduce this fort, no matter what it may cost. He is resolved to bring his whole force against you, sir, and if you resist, it will only be the worse for you!"

"That may be, Captain! But what terms are you authorized to offer?"

"General Taylor orders me to demand an unconditional surrender, sir!"

"What do you mean by that? Are we not to have the usual conditions allowed to prisoners of war, sir?"

"Your men will be allowed to keep their knapsacks, and your officers their private property."

"Well, Captain! I shall return to my officers, and

state to them General Taylor's proposition. If they agree to accept, I will notify you!"

"I give you ten minutes, sir, to decide."

"It is not time enough!"

"Well, sir! it's all I can give! If you send no answer within that time, we shall open fire!"

"Very well, sir! Let that be understood! And, on our part, sir, if we do not accept your terms, you will see yonder white flag come down, and our Union flag go up in its place. Good morning, Captain!"

Thus leaving this assumptious young rebel, after substantially, if not literally, the foregoing colloquy, I roll back on the hand-car to camp, and call my officers together. There is a general demur to the summary and insolent demands of General Taylor's shabby messenger.

"Very well, gentlemen!" I say to them. "Say but the word, and our flag of truce shall give place to a battle-flag."

But here Lieut. Kirby, of my own regiment, interposes. "Colonel!" he remarks, "The men are dispirited, since they saw our flag of truce up, and they won't fight."

"Well," remarks Captain Sanford, of the Connecticut regiment. "Let us take our time, and if the rebels choose to open fire, we can return it." Other officers express themselves similarly; and the result is, that we discuss the subject, not ten minutes only, but a half-hour, at least, without hearing any more from the enemy. But there are no more cheering auspices for us this morning than there were at our nocturnal council; and the finale of this last conference is a decision to accept General Taylor's terms, of protection to the private effects of officers and men. This finally settled, I appoint Captain Coe and Lieut. Kirby to meet Captain McNally again, and then repair, heart-sick, to my quarters.

But scarcely has the hand-car rattled off, with our envoys, than another flag of truce is displayed on the opposite shore of Bayou Bœuff. Col. Major presents himself at the dismantled bridge, and summons us to surrender, in the name of General Mouton. A short parley ensues, succeeded by the entry to our lines of the cavalry colonel and his staff, who cross over our broken bridge planks. Mounting " Black Roman," I proceed to the railroad, in season to see rebels coming in upon us from all sides.

Col. Major is a fine-looking officer, with the manners of a gentleman. He accosts me courteously, with an observation about the fortune of war, and expresses regret that he had not arrived in time to receive our capitulation, for General Mouton instead of General Taylor. He promises, however, that the terms made shall be strictly respected, and remarks that we have done well to avert a conflict.

" You had no chance at all !" says Major. " I supposed you had at least a thousand men, with ground well intrenched and fortified. But I intended to cross, above, and charge down the bayou bank on your flank, with twelve hundred !"

" We should have given you a reception from those double-shotted guns," I said.

" If we attacked your front, you might have given us something to do; but your few men never could have stood a charge on the flank here. What were you burning last night, Colonel !"

I pointed to the ruins of the sugar-house, yet smouldering and smoking, and replied: " An old store depot !"

" We thought it was the railroad bridge," said Col. Major. " It would have been the worse for you, if you had destroyed it. General Mouton wants all this road, for an advance on New Orleans."

"You think you will get there this time, Colonel?"

"We shall be in New Orleans by Saturday night, sir.
Nothing can stop us. We've driven your troops below
Lafourche, and shall follow them to Algiers."

Col. Major was not frank enough to tell me how he had
been repulsed, with all his force, at Lafourche Crossing,
on Sunday night; but he added, to his last words, the admission that our "Yankees" at Lafourche had made a
stout fight.

"We shall meet in New Orleans, Colonel!" said
Major, with a laugh, as he turned away to inspect our
camp.

"Shall I be permitted to retain a horse, for transportation, Colonel!" I inquire.

"Certainly," answers the Confederate officer, without
hesitation. "Have you other horses here, that you will
lend to my orderlies for the present? We cannot cross
our own over the bridge."

"I will order a servant to saddle my other two horses,"
I respond, quite satisfied, as well as surprised, with the
good-nature of our captors thus far. At this juncture,
my quartermaster, Lieut. Kimball, comes up, to prefer a
request. "I have a wagon of private stores and other
property," he says, addressing the Confederate chief—
"Will it be respected, like the rest? A few bottles of
wine, some cigars, and the like."

Our worthy quartermaster is very deaf. I hint this to
Col. Major, whereupon that affable enemy takes the trouble to raise his voice, in consoling assurance to Lieut.
Kimball that his "small stores," being "private effects,"
will be sacred from seizure. I begin to suspect that our
new friends are a trifle too generous in promises; but
the quartermaster, much elated, gets out a box of superb
Havanas, and commences a liberal distribution thereof.

Col. Major delicately declines to receive the luxury, pleading that he is no smoker; but subsequently consents to pocket a couple of bundles for his friends. Lieut. Kimball then proceeds to supply every interesting rebel, who has a grey cap, or a bit of gilt braid about him; and not a few of our own boys come in for a treat in the difficulty of distinguishing recipients. So opens our intercourse with Texans, of whom we conceive quite a favorable first impression.

But we are destined, I apprehend, to discover a reverse to this pleasant morning picture. Presently encountering my young *vis-a-vis* of the hand-car negotiation, Captain McNally, I inquire to whom I shall deliver the sword which still swings by my saddle. The rebel officer makes a courteous salute, and says, "Please to wear it, for the present, Colonel! You can resign it to General Taylor!"

At this moment, another Confederate officer advances, and demands my sword; adding, superciliously, to the young Texan captain. "You need not trouble yourself with authority, sir! I am commander here!"

This important gentleman, who wears a distinguishing quantity of gold braid about his grey suit, is Lieut.-Col. Phillips, a cavalry officer. I respond to his demand for my sword, by unhooking it from the belt which confines it to my side.

"I believe the belt goes with the sabre, sir!" remarks the chivalrous rebel; whereupon, unclasping belt and shoulder-piece, I hand over both. Lieut.-Col. Phillips coolly adjusts them to his elegant waist, and I take the opportunity to ride away from him. I have the satisfaction, long afterwards, of learning that he gets himself killed by a Yankee sergeant, at Donaldsonville, a few days subsequent to my capture, and that my sabre reverts to loyal possession, being awarded to the brave fellow who shoots its temporary custodian.

Returning to my tent, I find that it has been entered and ransacked by some of the rebels who are prowling about camp. My watch, gauntlets, and other articles, have disappeared. I look after my luggage brought from Brashear City, and find that one box, containing books, correspondence, and papers generally, has been broken open, and its contents scattered over the ground. I secure a trunk of clothing, and a few other personal effects, and get it, together with a trunk belonging to Col. Nott, placed on a mule-cart that holds our officers' baggage. This accomplished, I remove the saddles from "Black Roman" and another of my horses which a rebel has hitched near by. These saddles, one of them quite costly, immediately attract the admiration of our Texan rifle rangers. Several cluster about my tent, eager to "trade" for the articles. "Colonel," says one of them, confidentially. "Yer better sell me that ar' saddle! I'll give yer a right smart trade for *tt*."

I reply, that Col. Major has promised that I shall keep one of my horses, for transportation, and I will need a saddle with it; that I cannot just now say which I may keep, but will let them have one or the other at Brashear City."

"Now, Colonel," says the rebel, "Yer better let us boys have the saddles. Officers gets everything, and thar's no show for us. Yer better trust us than them. I'll give a hundred dollars for one o' them hides!"

I decline immediate traffic, but tell the "boys" they may look in again, after I see Col. Major. They retire, casting longing looks back at the saddles. I am now summoned by a sergeant to go out to Col. Major. I find him in company with one of the late engineers or firemen on the railroad, who, as I afterwards learn, has been accused of destroying the locomotives. Col. Major is in a towering rage, and accosts me in a high tone. "Do you know who ruined those engines, sir? They have been made useless, sir!"

I perceive that the subject is a delicate one; and reply diplomatically—"I suppose that must have been done by order, Colonel!"

"Did you order it done, sir?"

"I ordered the engines to be run off the track, sir!"

"It is an unwarrantable military offence, sir, to destroy transportation, when the post could not be held. It is against all rules of war. I would hang the man that destroyed those engines, sir!"

Here, turning upon the railroad man, who—brave fellow that he was—did not seem to blench at Major's menace— "If you don't put those engines in order, I'll hang you as sure as there's a heaven! Will you do it?"

"I don't know that it can be done, sir!" replies the engineer, looking our exasperated rebel full in the face.

"I'll make you know, sir. Here, take this man off!" cries Major, to a guard. "If he don't put those engines in repair, hang him!"

The man is led away. I do not recall his name, if I ever knew it; but he is evidently a bold fellow, and a true one; for, if he had been craven, he would probably have sought to exculpate himself by casting the responsibility of the order on me. I am convinced that Col. Major feels this, likewise; for the rebel officer well knows that the engines could not have been destroyed without my priority, as commandant. I get proof of this fact very soon; for the Texan colonel presently returns to me, and, with manifestly-strained politeness, expresses his chagrin that I must give up all my horses. "An order has come from General Taylor, to that effect," he explains. "Your General Banks or Bowen has ordered all registered rebels to leave New Orleans, and has restricted even delicate ladies to fifty pounds of baggage. In retaliation for this outrage, General Taylor orders that Yankee officers shall have no privileges allowed them."

"This is hard, Colonel Major," I reply. "I have lately been ill; and can hardly stand a march on foot for any distance!"

"I know it's hard, sir! I belonged to the old army, and we were accustomed to do things in better shape; but I cannot order anything here, against the General's will! If those engines had not been ruined, Colonel, we might give you transportation on the railroad, you know."

In spite of Col. Major's assumed courtesy, I could detect latent malice in his last observation. I was to be promptly punished for the loss of those locomotives to the rebels. I mentally pray that it may be found impossible to repair the damage.

"If I must give up the horses, may I retain my saddles, Colonel? They are private property, purchased by myself."

"I regret to say, the order is peremptory to take saddles also," answers Major. "I am very sorry, Colonel!"

I bow, and Col. Major turns away, laughing, perhaps, at this "retaliation," which leaves me the prospect of a long tramp, in what direction I know not. Bitterly do I regret, now, the confidence that I had placed in rebel assurances. I have seen opportunities of escape during all the morning, which I now wish heartily I had improved. Once over the Bœuff, I might have profited by my knowledge of the country, and of several places of shelter, to elude pursuit for some days, and, possibly, make my way to Lafourche or to the coast, at Grand Caillou. But it is now too late. Hardly do I regain my tent, before a guard comes for my saddles—thereby dissipating all hopes of the "trade" promised by rebel rifle-men. I perceive, likewise, that a guard is posted at the rear of my tent, near the rifle-pits ; an obvious hint that I am under *surveillance*.

To-day I have only tasted a cup of coffee and a hard-cracker. My lips are parched and skin dry and hot. It is evident that fever threatens me. During the forenoon no intimation of what is to be done with officers or men has been given. It is nearly two o'clock in the after-noon, when I get a hint that we are all to report at Brashear City. Pending an order to march, the prisoners are collected in a field, at the other side of the railroad, and obliged to remain there without refreshments, and exposed to the fierce sun, for several hours.

I see no more of Confederate colonels. About sunset we receive orders to get in column of march. We walk about four abreast, the officers in front. On either side ride cavalry, to the number of four score or more, armed with rifles, Enfield muskets, and pistols. The captain in command is an earnest, resolute-looking man, and con-trols his motley riders efficiently. After a few miles of progress, the fatigue of marching affects my enfeebled system sensibly, but I continue to keep up with my com-rades, till we get to Bayou Ramos. The bridge at this place, burned by Captain Hopkins, is passed, with diffi-culty, on its string-pieces. A Confederate steamer lies at the levee, filled with rebels. General Green has fixed his quarters in a capacious dwelling-house on the Bra-shear side of this bridge. We get sight of the old Texan campaigner ; a tall, plain, farmer-like personage, in homespun, with no insignia of rank. We are halted here, while our rebel captain accepts an invitation to sup Most of us are hungry, but nothing is offered to eat; and, we content ourselves with a rest upon the damp roadside, while a drunken trooper rides out from a neighboring camp, swearing horrible oaths, and threatening " Yanks" with all imaginable vengeance in future. This fellow, however, is solitary in his denunciation, and, failing to provoke a quarrel, finally rides off; while one of our Texan lieutenants remarks, apologetically, " That ar' cuss is a coward, I'll swar'—as well as a drunkard. Nobody but a coward would insult prisoners!'' This assuring verdict is endorsed by several of our rough guards, and we begin to have a better opinion of them.

When the order to resume our march is given, I find myself staggering as I attempt to walk, and, after proceeding a mile, am forced to fall out of line to the roadside. The captain of cavalry orders one of his men to dismount, and I take his place in the saddle, though so weak as scarcely to be able to keep my seat. The fever is gaining upon me; my senses wander. So confused become my faculties, that I ask the guard to give me a switch, while a handsome riding-whip, that I have been carrying, falls unnoticed from my hand. Dr. Hershey, a surgeon of U. S. Volunteers, who escaped from Brashear City only to be captured below, gives me a large dose of quinine, which somewhat revives my strength; and thereafter, clinging to my pony's mane with nerveless hands, I manage to ride slowly in the line, till we reach Brashear.

We are delayed at the depot an hour, and Dr. Hershey plies me with more quinine. Then, getting orders to march two miles further, to Fort Buchanan, I essay to walk with the rest. Arrived at our hospital, a moment's halt is made, and I take the opportunity to inquire, through the gloom, if Dr. Willets is there. A familiar voice responds, and I am presently greeted by the valiant surgeon himself, who informs me that Col. Nott, Lieut. Stevenson, and others of our regiment, are in the building. I accompany him up stairs, and the Confederate surgeon, remarking my nearly-disabled condition, invites me to remain at the hospital. But I am not permitted to accept this humane offer. Our Texan captain outside has orders to deliver his prisoners to Fort Buchanan, and he is a literal constructionist of all superior orders. Go I must, he says, to the fort, if I am to be carried bodily. The considerate rebel surgeon offers to procure an ambulance or carriage, but the captain is in a hurry ; he must return this night, to Bayou Bœuff ; so I climb once more on a pony, and thus finish the march to Fort Buchanan.

It is nearly midnight when we arrive and are delivered into custody of another commander. Our cavalry captain rides away, with his troop, and we are ordered to make ourselves as contented as may be possible on the bare ground. Dr. Hershey notifies the post-surgeon of my illness, and I am visited by the rebel doctor, who kindly shares with me his bed, my blankets having been left upon the baggage cart. Our couch has no canopy save heaven ; but the surgeon furnishes me with a cover, and administers an opiate, which ere long stupifies me into slumber.

CHAPTER XVIII.

A MARCH TO SHREVEPORT.

I AWAKE in a high fever, my senses wandering to an extent that renders me almost oblivious of past and present. I see figures moving about me, without caring to distinguish them. Toward noon I begin to recall events, but an acute headach bewilders me still. I mechanically swallow a dose of quinine tendered me by a Confederate surgeon. One of our captured officers enters the tent, and hands me a pocket-revolver, with a request to preserve it, if I can, as he is about to be marched away. I afterwards discover this pistol on my pillow, where it is seen, likewise, by my rebel doctor, to whom I deliver it. I faintly recollect that I murmur a few incoherent words of thanks to this surgeon, for his attention to me, and that I give him a bundle of cigars. Nearly all the day is a blank, save my grateful consciousness of kindness at the hands of a sergeant of the Indiana Volunteers, who brings me a bowl of tea and some toast. Next morning, I am less feverish. I hear that rank and file are paroled, but that our officers will be sent to the interior. The surgeon decides that I am too ill to undergo the hardship of a march, and must remain at the hospital. To the hospital, I am conveyed, toward evening, in an open cart, which passes through our old camp. I get a glimpse at my own tent, with several articles of furniture strown about it.

Arriving at the hospital, sick and sad, I meet Col. Nott,

our two surgeons, and Lieuts. Stevenson and Sherman.
Lieut. Stevenson is wounded in the foot, a bullet having
passed through heel and ankle.   He is the gallant officer
who made that last stand at Brashear, defending a field
piece. Col. Nott is in excellent spirits, and jocosely notifies me that no long faces are allowed in the mess. Besides
our officers, there are two citizen-prisoners quartered in the
room where I now find a cot.   The surgeon of our regiment, Dr. Willets, and his assistant, Dr. Throop, not being
held as prisoners, mess with their medical brothers, the
Confederate doctors, and assist in consuming the choice
" sutler" stores that were captured with this post.

Here commences the routine of hospital prison-life.
There are seven of us in this apartment, our beds occupying the greater portion of floor.   Two negro-women
wait on us, bringing our meals twice daily; meat, rice,
bread, coffee, and soups—well cooked.   No one molests
us, and we have the range of the hospital, visiting our
wounded boys in other wards.   A balcony, in front of our
two doors, looks upon the street and Berwick Bay.   We
have light, air, and good food, and are altogether as
comfortable as could be expected.   Col. Nott and myself
reclaim our trunks.   I have lost my blankets, wolf skin,
and many other articles, but console myself in the possession of necessary clothing.

We remain at Brashear till the Fourth of July. Meantime, our enlisted men receive their parole, and are
marched in the direction of our lines.   Our captured
officers depart, under a rebel guard, on the day succeeding my own transfer to the hospital.   Several come
to take leave of us.   Their destination is supposed to be
Texas.   General Taylor has ordered that only such baggage shall be allowed them as they can carry on their
persons, together with their blankets.   The stipulation

of "protection for private property," is thus adroitly
evaded, and our officers are obliged to abandon everything they cannot themselves carry. After journeying
with knapsacks and packs about twenty miles, they get
some relief; the lieutenant in charge contriving to impress an old lumber-wagon, with a couple of wretched
mules; thus securing transportation for such extra weight
as the more provident captives may have been able to
stagger under thus far. Marching progresses at the
rate of from fifteen to twenty miles each day; the prisoners walking between files of mounted guards. The
roads are heavy with dust, the sun scorching; and thus,
weary and faint, those Yankees plod through their hard,
dusty journeys, and sink at night to sleep in their garments, loaded with dirt and saturated with perspiration.
No opportunities occur for washing of clothes, and scarcely
for ablution of person, so that, before reaching New
Iberia, they find themselves in a pitiable condition.
There they are delivered to Lieut. Fuller, of the Confederate army, who is a bitter hater of "Yankees."
Under control of this officer they are marched all day
without rations. Indeed, the chances of getting adequate
food grow quite precarious. Detailed men are sent in
advance of the "coffle," to obtain and cook corn meal
into "pones." A prisoner's ration, distributed at the
evening halt, consists of a junk of bread four inches
square, and a slice of bacon an inch thick. To secure
his share, a man must be alert; and woe to the wight
who, weary or sick, neglects to attend the distribution!
He must go supperless, or beg from some reluctant
comrade. It is a spectacle alike curious and humiliating,
to behold our half-famished "Yankees" rush about the
"commissary," at his order: "Prisoners, fall in for your
rations!" True it is, that no other than prison-life can

disclose so frightfully the selfish nature of man. Such
crowding, pushing, and cursing of one another; such
swinish struggles for precedency in a throng of hungry
men; are never, it is to be hoped, encountered outside of
prison-gangs.

The diurnal march begins at seven o'clock, A. M.,
continuing till noon; and, after a halt during the "heated
term," it is resumed at four o'clock, P. M., and protracted
till the "cooking place" is reached. Often, when encamping at meridian, on the grounds of some "secesh"
planter, our "Yankees" are forbidden to approach the
shelter of a tree, and sometimes denied access to a tank
of water. Occasionally, they are regaled with a gratuitous
concert of songs by rebel ladies, and must listen, with
the best grace they can summon, to the "Southern
Avenger," "Bonny Blue Flag" and similar affecting
ditties. While in the yard of a rich planter, on the
Teche, a bevy of fair traitresses requested songs from
our officers and one of the dear creatures expressed
particular anxiety to hear a celebrated "National air,"
the name of which she could not recollect. She was
certain that it was neither our "Star Spangled Banner,"
"Hail Columbia," "Red, White, and Blue," nor any other
patriotic effusion, which the gallant officers mentioned;
and at length a wag of our party, Lieut. Page, suggested
to the southern maiden that the "National air" she
wanted might be "Old Bob Ridley." The intelligent
damsel joyfully exclaimed that it was; and "Old Bob
Ridley," being loudly called for, was presently given with
unction, to the evident satisfaction of an appreciative
southern audience.

But other interludes, differing from these roadside
voluntaries by rebel ladies, were met by our officers on
their weary march. Once they witnessed that "peculiar"

tropical sport, the hunt of a runaway negro, and saw the "game" brought down by bloodhounds, that, with gory jaws, and venting fierce yelps, leaped around and snapped at their naked victim.

Below Alexandria, our prisoners suffered much from thirst; the Teche water, rank with vegetable slime, seeming to aggravate rather than diminish the demand for drink. Once, when nearly sinking from fatigue, they were halted near the mansion of a planter on the bayou; but the "lady" of the house refused all access to her water-tank, exclaiming — "There's the bayou — good enough for any (here the gracious female used a word profane) Yankee to drink!" This woman claimed to be of an "upper class;" but had Mungo Park, the traveler, encountered her, he would, doubtless, have rated her far below those Africans of her sex whose native hospitality he extols so highly.

The Fourth of July passed by our prisoners was a gloomy and wet one; but when the march was over, and they reached the shelter of an old negro hut, the brave boys did not forget to give three rousing cheers in celebration of our national birth-day. The rebel guard could claim no share in such patriotic rejoicing. They turned away from those loyal captives, and, with customary southern taste, sought out the more attractive company of ladies in the negro quarters.

The arrival of our "Yankees" at Alexandria called out the population of that city, some to denounce, others to laugh at, and a few, perhaps, to pity the way-worn prisoners. At this point, Lieut.-Col. Clark, Confederate provost-marshal, assumed direction, and permitted our officers and citizens to remain exposed, under a fierce sun, without food or water, during the entire afternoon, while groups of delighted young ladies—including two daughters of General Dick Taylor—amused themselves with a survey of the "dirty Yankees," from a balcony at Head Quarters.

Late in the evening, the exhausted prisoners were marched to the upper loft of a building; an apartment seventy feet long by fifteen wide ; and there, to the number of nearly two hundred, they were confined till morning. Besides our captured Federal officers, there had been brought from Brashear City about one hundred railroad laborers and a few other stragglers. These men were held as "citizen-prisoners," in retaliation, as was claimed, for the detention as hostages of southern citizens residing on the Teche, who had been arrested by General Banks, in his advance through the Attakapas country. A common belief among the "secesh" seemed to be, that these poor fellows were "Northern planters," employed by Banks to work abandoned sugar estates; and it was almost diverting to witness rebel bitterness as displayed in their comments on the miserable fortunes of such "vandal speculators."

On the morning after their arrival at Alexandria, the half-famished prisoners were served with food, and permitted, under a strong guard, to wash themselves in the river. Returning to their quarters, they learned from rebel deserters (one hundred and fifty of whom were confined in a room below) that our forces under General Grant had taken Vicksburg. It was a morsel of news worth glorification; and our "Yankees" testified their joy over it by making their prison-house ring with Union salvos. This brought down maledictions on them from the rebel commandant, and at noon they were abruptly ordered to get ready for a journey up to Shreveport. Thereafter, having been marched through various streets,

"a show to all the populace," they were driven on board
a boat, and found themselves ascending Red River.

The passage to Shreveport was accompanied with daily
and nightly suffering. One hundred and seventy-eight
persons were crowded into a small flat-boat, with scarcely
room to lie, or even stand, without a portion being thrust
against engine and boiler. The heat became suffocating;
the stench was stifling. A rebel officer, named Lieut.
Dean, of the " Crescent Guards," was now in command,
and showed himself a cold-hearted tyrant over helpless
prisoners. Rations had been cooked in advance for the
voyage. They consisted mainly of corn-bread, destitute
of salt, and were placed in two piles of " pones" aft of the
boiler. The boat had been last used for the transportation of beeves and mules. The accumulated filth on its
deck was supposed to have been removed, when a shift-
less negro had seemed to shovel it off. But no fastidious
imagination was necessary to discover what had preceded
the corn-bread upon that deck. The passage from Alexandria to Shreveport occupied five days, but the " rations" became disgusting before half the distance was
accomplished. The stench from them grew intolerable.
Our men sickened with fevers. Even the strongest
turned from their filthy food in disgust. It was no relief
to drink the warm, red, river water.. That only aug-
mented thirst, and induced nausea and dysentery.

Both officers and men, thus suffering, grew reckless of
danger. One night, a rebel, claiming to be an adjutant
general of General Steward—a Prussian, and Lord somebody—presented himself on board, and began a series of
deliberate insults   The outrage was borne till " forbear-
ance ceased to be a virtue," and then, suddenly, one of
our brave boys ordered the poltroon to leave the boat, and
so resolutely did our ", Yankees" second this command,

SHREVEPORT PRISON.

that the Confederate retreated precipitately. Had he delayed a moment, our officers would have flung him bodily into Red River.

Our prisoners arrived at Shreveport on the day that a rebel legislature was commenced. As usual, crowds of citizens gathered to gaze at the " Northern planters." A little boy, brought by his father to see the spectacle, innocently inquired, " if they were members of the Legislature ?"

Assigned quarters in an old building in Texas street, the " Yankees" found themselves as badly situated as they had been at Alexandria. Their food, it is true, was better and more abundant, but the place of their abode was a place of torment. The yard of their prison-building, enclosed by a high wall, was one vast sink, full of abominations. The air which invaded their windows was loaded with noisome and poisonous exhalations. Every breeze from the south brought deathly effluvium into the crowded apartment, where one hundred and seventy men were forced to mingle their food, their drink, and the breath of their nostrils, in an atmosphere already charged with noxious gases. At night the vapors became dense, impeding respiration and banishing sleep.

Shreveport was the headquarters of Lieut.-General E. Kirby Smith. The rebel general's offices were located in the upper part of a small brick building, the lower story of which was devoted to those southern institutions a faro-bank and a liquor bar.

The routine of prison existence at Shreveport was dreary indeed. But in a few weeks, our Federal officers were notified that they were to be sent to Tyler, in Texas. On the morning of their departure, the " Northern planters" were separated from them, as, likewise, were two of their fellow officers, Captain Allen and Lieut. Page, both of the *Corps d'Afrique*, who, after an examination, were placed in chains, and, as was then reported, "reserved for execution." The parting from these apparently-doomed men was a painful one, as there appeared little hope on either side of another meeting.

The march from Shreveport, under guard of " Richardson's Texas Rangers," made our " Yankees" still better acquainted with the " tender mercies" of traitors ; for their new custodians let slip no opportunity of exhibiting their malignant hatred of Americans. Arrived at their destination, and confined in an ancient courthouse, the effects of hardships and ill-usage soon became apparent in a general prostration. Closely packed, as before, and denied exercise, the majority became feeble and hopeless, and many were ready to succumb to fatal disease. But, fortunately for their lives, they were at this juncture, on the 27th of August, removed to Camp Ford, four miles from Tyler ; where, in the open air, and with daily opportunities of movement and ablution, they speedily gained in health and spirits. Leaving them thus situated, let us return to Brashear hospital, where, with my fellow-prisoners, I am waiting an expected order to follow our comrades toward Texas.

CHAPTER XIX.

A BAYOU AMBUSCADE.

DAY at Brashear hospital begins, by each of us, except Lieut. Stevenson, making ablution in our common wash-bowl on the balcony. Breakfast discussed, the smokers indulge in cigars, and those who have books read them. Acquaintances call on Stratton and Parse, citizen prisoners. The former of these was lessee or agent of a plantation, the latter a hotel-keeper. Stratton has a wife, who brings him occasional luxuries, and is endeavoring to procure his liberation.

I visit our wounded soldiers in other wards. Some are badly hurt. The poor lad Newlan was shot through head and body, and his arm is fractured. He bears up nobly, and, clasping my hands, whispers—"Tell my captain that I tried to do my duty."

"You have done it well, my brave boy!" I respond; and the gallant youth sinks back, with a smile on his pallid lips.

Sergeant Deming, in another ward, is more comfortable, and in good spirits. Both he and Newlan were wounded, while defending the gun, with Lieut. Stevenson. In another room lies an interesting young man, belonging to the Connecticut regiment. He is of slight frame, and has features delicate as a girl's. Quiet and gentle, he lies reading his bible; or occasionally talks of his home and his mother. But the signet of death is on the

beautiful forehead of this poor boy. He will never see
his mother's cottage in New Haven again.

One of our attendants is the wife of my servant George;
a fat, good-humored damsel, who gets a mosquito-net for
me, and thereafter forages successfully for a tin wash-
basin. She is claimed, as a "fugitive" by some planter
on the Teche. Some of these captured "contrabands"
appear to take their fate philosophically, while others
bewail it bitterly. A free negro old man, who came out
from New York, as steward of the William Woodbury,
the transport which brought me to New Orleans, is now
detained as a hospital servant. We hear that many
blacks were murdered by the rebels during their attack
on Brashear City.

The town bears marks of thorough sacking. Rebel
steam-boats are constantly conveying plunder away.
Trains of captured negroes, mules, and horses, are
daily crossed to Berwick, thence to be convoyed to
upper Lousiana and Texas. The rebels claim to have
gained sixteen hundred prisoners, and three million
dollars' worth of quartermaster and commissary stores, by
their raid, thus far. They boast, likewise, of capturing
twenty-three flags. Our "Ironsides" regiment has lost
a stand of costly colors, which I had sent, previous to
my going to the Bœuff, to Col. Nott's quarters, for safe
keeping; a precaution that I now regret; for if I had
taken them with me, the enemy should never have captured them. I would have buried or burned them first;
but Col. Nott yielded them to rebel possession, in the
somewhat fastidious belief that, as our regiment had not
been able to defend its colors, the enemy were entitled
to demand them. I should not, I confess, have been so
scrupulous; for, in point of fact, our regiment was not
responsible for the loss of its flags; the greater portion of

our brave rank and file being at Lafourche Crossing, when B.ashear City succumbed to surprise.

Our surgeon, Dr. Willetts, makes himself actively useful, in attending both foes and friends, who need his skillful services. His zeal and discretion render him quite a favorite with professional "confreres" of "secesh" persuasion. Our assistant Surgeon Throop is paroled, and proceeds to the Federal lines, in order to settle the question of *status* regarding captured medical men, who claim to be "non-combatants," and, as such, entitled to their immediate liberation.

On the third day of July, we are notified by Dr. Hughes, post-surgeon, to get ready for a move on the morrow. Mrs. S——, having failed to effect the liberation of her husband, volunteers and receives permission to accompany him. Our arrangements for transportation being finished, we celebrate the "glorious Fourth," by embarking on a river steamer for our journey inland. I provide myself with a present supply of "Confederate money," for which I pay cent. per cent. in Federal currency, and then, after bidding farewell to our wounded and paroled who remain, proceed, with my fellow-prisoners, to the point of embarkation. Confederate Dr. Hughes shakes hands, gives me a parting "grip," donates a full flask of our quartermaster's "Bourbon," and then introduces me to a "jolly flat-boat" sort of skipper, who repeats the "grip" aforesaid, *con espressione*, as your music-teacher might say. Finally, after sundry delays and difficulties, we get ourselves embarked—with Lieut. Stevenson comfortably bestowed on a saloon settee—and before sunset steam away from Brashear City, and up through the Atchafalaya. Stratton and wife are allowed a state-room, and treated to coffee and a luncheon; and presently the boat-captain, approaching us mysteriously, beckons me to a corner of the cabin.

"Colonel," he whispers, "I've got just one state-room left, and I've kept that for *you!*"—Thereupon, opening a door, he discloses a couple of spacious berths, with white counterpanes and musquito-nets. I thank the rebel skipper heartily, and return his courtesy, in a like "fraternal spirit," by tendering a draught of my "Bourbon;" whereof, I must add, he shows excellent appreciation. Then, after exchanging intelligent glances, and a few words of friendly chat, we part for the night; our skipper to his steering-house and myself to tender a share of the "state-room" to one of my captured comrades. Col. Nott is already ensconced near the couch of our wounded officer, Stevenson; so Lieut. Sherman secures the extra berth and musquito-bar; and we are thus made comfortable for another night, at least.

The Atchafalaya, bordered by green woodlands, with glimpses, over intervening marsh-land, of lakes and forests that extend behind Brashear City, cannot fail to recall an earlier incident of this year's campaigning—the fight of our gun-boat Diana. In this narrow channel, the beleaguered steamer sustained a fatal conflict, till forced to strike her flag to the enemy.

It was in the latter days of March, 1863, before the first advance of General Banks through the Attakapas, that a little fleet of gun-boats steamed in Berwick Bay and its contiguous waters, under Commodore McKean Buchanan. There were the Diana, Kinsman, and Estrella, the flag-ship Calhoun, and, if I remember well, the Sachem. Brashear City had been captured by this armament during Butler's closing days, and about the middle of January our gun-boats met two rebel steamers, called the Cotton and Hunt, and chased them up the

Teche. A daily sea-engagement, thereafter, with a dogged marching forward of our infantry on land, resulted in a blowing up of the Confederate steamer Cotton, at a heavy price for us—the death of poor Buchanan. He was shot in the moment of victory, and left his name to that fort which was afterwards finished on the Brashear shore. Our troops fell back, the rebels followed, and regained their ground; and so the month of February passed; we occupying one shore of the beautiful Berwick Bay and the Confederate forces freely ranging on the other. In March we drew back to the Bayou Bœuff, a channel penetrating from the bay to lakes and water-sheets which intersected the marshes in rear of Brashear City. Our outpost forces still remained at Fort Buchanan; and, about the twenty-seventh of March, one gun-boat, the Diana, was dispatched upon a sugar speculation. I doubt if this fact be recorded in official reports, but it is certain that our stout little gun-boat, with her two thirty-two pound broadside guns, her Parrot and her Dahlgreen brass-pieces, and her crew of ninety, officers and men, steamed up, one pleasant morning, to the widow Cochrane's sugar-house, on the Atchafalaya, with two capacious barges towed behind her, and a document in somebody's hands, which purported to be a bill-of-sale for all the widow's sugar. Whether there was playing at cross-purposes or not has never come to light; but our good madame made a great outcry about her sugar, and declared the bill-of-sale a fraudulent one. Meantime, Captain Peterson remarked that rebel scouts were swarming round our pickets, stationed on the lady's grounds. Sharp skirmishing succeeded, and it soon became apparent that Confederate plotting lurked behind this sugar speculation. Some twenty hogsheads had been rolled on one of the barges, when our gun-boat captain

prudently resolved to wash his hands of the affair. The
sugars were re-landed, all hands piped on board, and the
Diana steamed for Brashear City. Widow Cochrane
saved her saccharine wealth from "Yankee vandals,"
and our gun-boat sheered off just in season to escape a
well-concocted ambuscade.

The bill-of-sale, a bait flung out to greedy quartermasters through the rebel spies who lurked within our
lines, had failed to compass the Diana's capture for that
day, at least ; but the Confederates confidently counted on
another visit of the gun-boat to secure the sugar which
had nearly been her prize. So reckoned Colonel Gray,
the rebel officer in command, and he prepared his ambuscade. Some hundreds of selected riflemen were sent
down to lie in wait below the widow Cochrane's premises; the Valverde Battery, of five brass pieces, took
position to deliver a raking fire across the bayou. Cavalry detachments, under Major Boon, a Texan Ranger,
waited under cover of the woods that fringed the water.
Every favorable point was made a cover for some squad
of sharpshooters, supporting six-pound howitzers. Thus
snugly ambushed, the Confederate trappers waited for
their game.

Meantime, unconscious of this scheming, Gen. Weitzel,
as our fate would have it, sent an order from his head
quarters at Bayou Bœuff, to make an armed reconnoissance of Grand Lake. The despatch was conveyed by
one of Weitzel's aids, Lieutenant Allen, who was also
charged to bring back a report of the reconnoissance.
The Diana was detailed, and detachments of infantry were
send aboard of her, as sharpshooters. Young Allen was
a gallant officer. I dined in company with him, in our
camp, the day before he started on this fatal expedition.
Captain Jewett and Lieutenant Kirby, of the 160th

New York Volunteers, Lieutenant Buckley and Lieutenant Laurie, of the Twelfth Connecticut infantry, and as brave a complement of officers and crew as ever manned a gun-boat, accompanied Lieut. Allen.

Grand Lake, as we know, is an expanse of water at the north and rear of Brashear City. With Flat Lake, Lake Pelourde and ather aqueous sheets, it bears the general name of Chetimaches Lake. Into these water-beds the Atchafalaya, flowing from Red River, disembogues its tide, and out of them debouches, to form Berwick Bay, and lose it volume in another lower bay, to which it gives its name. Fort Buchanan's guns, at Brashear City, commanded the mouths of both the Atchafalaya and the Teche, which thereabove unite; and near their junction is the town of Pattersonville. A swampy island, bisecting its waters, shapes two channels for the Atchafalaya—one through Grand Lake, and the other curving by the shore of Pattersonville, so that a steamer may sail up into Grand Lake on the Brashear side, and, passing round the island, may return by a channel on the Berwick side. The Diana started on her reconnoissance, with Fort Buchanan thus upon her right. She steamed through all the navigable waters back of Brashear City, saw no sign of rebels in their swampy range, and might as safely have retraced her course without encountering enemies. The ambuscade prepared by Colonel Gray was on the other channel. There the rebel gangs had lain in wait all night, expecting the Diana to revisit widow Cochrane's sugar-house. In the morning they beheld our gun-boat steaming up, but, to their chagrin, she was headed for the Grand Lake channel. Peering from their skulking-places all along the shore, from Pattersonville far down toward Berwick City, they could look across the woody island, and discern our steamer's smoke as she moved hither and thither, reconnoitering the lakes. Hour after hour they watched, wondering what occupied the Yankee gun-boat, and venting divers maledictions on her crew, until at length, as the day wore, they gave up every hope of getting her within their toils.

But Destiny was spinning her own web of mischance for the Americans. Our gun-boat had accomplished her reconnoissance; her head was turned toward Brashear; when, in an evil moment, some one said:

"Supposing we go round by Pattersonville, and give the rebs a shell or two."

"And stop at widow Cochrane's," added some one, laughingly.

The proposition was relished, it is probable, by all; for this monotonous duty of exploring muddy bayous had been wearisome enough. There were several hours of sun yet left, and they might give the enemy a "big scare" meantime. So Captain Peterson and Lieutenant Allen laid their heads together for a consultation, and the upshot was that they ventured to take the other channel. Discretion might demand that, having finished the duties of their trip, they should report without delay; but an adventure, with some dash of danger, tempted them, and so they turned the boat toward Pattersonville.

Merrily whirled the wheels, and our Diana dashed out of Grand Lake, and into the upper Atchafalaya, with flags flying, and guns all shotted, ready for the rebels. To run past Pattersonville and through the Teche mouth, bid good day to widow Cochrane, and, perhaps, have a flying skirmish with rebels and "bag" a few—these were incitements to freshen one's spirits; and so our gallant gun-boat was headed for a rebel ambuscade, and our brave sailors and soldiers rushed, unknowingly, into the toils which an adherence to their simple duty would have rendered harmless.

Meantime, the overjoyed Confederates followed, with their eyes, the course of the Diana. They watched her progress from the lake, her turn into the Teche, and her swift descent toward Berwick. Their cavalry could not restrain themselves, but dashed along the shore. Then a blue puff of smoke rose from our gun-boat's deck, a loud, metallic bark shivered the air, and half-a-dozen rebels in a group were stretched out, dying, on their dying horses. The survivors fled into the timber. A shell now curved in a sharp arc, and dropped amid the woods; a point-blank shot crashed through the thickets. No response was made from the rebel rifles. The Diana was allowed to come within short range before a shot was fired at her. Then, from long lines of hidden marksmen, and from all the brass artillery pieces, shot and balls were poured upon our doomed Americans, in an unbroken shower. The rebel cavalry, dismounting, crouched behind trees and bushes on the bayou bank, discharging their revolvers as fast as they could load them. No human force might stand up under such a hail of lead and iron as beat upon the Diana's decks from every quarter. Her cannoneers were driven from their pieces in the casemates; they scarcely fired a dozen times. Her infantry were powerless, exposed in mass to raking fires. They gave the rebels a few volleys, and then sought shelter between decks.

Now the exultant rebels grew frantic. Their yells and shouts mingled with the clap of howitzers and the crack of rifles and revolvers. The gun-boat's tiller ropes were shot away from both wheels. The engineers stood by their engines, working the boat by verbal orders, in default of steering apparatus. One moment her head was pushed to starboard, the next to larboard, to avoid encountering a bank. The channel was narrow, and rapid headway was impossible. Forward, the machinery was covered by defences; abaft, no part could be protected. The positions of Confederate batteries and sharp-shooters were changing constantly, to keep their sweep of the Diana. "There was no moment," said a rebel witness of the scene, "that a galling fire of six-pounders and Minie rifles was not poured into that boat." While one section of artillery sought some new position, in advance, another section hurled its shells and round shot without pause. Rebel rifles swept the decks of living combatants, while rebel howitzers crippled the craft.

Captain Peterson beheld his men driven from their guns, and rallied them repeatedly. The gallant fellows followed him to their posts, but only to be shot down mercilessly. The fight had lasted thirty minutes when the captain fell, struck by a round shot in the breast, and died instantly. Lieutenant Dolliver shared the fate of Captain Peterson. Lieutenant Allen was shot down soon after. Two infantry lieutenants sank beneath their wounds. Captain Jewett was stricken next. Lieutenant Hall commanded till he fell. Dead and dying strowed the decks. A plunging shot, penetrating double casemating, crashed through the pilot house, and Enfield bullets perforated the iron sheathing. A fireman had one leg cut smoothly off; a boatswain's mate received a shot which tore the bones of both his legs completely out. McNally, one of the engineers, was killed by a fragment which came crushing through the engine-room from a shell that had exploded in the wheel-house. These strange freaks of violence were noted amid clouds of scalding steam that filled the space below, to which all living men were fleeing for shelter.

So the fight went on, for nearly three hours, our devoted gun-boat making two miles down the crooked bayou.
Three officers directed successively—Lieut. Harry Western the last; and, during half the running of that terrible gauntlet, this gallant young commander strove to
save his boat, refusing to surrender. When the pilot
and an engineer had swum ashore, and all the working of
the engine devolved on Lieutenant Mars; when the ex-
haust-pipe had been severed, and the engine-room was
choked with vapor—steam at one hundred and twenty
pounds pressure, and the boat unmanageable; when, in
fine, all efforts to escape were plainly futile, then stout
Harry Western gave the signal of surrender. It was time.

Rebels on the banks were wild with joy. Our steamer's
boats had all been riddled, or shot from their davits, and
the Confederate officers came aboard in sugar-coolers.
One delirious ranger could not wait for transportation,
but leaped into the bayou and swam off to the Diana.
He was a Texan, and pealed out an Indian whoop. Then,
spying a violin belonging to the chief engineer, Lieutenant Mars, he clutched it, jumped again into the water,
gained a bank, and, mounting on a caisson, played and
danced the tune of "Dixie." Then his comrades paddled out in sugar-coolers, and began to swarm upon our
gun-boat.

But, in such a gun-boat as it now appeared, no one
might recognise our trim Diana. The scene, above and
below, was ruin refined upon. The upper works were
riddled like a sieve from stem to stern. Every berth
was cut in splinters. Chairs, tables, knives and forks,
books, broken glass and china, shattered panels, blood-
wet beds and pools of gore—and the dead and wounded—
were everywhere.

Such was the Diana's fight—a desperate and stubborn

effort to escape from overwhelming force and numbers. Had the odds been less unequal, or a chance left for resistance, those gallant youngsters who survived would have come off victorious, or sunk, with their vessel. But an ambuscade in Louisiana bayous! one might as well fight the air as attempt defence against a foe as impervious as ubiquitous.

CHAPTER XX.

FRANKLIN, ON THE TECHE.

ON the fifth of July we awake to discover ourselves at Franklin, on the Teche. Parting from my friendly steamboat captain, I follow the negro lad who shoulders my trunk, and soon find myself, with the other prisoners, at a spacious hotel; or what had formerly been one, but was now devoted to surgeons, nurses, and sick and wounded rebels. Lieut. Stevenson is placed in a lower ward of the hospital, and my fellow-officers, with Stratton and wife, are conducted to a rear gallery, on the second story, overlooking a quadrangular court. Three rooms opened from one side of this gallery, and Col. Nott, Sherman, and myself were assigned the middle one. Our married couple flanked us in one apartment, and the other, as we speedily learned, was occupied by two Federal surgeons and a Massachusetts officer, captured at Brashear City.

Our change of quarters had not been for the worst. Here we were comfortable and quiet; though strictly guarded, night and day, by half a dozen rebel rangers with loaded muskets, who patrolled, by turns, the gallery. They were civil fellows, however, bringing us water, and accompanying us, with cocked pieces, when we stepped beyond the gallery. Their unsophisticated back-woods traits were evident, and I amused myself with classifying them. One was a gay "Lothario," Russen, who skirmished continually, on the gallery, with "secesh" dam-

sels; another, "O'Neal," was a Vidocq in watchfulness.
If one of us turned over, in the night, this alert sentry
would click his gun-trigger at the window. "Miller," a
German, was inclined to Unionism, but the corporal, a
polite youth, was rebel to the spine.

Our fare, at this hospital, was excellent; coffee being
brought us at daylight, and a bountiful breakfast served
by a negro waiter about nine o'clock. Between four and
five, P. M., an ample dinner was brought up—cloth and
table being set, and coffee following the meal. A courteous
young Parisian, attached to some staff, as a lieutenant,
was very attentive to Col. Nott, whose acquaintance he
had made; and sundry bottles of choice Falkirk ale, with
other dainties, were consequential kindnesses thereof.
Opportunely, likewise, one day, a present of fresh butter
arrived from Madame P——, the lady whom I had met
at Dr. R——s house, on Berwick Bay, and who was an
acquaintance of Col. Nott's father—a captain in the staff
of General Bowen, in New Orleans. This lady's plantation was near Franklin, on the Teche. Altogether, our
fortnight at Franklin—apart from its close confinement—
was no unpleasant interlude of the prison-drama.

On the 19th of July, we left this hospital, for a march,
in charge of Lieut. Duncan, of Speight's battalion, and
nine guards. We parted from the two Yankee surgeons,
who were to be immediately paroled, but took with us
their room-mate, Lieut. Humble, of the Fourth Massachusetts Infantry. Outside of the hospital, we joined a
batch of Union prisoners, captured at Brashear City and
on the Lafourche bayou. They consisted mainly of
citizens, but there were three Federal officers, one of
them a fellow New Yorker, Captain Fred. Van Tine, of
the 131st New York Volunteers, and the other two
Lieutenants Basset and Wilson, of the 48th Massachusetts.

Infantry. They had been captured near Donaldsonville, on the Lafourche, and from them we received the welcome intelligence that both Vicksburg and Port Hudson were ours. It was glorious news, to inspire us for the march, and enabled us to step out quite manfully.

Port Hudson surrendered on the 8th day of July, and immediately afterwards troops were dispatched down the river, to Donaldsonville, which the rebels, who had captured Brashear City and the railroad, were then threatening in heavy force. Capt. Van Tine's regiment, the 131st New York Infantry, arrived at Donaldsonville, on the 12th of July, and on the same day marched, with remnants of several regiments, in a brigade of about fifteen hundred, to drive the rebels down Bayou Lafourche. Skirmishing and desultory fighting commenced at once, continuing through the day and night; and on the following morning our young captain was sent to the front, in a skirmish line of about fifty men extended a half-mile, on one side of the bayou—General Dudley and Col. Martin, with another brigade, being on the opposite bank. It was while engaged in a brisk skirmish with the enemy, at the front, that Captain Van Tine found himself suddenly charged by a heavy mass of cavalry, which, getting between the feeble and attenuated skirmish line and our main body, drove the latter back to Donaldsonville, and swallowed the former up bodily. Our captain and his brave boys fell into the hands of rebels of a scurvy character, who robbed them of watches, rings, and other valuables, beat the feebler ones with their sabres, and finished by marching the enlisted men within a few miles of our lines, where they stripped them of all remaining property, administered a hasty parole, and left them to find their own way to liberty. Captain Van Tine, and two Massachusetts lieutenants, were conveyed

to Thibodeaux jail, and thence to Brashear and Franklin,
whence they joined our party, for a tramp across the
prairies.

Our " coffle" was a straggling one. The rebel guards
on horseback rode in front and rear, and our motley gang
of prisoners tramped the dusty road between. We
marched fifteen miles that day, and camped about dusk
at a sugar-house, sleeping in wagon-bodies, which we found
under the sheds. We had one large wagon, drawn by
six mules. In this vehicle were carried our baggage and
rations. It was an ambulance, also, though a rough one,
for our wounded comrade, Lieutenant Stevenson, a couch
and six for Mrs. S——and an occasional stage for such of
the prisoners as gave out on the road. Our rations consisted of flour, corn-meal, and bacon. Bread was cooked
for us by negroes, at the halting-places, and our bacon
toasted at the camp-fires, on a forked stick, gave a savory
relish to the meal.

Starting next morning at daybreak, we halted, for dinner, on the banks of the Teche, where our corn was
cooked at a planter's house, in the shape of hot " pones,"
which we sweetened with " syrup." Here we met a
pleasant French physician, who examined Lieut. Stevenson's foot, and declared that its condition did not warrant our wounded officer to continue his journey beyond
New Iberia. Resuming our travels, I began to take
note of the "citizen-prisoners." Besides Stratton, the
"Northern planter," and Parce, the publican, there was
an old man, named Holliday, who had been the lessee of
a plantation near Brashear City, and was one of the most
garrulous and truculent of veterans, denouncing rebels
without stint, whenever they were out of ear-shot. He
showed himself a stout pedestrian, and kept among our foremost. Clark and Knowlton, who had been assistants of

Stratton on his government plantation, a young fellow named Emerson, accused by the rebels with having twice deserted their service ; a couple of old creoles, charged with having favored Federals, a negro who was said to have shot a rebel sergeant, and a noisy nondescript, who formerly sold newspapers in our Brashear camps—and was, doubtless, a spy--with] Haley, a clerk, made up our civilian party on the march to New Iberia. There had been another prisoner brought with the citizens, to Franklin, but he had escaped on the night before our departure, by descending a rope from the window. This man, named Thomson, had been arrested at his home, on the Teche, for having, as was said, displayed a Union flag when our troops marched up the bayou. The rebels at Franklin expressed much anxiety to recapture and hang this " Lincoln sympathizer."

CHAPTER XXI.

PRAIRIE TRAVELING.

I AM resting in the wagon, after a tramp of ten miles, and we are nearly in sight of New Iberia, when, crack! bang! pistols and rifles explode, and the air is suddenly thick with clouds of dust. Roaring, shouting, and a plunging of mules, confuse our senses, for a moment, and in the next we become witness of a general stampede among guards and prisoners. A vicious bull has broken from a drove of cattle near by, and, careering, madly, down the road, carries terror into the ranks of bipeds. Officers and citizens ingloriously disperse, and two or three over-vigilant guards, apprehensive of an attempt to escape, send bullets flying after the fugitives. From our rampart, the wagon, a few of us enjoy the sport; but for a minute or more, there really seems danger to the foot-farers. But the bull is brought to bay, our guards resume position, and we soon after enter New Iberia, and are halted in front of the Provost Marshal's office. Here we become a mark for rebel citizens, home guards, and such gentry, who make us aware of their rather unamiable disposition toward us, by significant remarks about hanging, shooting, and other summary modes of dealing with Yankee prisoners. We proceed thence to an old saw mill, near the river, where, having cooked our rations, we endeavor, in a heavy shower of rain, to get ourselves sheltered till morning. Lieut. Stevenson, who has suffered severely from his wound, during two days of tedious wagon-jolting, is here remanded to a hospital, and will remain, under care, till restored to a better condition for journeying. I spread my blankets on some boards in the saw-mill, and the rest dispose themselves as comfortably as possible, when an abrupt order arrives from the provost-marshal, requiring us to move. An ass, in the lion-skin of authority, named Brien, notifies Lieut. Duncan that no Yankee prisoners will be permitted to remain within the town-limits. Our Texan and his men are exercised not a little by this order, and visit no light maledictions on this Louisianian provost-marshal, as well as on Louisianians and provost-marshals generally. "If I had a hundred Texans, instead of nine," cries the bold lieutenant, "I'd clear out this one-horse town of all the mean 'Cagians in it!" But swearing is no help for us; so we load up, in the rain, and, with much grumbling of everybody, get started for another location.

Our provoked commander is determined to go no farther then compelled, this night; and we halt, about a quarter of a mile from our first location, at an old sugar-house just beyond the "Newtown" precincts. Here, unloading once more, in wet and darkness, we bivouac under the eaves of sheds, and, after a contest with fleas for possession, resign ourselves to the slumber of weariness.

At six o'clock, next morning, we have breakfasted, and are on the march, with lively remembrances of provost-marshal Brien. The day is hot, but we proceed twelve miles before halting, when we enjoy a good meal and noontime *siesta* at a farm-house pleasantly shaded with orange-trees. Turning off, then, from the Teche highway, we strike off toward the prairies, and after a tramp of seven miles, reach a roadside house of entertainment, called the "Texas Hotel," where we get an excellent

supper, at Lieut. Duncan's expense, and take shelter
from a night-squall in beds that, despite the fleas, prove
decidedly welcome.

Five o'clock A. M. finds us moving, next day; crossing
Vermillion Bayou at the outset, and pursuing our march
toward another stream, called *"Queue-tortue"* or "Turtle-
tail bayou." On this day, I ride a few miles on a pony,
loaned by one of the guards, and have the luck to discover a
bunch of onions hanging in a deserted hut on the prairie.

These guards of ours are good-hearted fellows; always
ready to accommodate, and, like their officer, inclined to
favor us as much as possible. "Gentlemen," remarks
Lieut. Duncan to the Federal officers—"I shall consider
you under parole, and place no guard about you. We
must watch these yer citizens, and if that deserter thar
tries to run, I'll put a ball through him right smart; but
you all, that are officers, may just consider yourselves
under parole of honor. That's enough between soldiers,
gentlemen!"

So we get on very amicably. Corporal Wiggins, or
"Corporal X," as his comrades call him, is our dashing
cavalier, who makes wild rushes off to right and left,
visiting houses in the timber. He is a capital rider, like
all Texans, but I would not back him as a sharp-shooter.
I think he discharged five barrels of his revolver at a
chicken, within eight feet, this morning, without any
effect but a crow of derision from the feathered biped.
We have another corporal, Handkomer, an honest,
genial fellow, and his brother, of the same stamp; "Bill
Clowes," a ranger, full of "yarns," who rides a silken-
hided mare, with the pretty name of "Red-bird;"
Caspar, a German, who likes to grumble; John Weed, in
green goggles, who keeps a sharp look-out for straggling
citizens, but is a simple, warm-hearted man; Weldon and

Chapman, young Texans; and a curious nondescript named Bell-air, whom the rest of them call a " 'Cagian,', and who has acquaintances among all the French creoles on our route.

I must here explain that a "'Cagian" is one of those dwellers on prairie or bayou-marge, whom we find composing a large portion of the population of Lower Louisiana. Many possess small plantations on lands reclaimed from the wilderness, or near a " timber-island," or the banks of a stream, which in rainy seasons overflows, and in droughts becomes a bog or shallow. The " 'Cagian's" isolated dwelling, " la cassine," often gives name to the small water course in its neighborhood; and he dwells with his family in almost patriarchal simplicity and primitive seclusion. Often, in traversing an extensive prairie, you will find the dwelling of one of these planters, encompassed with orange or peach trees, and surrounded by ploughed fields; his wife and black-eyed daughters engaged in spinning or lariat-twisting; his stout sons attending to herds of cattle on the prairie. Here the more, thrifty " 'Cagian" passes his days, content with simple comforts, and coveting no luxuries beyond his swift ponies and giant-horned oxen. The poorer " 'Cagian" builds his cabin in swamps or pine-barrens, and makes a precarious living by fishing or hunting. But neither the very comfortable planter, with his brace or more of slaves, nor the sallow-cheeked habitant of an isolated cabin, has much affinity with nabobs of wealthy Louisianian parishes ; those sugar-lords who number their human stock as our cattle-breeding " 'Cagian" counts his yearlings. The dogmas of " secession" and " state rights" have no charms for these independent denizens of forest and prairie, whose ranks have furnished, in other days, the Red River "*voyageur*," the bee-hunter, and the

trapper. Therefore, we find these people loth to follow
rebel-lead, and often in conflict with the military forces
which strive to drag them from their humble homes as
conscripts.

"But what is the " 'Cagian?" and why is he called by
this name?" I am asked; and reply, that, to the best of
my belief, he is the descendant of those original French
settlers who, under tempting promises of French prime
ministers, or magnificent scheming of Scotch John Law,
came out to New World colonies, to die of hardships and
poverty, and leave a like fortune as heritage for their
children. The wide-spread French possessions, reaching
from the St. Lawrence to the Gulf of Mexico, were once
known as "Acadie," and their creole inhabitants described as " Acadiens." An ancient French pronuncia-
tion is still retained in the corruption, " 'Cagians," used
indiscriminately by Texans, to designate the poor creole
Louisianians who dwell on prairie and bayou between
the Sabine and Mississippi.

Our third morning's march from New Iberia was a hot
and weary one, and we were glad, indeed, to reach, near
noon, a prairie " ranche," as the Texans called it, occupied by a " 'Cagian," who spoke excellent French, and
informed us that the spot was called " Tasso's grove."
The creole himself, who entertained us hospitably, on
rich milk, hot bread, and peaches, and accompanied us
several miles on our way, was an intelligent man, and
had a picturesque face, which, as if in conformity to the
name of his residence, resembled much our portraits of
Torquato Tasso. From this pleasant resting-place, we
proceeded, after dinner, to a piece of timber known as
Peach-tree point, where was situated the house, or " *la
cassine*," as our " 'Cagian" said, of one Miles Wells, for
whom our Texan commander had a message from some

rebel comrade. Here we replenished our canteens, but, finding no corn for the mules, pushed on toward another camping-place.

Bill Clowes had lent me his "Red-bird," for a "lift" upon the road, and I was jogging on, with the guard, when we were suddenly drenched by a heavy thunder shower. Striking into a gallop, with "Corporal X," we speedily made our way to a "ranche" which lay to our left, on the prairie, and, reaching it, found a deserted log-house, quite roomy and dry, with a contiguous cottage, likewise vacant, but containing a bed and other furniture. I proceeded to select a spot whereon to bivouac, discovered a shallow feed-trough, which I appropriated as a cradle, and therein spread my blankets, under a shed that sheltered the porch. Meantime, "Corporal X," "prospecting" for whatever might be "lying around loose," extracted an old wooden saddle-tree out of a dry water-cask, and presented it to me, as earnest of future "transportation." The wagon, with our supplies, presently came up. Stratton and his wife soon made themselves comfortable in a "furnished cottage," and, after a light supper, we all bestowed ourselves snugly.

The next day saw me "mounted." Corporal Handkomer had brought with him from Franklin a fine American horse, of great size and strength, which had been led, thus far, for lack of an extra saddle. But my prize on the night previous, in the shape of a wooden tree, of Spanish pattern, was speedily turned to account by our clever guards, who at once interested themselves in getting up an "establishment" for me. "Corporal X" manufactured a pair of tough stirrups out of a strip of ox-hide; Bill Clowes furnished pack-strings; Handkomer supplied blanket and girth; and in a short time I found myself once more of the "equestrian" order. I shall not venture to boast of · the figure which I cut, after climbing to a perilous altitude on the top of saddle, great-coat, and blankets; let it suffice that I realized an agreeable change from the weary foot-work, in jack-boots of previous days. Gayly enough, I trotted ahead of the wagon, that morning, and pushed on briskly to a roadside "inn," where I ordered breakfast for the party, and awaited their coming, like an independent traveler. We obtained a fresh and bountiful meal, at this place, paying for it the reasonable sum of a dollar *per capita* in Confederate currency; whereafter, ascending once more to my camel's hump, I continued the journey rejoicingly.

CHAPTER XXII.

CROSSING THE BIG MARY.

I SHALL never forget my journey over those Louisianian prairies that stretch between the Teche country
and Sabine river on the Texas border. It seems to me
that I can still behold the long, long miles of sun-burnt
road extending to a timber island, and the green, cool
shades on reaching one; the isolated ranches and dismantled log-huts; the continuous line of telegraph-posts,
decaying in their sockets ere a wire was fixed to them;
the herds of cattle and wild horses; the short, stunted
herbage; the low water-courses, dried-up springs, and
miry bogs, that in the rainy season swell to freshets—all
these features of the route are stamped on memory as if
branded by hot iron. Every foot of arid ground was
measured by the tread of weary prisoners, marching
through the parching hours, depressed, home-sick, and
hopeless.

I cut a grotesque figure, very likely, when mounted on
a mammoth horse, the loan of my indulgent guard. La
Mancha's errant knight would have been "nowhere" in
my company, and Ichabod Crane's dread charger, "Gun-
powder," was but a mustang-pony to my steed colossal.
I had my naked saddle-tree bound on the courser's spine,
above a blanket, with the piece of lariat. An ancient
overcoat served for saddle-cloth, and gave my seat a
level with the horse's ears. No bridle had I, but a lariat
noosed around the under lip and jaw of my poor barb

kept him in prompt subjection. Stirrups I boasted.
They were loops of ox-hide, pendent by two cords of
cotton from the saddle-tree. Thus mounted, and "ac-
coutred as I was," in dusty shirt, blue trousers, and
jack-boots, with hat slouched over my brows, I might have
seemed a melodramatic brigand going to execution, or a
jayhawker led out to be "lynched."

Lieut. Duncan was always a companionable fellow,
though "secesh" to the backbone; stern, when he chose
to be, and ready to draw revolver on a fugitive, but
courteous withal, and genial, in his way. He looked at
me with curious gaze, when first I met his eye, thus
mounted and caparisoned. A merry twinkle answered
my "Good morning." "I'll bet you," said he, "that
your own wife would not know you."

"Maybe not, lieutenant," I replied, "I wish I were
at home to try her, however."

"I'd like to send you thar," rejoined the Texan, "and
write your wife to *keep* you thar," he added.

So we jog on gently; for a trot or gallop would be
fatal to my equilibrium, perched upon this pinnacle of
horse-flesh. The lieutenant and I make detours on the
prairie, while our wagon, and the line of prisoners on
foot, and Texan guard on ponies, keep the half-obliterated
stage-road. In an hour we find ourselves a mile or two
behind, my fellow cavalier shooting several prairie-hens
and other wilderness game. We presently arrive at a
wide bog.

"Big Mary!" says the lieutenant, who has crossed this
prairie more than once before. "I swum my horse yer,
when I travelled this range the last time."

"What! swum that mud-hole?"

"I reckon *so*," returned the Texan. "There was right
smart o' water yer abouts the day I forded it."

This, then, I mentally repeated, is the "Grand Marie," marked on old Louisiana maps as a broad-flowing river. I looked around upon the muddy bottom, and could see wide hollows, where some shallow pools of water were yet lingering.   But no trace of a great river-bed was visible.

"You'd hardly believe it," added the lieutenant; "but 'twas a heap harder fording this yer Big Mary than Vermillion Bayou, that we've passed, or yonder 'Monteau river.   The water out yer riz a right smart freshet in the rains.   Here we are right on to whar the ford was. Thar's a heap o' mud yer.   I'll pick out a trail."

So saying, the lieutenant pushed his pony in advance, and crossed a sort of causeway, sinking fetlock deep in mud.   I followed in his track, my heavier animal getting almost mired in the first steps.   The Texan reined his steed on the solid prairie, and looked back upon my slipping charger.

"Try a small piece to the right! I reckon thar's a better place to cross!" he called to me; and, following his directions, I drew hard upon my horse's under jaw with dexter digits.   In another moment we were floundering in the bog, my boot-tops sunk below the mud level, and thick, adhesive mire half swallowing steed and rider.

Well it was for the man, that neither lariat girth nor ox-hide stirrup failed in tough tenacity.   Quite fortunate for the horse, that he was strong and resolute, or perhaps Big Mary had become a Yankee grave that day.

The brave lieutenant, who at first waxed merry over our deep wallowing, grew presently quite anxious for the safety of his prisoner.

"Hold on right smart!" he halloed.   "That's a great animal under you!   Give him the spur, right smart!"

But I could not give him the "spur," not being provided with those knightly appendages. I dug my heels into his flanks "right smart," however, and held on with bent toes and thigh bones tighter than the Old Man of the Sea clung to Sinbad's shoulders. Meantime, the poor beast, strong and gallant as he was, and struggling, as he did, most vigorously, was sinking deeper with each plunge, and I began to think of "dying in the last ditch," when, providentially, one giant effort lifted us to firmer ground. I felt the horse's forelegs planted, while he strained the veins and muscles of his neck, until they looked like ropes. I spoke to him in cheering tones, and with a noble leap he rose completely from the bog, and we were safe again. I glanced at our condition: mired from head to heels; my jack-boots half drawn off; my breeches showing a mud-line nearly to the waistband. I expected momentarily to hear a horselaugh from the Texan. But his voice was quick and earnest when it reached me.

"Look yer!" he shouted.

I looked as he pointed, and beheld an alligator, huge and ugly as any fabled dragon, slowly crawling through the mud, a rod or two beyond the spot where I had been "bogged." He was a monster, more than twelve feet long, with epidermis like an iron-clad gun-boat. He stretched his monstrous flappers out, and dragged his horrible hind legs and vast tail deliberately toward us. He evidently was hungry. His great upper or vertebral jaw was lifted from the lower one, showing such a *cheveaux de frise* of tusks as might have crumbled a small man easily.

"Keep quiet!" said the lieutenant. "I reckon that yer alligator would ha' liked a lunch off your pony. But I'll fix *his* flint sure!"

He leveled a revolver, as he spoke, at the ponderous head which was advancing. His arm and hand appeared rigid as a bar of iron. Not less steady was the red Indian pony which he bestrode, and which seemed to be eyeing the big reptile with a glance as cool as the lieutenant's. Then a flash darted from the pistol, and I heard a bullet whizz beside me. It struck the alligator fairly in one eye, which jetted out a stream of blood. The saurian made a wild plunge forward, and began to lash the mud with long sweeps of his tail.

" I think that bullet has got into his head," I remarked.

"I reckon *so*," rejoined the Texan, with his usual emphasis upon the little adverb. " I'll go another eye on him, this yer shot."

He loaded again, and fired. A second crimson gush, straight from the other eye, attested the consummate accuracy of the Texan's aim. I quietly reflected that a runaway prisoner might stand little chance of escaping scatheless out of a stern-chase, with this frontier marksman following him.

Our big alligator soon was quiet. After a few more flounderings, and a shot that broke one flapper, he lay wallowing, with short, dying gasps, in the bloody mire.

We rode on briskly, to rejoin our wagon. I mentally recalled my recent struggle in the mud, with such a neighbor as the twelve-foot alligator in striking distance. Never more am I ambitious of crossing the " Big Mary."

CHAPTER XXIII.

ENTERING TEXAS.

CROSSING the Mermonteau river, we encamped on a timber elevation, near Indian Bayou. Here we were overtaken by a Confederate officer, going home to Texas on furlough. He brought news regarding our regiment; having been captured at Thibodeaux, and, as he said, paroled, by Major Morgans, of the " Ironsides." Another day's march brought us to the Calcasieu river, a broad, deep-flowing, and picturesquely-wooded stream, which we crossed, upon a horse-boat, at "Clendenning's Ferry." We then entered upon "Piney Woods," losing the line of telegraph-posts, which had marked our prairie highway, but finding a shaded and sylvan road for miles along the river banks.

The Calcasieu is navigable for small steamers, one of which we saw upon its waters. Twelve miles below the ferry which we crossed, is another, at St. Charles Lake. At that point several steamers and small sailing-craft were captured by adventurous Federals, who penetrated the marshy river-mouth in launches. We encamped, this night, under pine-trees; after "Corporal X" had made prize of a mule, which he "lassoed," in true Mexican style. Musquitos here were legion, and I mentally thanked the fat wife of my servant George, whose good nature had provided me with a gauze shield against our ubiquitous torment.

On Sabbath day July 26th, we found ourselves; near

noon, at the "ranche" of an ex-postmaster, Mr. Escobas, who once kept a wilderness store, now closed and empty of goods. This intelligent creole possessed a comfortable dwelling-house, with several slaves, and was notably "secesh" in his proclivities. But I availed myself of his permission to boil some "Lincoln coffee," which our provident Lieut. Humble had purchased from the thrifty surgeon of his regiment, before leaving Franklin. An ancient negress, at the kitchen-outhouse, prepared a delicious beverage for us, in her French "biggin;" furnishing milk and sugar, *ad libitum*, and imparting her confidential prayers to us that "Massa Linkum" might sometime "clar' out" the rebels "round yer." Poor old soul! with sixty winters of slavery on her back, she endeavored to lighten their weight by the never-dying hope of enfranchisement.

Leaving West-Fork Post-office, as it was called, we rode a mile or two, halted for a chat with "old man Lyons," a Baptist, who dwelt with his family in the next ranch, and thereafter sought out a "camping ground," under the giant-pine-trees. Having enjoyed a good dinner that day, I made my supper on some dried, or "tassoed," beef, which Mr. Ex-Postmaster Escobas had presented to me.

We were on the road, next morning, before sunrise. Passing a Baptist church, secluded in the forest like a hermitage; halting at a roadside "tavern," noisy with Confederate travelers; and getting sight of a pine-woods school-house of rough logs, full of frightened urchins; we reached, about meridian, a small rebel camp, and shortly afterwards debouched from the "Piney Woods," and found ourselves at Niblett's Bluff.

Hardly were we fairly disposed, for rest and refreshment, in an old camp-ground, where Confederates had left traces of their presence, by brush shelters, and in a big tree, where they had "hung a nigger," than we were welcomed by a sudden thunder-storm, which, "fierce and fast, in ponderous rain, shot down, a sheeted flood." I had built a shed, with some pine-boards, and attempted to screen myself by crawling under it, upon my rubber-blanket. But the shower was too much for pine caves; and I was glad to follow the rest of our party, who had retreated toward the river-bank, and taken refuge in a dilapidated shanty once used as a "guard-house."

Lieut. Duncan had hoped to reach Niblett's Bluff in time for embarkation on a steamer, which, it was understood, left twice or thrice a week for Beaumont, to connect with cars that ran to Houston City. But there was no boat visible when we arrived, and none to leave for forty-eight hours, or more. We proceeded, therefore, to make ourselves as comfortable as possible, under the circumstances.

Niblett's Bluff is a muddy, barren, disconsolate village, of a dozen straggling huts and a steamboat landing. It is on a bank of the Sabine river, in Louisiana, and has served as a sort of *point d'appui* for Texan expeditions toward the Mississippi. Outside of our guard-house shelter, was a platform, where bales of cotton and hogs-heads of sugar were "dumped," awaiting transportation; and both guards and prisoners were soon as busy as bees collecting sweets from the saccharine deposits. With a broken cask of the "best clarified" at their door, one could hardly blame our Yankee boys for "foraging on the enemy."

Morning, at Niblett's Bluff, was inaugurated by a good breakfast at the "tavern," at the cost of $1.50 in Confederate paper. The landlady was a "host" in herself, and consented to let her sable laundress wash clothes for some of us, at the rate of $1,00 per dozen. "Yer kin pay that ar' price jest as well as yer kin pay a dollar a glass for whiskey!" said this reasonable female, and I agreed with her.

I was shocked to see, in an ante-room of the tavern, a young yellow girl extended on the filthy floor, sick with fever, and apparently dying. Scarcely sixteen years old, this unfortunate child had been married to our major's servant Albert, while they were with me, at Tigerville. She had left her mistress, Madame Turner, of Terrebonne, to follow the fortunes of a northern husband. But Albert, accompanying his master to Lafourche, could not protect his bride; and she became the prey of some Texan speculator, who had brought her to Niblett's Bluff. Recognizing the poor girl, I stooped, and called her by name. She turned her wandering eyes toward the voice, and appeared to know me, but relapsed immediately into painful apathy. I never saw her afterwards.

About dusk, that evening, the steamer Clotilda arrived from Beaumont, and we were ordered aboard of her. Spreading our blankets on the deck, we slept comfortably, and, at five o'clock, A. M., the following morning, found ourselves descending the Sabine. Toward evening, we reached the Sabine Lake, and came in sight of the "Pass," that scene of more than one disaster to our Federal forces. While threading the bay-channel, we grounded several times; and two negroes were constantly occupied in taking soundings. "Three and a quarter—scant!" and "five feet—large!" chanted momentarily by our dusky pilots, attested the shallowness of this intricate passage. Had our steamer drawn more than three feet, she must have struck fast in many places.

At twilight we reached Beaumont, a small, scattered

village, the terminus of a worn-out track called the New
Orleans and Texas Railroad.   Here we encamped under
trees; and, after an excellent supper at the "hotel," for
which I disbursed $1.50 (Confederate), I slept soundly,
as usual, and awoke refreshed.

Rejoicing, moreover, in the good fortune of another
substantial tavern-meal, I felt prepared for sumptuous
railway travelling; but my expectations were soon mode-
rated in considering the choice offered us by the surly
conductor—either to ride in a negro-car, already half
filled with blacks of questionable purity and unquestiona-
ble odor, or to climb the car-roofs, and take our chance of
holding fast thereon.   Good air, and a prospect of "seeing
the country" carried the day, of course; so we mounted
the car-roofs, where we found, much to our satisfaction,
that some freight, in the shape of several covered cabriolets and gigs, had preceded us.   I lost no time in
bestowing myself on the cushioned seat of one of these
vehicles, and, being nicely sheltered by its silk-lined
top, came quietly to the conclusion that this was an
improved mode of outside transportation.

At Beaumont, there was a general dispersion of our
guards; all receiving short furloughs, which they were
to improve by making hasty visits to their homes.   In
parting from some of these kindly foes, I gave them a
few tokens of remembrance; to Handkomer my pocket-
compass; for this quiet but sterling young man had
acted as my "orderly" more than my guard, on the march.
Indeed, I acknowledged good offices at the hands of all;
many an early cup of coffee tendered to me, and many a
cheering word or entertaining "yarn," that whiled the
tedium of the road.   Man is man, the world over; and
these Texans, doubtless, would have proved loyal Union
men, had their homes been north instead of south of our

Potomac lines. Even Lieut. Duncan, who, like officers
generally, displayed more rebel *animus* than the privates
do, was more mistaken, as I conceived, than criminal; but
the glamour of state pride and class arrogance prevented
his intelligence from comprehending his error. I left
him the bugle-frontlet of my cap, as a trifling mark of
my appreciation of his courtesy toward all of us; and he
seemed gratified, like a child, with the gift; remarking
that it was the first present he had ever received in his
life.

Forty miles of slow steaming brought us to Liberty,
a small town on the railroad. Here we saw the last of
our guards—"John Weed"—starting off over the prairie,
toward his "ranch" in the "timber." Lieut. Duncan was
to accompany us to Houston. Another stage of travel
brought us to the San Jacinto; where we discovered that
a section of the railroad bridge had been burned, by
accident, on the previous night, and was impassible.
Nothing could be done but cross the passengers on foot,
or by boats, leaving cars and baggage to await repairs,
which were progressing. The majority of "first-class"
Texans and their retinues went down the bank, toward a
ferrying place, but the prisoners mostly, myself among the
number, essayed to pass the obstacle. Never do I desire
to attempt another such a feat. The bridge was a half-
mile in length, at least, without planking, and the cross-
trees were so far apart as to oblige a wide step over each
intervening chasm. Encumbered with my heavy knapsack and bundle of blankets, weak in frame and giddy,
and certain that a mis-step must precipitate me fifty feet
into the rocky river-bed, I found that crossing of the
Texan Rubicon almost as perilous as Santa Anna proved
it. It cost me as much "balancing" as did my memor-
able passage over cypress-cones in the swamp of Bayou

Tiger; but, at length, it was happily over, and I threw myself—exhausted and grateful—on the other bank of *terra firma*.

Near this bridge is the old battle-ground, where Sam Houston and his little army defeated their Mexican invaders, capturing that wooden-legged hero who had led them across the entire breadth of Texas, from the Rio Grande, to get himself taken prisoner by the fugitives whom he was chasing. The "league of land," on which Houston encamped, was owned by an Irish virago, who, deeming her soil trespassed on, sent a peremptory order to the general, to "move off;" which, it is said, "Old San Jacinto" declined to do, till he had whipped the Mexicans.

Poor Sam! I shall learn soon whether he is really, as we have heard, a rebel, like the rest of these crazy southern leaders. I cherish my own doubts still; and would have almost guaranteed his loyalty at the beginning of Secession. Little, indeed, did I fancy, on receiving a last friendly letter from him, just before the war, that I should so soon look upon the field of San Jacinto, and under such circumstances as the present were. "If ever you come to Texas," wrote the old hero to me—"you will always find my latch-string out!" But as a prisoner-of-war, I must be greeted by another kind of latch, with the string quite out of my reach, I apprehend.

Leaving our baggage with the impeded train, and making "squatters" of ourselves on flat cars, drawn by another locomotive, we accomplished the remainder of our journey—twenty miles—before sunset. Arrived at Houston, we were detained at the railroad depot long enough to attract the notice of a violent old woman, who denounced us unsparingly. "Come here, you little dears!" cried this sad termagant; addressing—not us, but—a number of little children who were gazing timidly; "come, and the murderers of your fathers and brothers! .... O! if I only had the hanging of ye! .... Don't get too nigh the sarpints, children!, They'll p'ison ye all! .... Come away! they'll be hung sartain!—O! the Yankee murderers!" And, with her rheumy eyes revolving, and her yellow fangs snapping, the wretched beldame backed away, with the children, while we shouldered our baggage and followed Lieut. Duncan across a bayou-bridge, and up the main street of Houston, till we reached a block of buildings in which was located the provost-marshal's office. Here we were left standing on the walk, while our custodian reported his prisoners; and here we were speedily surrounded by a crowd of inquisitive Texans.

A bluff, off-hand sort of man addressed me at once, asking about our capture, and informing us that he was Capt. Conner, of the Texan navy, who had taken a noted share in the re-capture of Galveston from our troops some six months previously. The bold captain was anxious to show hospitality, and proposed to treat our party to refreshments at the hotel opposite; an offer which we should all have been willing to accept; but when permission was asked of Lieut. Duncan, who rejoined us, with a deputy-provost-marshal, at this juncture, we were told that he had no longer disposition of us. So, with suppressed anathemas against the new jack-in-office, who gruffly ordered us "forward!" we bade "good-night" to Captain Conner, and shook hands, in parting, with our pleasant Texan lieutenant.

That night, for the first time, I felt the consciousness of jail-incarceration. We were all thrust together into a ground-room of the stone court-house, its massy door locked upon us, while, in dingy gloom, we endeavored to dispose our blankets on the rough floor. We brushed its thick dirt aside, as well as we could, bought a few loaves of bread from the guard, at four bits apiece, and, washing them down with water, accommodated ourselves to repose. Next morning I was awakened by the earliest sunbeams striking through a grated casement. Breakfast, of bread, meat, and rye coffee, was brought by our guards, and we were gratified with the assurance of being speedily sent to a camp of prisoners in the interior.

The court-house at Houston was unfinished, but substantially built and having fine interiors ; a fact I learned, from being permitted to use pen and paper for a few moments in the supreme court-room, a handsome and spacious hall, filled with cushioned seats. About nine o'clock, A. M., we were marched from this citadel, to a depot of the " Houston and Navasota Railroad," where we were kept waiting in the street, under a hot morning sun, for an hour or two. It appeared, at first, as if we were to undergo hard usage in our day's travel; a filthy cattle-box being pointed out as the only unoccupied means of transportation. But, fortunately for us, the conductor was a gentleman, and we heard his clear voice soon ordering up an " extra car for the Federal prisoners." An extra car, accordingly, was furnished us; for which we were grateful to a considerate Northern man, and a former lieutenant-governor of the " Old Bay State" herself ; now transferred into an official of this Texas railway, but, I doubt not, with many a yearning in his soul toward the soil of loyal New England. Throughout that day's journey, as we rode in comfortable seats, and looked out, unmolested, upon the Texan prairies, we exchanged many pleasant words with our genial conductor, H. W. Benchley, of Massachusetts.

In the afternoon, after stoppages at several roadside stations, we reached " Camp Groce," our destination; having left at Houston one of our number, the alleged deserter, Emerson. Several of the citizen-prisoners had been previously left, upon the Teche ; and our party, on arriving at "Camp Groce," consisted of Col. Nott and myself, Captain Van Tine, Lieutenants Sherman, Humble, Bassett and Wilson, six citizens, Holiday, Parse, Haley, Knowlton, Clark and Stratton, and the wife of the latter.

At Camp Groce, I unexpectedly met old acquaintances, in Lieutenants Hayes, Dunn, and Curtiss, officers of the 175th Regiment of New York Infantry, who had been fellow-passengers on our transport from Fortress Monroe to New Orleans. Lieut. Hayes busied himself at once with the rites of hospitality, providing me with a bunk, and a seat at his mess-table. The other new-comers were likewise soon comfortably cared for, and we speedily found ourselves " at home" in the prison-barracks. It was Saturday afternoon ; the air was pleasantly tempered ; there were numberless questions to be asked and answered ; and, after refreshing ourselves with an ample meal, we sat on a bench, outside, and passed a couple of hours in retailing " later news." Thereafter, as if to recall us to the present fact of captivity, we were called upon to accompany a sad procession of the prisoners, escorting to its grave the body of a lately-departed sailor.

We were introduced, that evening, to many who were to be henceforth our prison-comrades ; and who had already passed weary months in various guard-houses and prisons. Here were officers of the Harriet Lane, captured in Galveston harbor, on the first day of the year, and of the Massachusetts Forty-Second Infantry, their partners in misfortune. Here, too, were officers and sailors of the Morning Light, blockading ship, taken by rebels at Sabine Pass, in January. A half-year of "durance vile" had rendered these brave men accustomed, though hardly reconciled, to their exile from home and service. Their eagerness to learn the prospects of " exchange," gave us a foreshadowing of prison-anxieties that had not yet definitely weighed upon us.

Col. Burrell, of the Massachusetts regiment, was expected daily to arrive from Huntsville, where, until lately, most of these Camp Groce prisoners had been confined, in the State Penitentiary. The Colonel, who had remained behind under an attack of fever, was now convalescent, and would probably join us during the next week. As the story of his capture involves that of a majority of our Camp Groce officers, I will devote the ensuing chapter to it.

CHAPTER XXIV.

THE GALVESTON SURRENDER.

In reviewing the "*index expurgatorius*" of historical chapters relating to South-western operations during 1863, that mysterious episode which inaugurated the year — the surrender of Galveston — must not be forgotten. Like other events transpiring after the recall of General Butler from New Orleans, our loss of this key city of the Gulf was glossed over with such official nonchalance as to completely hoodwink people into a belief that it was one of the inevitable casualties of warfare. Many of my fellow prisoners, however, involved in the catastrophe of this Galveston drama, are still living to relate, as they did to me, the real facts pertaining to it.

On Christmas day, Col. I. S. Burrell, with three companies of the Massachusetts Forty-second Infantry, finds himself landed on the wharf at Galveston. Commodore Renshaw, commanding the harbor, assures our Bay State Colonel that himself and his small force are protected by gun-boats, and he requests him to quarter his men in a large two-storied warehouse, under cover of protecting fire, in case the enemy should attack. What is this enemy? Let us go back.

Three months before, an expedition had left New Orleans, the flagship Westfield in advance, with Captain Renshaw in command; the Clifton, Sachem, Harriet Lane, Owasco, and some others following. Arriving at the rebel port of Galveston, the town was summoned to

surrender. No answer being returned, beyond a single
gun, our fleet ranged broadside-to, before the city front.
A flag of truce arose; a rebel boat appeared, and boarded
Captain Renshaw's ship; and, twenty minutes afterwards,
our sailors heard that their commodore had given the
town authorities four days of grace. All that day, and
during following ones, Galveston was alive with business.
Steam-whistles shrieked, wagons rumbled, cars rattled
over the long bridge, and steam and sailing craft plied
ceaselessly upon the bay. Meantime Confederate flags
were flying gaily. Truce having expired, the rebel colors disappeared, and Commodore Renshaw landed on
Galveston Island. The town had been deserted; every
article of value carried off, comprising guns and steam-
engines and public stores—whatever could be serviceable
to treason. With pompous ceremony, then, our Commodore hoisted the Stars and Stripes upon the Custom
House, and hauled them down some thirty minutes afterwards. A few poor Union men, who remained in the
city, gave three cheers, and so Galveston fell into our
hands, after its rebel population had been suffered to
strip everything of value from wharves and houses.

Here, now, this island city was our own. Its bay, and
sandy shore, and web-work of lagoons, that interpenetrate
the coast, on either side, to the mouths of many Texan
rivers, required but fortifications to become a *point
d'appui* for inland operations. Where bold Lafitte once
built a stronghold, darting out through covert channels
from his island ambuscade, it might be thought our well-
appointed fleet could easily make a nucleus for future
victories. Houston City and the thriving Brazos Valley
were in radii of fifty miles, and all the coastwise towns
and settlements seemed within our grasp.

But Commodore Renshaw, after capturing the island,

having seized a wooden gun, *propria marte*, exhibited his genius-furthermore by mounting it on the Westfield, and then sailed in pursuit of further glory to the bay of Matagorda. Anchoring off Indianola he ran aground; coasting southwardly, and coasting back again, he occupied ten days or more in "armed reconnoissance," meantime exploiting on sand-bars three or four times diurnally, so that a jest ran round his fleet that "Renshaw kept the Clifton as a tug to drag the Westfield off her soundings." So the month passed, and its last day saw the flagship fire some four or five score shells at a small mud fort near Lavacca, and, in doing this, burst her costliest rifle-gun. Thus ended Renshaw's naval expedition from Galveston.

The residue of hostile execution on that Texan coast was summed up daily, in gun-boat logs, by entries such as "lying on and off the bar at Galveston." No guns were landed for shore batteries; no earthworks thrown up; not a shot fired at the enemy's fortified camp, which, filled with active rebels, strengthening its defences, seemed to laugh at us beneath its still defiant flag. A railroad bridge two miles in length connected Galveston with the main land, and afforded ingress from the rebel rendezvous continually. Hordes of enemies were swarming in from interior Texas. Not a gun was trained upon the railroad bridge; not a section of its timbers shot away. The town was left to be a daily resort of our plotting enemies, while boats plied every hour between the shore and fleet, and rebel spies, disguised as wherrymen and farmers, were constantly supplying fish and fruit in exchange for Yankee greenbacks, and collecting scraps of information to subserve Confederate purposes. On the flagship Westfield all was gay and festive. Rebel officers came off to dine and wine at Captain Renshaw's invitation. Convenient flags of truce were ready to shelter everything, whether it were the passage of rebel soldiers, with arms and ammunition, to their camp at Virginia Point, or the convoy of rebel officers to Captain Renshaw's cabin, for a jolly carouse at his mess table. So the year waned, till a transport, with the Massachusetts troops, arrived on Christmas Eve, and Col. Burrell next day landed at the long wharf and took quarters in a wooden storehouse.

Here, then, Galveston City was occupied at last. Since October 8d—three months of *dolce far niente*—a fleet of serviceable war vessels had gambolled "on and off the bar," while rebel riflemen and cannoniers were making disposition of their forces in full view and unmolested. All this time a messenger-boat could bear dispatches twice a week between the island and New Orleans; but not till Christmas day does a small force of scarcely a dozen score infantry appear upon the wharf at Galveston. More troops are promised; Col. Burrell's other companies will shortly follow their commander and his little vanguard. Thus is this "nine months'" force doled out by piecemeal to possess Galveston.

And how possess it? Shut up in a warehouse on the wharf; four gun-boats lying near; in nightly expectation of surprise. Three companies of raw troops, staunch and brave, but inexperienced, are kept continually on duty; every day marched through the city, to be drilled and exercised, their picket lines thrown out to distant squares by day, and drawn around the wharves at night; some cautious reconnoitering indulged in, but to small account, because no adequate force can be detached beyond the narrow city limits. All the week, reports come in, of rebel preparations for attack. Three companies alternate in guard duty, day by day. Mounted scouts of the enemy are, meanwhile, scouring the inland shores. Cavalry squads hover in view of the town. The last day of 1862 finds all the Massachusetts men on guard, in three reliefs. These poor fellows, harrassed and worn, are hoping for the arrival of their comrades, to reinforce the post. Captain Wainwright, of the Harriet Lane, comes ashore, and with Colonel Burrell looks out, through field-glass, from a cupola, upon the rebel camp five miles away. "I will send a boat up from the Lane to-morrow, and shell those gentlemen!" remarks the naval captain. Night sets in, and Captain Proctor, with Lieutenant Newcomb and some sixteen men, dividing, make an expedition through the city streets, to look for rebel cavalry that are skulking thereabout. They meet with frightened Union people, who assure them that the town is to be fired that night. The mayor of Galveston asks permission to remove his family out of danger. The moon now rises on the scene, clear and resplendent.

Thus matters are progressing in the town on New Year's Eve. The fleet is quiet at anchor. The Clifton lies above Galveston wharves; the Sachem, and a little schooner called the Corytheus, just below; the Sachem undergoing repairs. The Harriet Lane swings close to shore, some two miles lower than the Clifton; and the Owasco anchors by a coal-barge, nearly midway. Captain Renshaw, in his flagship, occupies a sand-bar near the point called Pelican's Spit. Our flagship is aground, as usual. The moon rides high in midnight heavens, her beams flashing on that quiet bay, on the fleet at anchor, on our soldiers watchful upon the wharf, on the rebels gathering at Virginia Point, and stealthily advancing from all other points.

There are sharp eyes on the gunboats as well as on land; and at two o'clock a Clifton look-out passes the

word that a couple of rebel steamers are approaching the
channel roads above. Their dark hulls and smoke can
be seen distinctly in the moonlight. The Clifton signals,
"The enemy afloat!" and presently is answered by a
summons from the Westfield, to drop down to Pelican's
Spit, and tow her from the bar. The Clifton's captain
grumbles, as he well may. This channel, crooked as a
ram's horn, is hard to navigate even by day; and now
the moon is sinking to her setting. But at three o'clock
the Clifton warps a cable-tow alongside of our grounded
flag-ship, and about the same time the moon dips, and
rebel guns are heard, beginning their play upon Galveston
city. Captain Law asks leave to take his vessel back,
which Renshaw grants, but will not let his pilot go. So
the Clifton gropes through darkness, trying to retrace
her channel grounds a dozen times or less, and does not
reach Fort Point, two miles below the city, till broad
daylight. There she encounters a battery, which the
rebels have erected during the night. She shells and
drives them out of it in twenty minutes' time, and thereafter steams up beyond the town-point, shelling as she
passes.

Colonel Burrell, meanwhile, when the moon goes down,
begins to find things looking dark about his little camp.
The gun-boat signals are suspicious, and he calls his
Massachusetts officers together, for a council. The gun-
boats Clifton and Owasco are three miles away, the Sachem cannot help them much, and there is no other vessel, but the schooner Corytheus, nearer than the Harriet
Lane, two miles above them. Prudent Colonel Burrell
gets his companies in readiness to make their own defence as best they may, should danger threaten. Presently, Lieutenant Newcomb brings report of a rebel
battery erected at the market-house. The gun-boats

ought to be notified of this ; but no one can communicate with them.   Suddenly, at half-past three o'clock, the pickets fire their guns, and fall back to our barricades.

Those barricades of planks, some twenty inches wide, lying one upon another, had been opportunely piled breast-high, through Colonel Burrell's forethought.   They stood his men in excellent stead on New Year's morning.

Now began to ripen, very fast, the fruits of rebel plot-ting under guns of a Federal fleet and at the mess-tables of a Federal officer.   Magruder's time had not been wasted during Renshaw's farce of occupying Galveston.   His forces had been marched through the deserted city, night after night; piloted across that railroad bridge so courteously left for their accommodation in the transit to Virginia Point.   His heavy siege-pieces had been transported on that bridge to points which covered all the anchorage.   His railroad *ram*, armed with an 8-inch Dahlgren gun, and mounted on a flat, was pushed across that bridge upon the rails, until it bore directly on the Harriet Lane.   His cotton-bales, for breast-works, were conveyed by the same track.   That railway bridge, which half-a-dozen Federal shells could have demolished at any hour, became a rebel highway toward the re-cap-ture of Galveston.

When the moon went down, on New Year's morning, the scheme of politic Magruder sprang out to execution. While our fleet lay at anchor, its flag-ship hard and fast on a sand-bar ; while Burrell's handfull of infantry, with pickets compassing some two or three squares, were hud-dled in their quarters on a single barricaded wharf; the rebels had already, despite of all Yankee vigilance, suc-ceeded, under cover of night, in bringing down their heavy guns and field-pieces into the very city streets, as well as to commanding points above, below, and on a

water-base of two miles and a half. This was our "capture" of Galveston; which permitted rebel armies to collect under Federal guns, while their officers dined at flag-
ship tables, and the bitter sneer was common among our
sailors that "Magruder knows better than Renshaw the
number of men and guns we have !"   This was our "occupation" of the Key City, which held, during Christmas
week, a wharf four hundred feet in length, while all the
streets, and squares, and wharves, behind, to the right
and left, were undefended, and left to become, at last, a
deadly ambuscade of rebel rifles and artillery.

So, when the fight began, under grey obscurity of starlight, Magruder had six companies of dismounted dragoons, under Pyron, lying in wait with rifles, while a
regiment of artillery with field-pieces took position on
their flank at Fort Point. Further up, toward the city,
and within its limits, other batteries were posted on the
wharves. Six field-guns occupied the Centre Wharf; the
railroad ram was placed upon the Upper Wharf; a battery was planted right in front of the barricaded wharf
that sheltered Burrell and his men. This battery was to
cover an attempt to storm the barricade ; a project intrusted to five hundred rebels, commanded by artillery
Captain Cook.

These dispositions had been made since sunset of the
previous day; so well concocted were the rebel plans, so
actively the fellows worked, inspired by earnest treason.
Af half-past three o'clock, the centre gun was fired, as a
signal, by Magruder. Rebel pieces then began to blaze
along the water front. A simultaneous shower of rifle-
shots was poured upon the barricaded wharf and at the
warehouse used as quarters for our infantry.

Well was it for Colonel Burrell and his men that he
had formed their line upon the wharf so promptly. Fire

was directed against the warehouse incessantly. The
rebels believed that all our force was under cover of
that building, and they riddled its walls and casements.
When the fray was over, there could not be found a spot
of two feet square which was not perforated with bullet
holes.

But the Bay State boys, under their gallant officers,
were safe behind the barricade planks. After Lieut.
Stowell had burned certain signals, as agreed upon with
Captain Wainright, to indicate that rebels held the town,
the colonel ordered all to lie down on the wharf. Our
vessels now responded to the rebel fire. The gun-boat
Sachem and the Harriet Lane delivered shot upon the
town, but fired too high, their missiles crashing through
the roofs of buildings. A tempest of balls and bullets
now came dashing over the wharf, and presently the rebel
storming party hove in sight, wading through water to
assault our barricade. They carried scaling ladders, and
advanced in dark masses ; their sharp-shooters deployed
to the right and left. Colonel Burrell ordered bayonets
to be fixed in preparation for a charge. His men stood
up with pieces at a ready. They peered into the gloom,
but could perceive only a waving shadow on the water.
At that shadow they hurled a bright blaze, sending volley
after volley from their muskets, fast as they might load
and fire. The rebels could not stand that leaden hail,
but broke for cover of the neighboring buildings.

At this point of the conflict our enemies were repulsed
everywhere. While Burrell drove them from before his
barricade, the Clifton and Owasco had been silencing the
lower batteries. Fort Point was evacuated, and the cannon on the different wharves were dragged off at a gallop
under charge of General Scurry. Galveston become too
hot for rebel quarters.

Here it was that Leon Smith, "quartermaster-admiral," came steaming down the harbor with his brace of cotton-boats, the Neptune and Bayou City. Heading for the Harriet Lane, they ran into her on either side, and poured a murderous fire upon her decks. Four hundred rifles and three hundred double-barreled shot-guns swept the vessel's deck from stem to stern As Wainwright could not promptly cut his chains, he fought the ship at anchor like a hero. Such guns as might be brought to bear upon his foes did instant execution. The Neptune was quickly sunk, and the Lane's bows were turned upon the other boat, carrying away its larboard wheel-house by the shock. But overwhelming numbers, pouring un-broken sheets of musket flame upon the Federal vessel, from behind a cover of cotton bales, were not to be with-stood. Gunners fell at every piece on board the Lane. Bold Wainwright, foremost of her staunch defenders, sank beneath a rifle shot. His first lieutenant, Lea, was killed beside him. Then the rebels swarmed over their cotton-clad batteries, and our men, unable to make fur-ther head, surrendered.

It was a crisis of the battle. At every other point the rebels had been beaten. Even here, with Wainwright dead, and his fine vessel taken, it needed but a dash of our remaining gun-boats to have saved the Harriet Lane and gained a victory. His Neptune sunk, his Bayou City grounded, Leon Smith was master of the Harriet Lane, but he was still at the mercy of her consorts. Had the Clifton then attacked him he must have been lost. The Owasco did indeed salute him with a passing broad-side, but beyond this, no attempt was made against the rebel commodore.

It was not strange now that Magruder, foiled at every other point, withdrawing from the town front, and retreating under fire of our brave infantry, should hail the lucky stroke of Leon Smith as his salvation. Broad daylight now revealed the state of everything, and rebel strategy succeeded rebel ambuscades. White flags were run up on the Harriet Lane, and Smith dispatched two officers to Renshaw's stranded flag-ship, demanding a surrender of the fleet, and giving three hours' time to treat upon the proposition. The boat conveying this insulting message visited our other gun-boats likewise ; and an interchange of visits, under flags of truce, consumed an hour or two ; while half the time a fire of sharp-shooters was kept up on the barricaded wharf, which Burrell valiantly defended till he saw himself abandoned by the fleet, when he displayed a white flag also, and gave up resistance.

So the battle of Galveston was tricked away—" won half by blunder, half by treachery;" while that fool or knave, flag-officer Renshaw, fired not a single long-range gun, allowed not one of his eager men to volunteer on board another ship, and ended by capitulation as disgraceful as it was entirely needless. The Clifton and Owasco, at a word from Renshaw's lips, might have cut out the Harriet Lane, with Smith and all his horse-marines. Instead of being permitted to do this, our gun-boats, with their gallant crews, who muttered curses neither few nor choice, were ordered from the port, and, as a noble tar expressed it, in my hearing, " sneaked away with white rags flying." But the retributive hand of justice reached the wretched Renshaw ere his shame was fully consummated. He had given his men free access to the liquor-room, and then set fire to the Westfield, intending to escape in a boat which lay alongside, with Lieutenant Zimmerman and several sailors, ready to cast off. Whether the boat delayed till it could hail the

Clifton as she passed, or whether it was kept to take the recreant commodore ashore, can never be known. But as our other vessels, in retreating, steamed just abreast of their late flag-ship, she blew up, and Renshaw perished with her. He was not permitted to survive the sequel of his cowardice or treason.

Thus we lost Galveston—thus we lost noble Wainwright and the brave young Lea, whose rebel father was a major on Magruder's staff that day, and came on board the Harriet Lane in time to kiss his dying son. Thus Burrell and his officers were consigned to nineteen months' captivity in dungeons and corrals. And, above all, thus the entire Texan coast was lost, the rebel cause inspired and strengthened, and a rebel army organized at once from crowds of volunteers. Thus old Tom Green, Sibley, Pyron, Scurry, Majors, Leon Smith, Magruder, Baylor, and a dozen other leaders, were enabled to inflate the Texan mind with overweening pride of state and personal superiority. The gate of the Confederacy was thus left open, as it had been during the war, for food and clothing, arms and men, to pour from Mexican borders, over Texan highways, and through Louisiana rivers, to the Mississippi banks, and thence upon our loyal frontiers. Weak and disastrous as our subsequent campaigns against the Texans have turned out to be, their miserable results may be traced back to that unhappy New Year's day of 1863, when, in the language of a gun-boat officer, took place "the most disgraceful and cowardly action upon record."

CHAPTER XXV.

SABINE PASS.

Our quarters at Camp Groce were upon the railroad line, removed about two hundred yards from the road. The "camp" consisted of four stacks of barracks looking from three sides into a rhomboidal area. Beyond these buildings, a tract of wild country, wood, swamp, and prairie, stretched for miles around. The barracks were built upon grounds a little higher than the railroad grade, and, behind the particular stack of sheds appropriated to prisoners, a slope, covered with shrubbery and stunted trees, conducted to the timber-belt which formed a boundary for our rear. Another line of barracks running nearly parallel to ours, at a distance of one hundred yards or more, was occupied by the guard, a company of sixty or eighty militiamen, under command of a fat officer known as Captain Buster. Two deep wells supplied the post with water, which the prisoners brought for their own use from one of them, over a space of from six to ten rods, according to the locality of their quarters in the barracks.

One end, comprising less than a third of the barracks, was apportioned to the officers, and the remaining sheds, divided by three partitions, to enlisted men of army and navy. A large number of the sailors were men captured at Sabine Pass, on the 21st of January, who had, since then, shared the fortunes of their commander, Captain Dillingham, and the Federal officers previously taken at Galveston.

Captain John Dillingham, in command of the sloop-of-war "Morning Light," had been ordered to Sabine Pass in November, 1862. He had then with him two schooners, the Rachel Seaman and Velocity, and an old steam-scow called the Dan. The latter, being unserviceable, was soon after sunk and abandoned. While cruising at the Sabine mouth, Capt. Dillingham received several parties of refugees, whom he subsequently sent to New Orleans on board the gun-boat Owasco; by which vessel he first obtained news of the re-capture of Galveston by the rebels. About this time, he gained intelligence through Union men on shore, that an expedition was in preparation, with the design of seizing his own ship, the "Morning Light." On learning this, he at once dispatched the Velocity to Commodore Bell, his flag-officer, informing him of the fact, and asking for the assistance of a gun-boat. To this statement, a reply came from Com. Bell, directing the maintenance of a strict blockade at the Pass, and ordering the "Rachel Seaman" to Pensacola, for repairs. Complying with these instructions, Captain Dillingham remained at his post near the Sabine channels.

In the meantime, the rebels under Magruder, flushed with the success of their attack on our vessels at Galveston, were making new dispositions for another exploit. Major Watkins, Assistant Adjutant General, was assigned to the command of "all the land and naval forces operating on the Sabine River," and proceeded to improvise materials for an expedition. Two river-boats, the Ben and the Bell, were converted into gun-boats, by providing two 12-pounders, with some grape shot, for the former, and an 8-inch Columbiad, bored as a 6-inch rifled piece, for the latter. Infantry, with rifles and shot-guns, were supplied to each of these terrific war-vessels, and, thus equipped and manned, and panoplied with cotton-bales, they steamed through Sabine Lake, and down toward the Pass, where Captain Dillingham lay quiescent, with his ship of one thousand tons, on a sea as calm and glassy as the breezeless air might slumber on.

On the 20th of January, our Yankee captain descried his cotton-clad adversaries coming down the Lake, and not feeling inclined to await them, got under weigh and dropped out with the current. At daylight on the following morning, he found himself pursued. The Texan argonauts, assured by their easy victory at Galveston, that Federal fleets were not "invincible armadas," bore down upon our "Morning Light" with a directness that manifestly meant mischief. Captain Dillingham bewailed the calm. His ship could be manœuvred only sluggishly, at best, while the steam-engines of the rebels enabled them to choose positions. The enemy opened with his rifled gun when about two miles and a half distant from our ship, which returned the fire with a broadside.

The battle now began, and continued during an hour and a half, the rebel steamers gradually nearing our vessels. A rifled howitzer on the ship's poop deck exploded at the first discharge. The rebel craft, presenting their cotton-armored bows to Yankee missiles, offered but a narrow target, whilst their pieces, though handled awkwardly enough, were enabled to get a more effectual range as they approached. Our metal, though heavier, failed to keep them at a distance; and at length, arrived within one thousand yards, they poured a hail of musketry upon the decks of ship and schooner, which speedily cleared them of defenders. According to rebel accounts, the engagement was "concluded out of sight of land in the Gulf, and about twenty-eight miles southwest from Sabine Bar." The steamers ranged upon both sides to board our frigate; and, thinking to destroy one, at least, Captain

Dillingham veered ship, and discharged a broadside, at musket-range, with no more execution than if it had struck the iron ribs of a monitor. The other rebel boat then rounded, and began a murderous fire; when, deeming further resistance useless, Captain Dillingham ceased fighting, and surrendered.

It was a gallant prize for the rebel cotton-boats; though they were obliged subsequently to abandon and burn the ship, from inability to get her over the bar. The Morning Light had been formerly a clipper in the merchant service. She mounted, when captured, eight long thirty-twos, and a rifled Butler gun, and her consort, the schooner Velocity, carried two brass 12-pound howitzers, with boat and land carriages. About 150 stand of small arms, and 109 prisoners, were taken with the vessels. Such was the battle of Sabine Pass, in which Captain Dillingham lost ship and liberty. How much of his disaster is due to the neglect which left a wooden ship to be surprised, during a calm, by cotton-clad steam-boats, must remain, with other secrets, in possession of Commodore Bell and the Navy Department. The exploit, however, raised Texan pride and ambition to fever-heat, and the Confederate President at Richmond addressed a letter of laudation to General Magruder for his "noble enterprises" against the Yankees; whereat the classic Magruder made proclamation to the "army of Sabine," asserting his belief that it was destined "to astonish still more their enemies and the world, by such evidences of skill and audacity, as shall make Texan a better word than Spartan."

The "Morning Light" officers and men, were speedily transferred from the scene of their capture to a prison, at Houston, where our Federals, taken at Galveston, were still lingering. Eleven wounded, two killed, and twenty slightly hurt, comprised the casualties of this Sabine fight, on this ourside; while the rebels boasted that they lost not a single man.

At Houston, the Galveston prisoners had ·not been rigorously treated. Our officers enjoyed parole and liberty to walk the streets. The Federal loss in battle at Galveston comprised seventeen killed and wounded of the infantry, and sixteen of our naval force. The earlier days of captivity were marked by sundry courtesies from citizens, and our Yankee officers "fared sumptuously" on roast-pig, turkey, and occasional invitations to outside dinners. In a short time, however, the lines were drawn more tightly, and a consolatary leader, in the Houston daily journal, suggested the amiable experiment of hanging Yankee prisoners.

Houston, at that happy epoch, was a jubilant city. Magruder had made a triumphal entry, and been honored with a public reception ; on which extraordinary occasion a sword was presented to the hero, and a procession moved, consisting of about twenty-five horse-marines, on ponies, and seventy-five rangers, carrying shot-guns in every position. Pending this ceremony, our Federals were ordered into close confinement, which was soon shared by their newly-captured comrades from Sabine Pass. About this time, they received a definite account of the blowing up of the Westfield and asserted death of Commodore Renshaw. Rumors likewise reached them that our Federal troops in Arkansas had captured several thousand Texans at Arkansas Post, and that our army had suffered defeat at Murfreesboro, with a loss of 10,000 captured and a like number killed and wounded. About the close of January, Sailing-Master W. F. Monroe, of the "Harriet Lane," who had been shot in the face, after surrender, at Galveston, died, from lack of proper care and treatment. He was buried with military honors; eight officers being permitted to attend the funeral, and a rebel escort of sixteen firing a volley over his grave.

At Houston, our officers were visited by a noted rebel, Captain Chubb, of Galveston, who was recognized by a Massachusetts captain as a man who broke jail at East Cambridge, in 1837. About this time, the Federals were notified of Jeff. Davis's proclamation against Butler's officers, and it was intimated that several gentlemen would probably be handed over to the civil power for trial and punishment. But, though these and other unrefreshing scraps of news were doled out to them, our officers enjoyed occasional gulps of air and smacks of liberty (under guard) in tours of exercise and ball-sport, which were vouchsafed them.

Most of the Forty-Second Massachusetts regiment's rank and file received parole, and were forwarded soon to Baton Rouge Their officers, however, with many sailors, remained in prison at Houston, till the last of April. During their sojourn, General Houston visited the city, and achieved a speech to the assembled populace; and an Indian delegation from the Plains, all plumed and war-painted, held powows in the public square. At last a long-expected order came to march our Yankees to the Penitentiary at Huntsville; and, after being relieved of their watches, money, and such valuables, they were transferred on the Navasota Railroad, to their new and narrow State Prison quarters.

Our Federal officers protested; dispatching Dr. Cummings, of the "Forty-Second," (who, being a surgeon, enjoyed parole,) to General Scurry, praying redress. Meantime, for a day or two, they learned to relish cold corn-bread and water. But the Penitentiary Superintendent was an old Sam Houston man, and, moreover, a gentleman. He ordered hot meals to be prepared for our officers in his own house, gave them the privilege of exercise in the yard from eight o'clock A. M., to noon, and from one to five P. M.; and otherwise sought to lighten their annoyances.

In this Penitentiary 168 convicts were confined at labor. The first Sabbath saw our prisoners marched to chapel at eight o'clock, A. M., to attend service, with these convicts. On week-days the latter were called to work at five o'clock A. M., and relieved at six, in the evening.

The cells of this State-prison were not inviting dormitories, being overrun with cockroaches, and overbrooded by musquitos Their dimensions comprised eight feet by five. The yard in which our prisoners were allowed to pass the day, was two hundred feet square.

Various local entertainments assisted the time to pass. On one day, a convict would be placed in the stocks; another morning ushered in some negro, accused of attempting to kill his owner, while the latter was flogging him. Once, General Houston came—(he resided near the Penitentiary)—and talked "secesh" to our officers.

. But Col. Caruthers, the Superintendent, did not keep our Federals in convict quarters very long. He fitted up a large upper room, eighteen by twenty-five feet in floor area, with cots and mattresses, and gave our officers possession of it.

About the close of May, after encountering centipedes in their quarters, hearing news of General Hooker's defeat, with a loss of 30,000 Federals, and receiving a parting visit from General Houston, who was about going, for his health, to Sour Lake; a message arrived from Governor Lubbock, the Texan executive, expressing fears that the presence of our Yankees at Huntsville might attract a Federal expedition againt that important place. The brave Governor said the Yankees must be removed. The manufacture of 5,000 yards of cotton-cloth *per diem*, with sundry other items of Texan fabrication by Penitentiary machinery, must not be jeopardized through Yankee Jonahs. So, presently it transpired toward the end of June, that our prisoners were led out of Huntsville prison, and thence deported to Camp Groce, on the Navasota Railroad. More rumors, through rebel sources, accompanied their march; that Grant's army had been wofully routed in front of Vicksburg; that Banks had been driven from Port Hudson, with a loss of 7,000 men and three gun-boats; and that "exchange of prisoners" was totally stopped for the future.

CHAPTER XXVI.

CAMP GROCE.

SHORTLY after my arrival in Texas, I learned of the death of General Houston. He had passed from the scene of his triumphs and trials—his labors and strifes. It is yet a mooted point whether the old hero ever committed himself fully to the rebel cause. Certain it is, the ultra Secessionists never trusted him, while men of Union proclivities stoutly maintained that "Sam was only 'playing possum,' till a change come." In truth, Houston was a diplomatist, and his strategy had been learned in the lodges of red men. He was an "Indian fighter" in politics, and his personal nature had many aboriginal traits. I can understand very well that he might have appeared to favor the dominant feeling in Texas, with a latent design of recovering ground for a dormant Union sentiment. He held out nobly against the first billows of disloyalty, and it was not till the increasing tide had swept the gubenatorial chair from under him, and he saw himself about to be submerged and drowned by the fierce waters of rebellion, that we find "Old San Jacinto" apparently bowing before the storm, and content to abide its devastations. It was full time for Houston to compromise; for no man had more bitter enemies than he; and one more crime, though it involved the life of him who had been the saviour of their state, would have been a trifle to the traitors who usurped authority in Texas. Houston wisely stood aside. He had been wiser, perhaps, had he remained wholly reticent upon the question at issue; but it is difficult to comprehend his entire position. His household and many old friends were divided against him. He saw himself overthrown by triumphant rivals, and beset constantly by their secret plots. Already, too, it seemed that Southern Independence was *un fait accompli*. Reconstruction of the Union appeared impossible. What was the old Indian fighter to do? He must either become a traitor to the Federal Union, or permit himself to be deemed one. There are many stanch Union-men in Texas who maintain that "Old Sam" only feigned disloyalty, and I would rather believe their impressions to be correct than to denounce Houston as a sympathizer with Secession.

Doubtless, as identified with Texan history, Houston shared largely in State pride. Perhaps he might have halted between loyalty and treason, and, accepting Texan independence as his compromise, cast off, at once, from North and South. The "Lone Flag" would have been his stand-point, yet, who knows but that, behind it, he might have still kept folded the "old flag" of our nation, to be run up to the staff-head whenever a breeze should blow favorably.

Houston's old foes were active and wily, even after his retirement from public life. Two of these, whose names I do not now recall, prepared a scheme which they thought might entrap the old chief. It was when one of the first rebel regiments had been raised, and a stand of colors was to be presented to it. The two plotters procured an invitation to be sent to General Houston, to make "a speech to the soldiers." They anticipated a refusal, and hoped to make this a pretext for denouncing Sam as a "Union sympathizer." But to their astonishment, the invitation was promptly accepted. Houston promised to be present at the review.

The day of color-presentation arrived, and General Houston stood in front of the rebel regiment. The boys cheered him lustily, and everybody waited breathlessly to hear what he should say. The hero of San Jacinto straightened his tall form, and began:

"Boys!" he cried, in his trumpet-tones, " EYES RIGHT!"

The command, uttered with soldierly distinctness, was promptly obeyed. Every eye was obliqued to the right.

"Boys!" shouted the General, with a voice like Stentor, "Do you see anything of ——— ——— in your ranks?" He named one of the two men who had plotted to get him invited to speak.

A response of "No!" came from several soldiers in the line.

"Very well," said Houston—"Now, if you please— EYES LEFT!"

The soldiers shifted their regards to the opposite direction, and Houston thundered:

"Boys! do you see anything of ——— ——— in your ranks?" reciting the name of the other enemy who had sought to entrap him.

"No! No!" answered the "boys," who began to guess the meaning of Houston's orders.

"No!" echoed the ex-Governor. "And you never will see either of those fellows there!"

This sally of "Old Jacinto" against men who were known to be ancient opponents of his, and who, withal, were not personally over-popular, was received with shouts of laughter. When the merriment had subsided somewhat, the General's voice was heard again, in his tone of military command:

"Boys!" he shouted, "Do you see anything of YOUNG SAM HOUSTON in your ranks?"

"Yes! yes! yes! Young Sam's here!" were the rapid

responses which ran along the regimental line ; for the soldiers all knew that Houston's son had enrolled himself a few days previously.

"There I leave him with you!" said "Old San Jacinto," turning away from the soldiers, amid cheers and shouts which made the woods ring, and showed what a hold Sam Houston still maintained upon the people. The malignant traitors who would have entrapped him, did not venture to show themselves on the field that day.

General Houston, though fallen from power, preserved a great deal of Roman dignity in his obscurity.   On one occasion, while traveling through some portion of the State, a military official of the Confederacy demanded his pass-port.   "Pass-port!" echoed Houston, drawing himself up, and fixing his eagle eye upon the man—"my pass-port, sir, is SAN JACINTO!"   He was not challenged again.

But Houston has passed away.   His last conversations regarding our troubles were held with Federal prisoners, at Colonel Caruthers' quarters, in the Penitentiary of Huntsville.   Many of these, whom I met at Camp Groce, claim still that "Old Sam" died a Union man.

Col. Burrell and Captain Sherive arrived at our barracks a few days after I had become initiated and joined the "Forty-Second Mess."   A few extracts from my Diary, at this time, will show the routine of our prison-life.

"SUNDAY, August 2d, 1863.   Hot and dry.   Accompanied Lieut. Hayes to the woods, about a quarter-mile from barracks, where we bathed in a sluggish "brook."— Held religious exercises in barracks.   Col. Nott read the Episcopal service, and I assisted.—Another poor fellow, one of the 42d Massachusetts enlisted men, was buried to-day; burial service of R. C. Church, read by Lieut. Hayes.

"MONDAY, Aug. 3. Join 42d mess.—Corn coffee at 7 o'clock A. M. Today purchased a hammock, for $15 00, Confederate currency.—Slight attack of the prevailing summer complaint .. Assisted in digging new sink for officers.

"TUESDAY, Aug. 4. Suffering in head and bowels. Doctor attributes symptoms to change of water.

"WEDNESDAY, Aug. 5. Today, we get rumors, from Houston, that a new cartel is to be soon opened. "Exchange stock" rises in consequence. My sickness continues.

"THURSDAY, Aug. 6. Rainy. A dismal day.

"FRIDAY, Aug. 7. Still rainy. Showers heavy, penetrating our roofing, drenching our bunks and bedding. Col. Burrell and Capt. Sherive, of the 42d Mass. Reg. arrive from Huntsville. Col. B. is a tall, middle-aged, wiry-looking soldier.

"SATURDAY, Aug. 8. Weather clear again. Colonel Terry left camp, with the balance of his regiment; many having deserted. Col. Terry is the Confederate officer who brought our officers to Camp Groce from Huntsville.

"SUNDAY, Aug. 9. Religious services today. Preached a sermon to the officers, which appears to be well received. We shall have services regularly every Sabbath now. At request of officers, I have promised to conduct them.

"MONDAY, Aug. 10. Report that all exchange is stopped. We are annoyed by myriads of flies."

Such is a sample of the monotonous life we were now leading, varied only by the fluctuations of hope and despondency attendant on occasional rumors, regarding "exchange." Incidents there were of domestic interest, also, but not such as served to content us with our situation. During the month of August, fifteen officers, out of the thirty-five who composed our number, were prostrated by sickness at the same time ; and among these were our two surgeons, Dr. Cummings, of Col. Burrell's regiment, and Dr. Sherfy, of the "Morning Light." About the middle of this month, three sailors escaped from camp, in company, it was said, of some "Mexican" militia-men, who deserted. Lieut. Bartlett, of the Massachusetts officers, died at one o'clock A. M. of the 22d of August, and we buried him at 5 o'clock P. M., the same day; the burial service being read by Col. Burrell. Lieut. Bartlett was much esteemed by his brothers of the regiment. His disease was Typhus flux, which had become fatally prevalent among prisoners.

Our treatment by the rebels in charge of this camp was not, at this time, irksome, beyond the strict guard maintained. We were permitted to visit the neighboring woods, to procure fuel and brush for our verandahs, and for bathing purposes. Negroes and hucksters were allowed to bring us extra provisions, and commissions were executed for us at Houston and other places, whereby we procured Java coffee at $10 the pound, in Confederate currency, soda (for our bread) at $5.00, and tea at $20.00 the pound, molasses at $5.00 the gallon, and vinegar at fifty cents. Our corn-meal rations were also occasionally changed for flour issues, and we could buy sweet potatoes, eggs, butter, milk, and poultry, at comparatively reasonable prices, in Confederate money.

Thus the summer-months wore on. In September, we received "rebel news" that Meade's army, 20,000 strong, had been captured entire. We had already "chewed the quid" of such sweet morsels as the "capture of Washington," the "capture of Philadelphia," and the "Confederates marching on New York;" so we quietly digested our "latest Southern victories," with our customary diet of corn-bread. In the first weeks of September, however, the frequent passage of rebel troops, with munitions and artillery, on the railroad in sight from our barracks, betokened military activity in this quarter ; and we soon after were gratified with reports regarding the appearance of a Federal expedition off the coast at Sabine Pass. Six gun-boats and twenty-six transports, filled with "Yankees," were said to be near the bar, and an invasion of Texas was considered imminent.

It is not to be supposed that we remained emotionless waiters on the "impending conflict." But no one who has not known captivity can realize the absorbing interest with which, for two days and nights, we weighed every item of report, every scrap of rumor, that reached us, by the railroad, or through hints of friendly guards. On the third day, however, arrived news which did not comfort us much. Our expedition had been repulsed, our gun-boats captured, our Federal soldiers and sailors made prisoners by the rebels.

We had been attending the funeral of a brother officer, Dr. Cummings, and were returning to our quarters, when these ill-omened rumors took shape and substance in a telegraph message received by the rebel post-commandant, notifying him to get ready for the reception of two hundred prisoners. The details of our new Federal disaster were communicated speedily enough, thereafter, by its victims, who became subsequently our partners through many weary months of exile. To those details I must devote a chapter.

CHAPTER XXVII.

SABINE PASS AGAIN.

THE year 1863, though marked by many brilliant successes, was not a year of fortune for our Union. We boasted the capture of Vicksburg and Port Hudson, and the victories of Murfreesboro and Gettysburg, but we were forced to acknowledge, on the other hand, our reverses at Chickamauga, at Winchester, in Louisiana, and on the Texan coast, as well as the more vital perils of rebel invasion and sanguinary domestic riots. When the whole story of warlike operation and military councils shall be digested by unprejudiced chroniclers of another generation, then, and not till then, will many hidden things be brought to light and many suppressed chapters of facts become accessible to public scrutiny. In such a truthful *resume* of history the true story of Sabine Pass will not be the least astonishing disclosure.

I have before me the "official reports," as well as letters of "correspondents on the spot," concerning the disastrous finale of that expedition to the Sabine's mouth, which, directed by General Banks, and commanded by Generals Franklin and Weitzel, appeared upon the Texan coast, only to be driven off disgracefully, with the loss of two war-vessels and several hundred men captured by the enemy. From the "reliable correspondence" published in leading New York journals, claiming to give the account of an eye-witness, we obtained some curious and romantic ideas:

1. That, "considering the number of the force engaged, it is doubtful if any affair of the whole war can compare with the battle of Sabine Pass, in obstinacy of fighting, loss of life, and the amount of public interest."

2. That, "to the Union forces it was the opening battle of a most brilliant campaign."

3. That "the enemy's loss has been undoubtedly without precedent in the annals of war."

4 That "the enemy will tremble at a repetition of the attack."

5. That "the loss of the enemy was undoubtedly enormous."

6. That " a combination of those unfortunate accidents which no human foresight can prevent or overcome, turned victory into defeat."

7. That " the result of the entire affair will probably, and with justice, be ascribed to those accidents which so often determine the fate of armies as well as nations."

The foregoing seven propositions furnish a fair sample of the special pleading by which common sense was insulted, and a disgraceful failure, that should have been punished by prompt court-martial, was magnified into a gallant struggle against overwhelming odds. It is the same studied glozing of facts which deceived public opinion, though all the mishaps of Gulf affairs, from the loss of Galveston, on New Year's day, 1863, to the expulsion of our grand army from the Red River, and from all western Louisiana, before New Year's day, 1865. Yet of such mendacious statements, history, or, as General Sherman remarks, "what is called history." will be made up by those who must rely on contemporary authorities for the data where on they build their ponderous folios.

I think that, of all the "interest involved" in the projected capture of Sabine Pass, we poor Union prisoners who were, at that time, confined at Camp Groce, seventy-five miles from the Pass, had our ample share. With anxious hearts we had waited confidently for a different result; since none knew better than we had learned, the defenceless condition of Texas, and the certainty with which an ordinary Union army could, in one month, over-run the sea-board and lower counties, from Houston to Austin and from Sabine River to the Rio Grande. Lo-cated as we were on the railroad line, which brought and carried every rumor from the west and the interior, as well as from the eastern border and the coast, we had not only become apprised of events as they transpired, but we could form correct estimates of the amount of prepa-ration and degree of resistance which a Yankee invasion might expect in Texas. Some of us were in daily contact with guards whose sympathies were neither chary nor doubtful. Good Union men, in rebel homespun, and with Confederate arms in their hands, were daily whispering to us words of cheer; and when, in that first week of September, we had heard of a Federal force of six war steamers and twenty-six transports being off the bar at Sabine, it is no wonder that we had met each other with hopeful faces, and counted the hours which might elapse ere we should look upon our "Old Flag" flying over Camp Groce prison-yard.

Miserable was the reaction of our feelings, when, re-turning one evening from the Masonic burial of Surgeon Cummings, we heard the first report, scarcely credited by even the bitterest rebels, that our fleet and army had been beaten off, and several gun-boats captured at the Pass. I looked in the eyes of a Masonic brother, (honest Union man, though in rebel uniform,) for something which might deny the fearful rumor; but he shook his head, with a glance as troubled as my own. We found our worst fears verified. The American squadron and army, with its brave sea-captains and skillful generals, had retreated from the coast; not exactly   •

"Foiled by a woman's hand before a batter'd wall,"

but quite as shamefully driven off by forty-two Irish militiamen in a mud-fort with six ,pieces of artillery! The details, as I have said, we learned through the recital of prisoners like ourselves, fresh from the scene of their defeat, and burning with indignation against the authors of it.

They had come, those brave gun-boat-men and their gallant officers—those chosen sharp-shooters from the New York 75th and 161st regiments—to be flung ashore, into the enemy's hands, and devoted to long imprisonment, hardship.and privation. Pioneers of the Yankee fleets that were to follow, skirmishers in front of the Yankee army of six thousand men, in twenty-six transports, hugging the Sabine bar, these new prisoners— some four hundred in number—arrived a few days afterwards, to tell us the story of Sabine Pass, not "officially," or in the choice language of "special correspondents," but with plain, rough emphasis, such as men use when they feel that their lives and honor have been trifled with by those who should have cherished both.

In this wise, I gathered details concerning that Federal expedition of invasion. From log-books of naval officer, from yarns of man-of-wars-man, from recital of service-striped sergeant, I became possessed of truer information regarding this, as well as other affairs, than I could have gained out of all the red-tape documents at head-quarters.

Full of expectation, after re-conquest of Brashear City, the stout gun-boat Clifton, flag-ship of Captain Crocker, with her consort, the Sachem, Captain Johnson, steamed

out of the Atchafalaya's mouth, on the morn of September
6th, and, with the gun-boat Arizona and a dozen or more
transports, proceeded to the mouth of the Sabine. Here
they stood off and on, a while, no coast-guard being in
view. Propitious moments these for blockade-runners;
as never a Federal "warder" heaves in sight that day
or night, it seems. Next day flag-officer Crocker, standing on and off amidst the fleet, sends Johnson, with his
Sachem, to the Pass; and on his way the latter skipper
overhauls our missing blockade-steamer Granite City,
quietly returning from a trip off Calcasieu. That day
(the 7th) sees nothing further done; but on the 8th a
council is convened on board the transport Suffolk, whereat Generals Franklin and Weitzel, and their naval *confreres*, captains of the gun-boats, settle on a plan for
capturing the rebel fortress. Friendly shore-scouts have
assured them that no more than five or six hundred rebels
can be mustered in the fort or at Sabine City, and that
all the border force consists of two or three thousand conscripts. So it is decided to attack the place at once.
General Weitzel and flag-captain Crocker go ashore in a
small boat to reconnoitre for a landing-place ; the spot is
selected; the details of disembarkation are agreed upon;
nothing remains but to carry out the programme.

There are two channels debouching from the mouth of
Sabine River—a western one, called the Texan, and an
eastern one, known as the Louisiana channel. They are
separated by a shallow bank of shifting sands, horse-shoe
shaped, within the hollow of which a vessel striking
would be grounded. The channels, as well as the sand-
shallows dividing them, are commanded by the river
banks, so that a battery on the Texan side can sweep the
river to the Louisiana side. The Texan bank is curving,
and behind a rounding point are built the rebel earth-

works with a front of a hundred yards or more. The
Clifton is to follow up this bank, and run the batteries,
so as to bring her guns upon the rebel rear, which is not
fortified. The gun-boat Sachem takes the Louisiana channel, the Arizona following, while our blockáding steamer
Granite City remains below, to cover a landing of the
troops.

Well-planned thus far; and, to insure a prompt disembarkation, the boats belonging to both the Clifton and the
Sachem are borrowed for the use of our soldiers. They
are to be lashed, side by side, between the Granite City
and the beach; so that our troops, marching from their
transports over the gun-boat decks, may cross the bridge
of small boats and step dry-shod upon land.

All preparations made, two companies of our gallant
New York boys (from the 161st), and another detachment
from the veteran 75th New York Infantry, being sent on
board our gun-boats as sharp-shooters, a signal from the
Clifton, "up anchor," sets both upon the onset. Stout
Sachem-captain Johnson stands on his quarter-deck, while
the little war vessel that he has trodden in many a perilous
pass, ploughs up the Louisiana channel—the Arizona
steaming in her wake. At the Sachem's bows her pivot
gun points toward the enemy's forts, however devious her
passage. Her broadside thirty-two's are ready for business, but her Parrott speeds first across the quiet waters.
Meantime the Clifton, separated by sand-shallows, bears
up through the Texas channel, close to its winding bank,
and presently her nine-inch pivot sends a shell mid-air
and drops it plumply upon the rebel earthworks The
fort makes no reply. An ominous silence continues behind those rude defences, and our brace of gun-boats,
dashing head on, gaining length after length, already
threaten to run by the enemy in Farragut's good old

style. The Sachem's bold commander, looking back, beholds the Clifton in the opposite channel, striving to increase her speed. Flag-Captain Crocker is determined to run by those batteries; Sachem-captain Johnson must not fall behind. So his little gun-boat heads westward a bit, while the Arizona lags in her track.

There is a stake at yonder beach point, opposite a curving prominence of the Texan shore—a suspicious water-mark to Yankee eyes. The Sachem's crew discover it first, and the Clifton's lookouts note it as their vessel rounds the land point. The Sachem steams towards it, amid a crashing fire of all the rebel guns, which now have opened in good earnest. Six heavy pieces play at once upon our little steamer. For twenty minutes a shower of shot and shell rains down upon her deck. At last her bows are opposite the stake. A moment's pause is noticed in the rebel fire, and then a ball comes crushing through the gun-boat's boiler. A fierce explosion follows, and the hiss of liberated steam succeeds. White clouds of burning, stifling vapor drive our soldiers from their stations. Shrieks and groans resound from stem to stern. Thirty-four gallant men are killed outright, or scalded well nigh unto death, by that one terrible stroke of fate. Fear-stricken sufferers leap wildly overboard; dismal confusion ensues; the gun-boat swings around, disabled.

Not long are the rebels in discovering how cruelly that last shot told upon one opponent; and, leaving her to drift with her dead and dying, they turn their guns upon the newer foe. At this moment the Clifton, rounding that point which hid the rebel guns, appears resolved to force her passage upward. She advances swiftly, interposing between the rebel batteries and her crippled consort. She receives and returns their direct fire, and then essays a short turn for her gauntlet passage. But the Clifton's fortunes reach, at length, a turn as short as any channel-bend. Striking a sand-bank, she grounds, and lies unmanageable under the rebel batteries. A storm of rebel iron pours down upon her. She cannot bring her broadside into play. Its battery is pointed toward the Louisiana border. Only her bow-gun could be used with effect; till her 32-pounders, being whirled about, their shot plunged through her opposite bulwarks, speeding on the enemy. The fort, at this time, was within three hundred yards of our doomed gun-boat, and a rebel missile soon crashed into her steam-chest. Her rudder-chains were parted. She no longer answered her helm. Escaping steam scalded the sharp-shooters on her hurricane-deck. From this moment the rebels were masters of the channel. Our two gun-boats struck their colors. The enemy boarded them, in sight of our army and its generals. Three hundred gallant soldiers and sailors were suffered to be carried away prisoners, without a shot being fired in an effort to rescue them.

Why were they abandoned? Why were six thousand Federal troops, with arms and ammunition, with everything requisite for a successful assault of earthworks, permitted to remain on ship-board without an attempt to land them, for the dislodgement of our foes?

Why were the Clifton and Sachem deprived of their small boats, with which their sharp-shooters might have effected a landing, even after the gun-boats were placed *hors du combat*?

Why were not the small boats used as a bridge from the Granite City to the beach, whereby our federal troops could have been landed to support the gun-boats?

Why did not the Arizona, largest of these boats, make

fast to the Sachem, and haul her from her perilous position, after the perforation of her boiler?

Why were not our soldiers landed from the transports, and marched, as they might have been, from their point of disembarkation, to the rear of the fort (a mile or two only), and thus thrown into position to compass and assault the earthwork on its undefended land side?

Will it be credited that our attacking gun-boats were captured, their consorts driven off, and the whole expedition turned back, discomfited, by the resistance of forty-two men, working six guns, behind an earthwork?

Yet such is the case. We, who waited so full of anxious hopes, in our gloomy barracks of Camp Groce, know well the panic of rebels, suddenly threatened by invasion, and their wonderful transition from despair to triumph, when the astounding news came—of a victory at Sabine Pass.

I met the Confederate officer who arrived in charge of the Federal prisoners from our gun-boats; an intelligent Marylander, who had known me several years before. He was frank and honest in his admissions.

"Never were men more disappointed in the result than we ourselves," he said to me. "I fully believed that it would be my fate to march a prisoner, with my fellow-rebels, rather than to come to this post in charge of Yankee prisoners."

"You had no expectation of making a successful resistance, then?" I remarked to the lieutenant.

"We had made up our minds that every one of us must be captured, either at the fort or in Sabine City," he replied. "What other hope could we have—a raw company of Irish militia—the Davis Guards—attempting to resist your fleet and army?"

"Did you expect that a landing would be made?"

"We expected that, of course, and had no means of defending ourselves against it. Two hundred soldiers marching up to flank the fort, must have obliged us either to run or surrender. There could have been no alternative but to die in the fort, uselessly fighting."

"What did you think, lieutenant, when you saw our gun-boats apparently disabled and grounded?"

"We thought it was a stratagem, at first. It appeared to us as if your two vessels were put forward, like pawns in a game of chess, to be taken easily."

"Did you expect to get possession of the gun-boats after you discovered their disabled condition?"

"We began to have a little hope of escaping ourselves; but if a landing had been even then made by your troops we should never have ventured to board those gun-boats."

"Could not your armed steamers on the Sabine have aided your defence?"

The lieutenant smiled. "Your batteries," he said, "were stronger than ours, and in the hands of experienced artillerists. We had no reinforcements nearer than Beaumont, and you would have gained Sabine City and all the Louisiana coast for your base. We were lucky on our side, and you were—" My Confederate friend paused, abruptly.

"Well, lieutenant, what do you honestly think of our side?" I inquired.

"Excuse my answering," said the rebel officer, "You are a prisoner-of-war, and I have no wish to say anything unpleasant to you."

This significant response satisfied me, for the moment, concerning the opinion of our enemies regarding the affair at Sabine Pass. I asked only one more question:

"What was your loss, lieutenant? You know ours."

"We lost not a man," answered the rebel.

Having obtained this sum of information relative to that famous expedition of invasion, I parted from my rebel acquaintance, and went back to my quarters, to make a note of the conversation which is here reproduced. Bitter were my reflections, in common with all our despondent prisoners, new and old. Freedom had been almost within our sight; a Union victory had appeared to be an assured event. Texas might have seen the old flag streaming over all her hills and prairies. Instead of this — we could only bite our lips.

CHAPTER XXVIII.

LIFE AND DEATH AT CAMP GROCE.

THE "bad news from Sabine" reached us, as I mentioned, on our return from a Masonic burial of Surgeon
Cummings of the Massachusetts infantry. ` The ceremony
was an impressive one, and had been fraternally partici-
pated in by many Masons belonging to our Confederate
guards. Together, with white aprons, and bearing willow
wands, the men of North and South walked solemnly behind the bier; together they surrounded the grave, and
listened to the beautiful ritual of burial; together, then,
they cast the "ashes to ashes, and dust to dust," and,
dropping sprigs of evergreen upon the dead, as types of
an immortal resurrection, together they uttered the solemn
adjuration—"Amen! So mote it be!" In this Masonic
interchange, war and strife were for a brief space forgotten, and charity lovingly united the hands and hearts
of those who had been created one family by the Sublime Architect of souls.

The preliminaries of the funeral had been arranged at
a meeting of free-masons, called by one of our guards who
held high rank in the fraternity; and the following resolutions were adopted and signed by all.

CAMP GROCE, near Hempstead, Texas,
September 10, 1863.

To the Worshipful Master Wardens and Brethren of
Washington Lodge, Roxbury, Mass., Greeting:

At an informal meeting of the Masonic Brethren at

this place, Bro. A. J. H. Duganne, of Metropolitan Lodge, New York, being chosen chairman; Henry W. Washburn, of Union Lodge, New London, Conn., chosen Secretary; the following resolutions were read and adopted:

Resolved. That we attend in a body, as MASONS, and give our Deceased Brother, Ariel Ivers Cummings, of Washington Lodge, Roxbury, Mass., a Masonic funeral, as nearly as we are able so to do, and that Brother A. J. H. Duganne conduct the ceremonies.

Resolved. That a scroll, containing name, age, etc. be buried with our deceased brother, and that a copy of the same be forwarded to Washington Lodge.

Resolved. That we, as Masons, deeply sympathize with Washington Lodge, and believe its members have lost a most worthy and well-beloved brother; one who had the welfare of the Order at heart, and, to the best of our knowledge, always carried out the principles of Christian Masonry.

Resolved. That we hail the Masonic sympathy which characterizes this occasion of our deceased brother's funeral, at which lodges from the North, South, East and West are most harmoniously represented, as another illustration of the fraternal spirit which is continually adding strength to the foundation and beauty to the arches of our well-beloved Order.

Resolved, That we condole with the widow of our deceased brother, in the bereavement she has sustained, and, through Faith, hope that the Grand Master of all will, with Charity, uphold and protect her, until they meet in realms Above.

A. J. H. DUGANNE, Chairman.

HENRY W. WASHBURN, Secretary.

The first instalment of rebel captures at Sabine City
reached Camp Groce in the bodily shapes of two hundred
and thirty one soldiers and sailors, who were consigned
to a vacant portion of our barrack line. Shortly after
their arrival, our guard, under Captain Buster, were relieved by a company of conscripts, and ordered to Camp
Lubbock, near Houston. We heard no more from the
Federal fleet, and rebellion-stock in Texas grew obviously
higher day by day. About the middle of September, we
began to get acquainted with that peculiar visiter of this
latitude known as a "Norther."

A "Norther" gives little premonition of its coming.
Noon may be fair and cloudless skies may seem to promise a balmy evening, when suddenly a low wind sings
through the woodlands, whistles accross the prairies, and,
then, swelling into strength and fury, lashes the forests
like a flail, and sweeps with a roar toward the coast;
sometimes dry and cold, and freezing the marrow in one's
bones, and sometimes charged with gusty rain that de-
luges the country—swelling the rivers, flooding the
marsh-lands, and making the roads almost impassable.
Woe to the forlorn traveller who is overtaken by a winter
Norther while crossing a wide prairie. Horsemen have
been found in the saddle, chilled to death by this icy
wind; beef cattle and even herds of swine have perished
under the arctic cold of a December norther in Texas.

The routine of camp-life had been wearisome enough,
even if perfect health could have been assured us. But
with the sick and dying constantly in our midst, nightly
watches were rendered necessary, and a mental despondency began to prey upon many who were not physically
ill. Once a week, at least, we were called upon to follow the pine-coffin of some poor captive, and our rough
burial ground in the timber grew apace with graves of

Federals, marked by wooden headboards, on which Lieutenant Eddy, of the "Forty-Second," was accustomed to paint the name and age of the departed. The poor lieutenant was also an invalid, and sometimes obliged to prop himself on a pillow in his bunk, while he traced the sad record of death, in "silver-white" paint, kept carefully for such occasions by our provident and useful Captain Proctor, of the same regiment. I attended at our funerals, and usually read the service, sometimes making a few remarks befitting the solemn moment. The little mounds accumulated fast, and, one day, with some stout tars of the "Morning Light" and "Harriet Lane," and a few privates of the 75th New York regiment, Captain Van Tine and myself contrived to get a rude log fence constructed around our little "God's acre" of prison-dead.

Our Sabbath-day exercises continued; and we solaced ourselves occasionally with singing in our quarters; there being several excellent voices among the "42d" officers. Our militia-guards, who had replaced Captain Buster's company, were not all so friendly as their predecessors. We had occasion to note this fact a few evenings following their advent, when one of them deliberately fired at a sailor-boy, whose offence was, in the excitement of sport, pursuing a runaway ball to the guard-line. Without challenge or caution, the cowardly fellow drew up his gun, and discharged it at our sailor lad; and the bullet, whizzing past the latter, sped toward our barracks in dangerous closeness to the ball-players.

In the first week of October, Dr. Sherfy, our indefatigable surgeon, reported one hundred and twenty prisoners on his sick-list. We had fears, at this time, that our camp-fevers might be developed to a more malignant type, as Yellow Fever was said to be rife at Houston, and we were told that, on previous visits of this epidemic, the neighborhood of Camp Groce had been fatally ravaged. But we were happily spared from such aggravation of our condition. About this time, the citizen-prisoners who remained with us were notified that they would be speedily liberated. One of them, Holliday, had already succeeded in negotiating a "ransom," by paying some hundreds of dollars in specie to a Houston lawyer. Upon the fifth of October, we were abruptly ordered to make room in our quarters for the Federal officers captured at Sabine Pass, who arrived that evening by the railroad. This necessitated a general "doubling up" in our bunking arrangements, but we succeeded in accommodating the new-comers, who, at ten o'clock, P. M., appeared to be snugly bestowed for the night.

But rebel authorities are like their negroes—"mighty uncertain;" a truth which we experienced very soon; for, before midnight, an officer and file of men invaded our slumbers, with orders for all the "Sabine Pass" officers to vacate the premises, and repair to other dormitories. The post-commandant, it seemed, had overlooked an order from Houston, which required him to confine the new prisoners by themselves, and to allow them no intercourse whatever with the old ones.

So our later comrades in misfortune were now suddenly routed from their comfortable quarters, and obliged to tramp, in darkness, to some vacant sheds upon the rising ground that lay between our barracks and the railroad. There they were left, upon a floor of broken boards, to make themselves as contented as possible till daylight. Next morning, they were permitted to receive, through the guards, such rations as we could cook for them; and this arrangement continued until they succeeded, several weeks afterwards, in building chimneys and fireplaces to their dilapidated stack of sheds. Meantime, we heard various reasons assigned for the close confinement of these officers; among others, that they had thrown overboard the small-arms from their gun-boats, and that they had concealed a large amount of Federal money, which had been in custody of the Clifton's paymaster. Doubtless, the suspicion of a secret correspondence between these officers, who had so recently come from Houston, and some Union men lately arrested in that city, was the true cause of the "non-intercourse" orders; for, on a Sabbath morning, about twelve days after the separation, our barracks were abruptly entered by detachments of the guard, and our persons, trunks, and bunks searched rigorously. All papers that appeared suspicious, together with all our money, whether specie, "greenbacks," or Confederate currency, were taken from us, and we were notified that henceforth we should be allowed to purchase " extras," and pay our "washing" or other bills, only through drafts upon our funds, which were to be held in trust by the rebel post-commandant, Colonel Bates.

The "citizens" left camp early in October; it being supposed that they would be sent from Houston, across the state, to Mexico, and thence allowed to find their way to the United States. But they were hardly absent a week before we saw them returned to us; there being no means of overland transportation, and the wife of Stratton being, of course, unable to make a foot-journey. We now lost another of our officers, Lieut. Rumsey, of the 175th New York Volunteers. He had been lingering long, under dysentery and pneumonia, and was wasted to a mere skeleton. Shortly after poor Rumsey's death, we were called upon to lament the sudden loss of another officer of the same regiment, Lieut. Hayes, a favorite with all of us, and to whom I had become personally attached, attracted, by his many amiable traits of character. We had lately formed a small mess together, and I can never forget his attention and kindness to me, during days of indisposition; nor the bright smile with which he was wont to awaken me, at morning, bringing to my bunk a cup of "Lincoln coffee," that he usually prepared before our regular breakfast. He had been complaining of illness two or three days, but our surgeon did not suppose the least danger to be apprehended; deeming, as others did, that the young officer was only worn out with attendance upon others; for Lieut Hayes had been unremitting in his care of sick comrades at all times. But the inexorable messenger, who had summoned so many of our number, came likewise to my little mess, and divided its mates. Lieut. Hayes lay down, at night in my hammock, which he preferred to his cot-bed, and, in the morning, when Lieut. Stone went to awaken him, the heart of our brother was stilled forever. I know not if he had felt presentiments of death; but a few days previously he had related to me a dream, which I recalled to memory while following his remains to their last resting-place.

"I thought I was at home," he said, "and that a crowd of visitors were calling on me. They came by carriages-full, and stepped out on the walk before the house as naturally as if it were reality; and they were all living people; but their faces wore the faces of dead friends and relatives. Then I thought I fell asleep, and that my eyes opened, it seemed, upon another world, where there were thousands of angels floating in the air; and I saw the Virgin Mary, with a halo round her head, and her face and garments shining brighter than sunlight. She seemed to look smilingly down, as if calling me."

Lieut. Hayes was a devout Roman Catholic, and his faith, doubtless, gave color to his visions. But as I recalled his blameless character, his amiable demeanor, and the fine blending of seriousness and humor which made his society pleasant, I could not but hope that his dream would merge into reality, and that the Queen of Heaven might be indeed smiling upon him at that hour, far up beyond all clouds which overhung our dreary prison-house.

The low Texan forests were bending and sighing under the first blast of a "Norther," as we walked, in sad procession, two by two, to bury the remains of our genial comrade—the honorable, brave, and dutiful soldier; whose sudden death had fallen upon each of us like a personal bereavement.

Two by two, we followed the mule-cart, which contained a coffin of rough yellow-pine. The wagon-wheels jerked heavily over stumps and hillocks on the road that led through recently-cleared land to that small elevation, where we were accumulating graves, ranged side by side; the tablets of our captivity. The negro driver sat at one end of the coffin; we walked close behind it, and our ever-present guards, with loaded muskets, marched on either side. Climbing to the grave, that had been digged by the sailors of our company; standing at the edges, upon red clumps of earth; looking into the hollow, as the coffin was lowered down; listening to the rattle of the clods upon the pine boards; so proceeded the burial of our friend and comrade. A brother-officer of the dead, Lieut. Dunn, read the burial service, and we turned back, guarded by scowling rebels, in the face of winds that now came howling from the prairies. How we prayed, in our hearts, for a "NORTHER" that might sweep this rebel country like a tornado!

CHAPTER XXIX.

FALLING LEAVES.

THE rebel "powers that be" are becoming vigilant.
Post-Commandant Bates rides up and down on inspection
tours. Lieut. Col. Barnes visits our quarters periodi-
cally. Negroes are hauling posts, and digging a trench
around our camp-ground, for a future "stockade." Meanwhile the leaves are falling. The tree-limbs are swept
by raging "northers," that now blow more frequently,
laden with rain and hail. We look forward to a dreary
hibernation. We give up hopes of "exchange," and in-
voke patience to be our comforter. There is little oc-
curring to break the monotony of our captivity. We get
rebel journals from Houston, and hear the gossip of
guards, and note the passage of trains daily, sometimes
freighted with rebel troops and artillery. So the days
creep by. Occasionally we are visited by people from
Hempstead, curious to have a look at "the Yankees."
Among these come a few loyal souls, to sympathize with
us, as friends, and whisper low words of encouragement.
A couple of kind ladies have brought little comforts for
the sick, and books for the well. To one of these ladies,
Mrs. E——, of Hempstead, I loaned a volume of my
poems which I had preserved in my trunk. It contained
a silken marker, wrought with the "old flag." The lady
was so forgetful of rebel surroundings, as to open my unfortunate volume in the cars. A Confederate officer, behind her, peeped gallantly over her shoulder, and read,

perhaps, some sentiments not wholly in accordance with Southern predilections. He deemed it his duty to "report" the lady to General Magruder; and, the same night, many wakeful ones of our camp were startled by the apparition of a locomotive crashing past at midnight. Next day this unusual incident became a subject of much speculation. We conjectured, that some new conspiracy might have been discovered at Houston, or. that conscripts had risen in some rebel camp. Long afterwards, I learned the truth; that a special train had been dispatched from Houston to Hempstead, and that luckless Mrs. E——, arrested by a provost-marshal's order, had been taken from her bed, at midnight, and carried off for examination by Gen. Magruder; her husband being permitted, as a favor, to accompany her. Gen. Magruder was speedily satisfied, however, either that my volume of poems was no infernal machine, to blow up the Confederacy, or that the lady who borrowed it was not an incendiary; for he ordered Mrs. E—— to be restored to her home, and my book, containing the "Union marker," to be returned to its "Yankee" author.

But the winter days have come. Loud howls the "norther" over our barrack-roofs. There is no fuel in camp. Who will volunteer as "hewers of wood" to-day? cheerily sings the voice of Captain Dillingham, whilom of good ship "Morning Light," and now chief skipper of our prison hulks. Anon, the lumbering ox-team, dragging a wagon, and urged on by goading whip of a negro-driver, creeps across our prison lines, and we fall in, guarded by a rebel "detail," to our work of "log-rolling." Down past. the well, where captive tars and land-lubbers are waiting turns to draw their bucket-fuls of water for their breakfast meal; shivering wights, snuffing the keen north wind that whistles through their ragged garments; slapping their half-numbed hands together, and dancing on the cold turf, to impart some circulation to the chilled blood in their naked feet. A white frost clings to the grass and rimes the bushes with its glittering lace. The sun has not yet climbed those greyish clouds that race athwart the orient, and "it is a nipping and an eager air" which whips them seaward.

Down by the oaks and pecan-trees; under moss-laden cypresses, and through the scrubby mulberry and tea bushes; skirting that sombre hillock where we bury our dead, and following the cattle-path until we penetrate "the timber." Our ox-cart crushes through tangled vines and over rotten stumps, wheels round a fallen cedar, and is headed to the north again; the rebel guards squat here and there, with rifles on their knees; while we, with ringing axes, make short work of Texan timbergrowth. Down surge the youthful oaks; in scattered fragments fly the limbs and trunks of sturdy hickory; we emulate the woodmen of Virgilian pastorals, whose toils are scanned in schoolboy couplets:

"Trees on trees o'erthrown,
Fall crackling round us, and the forests groan."

Then "comes the tug;" to "pack" our heavy spoils; huge logs uplifted over wheels, and piled upon the wain; such loads as 'once we might have deemed Titanic burthens, now tossed lightly on the towering fuel-heap. Thereafter we march prisonward, to barracks, with our appetites well sharpened for the tough beef and "corndodgers."

In-doors the bunks are cold and damp. This keen wind searches through their gaping crevices. Our cook-house, with its stoves, allures a knot of icy-blooded invalids to cower beneath incumbent pots and pans of grumbling stewards. The barracks boast no stoves, but we have

digged two fire-places below our flooring line, at either
wing, and pierced some apertures in the wooden roof, to
serve as smoke-holes. So, like Hottentots in kraals, or
Esquimaux in snow-huts, we hibernate beneath continual
clouds of pungent vapor, eye-blinding and lung-choking.

Presently the whistle of the north-wind rises to a howl
around the barracks. Thick hurricanes, driving hills of
dust and banks of leaves before them, scud across the
railway cuts. Ere long, chill drops of heavy rain plash
down upon our roofs. The Dry Norther has passed, and
the Wet Norther comes roaring in his wake, with the
"noise of many waters." Plash, splash, dash! The yellow sands become wide pools of muddy rain. The blast
careers through bending tree-tops, wrenching knotty
boughs away, and threshing off their wet leaves as the
chaff is flailed from corn.

"All hands to caulk ship!" cries a watchful man-of-
war's-man, who, half cook, half caterer, chalks his number
in our officers, quarters. Timely call, O ancient mariner!
A score of leaks make known their whereabouts by dismal percolations, drenching berths and blankets. All the
roof, of shrunken pine boards, soon begins to ooze with
miry moisture. Rivulets of trickling rain wind down
from ridge poles. Streams descend into the bunks and
through their soaking contents. Lakes are mapped upon
the muddy floor. Meantime, *les miserables* patch up neglected holes, dam off incursive water-courses, mop up
embryo ponds, and shelter clothes and blankets with
what canopies they can command.

Rain, rain! through all the hours! Our hearth-fires
smoulder under incubi of smoke. Our greasy banquet-
boards of pine, that occupy the space between opposing
rows of bunks, are dripped upon incessantly. We snatch
our morsels out of dishes sprinkled on from juicy rafters.

Corn-dodgers are dough, our beef half boiled, our soup *soup-maigre*. So we shiver through the daylight, and at night crawl into damp repose, night-mared by water-sprites—all grim-haired Kuhleborns and no sparkling Undines.

Sorry nights, these; dim, dismal, dolorous nights, for wretched ones on beds of pain and sickness. I hear the poor consumptive's dying cough; I listen to the broken words of fevered sufferers; I catch the feeble sighs of manhood lapsing into infant weakliness.

How wearisome this night-watch with the sick, and yet how rife with healthful thought to one who ponders! My single candle scarcely penetrates the shadows which encompass me. The barracks are profoundly still. All sleep, except the dying.

A faint voice calls for water, and I wet the lips and forehead of a youth, who has confronted danger in a dozen battle-fields, and risen from the ranks to wear a captain's sword. I doubt if flaming batteries in his path have ever appalled him; yet he lies here now as tremulous and fearful as a girl. I scan my watch, and steal from cot to cot, with medicine to be administered at the midnight hour. I lift a comrade from his bed, as you would lift a baby. Three months ago this man might have wrestled with the strongest of us. Three days hence, we shall walk behind him, to the prison-graves.

I step out of our barrack door. The rain has ceased, but there is yet no starlight. The wind has lulled. The air is raw and clammy. A rebel sentry tramps on the dead-line.

CHAPTER XXX.

EXODUS.

THE monotone of prison-existence was broken by a few
outside rumors' during the month of November.   We
heard of Federal operations threatening the Texan coast;
of Union plots detected at Houston, and the consequent
arrest of sundry implicated citizens ; among others of
Dr. Peebles, and Judge Baldwin, whose loyalty to the
"Old Flag" was well known to many of our prisoners,
with whom they had conversed at Houston.   We learned,
also, that some of our escaped comrades had arrived safely
within Federal lines ; and we received occasional encouragement regarding a new cartel being agreed upon.
About this period, two privates of an Illinois regiment,
the brothers Smith, were brought to Camp Groce in irons,
charged with an aggravated attempt to escape ; the aggravation consisting in an appropriation of horses and saddles, wherewith the young adventurers made good progress from Houston to San Antone, before they were arrested.   Horse-stealing is a capital offence against the
Texan code of morals, which very seldom takes cognizance
of murder by pistol or bowie-knife; so, it was decided
that our two Smiths should be handed over to the civil
authorities for trial, on the horse-theft charge ; with a sanguine expectation, on the part of bitter rebels, that they
must both be convicted and hanged.   The two boys were
kept a few days under close guard at Camp Groce, and
then dispatched to Houston, to stand their trial.   We

felt, of course, great sympathy for them, as well as indignation at the rebel commanders who had transferred their examination to a civil court, in which their lives were sure to be jeopardized by a prejudiced jury; but we were powerless to interpose, and could only witness with sorrow the departure of our poor comrades, under a strong guard, and still manacled, for embarkation on the cars.

The stockade about our camp was now rapidly progressing; and we had made up our minds to close incarceration during the winter, when, on the 16th of November, after most of us had retired to our bunks for the night, Colonel Burrell came to our barracks from his own quarters, in a separate shed with Dr. Sherfy, and electrified all hearers by a brief and eloquent address: " Gentlemen !". (cried this bringer of "glad tidings,") " I have good news for you! We are all to be paroled and sent to our homes as soon as the papers can be made out!" It may easily be conceived that this announcement caused a general turning-out of slumbering prisoners. In a few moments the line of barracks was "all alive" with excitement. Officers embraced each other, exchanging mutual hopes and gratulations; Colonel Burrell traversed the men's quarters, repeating his little "speech" to hilarious audiences; cheers and shouts made every shed-roof ring; bonfires were lit, and the sailors sung patriotic songs till long after midnight. Very little slumber visited Camp Groce that joyous night. But on the next morning our happiness was somewhat tempered by supplementary advices. We were assured that the paroling officer might be expected immediately, but that we should be obliged to march several hundred miles to Shreveport, in Upper Louisiana, and there descend the Red River. No transportation could be provided for baggage. Hence, we

should be able to-carry only the garments that we might
wear, and such other "traps," as we could pack in bags
or knapsacks. We were counseled by the camp-commandant to sell off whatever property we possessed, in
order to free ourselves of all incumbrance upon the march.
But special orders were now reported in favor of four
officers, survivors of the Harriet Lane's disaster; Lieut. J.
A. Hannam, acting-master; Lieut. C. H. Hamilton, who
had been wounded; and two engineers, Lieuts. Plunkett
and Stone. These gentlemen were to be forwarded to
Shreveport by stage, and were to set out immediately.
With the departure of Lieuts. Stone and Plunkett, who
belonged to my mess, I was left alone; my kind mess-
mate, Lieut. Hayes, having been called away by death.
Another modification of the "exchange news" now dam-
pened our hopes to some extent; the paroling-officer informing us that his orders directed him to parole only
enlisted men. We began to entertain doubts regarding
a speedy liberation.

One of our citizen-prisoners, Mr. Parse, died on the
23d of November. He was an elderly man, who had kept
the hotel at Brashear. He had been a quiet, uncomplain-
ing sufferer, during most of the time since our arrival at
Camp Groce.

News of the capture of Point Isabel and Aransas Pass,
by a Federal force which had landed on the coast of
Southern Texas, about the close of this month, gave us
some indication as to the progress of American arms.

Our sick-list remained heavy; though diminished somewhat by the prospect of parole among the men. We began to experience much hardship in our barracks, from
excessive cold; and were obliged to keep our fire-holes
heaped with burning wood, which necessitated the endurance of smoke in stifling fumes. Meantime, daily, our

camp presented an appearance of great commercial activity. The prospect of a long march, with no wagons, had stimulated a desire to rid ourselves of all " impedimenta," and the rebel guards, with "outside customers," were anxious to relieve the "Yankees" of any superfluous clothing or other articles. Hence the guard-line became a sort of "Rialto," on one side whereof our sailors and soldiers displayed their "goods" upon the sand, while rebels clustered eagerly on the other, to cheapen and buy at " bargains" whatever was exposed for sale. I amused myself often in watching the varied groups engaged in these fancy-fair and rag-mart operations. Military and naval clothing, shirts, trowsers, gloves, stockings, boots, caps, needles, pins, thread, silk; with all kinds of knick-nacks, were ranged upon handkerchiefs along the line, the traders of each side on their haunches, buying and selling, while a guard, with his musket on both shoulders, sauntered up and down between the groups; occasionally making a bid himself, when some tempting Yankee "trick" attracted his attention. Competition brought out quantities of these "tricks," from Yankee trunks, valises, knapsacks, and bundles; and the market fluctuated like all markets. Sly "bulls" and "bears" were pitted on that guard-line, as on Wall or State street. The rebels, though coveting all our "tricks," were disposed to "fight shy," as our boys said; knowing that if an order to march should arrive suddenly, every thing for sale must be sacrificed. Our Federal traders, on their side, affected corresponding "stiffness," and "held on" for good prices. But the principal business soon became concentrated in the hands of a "heavy broker." Sergeant Wentworth, of the 42d Regiment, a shrewd and intelligent "Yankee," of the Massachusetts species, whose vocal abilities, and powers of entertainment generally, had lightened many a weary prison-hour, became, about this time, the very Mercury of merchandizing. Armed with a "special parole," which his "sweet charming" had obtained from Lit. Col. Barnes, the camp-commandant at this time, our bold Sergeant passed freely in and out of the guard-lines, lunching with rebel guards and officers, booking orders for " Yankee goods," selling on commission, with a handsome per cent. profit, and ultimately "commanding the market", to the general convenience of prisoners and no little profit to himself pecuniarily. Thousands of dollars, in Confederate currency, changed hands under his skilful prestidigitation, and, before the ides of December, our captive officers and men discovered themselves lightened of the greater portion of such little property as they had saved from previous forays.

Orders arrived to pack for the march, about December 7th; at which time I found myself prostrated by an attack of low fever that had been, during some weeks, threatening me. I had already made preparations for travel, in getting the promise of a pony, at the current price of three hundred dollars in confederate funds, or sixty dollars in gold. I had secured a bridle, and was in moderate hope to get a saddle; and had been relieved, through Sergeant Wentworth, of trunks and other "plunder," as a western man calls his baggage. But, when the day arrived for marching, I was lying, nearly delirious with pain and fever, on a cot in the shed which had been occupied by the citizens. Prostrated and helpless, my nerves unnaturally excited by Dover's powders, my stomach scarified from "heroic" doses of "Croton oil," I marked, with bewildered sense, the dispositions for departure, and was pronounced by the Confederate surgeon to be unable to travel, even in a carriage, which had been chartered by Colonel Burrell, and wherein a place had been secured for me. One by one, my fellow-officers seemed to fade into obscurity, as the fever grew more intense ; and at last, when Colonel Nott stooped over my cot, in parting, and remarked that he was compelled to leave me, now, as I had been obliged to leave him, at Tigerville—on a sick bed—I scarcely knew the purport of his words, and shortly afterwards sank back into an utter unconsciousness of aught beyond the fact of suffering pain.

Meanwhile, the march of our officers, and of the paroled enlisted men, proceeded under rebel orders. The soldiers and sailors started in advance, some forty hours, under a strong guard of cavalry; the officers and citizens following, under another escort, with a brace of army wagons provided by the Confederates, and two farm-wagons hired by those who still held property in "baggage." Five officers were mounted on hired mules, and four more, with Stratton and his wife, rode in the hired coach. On the first day of travel, they proceeded fourteen miles, and accomplished the distance to Anderson, nearly fifty miles, in three days. They continued at an increased average of miles, per diem, keeping the highway, but encamping generally outside of towns : in this manner passing through Huntsville, crossing the Trinity river, and reaching successively the Texan towns of Crockett, Palestine, Kickapoo, and Tyler. Camp Ford, the place of their destination, as it appeared, was gained after about twelve days' marching ; and, just before reaching it, they overtook and bade farewell to our enlisted men, who, with light hearts and light packs, were pursuing their road to Shreveport, and, as they fondly anticipated, at that time, to freedom.

At Camp Ford, our Camp Groce exiles received a warm greeting from the sixty five Federal prisoners who were there dwelling in huts, enclosed by a high stockade of split pine timber. Forty-five men, under one Captain Davis, constituted the rebel guard. At this post, the citizen Stratton was paroled and permitted to proceed with his wife to Shreveport. Winter now began to make itself felt, in fierce Northers, accompanied by snow, sleet, and rain, and the task of making themselves comfortable, by building new huts or repairing old ones, became an arduous one to our weakened and despondent emigrant prisoners. Leaving them for a space, at Camp Ford, I return to my personal fortunes.

CHAPTER XXXI.

HEMPSTEAD HOSPITAL.

LIFTED from the desolation of our evacuated quarters at Camp Groce, I am conveyed to the Confederate military hospital, at Hempstead. Here my symptoms speedily develope into an attack of latent Typhoid; and I am placed in a large room, containing twenty beds, occupied by other patients in low stages of sickness. During several days I remain in a very precarious condition, and my sufferings are of the most acute nature. For days and nights alternating between hopes of life and fantasies of death, I at length, under judicious treatment, emerge from immediate peril, and gradually struggle out of the vague idea of "life in death" characterizing this type of febrile disorder. At length the fever is declared broken. Slowly I resume my comprehension of surrounding things. I dream, one morning, that I am FREE; that I am in my camp, and stand before my regiment at dress-parade. The banners gleam; drums roll; the ranks divide in "open order;" the men and officers "present arms!" My eyes, meantime, are fixed upon the central flag of "stars and stripes." All other objects fade to indistinctness, while that flag grows larger in my sight, still larger, till it seems to fill the sky from zenith to horizon—till the very atmosphere appears a luminous medium of stars and glittering stripes, encompassing me. I awake from this celestial vagary, but still the stellar imagery fills my eyes. At length, by slow degrees, it takes a definite shape—no heaven-absorbing flag, indeed, but, nevertheless, the old, familiar emblem of our Union; in an inch-square painted brooch, upon the bosom of a female at my bed-side.

For a momemt I forget that I am in a rebel prison; that the cots surrounding me are occupied by men who betrayed and have stricken down our glorious banner. My eyes begin to overflow; I try to lift my feeble hand in salutation of that symbol of my country; I move my lips to bless it; then lapse into bewilderment, and sink back, fainting, on my bed of straw.

Next day I learn that the lady visiting my cot was the hospital matron, a Northern woman, holding her position simply because she is necessary to the rebels. Occupying the premises as her dwelling before the government appropriated them for hospital purposes, she was solicited to remain as a female superintendent, though known for firm attachment to her people in the Northern states. She performs her duties as a Christian woman, caring for the sick and wounded, with an ever-active zeal, and in a spirit of kindliness that is worth more than medicine. She claims one privilege only as her own; to wear the brooch that I had seen upon her breast; that plain enamelled impress of the "Stars and Stripes" which, gleaming over the poor prisoner's bed, had been transfigured through his dream and made to fill the heavens of sleep with rays of loyal glory. She wears that emblem of her country openly before the surgeons; and I well believe that many a dying Texan, loyal at his heart, although compelled to march in treason's ranks, has had his suffering soothed, his soul made glad, as mine was, by the sight of that "old flag" above his pillow, to bless his closing eyes and give his parting soul the hope that God would pardon a repentant rebel.

I thought it marvellous at this time that such an ornament should be permitted to be worn by any person in the Texan country; but I learned some stranger facts than even this, before I left the hospital. Of course, an order from the surgeon might oblige the matron to conceal her brooch, but she would have resented it at once by resignation of her charge, and this they cared not to provoke. They rather chose to ignore the harmless "whim," though, doubtless, had a man presumed to "show his colors" thus, the nearest "black-jack" would have had him dangling from it.

I said this worthy matron was a faithful ministrant to rebel sick; but that was in her line of duty, though impressed with every mark of kindness. It was easy to remark her deeper interest in Federal prisoners, as I had occasion to acknowledge for myself. There were two Northerners with me—a soldier and a sailor boy. The first, a Massachusetts man, sank very soon; the other lingered several weeks. Poor lad! I crawled out of my cot, at his request, to write his little will, bequeathing some few garments to the nurses, desiring that his mother's likeness should be sent back to "God's country!" as he fondly called the North, and praying that her parting present, a pocket Bible, might be buried with him, on his breast.

Poor Tweedy! Only twenty years of age, he has yet served through all the war—two years a soldier and the residue a gun-boat boy; a light-hearted youth, with few transgressions on the logbook of his simple life. He is a living shadow, lying on his cot, from which the nurses are obliged to lift him; for he cannot even turn without assistance. These rude nurses have taken a fancy to the "little Yankee," as they call him, and they humor him as if he were a child. He has "willed" his little "kit" of clothing to them, to be distributed after his death.

"Tweedy," I say to him, "are you prepared to die?"

"If it's the will of God," answers the poor boy, with quivering lip; "but I'm young yet. It's hard to go!"

He closes his eyes awhile, remaining silent; then whispers, feebly, "Do you think I'll be dying for my country if I die in a hospital, sir?"

"Surely you will, my boy," I reply; "as surely as if you fell in battle."

"I think I suffer as much," he rejoins—in a low tone. Then, after a pause, "I shall see my mother, sir, if it's the will of God."

One morning I hear Tweedy's voice just after I awake. He is talking with the matron, who sits by his cot. I hear her ask him about his family, and he tells her that he has been in the navy a year, and that his mother died four months after his enlistment.

"You have neither father nor mother?"

"No, ma'am," answers Tweedy; "and my sister is married, so she doesn't belong to me any more. I'm all alone in the world, ma'am."

I feel my eyes moisten, as the sailor boy's pallid lips murmur these simple words; but I am not prepared for the burst of grief which comes from the hospital matron. The kind woman seems literally to "break down" with her feelings. She bows herself over the dying "Yankee," and sobs with such vehement grief as I have seldom seen exhibited at the bed of death. "Poor child! poor child!" is all I can distinguish, in the intervals of her sighs and floods of tears.

It is a touching and curious spectacle to me, a prisoner: this Northern widow weeping over a Northern orphan. Stranger to her, his only claim is, that he is motherless. How much of long pent sorrow for her own beloved dead; how much of yearning for her native land beyond

the Mississippi; how many thoughts, fears, hopes, bound
up with loyalty and Union, may have mingled with this
Northern matron's tears and sobs.—He only knows who
reads all bosom secrets. I turned my forehead to the
wall, while one who occupied the nearest cot—a ranger
of Tom Green's command—called softly over to me, "She's
got a mother's feelings for that little Yankee!"

May heaven take sweet account of all such tender
hearts! The "little Yankee" sailor boy is dead. I gave
his Bible to the nurse, to be deposited within his coffin,
and I placed a shred of his brown hair within the cover
of his mother's ambrotype, to be transmitted to a sister
in New York. Let them be comforted, who loved the lad.
His latest hours were soothed by kindly cares, and his
last breath was drawn so peacefully that none might say
when his young soul passed upward.

A solitary tallow candle, fixed in an old tin sconce and
hung upon a post, throws a feeble glimmer through the
ward-room, where I occupy a cot among twenty others,
each the bed of suffering. December winds howl savagely
around the hospital—a large old building, once the principal hotel of Hempstead. A glazed door at my head,
loose-framed and creviced, gives ingress to the chill blast,
which, after whistling over the verandah, seems to moan
at this casement like a dying man. But there are real
moans of dying men within. A miserable conscript lies
some feet from me, in mortal agony. He has drawn his
knees to his chin, and is rocking up and down, muttering
incoherent words, and occasionally venting shrieks that
make our blood curdle to hear. This conscript has been
dying—so the doctors tell us—during forty hours. "He
cannot last till morning!" they say, and, God forgive us,
we hear the announcement with grim satisfaction; for the

poor man's constant cries and frenzied utterances have
driven sleep from us by night and day. It may be that
remorse is mingled with delirium in this case; for the
man rehearses, in his fevered way, continual memories of
fights and struggles. " Don't murder me !" he implores.
" Don't hang me yet!" and then calls men and women by
their Christian names—"O save me! save me !"—" Give
me a knife—a knife !"

In yonder corner a Texan soldier, of Waul's Legion, is
passing away. Three days ago, I heard him dictating a
letter to his wife. He yearns to see her " and the children," before he dies; watching the door with fixed gaze,
his eyes glassy and eager. The nurse approaches to ad-
minister a powder or draught. The patient mechanically
swallows, and then in a piercing whisper asks, " Do you
reckon she'll come ?—Do you reckon I'll live jes' to see
her ?" Poor fellow ! he passes away in a day or two, his
wife's name the last upon his lips; and a letter, arriving
afterwards, informs our surgeon that the widow is lying
near to death. Heaven help the orphans of this poor
Texan soldier, sacrificed, like his deluded comrades, upon the bloody altar of treason, which he hated; for he
was a " Sam Houston man" in old times, and voted against
secession.

The crazy soldier near me dies at last, and is carried
out on his mattress, to be stripped and placed in a pine
box, rattled away in a lumber-wagon by mules, under
whip of omnipresent "negro," and dumped finally among
hundreds of other bodies of poor soldiers, in the populous
grave-yard devoted to hospital victims. No prayers to
be said; no hymns to be sung! but clay to clay, as you
toss out ashes on your dust heap

Just after our gaunt tallow candle is lighted and hung
up, I hear a monotonous sound of talk from the wooden

settee near our stove. A Baptist conscript, detailed as a nurse, is mooting doctrinal questions with old Doctor Eastman, the Ward Master—a man of weighty arguments and deep quotations. These Texan conscripts and militia men are much addicted to ethical discussions. I have heard a brace of them disputing by the hour on "infant baptism," "free grace," and other dogmas. Old Doctor Eastman assumes to have the power of Boanerges in debate upon religious points. He tells us that his "specialities" are—1st, consummate knowledge of the science of medicine; and, 2d, a perfect comprehension of the Scriptures. Professional jealousy prevents a proper recognition of the first of these "good gifts," so that he is only ward master, instead of being chief surgeon. As for the other gift, he ·displays it in nightly fulminations of spiritual thunder which confound both doctors and patients.

"You see—I know all about this war, and how it's goin' to end," he drawls, in his deliberate manner, while the nurse, a big-boned bee-hunter, opens his mouth to swallow every word of inspiration.

"I'd like right smart to h'ar tell about that ar p'int," says the nurse.

"S'arch the Proverbs of 'Zekiel, and read Daniel and Revelations," pursues Doctor Eastman. "Alexander the Great was the Little Horn. You see there's to be periods, you understand—a time, and times, and half a time. That's Scripter!—Understand?"

"Sartin!" says the nurse, very much overpowered.

"The kingdom of Alexander was one time, and Napoleon Bonaparty's empire was another time—you understand?"

The nurse appeared quiet overwhelmed, and could only answer: "Edzactly—'nuther time!"

"Well, now, I'll make it perfectly clar, so as a child can understand it. Bonaparty ended the 'times,' and now we're in 'half-a-time.' This war is goin' to last till 1866, three years longer, and then there's to be a gineral war!—you understand?"

"Sartin!" says the bee-hunter; "a gineral war! All the ginerals is a-goin' in to fight."

"No, not that. I mean a gineral war—a universal war—in Europe and Ameriky. I'm not quite clar where the great battle of Armageddon is to be fought. Sometimes I think it's round the city o' Washington, and then ag'in I reckon it's to be in Italy. The blood, you know, is to flow stirrup-deep for six hund'ed furlongs, and that's about the space round the great city of Rome—old Babylon, 'cordin to Scripter. You understand?"

"Clar as a bee-gum!" asserts the nurse, professionally; and Doctor Eastman goes on with his lucid interpretations, till they drive me to sleep, and wake me up again, three hours later.

This old "expert" has written several books upon medicine, which are familiar in Western New York and in Illinois and Ohio. He has a ponderous manuscript volume of personal revelations, though he scoffs at spiritualism. This manuscript is filled with prophecies of his own, concerning the second Advent, which he expects to see, and the New Jerusalem, whereof he intends to be a citizen, reserving, perhaps, the Southern right of "secession." He is keeping his book to print in the "good time coming," as publishers of such light literature are now very scarce in Texas. Nevertheless, he tells us complacently that the work will probably revolutionize religious opinions throughout Christendom, and threatens some day, when I get strong enough to bear it, to bring down a few hundred pages and read them to me.

Among the rebel convalescents in hospital is a young man, twenty-eight years old, named Brock, a Missourian, who belonged to Sibley's brigade. Six years ago he quarrelled with and shot·or stabbed a cousin of his, in St. Louis, and was forced to leave his home, to escape trial for the crime. The breaking out of the rebellion found him on the Mexican frontier, and he soon afterwards enlisted in a partisan troop, commanded by one Damrell, if I recollect aright—a Yankee renegade.

Damrell was a guerilla of the Quantrell stamp, odious to friends and hideous to foes. He had picked up more than fifty reckless followers, numbering among them horse thieves, smugglers, and outlaws of the border. They ranged between San Antone and Austin City, were well-mounted and armed, and signalized themselves by hunting down suspected Unionists. Prowling around settlements and attacking isolated ranches, they scrupled not to murder and plunder wherever the weakness or unpopularity of victims promised them impunity. One of Damrell's gang, known as a dissipated and desperate man, was accused of murdering his own brother, by shooting him through an open window of his house, as he sat by the fire, fiddling, with his wife next to him and his children playing before them. The assassin was tracked through the timber by a squad of neighbors and the trail followed up to a remote ranche, where Luther (this was the guerilla's name) had put up for the night. The pursuers arrested him, but he denied all knowledge of the affair. It was impossible to fix the deed upon him, though all believed him guilty, knowing that he had quarrelled with his brother six months before   They contented themselves with warning Luther to leave Travis county within twenty-four hours and never return. He promised to do so, and was permitted to ride off. That very night the villain was detected in entering the house of his slain brother, by means of an opening he had made in the roof. He had climbed upon an ox-cart to the chimney, which, as is the case with log-houses generally, was built outside. Seized by one of the neighbors, who had tracked him in the morning, he attempted to lie himself out of trouble by asserting that he had some specie concealed in the loft. A few other neighbors arrived, however, and next morning Luther was discovered dangling from a pecan-tree in front of the gate. Nobody professed to know how he came there, and no questions were asked or answered about the matter.

When Damrell, the guerrilla, heard of this piece of summary justice, he swore vengeance. Before a month passed, several citizens, never suspected of Unionism, were shot on the highway, and the houses and barns of others set on fire. These outrages were laid to the guerrillas, and Captain Hunter, of the Texan Rangers, was bold enough to charge Damrell with the fact. The partisan leader heard of it, and gave out that he would have satisfaction of Hunter. In the course of a week he made several threats, and at last rode into Captain Hunter's camp, his person bristling all over with weapons. He had a six-shooter stuck in each of his riding-boots, two in his holsters, one in his belt, and carried one in his bridle hand. Besides these, a bowie-knife was at his side, and a double-barrelled shot-gun lay across his saddle.

Captain Hunter was on foot, when Damrell rode up and demanded, with a furious oath, what the Ranger had said about him. Hunter took his pipe out of his mouth, apparently to reply, but instead of doing so, he dashed its lighted bowl at the head of Damrell's horse, causing the animal to rear. This allowed him time to draw a pistol, with which he shot the guerrilla captain through his groin.

Damrell fell from the saddle and was dragged several rods on the ground. He never spoke again.

Another member of the gang assaulted Hunter, two days after this, and fired two shots at him. The Ranger then took deliberate aim and killed the fellow.

This is life—or death—in Texas!

So much for Major Hunter. I return to Brock, who had been one of Damrell's band, subsequently a ranger under Hunter, and afterwards a soldier of Sibley's brigade. He was rather an intelligent young man, and apparently of good judgment, though uneducated; but there was a wolfish expression in his eyes that indicated the evil of his disposition. Muscular and well-proportioned, his complexion darkened by exposure, his hair black, glossy, and redundant, he was a fair type of the conventional bravo or dashing guerilla.

Brock had been present at the battle of Fort Craig, where the Valverde Battery was captured from our soldiers, and where Lieut. Alexander McRae was slain. That battle lasted all day, and was far more disastrous to rebel life and limb than our official accounts have ever been able to report. Brock related to me how the gallant McRae stood to his gun.

"We just wanted to save that ar' Fed.," said the Ranger. "He fou't like a painter. It warn't no use; but he toed the line till all wor blue, Yank! He never guv in. He wor cl'ar blood!"

I inquired if McRae had been offered any terms before surrender.

"Surrender!" echoed the Missourian. "Gineral Sibley would ha' guv his best hoss to save that Yank's life. You see we picked off them battery chaps like as if they wor stuck up at a turkey-shootin'. An' thar stood that Yank, McRae, sightin' his guns, an' never mindin' grape nor shell nor bullets, more'n you'd mind a dose o' quinine fur fever an' agur.   Thar he wor, when we'd killed every man of his command, and thar he wor when we charged on to him.   'Surrender, captain!' says Gineral Sibley.   'You are a gallant man.   I want to save your life!'

"Then we seen him jes' smile, an' he riz his head up, an' p'inted to his breast an' body, that wor kivered all over with shot holes, and bloody as a bullock.

" 'It's too late!' wor all he said; and then he reeled an' fell across his gun.   We lifted him up, but it *wor* no use.   There wor a dozen mortal wounds, if there wor one, in that ar' Yank."

Such was the account which I received from this wild Missourian, concerning the death of that noble Union soldier, Lieut. Alexander McRae, of the regular army.   He defended his pieces to the last—till all who had served them were killed or wounded—and then he sank down himself, the last victim upon an altar of sacrifice.   Gen. Sibley's victory was dearly bought, though he took the six pieces that have since served the rebels in a hundred fields.   But who shall say how much *we* lost in losing brave McRae?   Peace to the loyal soldier's ashes!   Undying honor to his memory!

CHAPTER XXXII.

HOSPITAL PHYSIOLOGY.

FORTUNATE was it for me that, in a Confederate hospital, I fell under skillful treatment and kindly care. Dr.
W. H. Gantt, the chief surgeon, recalled to my memory
that we had met, many years before, when he was a young
disciple of Hippocrates in Philadelphia. I found in him
a scientific physician, and a gentleman, who treated me
more as a friend than as a prisoner. Dr. G. W. Neely,
assistant surgeon, was likewise a sympathetic man, and,
indeed, among the different surgeons and nurses, I remember no one who, whatever might have been his political bias, ever manifested toward me aught that savored
of bitterness or rancor. The nurses, principally invalid soldiers detailed for hospital duty, were civil and attentive,
and to the good lady of the house I was indebted for many
kindnesses, that I shall always dwell upon with pleasure.
Mrs. E——, who had lent books from her library to my
fellow-prisoners at Camp Ford, visited the hospital ward
several times, and kept me supplied with mental pabulum,
being not forgetful, in her goodness, to tender an occasional *morceau* of more material food, in the shape of a
bit of chicken or other delicacy. As I progressed in
convalescence, Dr. Gantt permitted many indulgences to
returning appetite; and, as the hospital larder, furnished
by contributions from a large neighborhood, was by no
means an empty one, I cannot class my sojourn at Hempstead among the "jours maigres" of prison life. Here

was black tea in store, sufficient, as the matron said, to last for two years; white bread was received from Houston once or twice a week; flour, sweet petatoes, beans, sausages, poultry, and eggs were brought in by farmers, anxious to make favor with surgeons, who might be called upon to pronounce as to the physical condition of conscripts; and finally, there were "medical stores" of whiskey and wine, which, at intervals, and by spoonfuls, tempted our convalescent lips, in the disguise of egg-nogg.

The patients were representatives of various military and social classes. In the ward-room, where my bed was located, there were nineteen other pallets, each with its occupant, until a discharge, by death or surgeon's order, made a brief vacancy, to be filled by some new-comer. Soldiers from nearly all the regiments or brigades of Trans-Mississippi Confederate troops were either received for treatment, or transiently reported, at this Hempstead hospital; and it was my custom, when able to rise, to mingle familiarly in conversation with all who appeared sociable. The death of my two fellow-prisoners, Parker and Tweedy, left me a solitary Federal among the rebels; and when, at dusk, as was my habit, I crept, blanketed and capped, to a settee behind the stove, my presence soon collected a group of other invalids, who liked to hear the "Yankee officer" talk, and were glad to ask and answer many a question. With these soldiers, who had seen service from the Rio Grande to the Mississippi; who had marched and fought under Generals Green, and Sibley, and Magruder, and Price, and Waller, and Waul, and Kirby Smith; who had hunted recusant conscripts in swamps, foraged with Quantrell's guerrillas; ranged the borders with Major and Pyron, and kept the coast with Leon Smith and his amphibious cow-boys; among these wild fellows, now stranded, like myself, on hospital cot-bed, I held many a chat, mingling whiffs of tobacco-smoke, and exchanging divers items of fact and speculation.

They were genial fellows, in the main, my rebel comrades of this ward-room; and their brief stories, shrewd observations, and unvarnished opinions, afforded me a clearer insight to the internal workings of rebellion, than I could ever have gained by other means. Clustered around our iron stove, into which we thrust great clumps of fuel, fetched by attendant blacks, we whiled long hours, often from early candle-light to midnight, in comparing views upon "secession," its causes, its merits, its effects, and its prospects. It would require double the number of pages that must suffice for the limits of this book, to rehearse one half the matters of interest that formed the topics of our prison converse; and the relations of personal histories and adventures which I heard might constitute a volume of frontier romance; but my chief enjoyment was in drawing out the real feelings of these rebel soldiers, regarding what they termed their "cause." Need it be added that I felt, at times, repaid for every hardship or peril that I might endure, when, in the dim light of that hospital ward-room, I read the glow of honest loyalty on some dark Texan visage, and felt the grasp of a hard but warm hand, and listened to the low-breathed whisper—"Colonel—I was always a Union man—I'm for the Union still!—May God speed the day when I can openly declare it!"

This from a rebel soldier; with the brown rags of Confederate clothing on his stalwart limbs; but having a heart beating under them for that "old flag" which Rebellion had trampled under foot in Texas. And it was not from a single mouth, or on one occasion only, that wishes and prayers for the restoration of our government

over the land, cheered my heart in a prison-hospital. I
have looked about upon a dozen, and counted a score, of
enlisted soldiers in the Confederate service, with whom
I felt that I could trust my tongue to talk of Union—and
of Freedom—as freely as I could speak of them on my
own northern soil. Many a time has my sympathy responded to a simple but touching recital, like the following—

"Colonel! I wor ag'in this secession, from the start!
I wor an old whig, and a Sam Houston man, when he run
last; but when he caved in, what wor I to do? I stuck
out, to the last, and voted ag'in the state goin' out; but
I'm a poor man, and poor men can't stand the pressure!
I had to make up my mind to volunteer, or be conscripted.
My hogs would have been seized, and the old woman
turned out of doors, if I'd held back, Colonel! So, I jes'
'played possum,' and j'ined the army."

"But, could you not have left the state?" I inquired.

"Whar to go, Colonel?.... Wife and three young critters are jes' like a ball and chain fur a poor man. I own
a piece o' land, with a hog-range in the timber clus' by.
S'posin' I'd undertook to make tracks out o' the state,
who'd bought my log-pen? who'd paid me a cent for hogs
or ye'rlin's? No, sir! run or swing on a black-jack limb,
would ha' been my choice; an' I tell you, Colonel, a feller
can't run far nor fast, without money, and with a wife and
three helpless young 'uns hangin' onto him, sir!"

I could not but confess the truth of this remark; but
I proceeded with my questions—

"How does your wife get along without you, the children being helpless, as you say?"

"O badly enough, Colonel. The poor woman has to do
everything herself; though I did leave right smart o'
hog's meat an' meal in our log-pen. But, my cattle—I

had fifteen head—they're all stampeded; and the old woman couldn't 'tend to markin' the ye'rlin's! Besides all
that, thar's a mean cuss of a neighbor, a desarter at that,
who's been muddyin' our spring, so my wife can't git
water, without going three mile for it.—Blast him, if ever
I get him, there'll be one less cowardly reb. in the Lone
Star State!"

The story of this soldier might serve for hundreds of
his class. Men with families of young children, dwelling
on some wilderness farm; which they had purchased and
cleared; owning perhaps, ten or twenty head of stock,
and some hogs; striving, by honest labor, to earn a home
for later years; such men are the saddest victims of the
wretched delusion which has ruined our Southern states.
The wealthy notables, whose ambition begot, stimulated,
and precipitated the unholy strife, have been comparatively unharmed, as yet, by its effects. The two orders
of citizens who really suffer, at the South, and more especially in the Gulf states, are, on the one hand, the wealthy
and honest enthusiasts for State rights, who plunged into
the contest with a self-sacrificing zeal which would have
sanctified a less atrocious cause, and who abandoned homes,
professions, station, and even their families, in order to
give service, money, and life itself to the Confederacy;
and on the other hand, that immense class of non-slave-
holding, laboring, and producing Southerners, who never
really sympathized with Secession, but who were drawn
in under the "pressure" of various influences, to become
the bulk of rebel armies and the victims of every battle-
field. A majority of the ancient members of whig and
American parties, and a very large proportion of even the
Democratic party of the South, who were either small
land-owners, or artisans, cattle-drivers, and proletarian
operatives generally, had no more interest in the issues

whereupon the Southern orators were blatant, than they possessed in the stock of banks or railroads. On these poor men—forced by the accident of birth-place or location to cast their fortunes with Rebellion—the hardships and horrors of war have borne with crushing weight. To this class a majority of Texans belonged; but it is a truth not now to be denied, that this majority never voted for the secession ordinance which carried the Lone Star State out of the Union that had done so much for her welfare; that had incurred for her protection a war with Mexico, replenished her bankrupt treasury, fostered her growing institutions, and defended her from savage foes.

"What is the reason," I one day asked, of a young Texan, who belonged to Waul's Legion, and whose Union proclivities were known to me—"What is the reason that you, who have no family to encumber you, do not make your way to the Federal army?"

"Well, Colonel," answered the ranger, with a humorous expression in his fine eyes that announced a jest he was about to utter—"to speak candidly, I've never had a chance to get near enough to the Fed's. They were always running away from us Texas boys!"

I smiled at the retort, but could not help wincing under it; for it is a lamentable fact that our troops have invariably encountered reverses in their several expeditions against the Texan coast and borders. It is no marvel that those rough-natured, courageous men, who compose seventy or eighty regiments which Texas has raised for service beyond her frontiers, should have become vain and self-glorious concerning their invincibility, or that the nourishment of their local pride should prove a potent aid to rebel leaders in their discipline and handling of conscript masses. Mankind is the creature of gregarious affinities; and camp life, coupled with victorious associations and mutual experiences, may mould an army of men who entertained very incongruous sentiments into a military homogeneity that must soon eradicate all dividing lines. If more than half the people of the South were Union-men when the Rebellion broke out in South Carolina, so, at various stages of the war, Unionism has pervaded Southern armies, or has been seemingly crushed out entirely, just as the barometer of success or reverse, of hardships or hopes, has indicated the future to be for or against the principle of Secession.

Discussing facts like these, with rebel volunteers, in Hempstead hospital, modified many former views which I had harbored regarding Southern Secession. I, a prisoner, alone in the heart of a seceded state, discovered secret friends in men who might have before encountered me in deadly conflict, or might do so in the future, and yet whose hopes and sympathies were akin to my own. This poor German soldier, who shares with me the white bread and savory sausage brought by his good wife from their little farm, some twelve miles distant; brought in a basket upon horse-back, by that good wife, through sleet and snow of a January norther; this poor fellow, whose eyes gleam when I speak to him, is no more a rebel in heart than I am; but he must, nevertheless, shoulder a Confederate musket, and march out, from the little home which he has built up by hard toil, to brave the perils of battle and suffer the pangs of disease, for a quarrel that must make him poorer day by day, and which, if successful in its quest, could never insure him a jot or tittle of property in the future. This rude but kindly nurse, who wishes that he could go with me to the North, when I shall be exchanged, and who shows me a letter from home that tells a story of privation and struggle, would fervently hail the return of peace and government, under that

grand banner which can alone secure their permanence
This ranger, who smokes his pipe on my right, and whose
little property has been eaten away by rebel tithes, would
gladly, as he says, give all that is left to him, if Union
could be restored, and the Nation keep step, once more,
to the old, beloved music. And this intelligent cripple—
a Methodist preacher who became a military wagon-master,
and lost his leg under car-wheel on yonder railroad—has
too much judgment to share in the illusive dreams of a
baseless, friendless, and hopeless Southern Confederacy.
These men are only types of the great family of loyal
men whose hands are wielded, not by their own volition,
but by an extraneous power, born of folly, and strengthened with arrogance, but inevitably, doomed to perish,
and become

            —" A thing
O'er which the raven flaps its funeral wing."

Abruptly on one of the latter days of January, 1864, I
receive orders from the post-surgeon—Dr. Gantt being
temporarily absent—to pack up and get ready for travel.
The nurses congratulate me on a prospect of speedy liberation; the rebel invalids, and convalescents, with whom
I have been familiarly domiciliated, crowd around, and
tender hearty wishes for my future health and happiness.
I grasp several rough, warm hands, but the locomotive
whistle hurries me, and I must call out, in parting, that
"I wish I could shake hands with all of you, boys!" and
so, after brief adieus to our kind matron and Dr. Eastman, I find myself hastening to the railroad, with many
a Texan "God bless you, Colonel!" lingering in my ears.

A rebel lieutenant, who has charge of Camp Groce,
meets me at the cars, and says that I am remanded to
that post, instead of being, as I had hoped, permitted to
proceed to Shreveport, where I suppose my fellow-officers

to have preceded me. A few minutes of steam-travelling
conveys me to the well-remembered stockades, within
whose unfinished lines are our desolate barracks, that recall to me many melancholy reminiscences of sickness
and death.

But I am not to be confined in the old buildings. The
lieutenant stops at the sheds once occupied by our Sabine
Pass officers; and I am ushered into one of them, where
a fire-place is roaring with great hickory logs a-flame, and
where some half-dozen guards are watching a huge pot
of beans that boils before them. Here I am at once fervently greeted by the welcome tones of "Yankee" voices,
proceeding from the brothers Smith, whom I had feared
were still in chains and jeopardy. But the brave boys,
still wearing Federal uniform, seemed in excellent heart
and bodily condition; and speedily made me quite at
home in their quarters, which they shared with a good-
humored set of rebel conscripts. I took my stool in their
circle, and discussed some palatable bacon, sausage-meat,
and biscuit, with an appetite that gave warrant of returning digestion.

The Smith brothers had been looking for my arrival,
in hopes that it would announce their own speedy parole
and transfer to Shreveport. They related to me the incidents of their trial by the civil authorities at Houston,
on a charge of horse-stealing. It appeared that they found
friends and sympathizers in quarters where they expected
harsh usage. The sheriff, in whose custody they were
placed, and whose duty it was to empannel the jury, had
shown them especial favor ; and they had been ably defended by a volunteer counsel; while the court, instruct-
ing the jury, had declared them amenable, as Federal
soldiers, to military law alone. "When these prisoners-
of-war escaped from their guards," said the Texan judge;

"they became at once hostile belligerents, and possessed the right, as such, to take up arms against us. It was their duty, moreover, to rejoin their regiment as speedily as possible, and to make use of every means to escape from an enemy's country. They exercised their right, as military belligerents, to appropriate horses or arms of an enemy, in order to facilitate their own return to the government which claimed their allegiance. If they are to be punished for this, the punishment must be inflicted by military law."

Under such sensible ruling our Smith boys were acquitted of civil offence, and remanded to the military authorities, by whom they were sent to Camp Groce, where I now encountered them. So these brave fellows have contrived to see a great deal of Texas at rebel expense. Captured at the prairie-edge, near Vermillionville, in Louisiana, while out on a foraging jaunt, they were, at first, taken to Houston and incarcerated in a guard-house. Escaping thence, they helped themselves to a couple of horses from a roadside barn, which was sentineled by a sleeping dog, obtained a saddle for one from a farm-house porch, where slept another mastiff, and borrowed two bridles and a second saddle from some other neighboring ranch. Thus mounted and caparisoned, they kept the public road, without money, and in Federal uniforms, stopping at rebel houses, and passing for Confederate soldiers on furlough, till they traversed the entire distance between Houston and San Antone, across the heart of Texas. They supped with the families of rebel officers, dined at the tables of rebel parsons, and told rebel "news" to everybody who questioned them. Had they succeeded in getting beyond San Antone, they might have escaped to the Mexican border; but, just before reaching that city, they were so imprudent as to make themselves known to some Texan wagoners whom they overtook, and who appeared to be favorable to the Union. These men betrayed them, and they were arrested in the streets of San Antone, cast into prison and chains, and subsequently, as we have learned, returned to confinement in Houston. But they were full of pluck and determination still, and assured me, in a whisper, that they were not the boys to be kept long in any rebel prison.

But our sojourn at Camp Groce, with the queer personages whom, by courtesy, we called our guards, was quite unlike imprisonment. We were our own masters, to a great extent, being allowed to range quite freely over surrounding localities. Many a tramp about the old barracks, and within the woods, and over to the Federal graves, did I have, in company with some sociable conscript, or with the Smith boys; and we felt no galling of a " captive's chain" either in or out of our quarters. The Smiths and myself occupied a shed, with one or two conscripts, and we read, played chess, or sunned ourselves, or gossipped by the fire, like favored guests in the rural districts.

The conscripts were all characters. We had our Missourian cattle-driver; a very Fallstaff of a man; with that venerable swash-buckler's traits of morality improved upon; a salacious old dog, who smacked his lips over the recital of scapegrace adventures, with as much unction as Sir John, when he vapored with Shallow about "St. Clement's inn" and the "bona robas." Many a quaint tale did this strange, white-bearded sinner relate, while his ponderous paunch shook with deep quakes of laughter. We had a sober citizen, on the other hand, who never smiled, but vented the most mirth-provoking expressions without a single grim muscle being softened by them. Then we had our disputative conscript; our growling conscript; our Jeff. Davis-hating conscript; our substantial conscript; and our conscript with no substance at all; about a dozen, perhaps, in all, coming and going, during our stay of three or four Sabbaths; and I must do them the justice, to say, that a better-natured, merrier set of grumbling foemen I never wish to encounter. There were good Union men among them, moreover; and a few with minds and cultivation much above the average of the conscript-class. With the loyal-hearted ones, I could talk freely, on loyal themes; and it thrilled my heart more than once to hear the earnest expression of hopes and longings for the Union that had been flung away by reckless political gamesters. "Would to God!" cried one of these men, to me—"that Lincoln could hurl a million of men on this accursed Confederacy, and blot every traitor from the face of its earth!" These were the words he uttered; and, as I recall them, I can almost see the man, as he stood before me, with indignant look, and hands clinched, as if to emphasize his adjurations. How I wished, then, for a regiment or two at my back, as a nucleus for ten thousand such gallant Union Texans as this, to rally around. How I mentally anathematized the folly or supineness which had left such men to be segregated, dispirited, hunted, and conscripted to rebel service, when they burned to organize and strike for the rights which a bullying minority had wrested from them.

It was by conversation with Texans of this stamp that I learned the fact, studiously ignored or suppressed by Secessionists, that less than half the actual voters of the State cast ballots when their "Lone Star" was obscured by treason's red eclipse; that less than sixty men and boys constituted a "Convention" which had drafted the Secession audience; and that only a "Reign of Terror" had dragooned the people into their mute acquiescence with Rebellion.

Some stout hearts held out against threats of death and under actual persecution and imprisonment. Judge Baldwin, a leading citizen, Dr. Peebles, a wealthy and influential gentleman, Attorney-General Rosenbaum, Judge Whitmore, and other members of the Legislature; with many more gallant souls, of all conditions and positions; kept their testimony of faith in our Union through all perils and temptations. May they be recompensed and rewarded in the "good time coming!"

The few weeks of my second stay at Camp Groce were marked by genial Spring weather, which recruited my energies rapidly. Two mails came to me, one day, and my heart throbbed, for a moment, in anticipation of "home news;" for I had received but one letter from my wife since the capture of Brashear; but the epistles were both postmarked in Texas. One was from Col. Nott, at Camp Ford, giving me items concerning his new prison, and dissipating every hope that I had cherished regarding the exchange or parole of our fellow-officers. The other was a courteous note from Mr. Cushing, editor of the "Houston Telegraph," conveying a kind tender of service, and accompanied by some New York papers, which were richly acceptable. This unlooked-for attention from a stranger was, I need scarcely say, very grateful to a prisoner, as were the friendly words which prefaced it: "Recognizing your name as that of one whose writings I have in times past admired, I obtained permission from Gen. Magruder to send you a newspaper, and also to tender you any assistance it may be in my power to render, consistent with the relations that exist between us. Should you wish for money, I can advance you a limited amount at any time, subject to the approval of the Provost Marshal General."

I hastened to procure a sheet of writing-paper, and a well-worn pen from one of our "guards;" and lost no time in acknowledging Mr. Cushing's polite offer; telling him that, though I was personally provided with funds for economical use, at present, I would not hesitate to avail myself of his liberality, should a long extension of captivity render it necessary, for myself or comrades. I added a small literary contribution for his journal, and soon afterwards received a welcome reply, in the shape of another instalment of "Yankee" newspapers.

Meantime, our Smith boys, getting restless under delay and inaction, were projecting another attempt to escape, from which I succeeded, however, in dissuading them. Our quarters were often visited by Texan volunteers, who, intending to take the cars at this water-station, would present themselves in camp, mounted upon fine steeds, and accompanied by negroes who were to go back with their masters' horses. Sometimes, one or two of these cavaliers would "bunk" with us; leaving their animals, with saddles and bridles, tethered in a shed at the rear, and often hanging up their pistols, or depositing their guns, within reach of our "Yankee" hands, till morning. The brothers Smith were sorely tempted by such opportunities, and I think that, if I had not discountenanced the venture, those brave *garcons* would have improved a moonlit night by riding away once more, on "borrowed" chargers, with rebel arms and haversacks slung at their saddle-bows.

But, at length, one morning, just after I had returned from a long stroll, with Mr. Rowe, an intelligent and agreeable "chum" of mine, the train from Houston rattled up, and a snuffy-looking Hessian Confederate reported orders from Head Quarters. The Federal prisoners were to be at once removed to Camp Ford. The Teutonic gentleman, of drill-sergeant aspect, was to take charge of us, and we were expected to get ready while the cars waited. ·

Short leave-takings were necessary; much bustle to get "tricks" together; resulting in my bestowal of several cumbersome "traps" on our guards, as keep-sakes; inducing, also, the relinquishment, on my part, of a costly military cloak, to the Hempstead telegraph operator, in consideration of some three hundred and odd wretched Confederate dollars; and thereafter, with my comrades, the Smiths, and a fresh half-dozen of Federal sailors from Houston, who were consigned to Shreveport, for parole, I found myself whisked over the railroad, some twenty miles, to Navasota.

At that place steam-transportation ended, and we were to finish our journey in stage-coaches. I purchased a pound of "Lincoln" coffee, at fifteen dollars—last token of abandoned civilization; and then, at the word of our custodian, orderly sergeant and brevet-lieutenant of provost-guards, I took seat among six, in the coach, and was rolled away to Anderson, the capitol of Grimes county, where we tasted a frugal supper of fat bacon and hard bread, rations carried with us on the coach.

That night we passed on the road, toiling slowly through heavy mud, and making but one stop, near midnight, to change horses and swallow some coffee at the moderate price of one dollar and a half a cup.

CHAPTER XXXIII.

STAGE-COACH STORIES.

THE stage-coach, lumbering heavily over ruts and ridges; dragged by laboring horse-flesh, night and day; that vehicle almost obsolete for Northern transportation; is still the principal public means of travel in south-western regions. I sat beside the driver during much of my Texan transit, and was thus enabled to look out and over points of interest. Our first Jehu was an admirable "whip," and manifestly plumed himself thereon. His lash, describing aerial battle-fields by segments, tangents, arcs, and curves, could lasso gadflies on his leaders' ear-tips, or fire a fusilade of snapper-cracks with such rapidity as Lonjoumeau's renowned postilion might have envied. He was literally an "old stager;" for he had driven his "four-in-hand" upon the Blue Ridge and through Californian canons, over western corduroys and in the southern cypress swamps. He had "run a mail" *via* northern Texas and the Indian trail, until his fellow-drivers were all shot or tomahawked by Camanches; and he "drove express" through western Louisiana till the Federals entered New Iberia, and he was obliged to rattle off his last coach at "double quick" in advance of the rebel couriers. "Full of strange oaths, and bearded," this roving chari-oteer now made Texas his *curriculum*, and rejoiced as an "exempt" from military service. His conversations were on "hair-breadth 'scapes" and imminent highway perils, that would read, if printed, like a yellow-covered novelette. He knew the legends of a hundred wayside melées, with ball and bowie-knife, and pointed out, on our journey, here and there, the spots which murders, lynchings, or waylayings had made historical.

"Down yander cross-pike, thar"—he indicated with his whip-handle a narrow turning from the road, through sombre woods—" old man Larew was sot on for his money, nigh on to a mouth ago. Some say it wor jayhawkers got him; but I reckon 'twor the sojers. Thar wor a heap o' conscripts in the timber, skulkin', and old man Larew wor used to keep right smart o' plunder in his log-pen."

"You say they killed him?"

"Dog-on if they didn't—cut and shot the old man orful: sot fire to his log-pen; and the body mought ha' burnt too if the niggers hadn't woke up just in time. The varmint got the old man, shore, and got his specie, I've heern."

We rode a mile or two, and passed a belt of woodland, bordering on a prairie. The driver pointed to a clump of timber at a little distance. "Thar's the place," said he, "they hung a chap for waylayin' two travellers in a wagon. He shot 'em in the back, and tried to *caché* the'r bodies underneath them red oak yander. But the hoss an' wagon wor his ruination; for a nigger seen him drivin', an' the county raised and hunted him. They got sign o' the varmint past Trinity river, an' treed him in the Big Thicket with dogs. He wor fotched back yer, to them dientical oaks, an' hung right over whar he got the men. His carcass is buried out yer, jas' whar he dug the grave, and tried to cover his trail, you see, but he couldn't; 'cause murder'll out, shore's shootin'!"

He touched up his nigh leader, and indulged in sundry resonant lash-crackings, which startled woodland echoes all about us. Stage-wheels began to spin, and, steadying myself upon the precipitous box-seat, I had only time to cast a parting glance across the murderer's grave before we whirled into a hollow. But, arrived at the next hill, and slowly climbing it, I ventured to inquire if these assassinations were as common now as formerly in Texas.

"I'm not clar as to that," the driver answered. "I've heern o' right smart shootin' an' cuttin' when them Regulators and Moderators fou't ag'in one another so long 'go as Murrel's gang—that 'ar cussed nigger thief 'an land pirate. Talkin' o' nigger thieves, jes' look yander, through the oak-openin,' an' you'll sight a blazed stump— out yer, whar the road forks."

I glanced in the direction indicated, and beheld the charred remains of an oak-trunk, with its extended limbs, like skeleton arms, blackened by fire, which had probably consumed the upper branches.

"That wor the spot whar a nigger thief and Linkin spy wor burnt," quoth the driver.

"Burnt alive!" I ejaculated.

"Hide an' har," returned my matter-of-fact colloquist. "Yer see, the committee diskivered a heap o' brimstone, kreosote, an' strichnine in that chap's log-pen, hid in a bar'l; an' thar'd been right smart o' well-p'is'inin' an' cabin-burnin' goin' on roun' Trinity Timber; so the citizens jes' up an' got this man, some whar' 'bout this yer range. He wor a Baptist preacher, an' a sort o' doctor, an' allowed it wor a sin to lick niggers; and so the people jes' sot on his case, an' fotched him guilty o' p'is'inin' wells, an' house-burnin', an' spyin' for old Abe Linkin. Some said hang and some said shoot; but the majority wor fur burnin' the cuss; an' out yer's whar they kerried the sentence into execution, you see."

"It was a mob, I suppose?"

"Yes, it wor a mob, shore; an' the sheriff o' the county

wor at the head. That's nigh on to a y'ar ago, an' I
heern nothin' about Linkin spies roun' sence that 'ar burnin'. Clar'd 'em out, shore!"

"Are there no regular courts and juries, driver?" I
asked.

"Mighty skerse, you bet. What wor that you axed
me, about these yer killin's—if they wor common yerabouts? Now I'll jes' tell you what wor told me by an
old Texan; an' he's lived in these yer diggins, man an'
boy, nigh on to sixty y'ar. We wor a-talkin' consarn-
in' shootin's, an' cuttin's, an' sich things, an' sez he—
'Wor you ever in Mexico?' an' I told him I wor, menny
a day. 'Then,' sez he, 'you know, when a murder's
trailed down thar, an' they git sign o' the body, they jes'
stick up a wooden cross to p'int out the place whar the
job wor done!' 'I know all about that,' sez I, 'for I've
sighted a heap o' them crosses.' 'Well, then', sez this
old Texan to me, sez he, 'if you wor to stick up a cross
in Texas for every murder an' killin' as hez been done
yer, thar'd be wooden mileposts all the way from Sabine-
town to Brownsville!' That's what an old Texan said,
strangor."

"No doubt 'tis true!" I responded.

"Law an' gospel, shore!" rejoined the driver. "I
heern a squire down in Crockett say he didn't know a
single cussed town in all Texas whar thar hedn't been a
murder, or shootin', or killin' o' some sort—an' he didn't
know only one case whar anybody was hung for it, an'
that wor only an old Mexican woman which p'is'ined and
robbed a soger down yander at San Antone. G-e-t up,
yer lazy critters!"

Passing rapidly through Huntsville, capital of Walker
County, and the seat of that State Penitentiary, wherein

Col. Burrell and his fellow-officers had been incarcerated, we rode all day through a well-timbered country; getting sunshiny glimpses of rolling lands, devoted to the culture of corn, tobacco, and cotton. We crossed the Trinity river, after about fifty hours' travel from the railroad line; and, having stopped to dine at a tavern, I noticed, when the stage rolled on, that another' passenger was added to our "deck-load;" a venerable old gentleman, whose face bespoke intelligence and whose garb betokened comfortable circumstances.

The talk was upon that never-ending theme—the war. A heavy-headed, beetle-browed Confederate officer was my *vis-a-vis*, and a saturnine secessionist, who wore a threadbare coat, was helping him to curse the "Yankee tyrants." Not caring to embroil myself with either of these worthies, I turned my eyes and thoughts upon surrounding scenery, and only caught a word, occasionally, till the name of "Mr. Lincoln," uttered by the elder passenger, attracted my attention.

"I knew him very vell. We were young men and boys together....I recollect a curious circumstance—"

The old man paused, but it had been sufficient. All other conversation ceased, and our curiosity waited for a story.

"We were young men together, and I bring to mind, as if it were but yesterday, how several of us—Abraham Lincoln with the rest—were one day listening to a strolling fortune-teller, who pretended to predict our destinies. To some of us were promised wealth, to others station; and others were to have more checkered futures; to be crossed in love or placed in dangerous straits. The only one who seemed to take no interest in the matter was young Lincoln. He was not a beauty, then, no more than now, and hardly calculated to be marked for special favors;

so he kept within the background, while the rest of us were sharing fortune, good and evil. At length, however, some one pushed him forward. 'Here, tell us this one's fortune,' cried we all; and Lincoln, laughing quietly at the joke, held out his hand.

"The scrutiny was long, and amused us yet more with its seeming earnestness. The lines upon the young man's hand were studied over, and his face perused as if it were a book. At last the fortune-teller spoke:

"'Yours is a mighty destiny!' We all laughed outright at these words, but that did not prevent the seer from going on. 'You will be raised to honor and renown! You will be President of the United States!'

"The fortune-teller stopped and seemed to hesitate. We laughed the louder, calling out, 'Go on! go on!'

"'I see a river of blood! There will be war—a terrible war between the North and South—while you are President; and—'

"'Nonsense—that's enough!' cried Lincoln, turning off abruptly; and, in merry mood, we left the prophet of our future to himself.

"Years after this, I heard the incident recalled by Abraham Lincoln, as a folly of his early days. We were then middle-aged and sober men, but both laughed heartily as we dwelt upon the recollection.''

The old man finished his relation, and a silence followed until some one muttered:

"What a pity!"

It was the saturnine secessionist.

"What is a pity?" asked the elder passenger, mildly.

"That you didn't let your fortune-teller finish that prediction, sir," said the saturnine secessionist. "He might have told Lincoln how long the war would last, and who'd be whipped."

We all laughed at this sally, and our driver touched up his horses with a double crack of the whip-lash. Shortly afterwards, we came in sight of the town of Crockett; and the old friend of Abraham Lincoln alighted at a respectable mansion by the roadside.

And as I looked back, from the stage-top, scanning the Texan country that stretched far away beneath the high hill we had crested; as I caught a parting glimpse of the ancient traveller, who had related his story about Lincoln, in hearing of a "Lincoln prisoner," I pondered upon the mysterious sequences of events which had brought us together on this Texan highway. Is there, really, a DESTINY, in mortal lives? was the "star" of Napoleon a real planetary indication of his wondrous fortunes? and has our Illinois back-woodsman a "star" likewise?

"Git along, yer lazy critters!" said the driver, cracking his whip.

CHAPTER XXXIV.

ON THE ROAD.

SPRING in Texas gives a promise of beauty which Summer fulfils abundantly. Wide prairies and broad hill-slopes, sprinkled with a charming variety of early flowers; grand parks of woodland, peopled by herds of wild deer; grazing-ranges, resounding under the flight of cattle-droves; live-oak groves; cedar-clumps, and "timber-islands" of every déscription; meet the well-pleased eye on either side, as the coach lumbers on, over hills and through valleys.

The Texan Flora is magnificent. Dahlias are indigenous to the country about Camp Groce. Geraniums grow wild in all quarters. The blue passion-flower, (*passiflora cærulea*,) and the fringed-leaf variety, (*passiflora-ciliata*) are discovered by the roadsides, and the ever-blooming rose, (*rosa-semperflorens*,) and modest primrose, which Linnæus called *Primula veris*, the "firstling of Spring," peeps out from the green meadows, in tints of lilac and red. The sweet-jonquil, (*Narcissus odorus*,) the oriental hyacinth, and our Northern lilac (*syringa vulgaris*) flourish in the low wood-lands, while water-lilies rise dripping from the swamps, and the shrinking sensitive plant (*mimosa sensitiva*,) expands its delicate petals under the first kisses of Aurora. All these, and an infinite variety of other flowers, regale the wayfarer's senses as he journeys amid half-reclaimed wildernesses; while mocking-birds trill their oratorios, the Southern oriole and blackbird tune their cantatas, and the whippoorwill joins its plaintive refrain, as the twilight shadows darken. Our sailor-prisoners were ever on the alert to snare the rich-toned mock-birds, and they caged many beautiful specimens of the red-bird, to bear home to their Northern friends, as trophies of Southern captivity.

But it would require pages to touch upon the wonderful insect-life of forests and prairies; wild honey-bees, hiving in hollow-trees, and amassing great stores of melliferous sweets, to tempt the roaming "bee-hunters;" wasps, building fortresses on high oak-limbs; striped spiders (*Salticus scenicus,*) hunting their prey on the leaves below; green wolf-spiders (*lycosa saccata,*) darting from swamp-pools on "the small gilded fly;" tarantulas, hiding their hairy ugliness under rotten stumps; scorpion-tribes burrowing in the sands; black pill-beetles, or muck-bugs, (an American type of the Egyptian *Scarabeus sacer,*) rolling their dirt-balls before them, under supervision of some gorgeous king-beetle, in a steel-blue coat-of-mail, green, purple, and violet wings, golden-crowned head, and silver antennæ; with multitudinous families of bright-winged *Lepidoptera*; from the little gold-dusted moths and tortoise-shell butterflies—through all brilliant reflexes and quarterings of azure, vert, argent and or—up to the royal enrichments of full-armored chrysalides, rivaling the *curculio regalis* of Brazil, whose scales of sapphire, emerald and ruby, are like "an illumination of all gems."

But, I could never weary in recalling the innumerable living-jewels of Texan woods and fields, whereof I caught but transient glimpses, during brief snatches of liberty in wood-land walks. Doubtless, my condition as a prisoner made me more eager-sighted and receptive of attractive imagery in flowers, birds, insects, and even leaves; yet I cannot but remember many of these objects as the most curious that I ever noticed. I am sure that Texas must be a mine to the naturalist, wherein, by "glow-worm lamp," he may explore new worlds of painted and breathing beauty.

Looking out, from stage-coach top, into vistas of Texan woods, or over stretches of prairie, I could not refrain from reflections on the folly which now constrained the abandonment of plough-furrows for cannon-ruts, and the peaceful germs of harvest-field-life for fiery seeds of battle-field death. Here, by the hedges, and clambering on the trees, as far as one's sight may reach, are leagues of vines, putting out bulbs which are to swell into myriads of grapes, that shall yield their purple wine only to sun and earth; while the owners of them are pouring out richer wine in the life-waste of a doomed and desperate cause. Here are buried treasures of corn, that must fructify for idle decay; here are herds of wild cattle that may perish before a drover shall claim them; here are hundreds of square miles that must bear no usufruct for years to come; and all because a few demagogues have undertaken to reverse the laws of nature, and to declare that Slavery, instead of Freedom, shall be the corner-stone of our Republic.

But the stage rolls on. We halt at Crockett, the capital of Houston county, for a night's rest, and I there become a cynosure for the eyes of inquisitive Texans, who have been apprised of my "Yankee" antecedents. Here, after sound slumbers in a bed whereof my Hessian guardian occupies the "outside" half—in order, as he says, to "protect his prisoner with his life"—I rise to devour, with good appetite, a substantial breakfast; and, thereafter, bid farewell to my comrades, the Smiths, who are to pursue the highway to Shreveport, while I must diverge toward Tyler and Camp Ford. So, the light-hearted brothers give me a parting hand-shake, and roll off, in an extra-coach, to the Louisianian border, there to abscond suddenly, (as I subsequently learn,) and make good their escape into Federal lines upon the Mississippi. Meanwhile, with my Teutonic conductor, and another traveler, I find myself in another stage, on the road to Palestine.

Our new companion is a Confederate colonel, on detached service. We speedily strike up a free conversation, and I discover my colloquist to be intelligent and agreeable; but it is not till we spend some twenty-four hours in company, that he becomes enlightened as to my military status.

"To what command are you attached, sir?" inquires the gentleman, during some chat which renders his question a pertinent one. "Are you in General Kirby Smith's army?"

"No, sir," I reply, quietly—"I belong to Gen. Banks's department"

The Confederate looked at me, with a puzzled expression of countenance. "Gen. Banks!" he repeated.

"Yes, sir," I rejoined, with a smile, at the same time unbuttoning a shaggy over-coat, and disclosing my Federal uniform-coat—"I belong to the other side! I am a prisoner-of-war, travelling on parole, at present."

We joined in a laugh, and the officer remarked, quickly, that he hoped he had not, unintentionally, made any remark calculated to wound my feelings, while ignorant of my position; to which I replied, that I had noticed how singularly free his discourse had been from anything which could give offence; and, with this mutual and somewhat Pickwickian understanding, our converse proceeded as sociably as before.

The rest of my journey, through Palestine, the capital of Anderson county, and by way of Kickapoo and other towns, to Tyler, was rapidly and pleasantly accomplished. At Tyler, I was presented to the Provost-Marshal, a young gentleman in spectacles, who looked like a Yankee school-master, and who generously informed me that Confederate armies were annihilating Federal armies, in all quarters, and that it was very probable that Lincoln would soon sue for peace to Jeff. Davis.   From this entertaining gentleman, my brevet-lieutenant guard obtained a wagon to transport us the four miles which intervened between Tyler and Camp Ford; and, parting from my stage-coach acquaintance, the Confederate colonel, who promised to write to me, I was bowled away, on a rough board seat, to the stockade that was to become my future quarters in Texas.

CHAPTER XXXV.

CAMP FORD

IT is dusk, when I enter the wide gates of the prison-corral. I have parted from my Hessian, who promises to send me a badge which belonged to valiant Captain Wainwright, killed at Galveston. This little Teuton seemed shrewd enough, but is a desperate rebel; a thankless distinction for any alien to the soil; since it is a fact that "Know Nothing" prejudices are still quite rife in Texas. "That ar' Dutchman," says a guard to me—"aint o' much 'count yerabouts. We got no use for Dutch or any other furriner in this yer fight."

Stumbling under knapsack and blankets, I pass several ten-foot-log structures, which, from the hill above, where I reported at Head Quarters, appeared to be pig-pens, but which I now see inhabited by Federal officers. Arriving at the hut of Col. Nott, I find its bunks all occupied, and thereafter perambulate in divers quarters, seeking shelter, till at length, I get lodgings in a demi-subterrene "shanty," whereof Lieut. Peck, of the Twenty-Third Connecticut, whom I last saw at Bayou Bœuf, is co-proprietor with Lieut. Root, of the Seventy-Fifth New-York volunteers.

Next morning, after being invited to mess for the present at the "Fifth Avenue Hotel," tenanted by Messrs. Nott, Dillingham, Crocker, Johnson, Dane, and Dana; a snug coterie of six; I look about me, on the "corral," and "prospect" for personal accommodation in the future.

Quartermasters
Grave

My Real Estate

Land is not all appropriated, though buildings are ; so I presently "preempt" an eligible site for improvement on a lot upon the "Avenue," opposite that principal hotel at which I take my meals. Thereafter, I make a building contract with "Dawe and Hicks" from Kansas, who bear the reputation of having erected the best house in town, and who agree, in consideration of one hundred dollars, legal tender in Confederate currency, to rear me a palatial mansion twelve feet by ten inside, with a good stone fire-place, and a substantial clay chimney. So, then, relieved of anxiety as to shelter, I prepare to adapt myself once more to gregarious prison-life.

There are many old friends to greet, and new acquaintances to make. Here are my fellow-officers of the "Ironsides," eleven of them ; our quarter-master, Lieut. John F. Kimball, having died on the 3d of September, last year ; and an ex-lieutenant, Fry, having been discharged as a citizen. Poor Kimball declined rapidly upon reaching Camp Ford, as a prisoner. He yielded his life, after long suffering, and was buried, near sunset, under sombre clouds, sprinkling their tears upon the mournful procession which followed his pine coffin to a grave that loyal hands had hollowed at the base of a branching oak. But as our comrade's dust was mingled with Southern earth, the last beams of departing day broke forth in a flood of splendor; cheering survivors with golden promise, not only for the spirit which had passed away, but for our beloved country, toward which every prisoner yearned continually.

The death of Lieut. Kimball was followed, later in the fall, by another and very sudden summons of a prisoner to eternal enfranchisement. The prison-grounds had not at that time been stockaded, and our Federals either bivouacked under trees, which grew thickly, or slept in a small barrack-stack, within their allotted limits. But the approach of winter stimulated an effort to house themselves more comfortably, and details were formed for the work of cutting and drawing timber. Under supervision of guards, outside-details were allowed to go beyond the grounds, and drag or "back" their wood to the guard-line, where other details received the loads and transported them to the sites of log-cabins. A private, of the Twenty-Sixth Indiana regiment, named Thomas Moorehead, was, one day, near the guard-line, waiting for wood, when he was abruptly commanded to fall back. The Federal soldier was aware that an order had been promulgated, forbidding prisoners to approach within three paces of the line; and he had halted, therefore, at a distance much greater; nevertheless, in compliance with the sentry's command, he was turning back, when the brutal rebel, whose name is remembered as "Frank Smith," deliberately fired at Moorehead, the shot passing through the latter's body, and shattering the arm of another prisoner who stood behind him. Moorehead, fatally hurt in the bowels, died the same night; the wounded man was left without surgical assistance, other than could be afforded by a hospital steward, captured soon after.

This cruel and unprovoked murder exasperated the Federals beyond measure, and they threatened to rise, massacre the small guard, and sack the neighboring town of Tyler. Happily, the counsels of Lt.-Col. Leake, of the Twentieth Iowa regiment, calmed an excitement which might have resulted in a rash outbreak that could only end in the destruction of all.

The temper of Camp Ford custodians, at this period, was bitter in the extreme. "Richardson's Guard," a company of partisans, who had never known real service, but had signalized themselves as kidnappers of conscripts, bore no good feeling toward the Federals under their charge; and the assassination of Moorehead was succeeded by repeated attempts to "shoot a Yankee." One morning a sentry suddenly levelled his piece at a soldier, who had merely looked at him, and the Federal only escaped by falling flat on his face, and letting the bullet whistle over him. But the boy was plucky, and gained his feet with a heavy fragment of stone clutched in his hand; and the next moment there was a rebel knocked down, while our Yankee fled among his fellows, and could not be recognized when the guard turned out to arrest the delinquent.

Lieut.-Col. Leake, here mentioned, was one of the most genial and intelligent officers that I met at Camp Ford. He was captured at the battle of Morganza, or Fordoche, which took place on the 29th of September, 1863. Previously to this engagement, Col. Leake commanded an advanced guard of Gen. Herron's force, the Second Division of the 13th Army Corps, which had landed at Morgan's bend, two miles below Morganza, on the 17th of September. Gen. Herron, after throwing out reconnoissances which satisfied him that the enemy occupied the Atchafalaya banks, in a force of about five thousand, remained near his transports, while Col. Leake, with 208 Indiana infantry-men, Lt.-Col. Rose, of the 26th Ind. Volunteers, with 241 more, Major Bruce, with 150 cavalry, and Major Montgomery, with 25 mounted infantry; besides a section of the 1st Missouri artillery, with 34 men; the whole forming a detachment under command of Col. Leake, took possession of Norwood's plantation grounds, at the junction of Bayou Fordoche road with a road leading to the Atchafalaya river. Col. Leake's instructions were to engage the enemy's attention, in order to mask operations on the river. Obedient to these, the colonel occupied his little force in reconnoissances, send-

ing his cavalry to annoy the rebels, and advancing his
infantry and artillery into positions which might attract
their fire.   Sharp skirmishing took place daily, and the
Confederate out-posts were frequently driven in.   After
holding the junction about a week, Col. Leake shifted his
position some three quarters of a mile to the Sterling
plantation, Botany Bay, leaving his cavalry pickets still
at Norwood's.   From this point, the colonel made divers
demonstrations, driving rebel pickets on several occasions,
and skirmishing, more or less, daily.   But Gen. Tom
Green, was in command of the Confederates; and though
Col. Leake succeeded in arousing the old fighter to action,
he could not conceal from that fox-like foe the weakness
of Federal defences.   Of this weakness our Iowa colonel
was too well aware himself, and so demonstrated to Gen.
Vandeveer, who visited his camp about this time.   But he
was ordered to remain at his post, and did so; the consequence whereof was the sudden pouncing down upon him
of crafty Gen. Green, with all his rebels; who, crossing
the Atchafalaya, and filing through woods and swamps, in
their customary Indian manner, appeared abruptly, one
morning, within a mile of Leake's head-quarters.   By a
detour through timber-lands, the rebel cavalry cut ours
from their base; and, about noon, the men of Speight's
Brigade, 900 strong, under Harrison, broke out through
cane-fields, and advanced upon the Federal reserves.   Col.
Leake, forming his lines behind fences, received the
Texans with a withering fire, which drove them back.
They then attacked his right flank, but, soon changing
front, our gallant Iowan met them there with equal success.   They then charged on his left flank, where the
little battery was stationed, but another rapid change of
front again drove back their lines, discouraged.   At this
moment, a body of cavalry appeared, advancing from the

front. Their uniform was blue, and the cry rose that these were our Federal pickets falling back to reinforce the post. But that report was false. It was Gen. Green, with his Texan rough riders, clothed in the spoils of Brashear City. Heeding them not, Leake was moving on Harrison's retreating ranks, when another rebel brigade, posted under the levee, suddenly showed levelled arms, and demanded the Federal surrender. Col. Leake then looked about him, to discover his post completely surrounded. His cavalry pickets, under Montgomery, had taken the "back-track" of escape, through canefields, without notice of discontinance; his infantry pickets had been flanked by the rebel march, and our Federal commander now found himself *hors du combat*. The fight had lasted more than two hours, under a drizzly rain, and resulted in a loss of 14 killed, 24 wounded, on our side, while the rebels owned from 45 to 75 killed, and from 120 to 145 wounded. The prisoners, upon surrender, were marched across the Atchafalaya, and thereafter found their way to Camp Ford. Thus, through agency of the same rebel forces—comprising brigades under Green, Major, Speight, and Mouton, Col. Leake and myself were introduced to prison-relation ship in Texas.

The industrial resources of Camp Ford, or "Ford City," as we called it, are turned to notable account. With a half-dozen axes and hatchets, three spades, a dull saw, and our jack-knifes, we contrive to multiply tools, erect machinery, and establish manufactures, agriculture, and the mechanical arts. Supernumerary knife-blades are forged into chisels; a stray file is sharpened into a centre-bit; lathes are built, with foot-boards and hand-wheels· In spite of all obstacles, Yankee ingenuity finds means to assert itself, and the long hours of our imprisonment are

whiled away by many shrewd workers, with no small returns of pecuniary profit to themselves.

Here, near the great gate, under most dexterous digits
of Master's Mate Fowler, a sea-genius, who knows the
forest trees as well as he does the cross-trees, we have
basket-weaving out of peelings of ash wood, and chair-
making from grape-vines; not to speak of table-mats,
drinking-cups, and chess-men, carved with a pocket-knife.
Not many paces off, sign-marked by upright frame-work
of a wooden ash-filterer, our chemical laboratory is seen,
where Citizen Haley, much travelled and Spanish-talking,
beguiles captivity by charitable soap-making *por los po-
bres*. Yonder, by "Big Mess" kitchen-house, Lieutenant
Woodward, always busy and useful at his foot-lathe, is
turning chess-sets, which are models of artistic taste.
Stout Sachem-Captain Johnson, of "Fifth Avenue Mess,"
is meantime fashioning a splendid arm-chair for his naval
brother, Captain Crocker, of the Clifton; while Lieutenant Mars, just opposite, is stringing his new banjo,
wrought from ash and hickory. Another famous lathe,
revolved by wheel and crank, is wrought at skilfully, by
Engineer Johnson, a Diana man, who scans his work with
a single eye, ('tis all the rebels left him,) while he deftly
turns a goblet out of holly-wood. Down yonder street,
the potters mix a reddish clay, which constitutes our subsoil, and shape bowls, plates, coffee cups, and smoking-
pipes. Pipe-carving, out of various materials, is quite a
favorite employment. Rich and intricate designs, quaint
forms, and really beautiful workmanship, give value to
these tokens passed from friend to friend. Our half-breed
Cherokee, Hicks, a nephew of John Ross, the noted chief,
displays his aboriginal handicraft on a handsome calumet,
delicately traced with flowers and tomahawks *in relievo*,
which he gives to me. The elegant ornamentation of our

chess-men, made with knife-blades, is marvellous to see.
Two exquisite sets, carved by Lieutenant Morse, as presents for his family, look like Cellini models done in
wood.

Thus wears on the time, captivity cheated of much irksomeness by hours of well-spent labor. So our log huts
have been built, their chimneys stacked with clay and
strips of oak, their chinks and bases plastered up with
mud, which hardens like adobes. So hoes, rakes, axe-
helves, tubs, doors, dining-tables, bunks, and bedsteads
have been wrought by skill and industry from literally
nothing; for the rude materials were first to be "packed"
in from distant woods, to which we could have access
very seldom, under pass of the commanding officer and
a guard of rebel riflemen. Sometimes lines of eager
prisoners stand waiting for hours at the great gate, without obtaining the desired permission to go out for timber.

I must not forget our newspaper—not press-printed,
but written in minute and legible Roman letters by that
general genius; Captain May, who draws with pencil, as
with fiddle-bow, to excellent conceit. "The Old Flag"
is a popular sheet, the organ of American opinion at Camp
Ford. Its advertising columns show the thrift and progress of this loyal city in extreme Secessia. Doubtless,
if we felt ourselves located here for the duration of a
Trojan war, we should find means to build a press and
cast or cut out types, like Faust and Guttenberg. I venture to affirm that it would not surprise our rebel guards
if we built paper mills and steam-presses, and set up a
daily paper in our corral. They tell us now, with open
mouths, that our Yankee armies have "right smart 'o soldiers that kin git up sich tricks."

The *entours* of our camp—those free surroundings outside of stockades—consist of prairies, interspersed with

timbered hills.   The north gate of our prison yard, or
"corral," gives egress on an open plain, where sheep and
hogs are herded, where the deer and wild fox rove, and
cattle crop scant grasses.   On the east are woods and
cultivated lands.   The west is hilly, crowned with scrubby oaks and ash.   A rebel camp of cavalry and the huts
of conscripts hide behind those eminences.   Upon the
south a hill abruptly rises, with a streamlet at its base,
which flows within our southern stockade, and is called
"the spring."   The rebel commandant's headquarters—
two or three log-houses—look down upon our corral from
that hill.   A gate stands midway of our western stockade,
and is usually open, guarded by a sentry.   Just outside
this gate, the rebel guard-houses are situated, with some
cabins used as quarters for the guard.   One frame of logs
is called the "wolf-pen."   There offending Yankees are
confined on corn and water.   There, usually, some dozen
rebel conscripts, apprehended for desertion, are immured.
There, also, several citizens accused of "Union sympathies" await removal to the provost prison of Tyler, or
to Houston, where they can be tried for "treason" to
the "Southern Confederacy."   We Federals have an
unsuspected method of communicating with those "Union
men."   Our boys take turns in being late at roll-call, or
transgress some other rebel rule, and so are ordered "to
the guard-house."   This is our "police telegraph," and it
works admirably.

Our "spring" is a wonderful one.   It gushes out of
the clay-bank, cool and crystaline.   It is impregnated with
iron and sulphur, and the water is a perpetual tonic.   We
have several wooden reservoirs, to which the prisoners
resort for washing purposes.   The upper one contains our
drinking water.   This single stream supplies the wants of
near six thousand men, comprising prisoners and their

DEPARTMENT OF THE GULF.

guards. It threatened failure once, but Northern ingenuity sank the reservoirs and guarantied perennial supplies. Shrewd Captain Johnson, a notable mechanical and scientific genius, was our "Commissioner of Aqueducts." He trod the Sachem's decks, her bold commander, on the salt sea, but has proved himself as useful here in "fresh water" matters. To him we owe our earliest turning-lathe, and he inaugurated chair-making, which now supplies the camp with seats of every pattern—Gothic, rustic, cane-backed, willow-woven, grape-vine-wrought, and oaken-ribbed.

So "Yankees" lead the "march of improvement."

CHAPTER XXXVI.

A CELEBRATION.

I ARRIVED at Camp Ford about the middle of February, 1864; at the time a caravan of wagons— forty-five in number—filled with negro families, was passing the stockade, while its migrating owners, on horseback and in coaches, led their chattels into exile. I had encountered many other corteges and coffles on the road; for this Lone Star State has become a general refuge for rebels now, as in former days it was a refuge for malefactors of all descriptions. The corral, at this period, was not so densely populated as it afterwards became, and I soon grew familiar with its bounds and inhabitants.

The latter were as varied in character as they were motley in appearance. A hundred officers, who had abdicated all pretensions to rank, as they had worn out all insignio of it; a score of Kansas privates and Louisiana "citizens;" and a couple of venerable mules, the property of two gallant sea-captains; these constituted the population of Camp Ford Borough, as it was called in the local newspaper.

Does not a newspaper follow a Yankee march everywhere? So, of course, Camp Ford possessed its journal; though we boasted neither types nor printing-press; so, notably, we discussed our prison-affairs in editorial columns, and trumpeted the merits of our small wares in flaming advertisements.

Captain May, of the Twenty Third Connecticut regiment, who had been "gobbled" by rebels at his sick-quarters in Terrebonne; Captain May, whose musical skill brought to us "Sounds from Home" through the deftly-fingered chords of his violin; Captain May was our publisher, printer, and general advertising medium. For this accomplished captain acted as "admirable Crichton" in the entertainment-line. He could write a sensation-story, and illustrate it with his pencil; and he could print a mezzotinto in writing-fluid or imprint a newspaper with the steel-pen. So, betimes, we presented our Connecticut "confrère" with a fiddle; purchased notably from speculating guards for a hundred Confederate dollar-promises. So, moreover, we furnished paper-stock, to the bulk of a half quire, or less; and, on the score of literary antecedents, I was myself impressed as a contributor to the "Old Flag" columns.

Thus I became, very speedily, one of the leading citizens of our Federal "borough." My "real estate" entitled me to be classed among men of substance, though corn-bread diet lamentably failed to make me personally substantial. But it is sufficient that I became a householder, and, after inaugurating my "log-pen" by Sabbath-services at the door, settled down to the monotone experience of prison-life.

But "public men have public duties," we are told; and one of mine, presently, was to figure in that peculiarly American entertainment—an "order of exercises." The Twenty-second day of February drew near, and, as dutiful scions of a patriotic stock, we resolved to "celebrate" the birthday of our *Pater Patrie.* I need not dwell upon the momentous preliminaries to this great event. Are they not written and published in a fac-simile edition of the "Old Flag," whereof Captain May hath copyright? Let it suffice that I extract from that enlightened organ.

(From the " OLD FLAG" of March 1st, 1864.)

THE CELEBRATION.

"At about eleven o'clock, A. M., of the 22d of February, the buildings and squares about FIFTH AVENUE and 42d Street, were literally *blue* with the "Yanks" assembled preparatory to some remarks from LIEUT. COL. T. B. LEAKE and an original POEM, from LIEUT. COL. A. J. H. DUGANNE.

In the remarks made by LT. COL. LEAKE was exhibited and communicated through the entire assembly a flow of pure patriotism that was virtually a powerful appeal to all to imitate the glorious example shown in the life of Gen. GEORGE WASHINGTON ; to remain, in the hour of trial and darkness for our Good Cause, firm and true to the principles of our Government and to its administrators—placing faith in the moral power of the Union for final and complete success, till its restoration shall make the nation mightier than it ever was before.   It was no elaborate and prepared Oration, yet lacked nothing in interest or delivery from the fact of its being extempore.

"At the conclusion of this address, LT. COL. A. J. H. DUGANNE arose and delivered the following POEM:

WHO bids me sing?   What theme my soul dilates?—
A captive whispering to its captive mates!—
Can Glory's raptures thrill the fettered thralls
Whose flags are trophies now, on Treason's walls?
Can Valor's story nerve the shackled hands
Whose broken sword-blades rust in rebel sands—
Or lifted, murderous, threat with cruel strife
Our Nation's Union and our Freedom's life?
In vain my harp the charms of home would sing;
Quick-gathering tears from answering eyelids spring;
And all the heart's deep fountains, softly stirred,
O'erwhelm our manhood, at that one dear word:
HOME! where the Wife sits, numbering, day by day,
The long, long hours that steal her hopes away;
With low-drawn sigh, and voiceless prayer, to wait
The step that COMES NOT to her lonely gate!
Home! where the children, prattling War's acclaim,
Through mimic trumpets lisp their father's name—
But, wondering, pause, to note, with childish fears,
The eyes that watch them dimmed with sudden tears,
And, trembling, ask, of lips that must be dumb,
Why Mother weeps?—why Father will not come?

WASHINGTON.

Dear Home! sweet Home! how many a warm heart beats—
How many a lip the loved one's name repeats—
Where MAINE exults, on stormy Ocean's brim,
And HAMPSHIRE lifts to Heaven her mountain hymn;
Where MASSACHUSETTS sits, like matron free,
And fair RHODE ISLAND slumbers at her knee;
Where dwells CONNECTICUT, midst emerald vales,
And where MANHATTAN spreads her snowy sails,
And rolls her iron chariot-wheels, and shakes
Her golden garners o'er the Northern lakes!

God bless our Homes! from East through boundless West—
The hallowed shrines of all the heart loves best;
From blue OHIO to COLORADO's marge,
And over IOWA's prairies, green and large,
And where the winding ILLINOIS outflows,
Or INDIANA, with silvery harvest glows,
And fair ARKANSAS skirts the Indian land—
And where the Red Men's loyal wigwams stand—
There sleep our Homes, where tender hearts, like doves,
Brood o'er the memory of their absent loves!

Awake, my Harp! Thy song to Heaven aspires!
A Nation's memories climb thy sounding wires!
Awake, my Harp! and thrill with loftier sway:
A Nation's Father bends from Heaven this day;
From Heaven's high hills, where Freedom's angel waits,
Closest to God, within the eternal gates—
Where Freedom's martyrs, wing'd with crimson scars,
Gleam through the azure fields of endless stars!
From Heaven the HERO comes!—his awful mien
Troubled, yet calm, and sorrowing, but serene.
With trembling glance his kingly shade I mark
Break through the storm and cleave the midnight dark:
O'er ice-browed Andes leans his sworded hand—
His rushing footfall spurns Pacific's strand:
His helmet gleams o'er Alleghanian snows—
His lifted shield o'er hushed Atlantic glows;
His breast I see, beneath celestial wings—
And there—O! there—my bleeding Country clings:
Clings as a mother to her first-born son—
Her Hero-Child—her god-like WASHINGTON!

Land of the NORTH! where loud Niagara's roll
Voices to Heaven a free-born Nation's soul!
Land of the NORTH! where wild Atlantic waves
Baptize for Freedom's faith the souls of slaves!
From all thy plains, on all thy breezes borne,
How swells the exulting song this sacred morn!
Where Manhood's shout and Childhood's lisping sweet
The dear-loved name of WASHINGTON repeat.
By tranquil Hudson's sunlit waves they kneel,
Where Washington first turned the invader's steel;
On TRENTON's plain and MONMOUTH's field they pray,
Where Washington retrieved the eventful day;
And roll their hymns through Schuylkill's wintry gorge,
Where once arose HIS prayer—from VALLEY FORGE!

And thou, imperial WEST! whose sylvan tongue
Hymned unto God while Saturn yet was young;
From voiceful symphonies of waving woods,
And solemn calms of silent solitudes;
And low, soft melodies of breezes bland,
And rolling harmonies of rivers grand:
Thou Nurse of Empires! at whose fostering heart
All nations drink, and all have equal part;—
Enthroned on harvests—girt by garners wide—
Thy wealth our wonder, and thy power our pride!
Majestic WEST! thy millions kneel, this hour,
To praise the Eternal for their Freedom's dower:
By Mississippi's shores their anthem flows,
And where Missouri laps her mountain snows;
And where the Ohio, nursed by crystal rills,
Leaps to thine arms from Pennsylvanian hills;
There shalt thou kneel, O! mightiest WEST, and tell
Where Washington survived and Braddock fell—
When the young hero jarred, with mailed hand,
The mystic gates that sealed our sunset land!

Land of the SOUTH! whose glorious life distils
Balm from thy vales and odors from thy hills!
Thy brow all sunshine, and thy heart all fire,
Thy breath a vintage, and thy voice a lyre;
Land, where the air with wildering fragrance swoons,
And all the woodlands thrill with golden runes;

Land, where the Morn with nectar'd kisses woos,
And where the soft Night weeps ambrosial dews'
O, queenly Southland! crowned and gemmed with flowers;
Thy silken dials, that mark the year's sweet hours;
Lilies, whose silvery moons no tempest mars,
Roses like suns, and violets like the stars!
Thy throne the summer, and thy realm the soul,
Whose charmed senses own thy soft control:
All-beauteous SOUTH! thy heart must share and claim
Our Father's kindred and our Hero's fame!
Thy myrtle blooms his radiant brows to twine—
His name, his heritage, his birthplace—thine!
We yield thee this, bright Mistress of the Sun!—
Thy bosoming flowers first cradled WASHINGTON!

VIRGINIA! from whose breast the milk outran,
That nursed with godlike strength the immortal man;
Whose sacred groves enshrine the hero's clay,
Where wondering pilgrims pause and patriots pray:
Virginia! underneath whose trampling heel
Sceptres lie crushed, and crownless tyrants kneel;
From thee, from thine, he drank his impulse brave;
For thee, for ALL, this broad, free land he gave!
From thy blue hills his soaring sense he caught:
They share his fame—but all the world his thought!
Thy gates the portals whence his soul outspeeds—
But all the earth a temple for his deeds!
Thy hero-chiefs the priesthood of his shrine,
That all mankind might learn his faith divine:
The faith that shatters thrones and sunders chains,
And floods with Freedom's tide the bondman's veins,
And shapes from freemen's souls the Almighty's fanes!

O, proud Virginia! loftiest was thy trust—
His grand example, and his peaceful dust.
Thou wert our Mecca, thou our Delphic ground,
Where kneeling seers were awed by voice profound.
Thee clustering round, uptowered the shielding States,
And young Republics kept thy sunset gates!
From Northern mountains and from Southern leas,
From orient headlands and from westering seas,

Each gladsome breeze new freights of blessings won,
For OLD VIRGINIA—Nurse of WASHINGTON!

And o'er thy hills it stoops, O, perjured land!
Through Vernon's shades, and by Potomac's strand;
And o'er thy vales it broods—that form of might,
Parting the Storm, and towering through the Night!
That awful Presence, moving from above;
Grief on its brow, but in its glances—Love!
From Heaven it comes—through Vernon's gloom descends,
And where my mournful Country kneels, it bends;
And softly murmurs—sheltering her head—
"What ails thee, Mother? Are thy children dead?"
She hears his voice, and wakes from swooning trance,
Her ebbing life-tides swayed beneath his glance.
That mailed breast, that soaring helm she sees,
And the strong hand that lifts her from her knees.
And now she speaks, whilst all my fluttering breath
Waits for her voice, but hears no word she saith;
For muttering winds upswell, and thunders roll,
And the wild tempest frights my listening soul:
I only hear—around Mount Vernon's dells—
The roar of cannon and the crash of shells;
I only hear—upon Virginia's air—
The drum's wild rattle and the trumpet's blare;
While charging armies shake the shuddering meads,
And the hills reel with mingling men and steeds,
And the wide land with mortal wound outbleeds!
I only hear the shout, the curse, the groan;
I only hear a low, sad, shivering moan,
Where sinks my Country's heart, where droops her head,
And the great Voice demands, in whisper dread,
"What ails thee, Mother? Are thy children dead?"

Dead? worse than dead!   The child is worse than dead
Who scorns the fount where first his fondness fed!
O, worse than dead! whose heart, untouched with ruth,
That mother hates who watched his tenderest youth!
Dead! worse than dead! the impious and unblest,
Who tears the mantle from his mother's breast—
Who spurns the matron crown that mother wore,
And leaves her sorrowing for the sons she bore!

And whence the gain ?   What heritage survives
O'er wasted treasures and o'er squandered lives ?
Are Hatred's heirlooms, hurled from sire to son,
More dear than Loves, that linked all hearts as one ?
Can sundered hearthstones gleam with ruddier blaze
Than the old fireside of our fathers' days ?
Can alien halls the old, old HOME replace,
Or alien births our kindred's graves efface ?
In vain Rebellion strives !   Would Balaam curse ?
His trembling lips God's blessings still rehearse !
Would Korah rule ?   The earth drinks Korah's cries,
And plagues descend where Israel's rebels rise.
Sanballat's seed may drop from Judah's stem,
But Israel dwells where dwells Jerusalem !
Samaria's shrines may rise on rival sod,
But Mount Moriah is still the Mount of God !

O, WASHINGTON ! thou drewest our faith from Heaven !
By Heaven, through thee, our freedom's life was given;
Thy goal our Union, and our homes thy gift,
To thee, this day, our Nation's Soul we lift !
Thy God is ours !—on HIM our hopes we cast:
We trust the Future, as we read the Past !
While Truth is steadfast, and while Time is just,
Thy path we tread, and in thy faith we trust !
Though man be weak, we know that God is strong,
And come what may, the Right shall rule the Wrong !
For ceaseless still, o'er traitors quick or dead,
Our Nation's feet their destined course must tread;
And where the ARK OF FREEDOM heads our march,
God's Pillar leads, and Angel wings o'erarch !

CHAPTER XXXVII.

BLOODHOUNDS.

ABOUT the "ides of March" exciting rumors came to us from the Red River. We became aware that General Banks, with a new and powerful army, had advanced from the Mississippi, captured Fort De Russey, occupied Alexandria, and was marching up on the Texas borders. How our pulses beat wildly once more! how we talked of liberty by day, and dreamed of it by night! How some of our gallant fellows resolved that they would strike for it; or, at least, endeavor to strike some path that might lead to it!

There had been much "underground" work proceeding within our stockade lines during a month past. We had speculated—or, at least, numbers had—upon attempting a stampede from the prison corral, through a tunnel, and thence dispersing to the woods and swamps. The project was hazardous; for, though an escape from the yard might be comparatively simple, there was an "undiscovered country" outside of our camp which threatened many an obstacle between us and deliverance. But some among the leaders had been prisoners sixteen months, without a word from "home" to tell them whether their dear ones were alive or dead. Others had been so often disappointed in the hope of an exchange that any risk seemed preferable to awaiting tardy action by our government.

So, big with secret preparation, weeks had passed. Alternate gangs, in regular reliefs, were digging in the tunnel. Ground had first been broken in a large "shebang," or log-house, occupied by stalwart Western officers, who rejoiced under the *soubriquet* of "Hawkeye Mess." The shaft was sunk some eight feet deep, and it was proposed to tunnel out below the northern stockade to a small enclosure, just beyond the line of sentinels, where we had buried poor Lieutenant Kimball, the quartermaster, in the shadow of two lofty trees. Our work went on incessantly, and we disposed of all the excavated earth by dragging it in a box to the shaft-opening, thence transporting it in water-buckets to the different cabins, and depositing it in fire-places, to *raise the hearths*. This process awakened no suspicion, and the work proceeded from day to day.

There were some, however, who had little faith in "underground railroads" or a general stampede. Lieut. Col. Rose, and several other officers, determined upon attempting their enlargement in small squads. The scheme was confined to but few beyond those actually contemplating escape. I did not feel great confidence in the successful *finale* of this undertaking, but accorded it my sympathy and help, of course. An old box coat, a hundred dollars, and some odd ends of disguise were my own contributions to the stock of preparations. Six officers were in the party, but this number grew to fifteen before the "break" was made.

Our "band" and "singing club" were wont to practice in my cabin, which was a more pretentious edifice than most of our "shebangs," built as it had been by log-raising "experts," and by "days' work" (as carpenters say) for cash, in Confederate currency. Here, before a fire of hickory logs, and with a dip candle or grease lamp upon my table, covered by a Mexican blanket, the sons of Massachusetts and Connecticut, with "*bassi*" and "*tenori*" from the Great West, would meet in harmony, with a vio-

lin, two banjos and a triangle; and here, "soon as the
evening shades prevailed," the rafters rang with "Glory
Hallelujah," "Massa's Runn'd Away," and " Rally Round
the Flag, Boys!" rendered in such vocal thunder as no
rebel throats might ever master. Meanwhile, recumbent
in my hammock, stretched between two logs, I smoked
my calumet and mused on Northern friends and fortunes.

This night, however, calls the "band" to other quarters. It has been raining, and thick clouds are lowering
still. It is a night for enterprise, and the word comes
that our comrades have concluded that their time is "now
or never." So, as the evening darkens, we steal, one by
one, to a "shebang" hard by our southern stockade, where
the "break" is to be made. Our would-be fugitives must
creep across the spring, or brook-bed, thence crawl up
some thirty feet to the stockade, and then. by main
strength, lift a sixteen-foot post out of its socket, and so
separate it from a contiguous one as to create a gap suffi-
ciently wide to give a human body passage through it.
All the while a line of rebel sentries guards the outside
of this stockade. The tread of each man, as he walks,
the ringing of his piece, strike momently upon our ears.
A single false move on the part of one among the escaping
prisoners-may jeopardize the lives of all. Should a suspicion of the plot be entertained, the guards may all be
watching. They might peer through all the interstices
and detect a moving body even in the shadow. If the
dirt crumble noisily, if the uplifted post fall or strike
against another, if the sudden width of space be observed
by eyes accustomed to all "signs of woodcraft," woe be
to our venturous comrades! Half-a-score of rifles may
give tongue at once. Nay, we might have a volley fired
at random into our midst.

But these Yankee boys have made up their minds to

"take the chances." One after another they emerge from their respective cabins and rendezvous in the rear of Col. Leake's "shebang," which is the nearest to the southern stockade. Inside of this hut our "band" and lusty singers have already collected. They tune their instruments and voices. They strike preliminary notes. At length they burst out, in a jubilant African chorus:

"Ole massa's runn'd—aha!
De darkeys stay—oho!
It mus' be now dat de kingdom am a comin',
An' de year of Jubilo!"

The rebel guards, not forty feet away, tramping their beats in mud and darkness outside of the stockade, hear this unusual din from Col. Leake's "shebang," generally a quiet one. They peep between the stockade posts and discern nothing—remark nothing in the wet corral out of doors. But presently the music—fiddle, banjos, triangle, voices, all combined in an orchestral "norther"—sweeps across the brook gully with tenfold vehemence. The Yankees are on a musical spree, "reckons" the Texan "Johnny," as he listens, on his gloomy post, to the really-melodious execution of our vocalists. Presently he "orders arms," and gets his ear in closer contact with the stockade, wishing, perhaps, that he were in that Yankee cabin, listening to good music by its blazing hearth, instead of being an "outsider" waiting for the "first relief," and shivering beneath his ragged blanket.

Very soon, our "Johnny," hearkening to the Yankee banjos, forgets about stockades and prisoners. Quite unconscious of a trick, he calls out—"Give us Dixie, Yanks!"—and presently that "patriotic" melody regales him. "Johnny" is enraptured. "Johnny" joins in the refrain—

> " O we all will sing together—
> Dixie's land !
> In Dixie's land I take my stand,
> To live and die in Dixie !"

Meantime, covertly stooping through the gloom, a Yankee form glides from behind our musical "shebang." It is Col. Rose, doubling his six-foot length, as he crosses the spring and crawls on hands and knees to the stockade. He carries a bag of flour and sugar, mixed and burned in pellets, with some twists of dried beef and hard tack, as provisions for the road; a blanket and a pair of socks as extra clothing. Following him, creep Captain Adams and Engineer Mars, and, one by one, a dozen other aspirants for liberty, each with his little bundle and big stick—time-honored helps to fugitives in Dixie's land. They gain the stockade, and lie down, in shadowy silence, at its base, to listen for the sentry's tramp.

But rebel "Johnny," with his ear inclined, still listens at a gap some twelve feet distant. Meantime, a brace of stalwart "sympathizers" with our fugitive boys have lifted up a post, and, leaving one end partly in its socket, bend the tall log inward, leaving room for egress. Round the post a cord is fastened, with a loop outside. Col. Rose peers through the aperture, and takes one step past the post. Just then a loud burst of the vocalists, a choral swell upon " Dixie," rises from our "shebang." The long colonel's figure disappears; another glides behind him; one by one, our fugitives dart out and lose themselves in murkiness. The last one is to pull the cord, and thus draw back the post into its socket. But he forgets, or fears to linger, and flees outward, after his comrades.

"Huzza!" we almost shout, mentally, without a tremor of the lips. "And now for a rousing chorus! Now for 'John Brown' and 'Rally round the Flag, boys!'"

"Have they escaped?" "Did all get out?" The eager questions pass from lip to lip. Our younger captives wish that they had seized this chance. Old prisoners wag their beards and smoke. Croakers prophesy misfortune.

Two hours wear on, and taps have sounded. It is dark and cloudy yet. Our music is dispersed. We hear the rebel call for "second relief" to turn out. Presently a heavy shower descends. We think of our poor comrades drenched and wandering.

"Happily," one says, "the rain will make pursuit more difficult."

"Should there be dogs—"

Ah, dogs! the negro-dogs! the bloodhounds! the man-hunters!

"Oh, there is no danger in that quarter!" cries a young lieutenant. "Colonel Allen says he would never set a dog on a white man's trail."

"And I heard him say," says another officer, "that a prisoner's right was to escape if he could, and he should only use civilized means to recapture him."

"That speaks well for Allen, if he is a rebel," asserts another speaker. "But you never can depend on the word of a traitor, gentleman! I shouldn't be surprised to hear the hounds out to-morrow, ·when the rebs discover this stampede."

"What's that?" suddenly asks a western man, pricking up his ears, as the tramp of men came to our ears, through the door of the cabin which was wide open.

"Only the second relief going its rounds," was the answer.

But at this moment a sound of some wind-instrument arose on the night air.

"That's a cavalry bugle!" exclaims a young infantry

lieutenant. "Wouldn't I like to see Grierson dashing down on the rebels here !"

"Cavalry bugle !" cries an old dragoon. " It's more like a cow-horn ! What sort of a call is that, I'd like to know ?"

"I'll tell you what it means," responded a Massachusetts captain, captured at Galveston, who loved the rebels as Satan is popularly said to love holy water. " Cow-horn or bugle, it means that old Allen is a cursed liar, and that he's going to set the dogs on our boys—that's what it means !"

We started up directly, for the truth of this observation flashed upon us. The horn continued to sound, shrill and loud, and presently the deep baying of dogs began to answer it. We looked out into the rainy darkness, and could see lights moving to and fro on the hill, at rebel head-quarters.

" They've got track of the stampede," says our Massachusetts man. " See the pine-knots dancing on the hill ! That's young Allen and the officer of the day, I'll bet a shad ! They're mounting horses and calling the dogs, I tell you."

And to this conclusion we all arrived, without contradiction; for a jargon of oaths and exclamations sounded on the hill, and at the guard-house gate; while the horn was wound incessantly, and dogs barked furiously. In a few moments, we could see, by the glare of pine-knots outside the stockade, a number of mounted men riding down the road, followed by a pack of hounds. We began to fear that it was all over with our fugitive comrades.

That night was an anxious one to many in the corral. Rain poured down, at intervals, in torrents; the thunder rolled; the lightning flashed so vividly, and with such rapidity, that it seemed like an unbroken cannonade. I lay awake, in my hammock, thinking of the dreary night, as I listened to dashing floods upon my cabin roof.

At roll-call, next morning, Lieutenant Ross, a rebel officer, whose heart was more in his vine-yards and grape-vines than in politics or camps, read off the list of pri-soners. Whenever the name of an "absconded" one was reached, some wag would shout out "furloughed," or " on leave," while, as the number swelled, this poor lieute-nant's eyes grew larger with astonishment. We thought the rebel commandant's shrewd son, Lieutenant Allen, had departed with the hounds, but he appeared before roll-call was over, and began to check the absentees. I can recall his look of ludicrous dismay when fifteen offi-cers were reported "missing." "Fifteen—!" He closed his comments with a Southern oath, and then, like a true " Christian gentleman," sprang on his horse and rode away for a new pack of bloodhounds.

We learned soon that our boys had a start of nearly thirteen hours. The bush had been beaten with men and dogs; but the pack was put speedily at fault, it appeared, by the rain, and no traces of the runaways had been found. We gathered news by scraps from friendly guards or growling sentinels. It seemed that the stampede was discovered scarcely fifteen minutes after it took place. The new relief had passed, the sergeant carrying a lan-tern, and its light, reflecting on the stockade, revealed the post displaced, with a rope hanging from it. The be-wildered sentry could explain nothing; his muddy brains were still full of "Dixie," which our courteous Yankee band had played for him; so "Johnny" was "toted" to the guard-house, there to answer for his lack of vigilance.

But now the rain had ceased; the clouds disappeared; a Southern sun rode high. We heard the tramp of horses. Lieutenant Allen and another rebel officer, and half-a-dozen mounted privates, armed with guns and pistols, rode off swiftly from headquarters. In advance gallopped "Chilicothe."

"Chilicothe" was an "expert" among rebel scouts and forest-men. It was his boast that he could "out-Indian Indians." Never was a truer shot, a tougher campaigner, a more unerring hunter either of beast or man. Little cared "Chilicothe" whether dogs led or followed. His own infallible craft, half skill, half instinct, guided him by sun or stars. On him, this prairie-scout and wood-land-spy, devolved the task of tracking our poor Yankee officers. White man on white man's trail, with a new pack of staunch sleuth-hounds, from Tyler, made up a pleasant hunt for rebel officers. We saw them set off at a canter, and awaited anxiously that day's developments.

Night came again, and with its shadows came some three or four poor Yankee officers, recaptured, fatigued and leg-weary. Col. Rose was one of them, and Lieut. Lyons, of my regiment, whose rosy face bore sundry weather-marks. They had been floundering all the night in swamps; had gained a score of miles, and lain down for a nap, to be awakened by the voice of "Chilicothe" calling his hounds. Next day, another batch of runaways arrived; on the third, more were captured; till, at length, thirteen rejoined their bantering messes. All had been run down by "Chilicothe" and the dogs. All were in woful plight; their scanty clothing shredded off by con-tact with the thickets; their feet and hands sore and wounded; their skin scratched in a hundred places. They had lost their route; had doubled on their trail; had va-gabonded from a score to sixty miles; and yet not one had crossed the Sabine, which was scarcely one day's march from camp. So much for the *stampede*.

Yet two of the fifteen escaped, in spite of dogs and

"Chilicothe." They lost their clothing, food, and even their canteens; but, with dogged obstinacy, kept the swamps, emerging only in the night, to glean a corn-field. Thus, for days and nights, and weeks, they plodded forward, till the Louisiana line was reached, and Red River. We heard from them, at last, through prisoners taken at the fatal fight of Mansfield. They had gained the Union lines, on Red River, some days before the battle, and were forwarded to New Orleans in safety. Afterwards we heard the story of this bloodhound chase from many lips. Lieut. Collins, a fine western officer, was nearly murdered by them. He had stopped to rest, when the deep howl of dogs apprised him of pursuit. Ere he could make away, two rebels rode upon him. A brace of six-shooters were levelled at his breast, and the accustomed threat—with a huge oath—of shooting on the spot, was flung at him.

"I am unarmed, and hardly strong enough to stand," said Collins.

Another oath was hurled at him. "We'll give the dogs a taste of your infernal Yankee blood. St-boy! smell of him, boy! St-boy! Seize him—shake the Yank! Stuboy!"

The furious hounds, thus encouraged, sprang at Lieut. Collins. Their glittering teeth, with white foam gathered on the fiery gums, met in his ragged uniform. He felt the tearing of his garments, and expected momently to bleed; when the rebels, with malicious laughter called off their hounds.

"You see, Yank! they'd as soon eat Yank as nigger! If we had old Kangaroo Abe out yer they'd got him, shore, hide, har, and tallow! Now, jes' tote yer carcass, Yank, or we'll shoot yer on sight, by ——!"

So marched Lieut. Collins back, thirty miles, at horsetail, with his weary pace accelerated by curses. And, to tell the truth, our officers themselves "swore terribly" when their reminiscences were mixed with bloodhounds.

To fully realize and appreciate these "dogs of war," one ought to be hunted and fugitive, like Lieut. Collins and his compatriots. While sinking with fatigue, spent with privation, hopeless of escape, to hear the wolf-like yelp and long hyena-howl of these trained men-hunters, is something to experience, even for "used-up" Sir Charles Coldstream. I warrant it as a "new sensation" for the most languid disbeliever in emotions. Some hounds will track a human being, day and night, for weeks, and follow his scent, especially if it be a negro, hundreds of miles through swamps and woods, and over water-courses. They run at times, like game-dogs, smelling the ground, at intervals making deer-leaps, springing up to touch the overhanging leaves and branches with their noses. They double and dart round in circles, cross a stream, and then, with a few sniffs of the air, rush up or down the bank to find their broken scent again.

The quickness of their smell is quite as wonderful as its tenacity. When a negro, or a white man, is to be pursued, the dogs are simply taken to the trail and made to nose it. On the night of the stampede, a pack, as we discovered, was called immediately, and placed upon officers' tracks, just outside of the gap by which they had passed through the stockade. This pack of hounds was not a good one. Though the breed was fair, the dogs had been permitted to run after deer and foxes. Consequently, though they opened on the human trail, their scent was soon diverted by the tracks of animals in the miry woods and fields. This was the reason the nocturnal hunt had been unsuccessful. In the morning, a fresh pack of real man-dogs was procured from Tyler, and these tracked

Collins and the Bloodhounds

Punishment of Capt. Reed

our officers, even after eight or ten hours' rain had intervened.   The real hounds are never allowed to hunt down
any game inferior to man.   When not in use, they are
chained up and kept on starving rations.   They grow
fierce as tigers, with forced abstinence, and their scent
becomes acute in the extreme.   Woe to the hunted man
if hunger-maddened hounds overtake him, in swamps or
timber, while the mounted pursuers are too far behind to
call them off or moderate their savage eagerness.   Woe
be to a fugitive if the sleuth-dogs once taste his blood!

CHAPTER XXXVIII.

RED RIVER ADVICES.

SHORTLY after the abortive attempt at a "stampede" chronicled in my last chapter, Lt.-Col. Leake received sudden orders to march, with his officers and men, under guard, to Shreveport, there to be forwarded for "exchange" to the Federal lines near Alexandria. Though parting from the gallant Western men with regret, we rejoiced in their prospect of speedy enlargement, and hoped that our own would soon follow. Meantime, the news which we received almost daily, in reference to affairs on the Red River, served to elevate our spirits wonderfully.

Mr. Cushing, of the "Houston Telegraph," had been as good as his word in extending many acceptable courtesies to our officers. To Captain Crocker and myself he sent his paper regularly, and its news, although colored, of course, by rebel sympathies, was usually very reliable. I was indebted, subsequently, likewise, to this editorial friend, for a welcome gift of a real treasure to prisoners— a half-ream of good writing-paper, which not only replenished my own exhausted stock, but served to supply my comrades with a medium for conveying their thoughts to the beloved ones at home. I shall pleasantly recall the kindness of Mr. Cushing, in this and other disinterested attentions toward a stranger and prisoner, as a guaranty that his heart is right, whatever may be the errors of his head upon the questions which make up our conflict of opinion. The "amenities of literature" were happily illustrated to me, through such intercourse as it was my fortune to have with Mr. Cushing and other friendly spirits in Texas.

With my accession of writing materials, I found myself enabled to transcribe various detached jottings and journalizings, as well as to take down the verbal relations of fellow-prisoners, concerning many interesting events and experiences, which the limits of this book will not permit me to include in its pages. Few among the multitude of incidents connected with our war will ever be told veraciously in official documents. Reports by commandants of posts, or colonels in command, are in general more elaborate than correct, and yet of such is history made. No mortal eye can trace the fortunes of a single battle-hour in all their shifts and changes; no single record of a conflict, though it be endorsed by the commander-in-chief, and vouched for by an army corps of generals, can ever comprehend the fight in its details; the sudden dash, the quick recoil, the giving and disputing ground, the fierce melée, the isolated grapple, the death-shot, the last agony; with all their infinite phases of wild excitement, iron hardihood, cool forecast, and deliberate purpose, veiled and canopied with a lurid haze of smoke and dust and blood; now dense as thunder clouds, now torn and rifted by the dreadful shock of cannonry. We may believe no bulletin reports a tithe of what one dying soldier beholds with closing eyes, within the compass of his regimental line. It is well, perhaps, that all this terrible minutiæ of a human battle should be left to the imagination to depicture, and that every fighter should be so involved and swallowed up in the great action of the strife as to remain quite noteless of all scenes or acts beyond his individual part in the wild drama. Nevertheless, when, here and there, apart from the red-tape-bound formula of war-office reports, we read or listen to some personal story of a soldier's battle-life, some episode of peril or prowess in the fiery heat of conflict, we are fain to linger over the unstudied sentences, and wish that history were wrought from such materials.

So, when the simple reminiscences of soldiers found expression in as simple words, and the representatives of many a fight exchanged opinions around our log-house hearths, I often gleaned a better knowledge of the battle or campaign than I could gain from all the papers of the War Department. Here, in the rapid crayon-dashes of a personal story, I realized groups of cannoniers, all grim with powder, standing round their gun, and charged upon by rebel horse; and presently a double-quick step behind them, and a blaze of musketry from the supporting infantry column, driving back the grey-coats in disorder. There, sketched rudely on our clay-floor, with a pointed stick, I traced the flanks and centre of a line of battle, with the enemy's direction of attack and the position of our own artillery and reserves. Meantime, the observations, "We were here," and "Thus we moved," and "Here the rebels showed themselves," with quick rejoinders and additions by a score of mutual actors on the field, were worth, to one who would compare and "inwardly digest," much more than all the multiplex reports of aids or adjutants on regulation-paper.

Meantime, I could study character at my leisure; and there is a variety of it to be found among prisoners, at all times. The "wise and simple" are closely proximate in such quarters as ours were. Nor were my many chats with enlisted men, and conversations with officers, productive only of time-killing. I gleaned food for after-speculation in much of my daily intercourse, and recognized, in the attrition of mind, devoid of conventional lubrication, a healthful stimulus to my own mental faculties.

Chess-playing amused, labor occupied, but social converse was, after all, our chief enjoyment. There were many strong intellects among my comrades, with whom it became interesting to discuss both men and books. Among the "oldest inhabitants," of Camp Ford, were Col. Leake, whose professional schooling and quick wit made him sound in argument and ready at repartee; Mr. Finley Anderson, a correspondent of the New York Herald, who was exchanged before my arrival at the corral, and who subsequently, I think, became attached to Gen. Hancock's staff; Lieut. Louis W. Stevenson, of the "Ironsides," who was wounded at Brashear City, and whom I had left at the hospital in New Iberia; Captain Torrey, of the 20th Iowa regiment, Col. Leake's command; and many other choice spirits, whose discourse wiled prison-life of much of its irksomeness.

Captain Torrey, with his regimental brother, Captain Coulter, were captured at Aransas Bay, on the Texan coast, in December, 1863. He had reached Texas with the expedition that landed at Brazos Santiago and Point Isabel, taking Brownsville, on the Rio Grande, soon afterwards. A force of land-troops, disembarking at Mustang Island, and Corpus Christi inlet, marched twenty miles to Aransas Bay, capturing there about one hundred prisoners and three pieces of artillery. Reinforcements following, an expedition was marched the entire length of St. Joseph's and Matagorda Islands, which lie along the Texan main-land. These advances accomplished the seizure of Fort Esperanza, whose garrison succeeded in a timely evacuation of the place. Our troops held Matagorda Peninsula, and the town of Indianola, during several weeks, and occupied the town of Lavacca repeatedly.

During this campaign of winter and spring, inconsidera-
ble damage was done to the enemy, and many casualties
occurred among the Federals.   A worthy and intelligent
sergeant of my regiment, accompanying Col. Kempsey,
the former chaplain of our "Ironsides," who had obtained
command of a negro-battalion, was drowned in one of the
bayous, while swimming his horse.   Poor Vassar was an
earnest, loyal soldier, and had earned a better fate.   It
was during this period of coast occupation by our forces,
that Captains Torrey and Coulter were made prisoners,
together with three privates and some citizens, upon the
schooner Gen. Ransom, taken near Lamar, in December.
In January, a Federal corporal and three privates were
surprised on the prairie, near Lavacca, while they were
hunting beef; and other squads of our soldiers were captured while "prospecting" for fuel upon the shores of
Aransas Bay.   Delays and disappointments continually
harrassed our forces.   Sometimes, for days, no rations
were provided for the men, owing to insufficiency of
quartermaster's supplies; and, during weeks, the poor
fellows shivered and froze in their bleak camps, on barren
stretches of sand, without a stick of wood within miles of
them.   The whole account of Federal operations on the
Texan coast may be summed up by a large expense of
fleets and armies, life and money, in holding a useless
tract of sea-shore, during five or six months; balanced by
a few hundred bales of cotton seized at Brownsville.   The
Rio Grande campaign, like its "supporting" campaign on
Red River, was a lamentable waste of time and treasure.
Generals and commanders have been superseded and disgraced for much less disreputable failures.

   We have now to speak of the Red River campaign,
whose disastrous results speedily became felt at Camp
Ford.   Col. Leake and his expectant comrades had been

gone from us scarcely a week, when, instead of pleasing advices concerning their "exchange," a very different sort of news arrived to dishearten us. We learned of the battle of Mansfield. Dispatches, from Kirby Smith to Col. Allen, our rebel post-commandant, notified him to prepare for the reception of three thousand Federal prisoners. We were indignant at this outrage on our good sense. We spurned the report as a "weak invention of the enemy." But it was too true. Corroborations of a woful repulse of Gen. Banks's grand army of invasion came thickly and fast. Conviction forced itself upon us; and bodily proof arrived, soon enough, in the shape of a first instalment of 1186 Federals, captured at Mansfield, on the 8th of April, 1864.

It is no marvel, at the opening of the year 1864, that Gen. Banks, Commander-in-chief of the Department of the Gulf, should desire to twine some Augustan laurels over the Cæsar-like baldness of his administration, thus far. It is true, he had the credit of reducing the rebel strong-hold of Port Hudson; and it may be that his approaches, assaults, minings, and forlorn hopes, necessitated the surrender of that place, after the suggestive example of Vicksburg, some days previous. But, with the exception of Port Hudson conquest, and the Teche raid, our General's military triumphs had not been brilliant ones. The swoop of Texan legions on Opelousas railroad lines, and their menace of the Crescent City itself, were only opening moves of an intricate chess-game which has been played on the Trans-Mississippi board, since midsummer of 1863. Gen. Tom Green and his tattered regiments, repulsed at Donaldsonville, which Green attacked just after the capture of Brashear City, (and where his subordinate, Lt. Col. Phillips, lost his life and my

sword), posted their batteries on Mississippi curves, and
waged destructive ambush-war upon river-boats for many
a month thereafter. Meantime, rēoccupying the rail-road
to Berwick Bay, which the rebels had evacuated after a
month's possession, Maj. Gen. Banks organized and dispatched that famous expedition, of gunboats and transports, which, under Gens. Franklin and Weitzel, were
driven back so ingloriously from a mud-fort at Sabine
Pass. Subsequently transpired the coast-wise operations,
which nibbled at the edges of Texan shores, till they
served to stimulate the organization of a large defensive
force through all the State. Then took place sundry
bloodless explorations into Calcasieu morasses, begetting
much astonishment among vagrant "Cagians," but little
result otherwise. Finally loomed up—"*graviter commo-
dus*—" the Red River Expedition of 1864.

This expedition was, without doubt, well-planned, and
effectually preceded by organization and preparation. The
mortar-fleet and gun-boats of Com. Porter were to co-
operate with the army. Numerous transports carried the
troops. Abundant commissary stores and munitions were
provided. Veteran regiments, with officers of tried skill
and courage, made up a majority of the forces. What
was lacking for success? Nothing—but a Chief

For it is unhappily the fact that Gen. Banks, however
capable as a financial or civil executive, has too little of
that iron in his nature which is requisite for a great military leader. Gen. Banks is not a good Commander-in-
chief. He will take care of his army's subsistence, and
he is equal to an intelligent comprehension of warfare;
but he is not a Dictator, as every General charged with
the responsibility of a Department or a Campaign ought
to be. He cherishes the *suaviter in modo* to the neglect
of the *fortiter in re*. Hence, where the General should be

supreme, we find the staff omnipotent; where the Commander should ordain, we find the subordinates overruling. I need not dilate upon a matter that is patent to the army of the Gulf; but I might fill chapters with testimony which shows that our reverses and disasters in Louisiana have been the result of wrong-headed and arrogant intermeddling of staff-officers and other inferiors, who should have been kept in their position, under curb-reins, and, if necessary, under the whip of a Commander's discipline.

But the Red River Expedition moves, and its first steps are victorious ones. The rebels retire before its fleets and forces. Fort De Russy, with an iron-clad water-battery, surrenders, after a brief resistance, yielding garrison and guns. Alexandria is speedily occupied. Red River is illumined by Stars and Stripes. Yankee craft crowd its waters, from the Atchafalaya to the Mississippi mouths. Amid all this blazonry of Federal success, Gen. Banks arrives from his seat of Government, and prepares for an advance on Shreveport, by land and water.

It is a brave sight, this march of our grand army, on fine roads, and by a broad river, past the beautiful city of Alexandria, which crowns her lofty water-front with rich villas—the homes of luxurious planters. Gen. Franklin arrives, preceding his army-corps, all reported in good health and spirits. Gen. Smith's troops defile through Alexandria streets. Gun-boats and transports, propelled by steam and canvass, move gallantly under the bluffs. Cane River is crossed by a pontoon bridge. Natchitoches is occupied by our forces, under Gen. Lee. The rebels burn their cotton-bales, and the smoke thereof becomes a beacon for Federal advance. Gen. Banks's progress up the Red River, escorted by gun-boats and transports—saluted by cannon-discharges—is like that of a conqueror.

Porter precedes him, occupying Grand Ecore. Porter selects a van-guard of gun-boats, and pushes up the river toward Shreveport. On the third day, he reaches Spring-field Landing, but finds that the rebels have sunk a large steamer across the channel. Porter is stopped, but he sets vigorously at work to remove the obstructions, and is about succeeding, when a courier from Gen. Banks reaches him. He hears "unpleasant and most unexpected news." Our "army has met with a reverse." In fact, the battle of Mansfield has been fought, and Gen. Banks, defeated, is falling back to Pleasant Hill. Let us trace the BATTLE OF MANSFIELD.

Picture a nearly triangular space, broken by woods, fences, and fields; its base a long fence, running from south-east to north-west; its lower side traced by a line extending westerly to a line of woods that forms the left rect-angle, as you approach the area, by a road—the Mansfield highway—which intersects that area. Fancy your march advancing from the south, through a narrow defile of the woods, and suddenly entering on the com-paratively open triangular area I have described. This was the manner and route of march of our cavalry sent forward by Gen. Banks to occupy the enemy, who were understood to be in force on the road near Mansfield, but who, it was supposed, would not make a stand at that place. The cavalry rode on, through the woods, until they debouched into the open space, called Moss's Planta-tion. They left their supply wagons halted, in a long line, on the narrow woodland road, while they galloped on and engaged in desultory skirmishing with Texan horse.

Fancy, now, the advance of our Federal infantry, with some artillery, arriving upon Moss's fields, and engaging with the enemy, who are massing between the plantation and Mansfield. The left of our line of battle rested upon woods, west of the Mansfield road. There Col. Dudley's cavalry brigade had been skirmishing with rebel horse. There was the 23d Wisconsin infantry, supported by a section of Nims's Battery. On their right stood the 57th Indiana regiment, backed by another section of Nims's guns. Next to the Indiana men were stationed the 77th Illinois veterans, not in line, but at an obtuse angle, retiring toward the right. The 48th Ohioans came next; at their right, the 19th Kentuckians, and next to these the 83d Ohio volunteers, flanked by a cavalry force under Col. Lucas. This was the first line of battle, just within an open piece of wood-land; from its advanced left, on the Mansfield road to its receding right, extending southeasterly. Before it, at a distance of a hundred yards, was a high fence, and beyond this fence, at about the same distance, rebel lines were forming. Behind our line of battle, on rising ground, were clear fields, in which were stationed the Chicago Mercantile and the 1st Indiana Batteries. In rear of these batteries, Maj. Gen. Banks, with Gens. Franklin, Lee, Stone, Ransom, and other commanders, took post at intervals. A fence enclosed the base of these fields.

Now, the battle has begun in earnest. It is nearly four o'clock in the afternoon. Our troops have been marched from Pleasant Hill; some of them had to fight their way, in skirmishes, over eight miles of road; others have been double-quicked more than that distance. They passed, on their route, long lines of our cavalry force at a halt, and have had to file by the wagon-trains that occupy the narrow road between Pleasant Hill and Mansfield. The fight waxes warm. The foe bring heavy guns up. It is now found that a whole rebel army is in front, where it was fondly fancied no opposition would be made

to our march. Presently, our skirmishers and cavalry
fall back. At the same time, a movement of the enemy
is noticed. They are coming at double quick, to gain
the fence in front of us. That must be prevented. The
word is given for our line of battle to advance. The line
pushes forward, through heavy timber, and over broken,
uneven ground, to reach the fence. It is a race for position; but our side wins. We gain the fence, and pour
a volley from behind its shelter, that carries death into
rebel ranks. But, meantime, the enemy's right has swept
in contact with our left, which was somewhat advanced.
At that point the rebels reached the fence first, and, from
it, drove back our infantry. That left was the weakest
portion of our line. It should have been the strongest,
for it was to hold the Mansfield road. But when our
first line of battle was formed, the 19th Kentucky volunteers were shifted from the 1st brigade, which held our
extreme left, to the centre of the 2d brigade, in order to
strengthen that wing. Hence, in the 2d brigade, our
right, there were five regiments, while but two regiments
remained in the left—our real front. The enemy massed
heavily on these two battalions, compelling them to fall
back, just as our right won the fence. We maintained
our line at that fence nearly two hours, delivering volley
after volley on the rebels, and repulsing their repeated
charges. It was not until the enemy's left, extending
beyond our front, succeeded in flanking the position, that
we fell back, in order, to the open fields at our rear.
Meantime, the enemy's right, having broken our left flank,
capturing Nims's Battery, swung to the rear of our first
line of battle—occupied the road, which had been left
with only a small guard of cavalry—and then prepared to
charge our boys from a new position.

The Mercantile Battery had been stationed, as before intimated, at the north-west edge of an open field in rear of the original line of battle. When our two left regiments fell back, part of them, together with some of the contiguous brigade, being made prisoners, the battery shifted to position in a peach orchard, at the left of the Mansfield road, about eight hundred yards behind its former ground. Two regiments of our cavalry, that had retreated, likewise, before the enemy's left wing, took post at the rear of one section, which began a brisk artillery play upon the rebels. One piece, however, was soon disabled; while the Indiana battery, which had occupied the right of the Mercantile and fell back with it, left three pieces to the foe, and became, thereafter, *hors du combat*.

This was substantially the end of the battle. The 3d Division of the 13th Army Corps had, after marching out of Pleasant Hill in the forenoon, turned into camp about two o'clock, P. M., and remained thus till half-past three o'clock, P. M., when it received orders to advance toward Mansfield. This force did not reach the scene of action till five o'clock P. M.; when, under direction of Gen. Banks, its first brigade formed on the right of Mansfield road, its second brigade on the left. The division was then moved forward, to the edge of the open field, over which the enemy was, at this time, moving in force, to attack our wearied troops in rear. When a distance of about three hundred yards intervened between the rebels and our new line, the latter opened fire and drove the former. The enemy rallied, and was again repulsed. Another force now massed on the rebel left, to flank our right. Lt. Col. Florey, who commanded the 1st Brigade, forming our right, dispatched Adj. Watts, to inform Gen. Cameron, Acting General of Division, of his peril. Not finding Gen. Cameron, Lieutenant Watts reported to Gen. Franklin, who immediately ordered Col. Florey to hold

his position, assuring him that the enemy would receive
due attention. Subsequently, finding his flank imminently
menaced, Col. Florey sent Capt. Wells to Gen. Banks;
who repeated an order that the position should be held,
as Gen. Emory was moving up to check the enemy. At
this juncture, heavy firing was heard in front, the 2d
Brigade fell back, flanked, and a rebel force of cavalry
advanced upon our left. Col. Florey then directed his
brigade to give ground; when the enemy's column, that
had massed on our right, closed in suddenly, and the
colonel found his force attacked at once on both flanks
and in rear. Another line of the enemy advanced, meanwhile, at the point of the bayonet. All the late battle-
field was now overwhelmed by rebel reserves. The whole
Confederate force, after sweeping roads and fields, and
swallowing up regiments of our previous line, which had
continued their resistance, now concentrated on Moss's
fields. An unavailing rally of scattered forces was made
at the line of woods, but the mass of our discomfited
Army Corps retreated in wild disorder on the Mansfield
road, impeded by cavalry wagon-trains. We had lost
the battle.

The 13th Army Corps had sustained the brunt of this
conflict, and suffered terribly. Its 3d Division numbered
no more than 1200 men in the fight; its 4th Division,
under Col. Landram, comprised about 2000. Col. T. E.
G. Ransom commanded the entire force, and bore himself gallantly, till he received his wound in a skirmish
near the peach orchard.

Our 19th Army Corps remained at its camp, six or
eight miles back, upon the road. This corps was composed of 7000 effective soldiers. Behind, not yet arrived
at Pleasant Hill, was Gen. Smith's corps of 9000 men.
Yet our van-guard, repulsed at Mansfield, was so de-

moralized, it would appear, that the entire army was obliged to retrograde, the Red River expedition was abandoned, and our fleet and forces barely escaped annihilation at the hands of pursuing rebels.

Is this creditable? Yet it is a fact! And it is a fact, also, acknowledged even by Texans, that the rebel army, though nominally masters of the field; though in possession of guns, colors, and nearly four thousand prisoners; was, in reality, terrified at its own temerity. It dared not remain upon Mansfield battle ground. It fell back, at the very same time that our Federal army was retreating upon Pleasant Hill.

Why was not the 19th Army Corps brought up to retrieve the fortunes of Mansfield? Even though utter lack of generalship had attenuated our march, through an enemy's country, to such an extent that Gen. Smith's corps was left far behind; even though the fatal mistake was made of underrating the enemy's force, and deciding where he ought to fight and where he ought not to stand; even though mere regiments and depleted brigades were thrown forward on a powerful hostile army, without supporting masses within immediate handling; yet, after all these blunders, Mansfield defeat might have been converted into a success. Had our general possessed a just knowledge of his foe; had he "plucked the flower safety from the nettle danger," and brought up his fresh reserves, to give the rebels a Blucher upon their half-won battle-field—Gen. Banks might have regained his ground; might have driven the rebels to Mansfield village; in a word, might have pursued his march triumphantly; but he chose rather to adopt "discretion as the better part of valor," and to lose instead of win his Red River campaign.

The pages of this book are not the place to discuss all, or to relate all, that is familiar to my comprehension regarding that barren march of our army on the Louisiana and Texan borders. History will weigh its merits and its demerits.

But what mighty results hung upon that Red River expedition! "Texas," said General Magruder, "is the Trans-Mississippi Department!" Texas, during years, indeed, was the gate and outer wall of the Confederacy. It was a prize worthy of our best steel.

But what is the history of our campaigns against Texas? We captured Galveston, the key city, and lost it, disgracefully. We menaced Sabine City, with a fleet and army, and were repulsed by two score of militia men. We directed our columns toward the Attakapas prairies, and penetrated the Calcasieu with gun-boats, only to withdraw irresolutely from both. We threw ships and forces on the southwestern coast, and occupied the Rio Grande; pawed at an edge of the Nueces wilderness; alighted, like the water-fowl, on Decrow's Point; remained ingloriously squatting on bleak sands during a winter; and then returned, without accomplishing anything; without a single raid into those rich interior counties, lying coastwise; Matagorda, Brazoria, Wharton, and the populated bottoms further inland. Yet a true occupation or menace of Central Texas might have kept Red River clear for our expeditions to that border. An effective army corps on the Rio Grande might have occupied Magruder with work at his door, so that his famous "plan of defence" could not have been solely devoted to eastern frontiers. But our Federal Commander-in-chief, slowly dribbling out his operations, like his armies, by piece-meal, gave Magruder and Kirby Smith ample time to consolidate their several programmes. So much for our invasions of Texas. I shall not discuss the "Generalship" which directed them.

CHAPTER XXXIX.

IMMIGRATION AND POPULATION.

ONLY a short time previous to the immigration of Red River prisoners, our numbers had received a large accession by the return of more than seven hundred men from Shreveport, including our sailors and soldiers who had been paroled at Camp Groce, and whom we supposed had long since been forwarded to Federal lines. With the Camp Groce enlisted men came others, who had formerly been confined at Camp Ford, and sent thence to Shreveport on Christmas day of 1863. Dismal had been the experience of the latter poor fellows; bitter their sufferings during a severe winter in a shelterless camp near Shreveport. Even while at Camp Ford, before being marched to Louisiana, these men were destitute of cooking utensils, as well as clothing, and could only prepare mush, instead of bread, in pots loaned them by the guards. On that cold Christmas morning when they left their prison quarters, cherishing delusive hopes of speedy liberation, the half-clad and shivering fellows were obliged to march over the snow and ice that covered the roads. Of the six hundred who started, not two hundred had shoes, or other covering to protect their lacerated feet. They had been constrained to part with their scanty clothing, months before, when, nearly starved, on their marches from the Mississippi into Texas, they gave everything not absolutely necessary to decency in exchange for food wherewith to stop the cravings of hunger. But they were American soldiers—these suffering captives; and, inspired by longings for liberty which almost banished the sense of pain, they trod manfully forward, tracking the road with bloody footprints. Two days after their departure these mournful impressions of patriot feet could be traced on the snows that surrounded Camp Ford.

Arrived near Shreveport, to which place they were hurried by forced marches, the Federal prisoners were halted at an ice-bound spring, and thereafter told to shelter themselves as they might in the open fields and woods. The arrangements for "exchange" had not been effected; so they were notified; and yet no provisions were made for their comfort or shelter. Bare sustenance was furnished them, in rations of meal, with occasional beef or bacon. In this condition they were placed under a strong guard, and left to shift for themselves.

No one who did not participate in the endurances of these brave men, can realize or depicture those winter-months at Shreveport. Some of the naval prisoners, warrant officers, who were confined in the guard-house at Shreveport, were subject to many hardships and privations; but their sufferings were mild in comparison with the exposed dwellers in that bleak camp near the Four Mile Spring. Many were the attempts made by rebel emissaries to seduce our loyal soldiers and sailors from their allegiance to the Union. The seamen, particularly, were approached by every inducement which it was in the power of Treason to present. They were reminded of their daily cruel life, as prisoners, and promised position and liberal wages as workmen on Confederate gunboats. But our noble tars were steadfast in fidelity to their colors. They had seen their comrades dying of fever, cold and famine. They had been marched over snow and ice, while their blood tracked the path. They were forced to drag fire-wood for miles, in order to cook their scanty rations. They were shot down and hunted by bloodhounds at every attempt to escape! But, God bless them! In Shreveport woods, at night, a score or so would steal off, in groups—under a clouded sky—and, while some acted as pickets, a gray-headed tar would draw from his bosom the "Old Flag"—the "Stars and Stripes," and hoist it on a pole, to wave in a fierce "norther;" while the full hearts of his noble comrades were relieved by a hearty hurrah that startled rebel sentries on their posts, with sudden fear of Yankee insurrection. Then Jack would hide away his flag again, and creep back in the gloom, to his bed on the hard ground, and his breakfast, next morning, of corn-meal, salt and water.

When, in March, these hopeless captives were again removed from Shreveport to Camp Ford, in order to prevent their recapture by the advancing army of General Banks, they presented a spectacle which beggars all effort at portrayal. Numbers were literally naked, save blanket rags fringing their loins. It was like an irruption of squalor and pauperism on Camp Ford. Several log-houses, which they had built before their exodus in December, were restored to them, and a space of about three fourths of our camp-ground was appropriated for their use. More than half their number, however, received speedy orders to take the road again. These were the enlisted men of Lt.-Col. Leake's command, who, as I have before stated, were paroled and reported for "exchange." We bade farewell to them a short time previous to the first arrival of Red River prisoners.

But the influx of immigrants, by the thousand, which followed the disasters to our armies, not only absorbed all the area of "Old Ford Borough," but rendered expansion a public necessity. An order soon came, therefore, to enlarge the limits of the stockade. This was effected, under Col. Allen's direction, without much expense, by the ingenious expedient of "docking" eight feet from the sixteen-feet split logs that confined us, and using the upper halves as new stockade-posts to enclose the necessary enlargement. Our population swelled rapidly; though materials for building or shelter did not augment proportionably. But, fortunately, the warm weather was at hand, and our new-comers were, as yet, in a healthy condition. They were fresh from camp-life and service; captivity was novel to them; and they soon constituted themselves into messes, arranged their bivouacs in streets, and began to amass green boughs for wigwams, or dig cavernous vaults for troglodytic dwelling. In a short time, Camp Ford, in its increased proportions, began to wear the aspect of an immense bivouac-ground, stretching from side to side of the low stockading.

We had cherished "great expectations" of our agricultural interests before Spring set in. As gentlemen-farmers of the old "Borough," we had laid out kitchen-gardens very extensively. We planted corn, rye, lettuce, sweet potatoes, water-melons, beans, peas, cabbages, and red peppers. We hedged in plots, dug drains, made beds, and fixed our vine-poles. A propitious season and abundant garden-sauce were much prognosticated. But when the ides of April came, and with them General Banks—as far as Red River; and, when three or four thousand of his troops came some hundreds of miles further, breaking, like an irruption of the Goths, on our peaceful prison-yard, then, alas! our vegetable speculations were nipped with "morus multicaulis" frost-fingers. Sandals of zou-zous, boots of cavalry-men, trampled unheedingly over embryo garden-crops. A clump of tall corn long remained to mark the spot where Captain Ham-

mond used to dig betimes on February mornings; some
green sprouts peeped out afterwards from Capt. Fowler's
sheltered beds, hard by his log-hut. But all else in the
agricultural line yielded to the invaders. Our kitchen-
gardens became a reminiscence of the past.

Fancy—but no! one cannot fancy a resemblance 'to
our grotesque city of captivity. It is a place of Suc-
coth—of booth-dwelling in the wilderness. It is a gipsy
rendezvous. It is a wigwam metropolis. It is a Tartar
encampment, without horses; a Boschman village, without oxen.

Fancy, then, a space of half a dozen acres, enclosed
with a stockade of timbers eight feet high. One-sixth
of this area is allotted to the officers, who dwell in log-
cabins, erected by themselves or purchased from some
former tenant. Each cabin hut, or "shebang," as we
term it, shelters and accommodates a mess. The numbers of a mess are various; some messes have no more
than three, and others muster ten or twelve. These
"shebangs" are arranged in streets, right-angled with a
central thoroughfare called "Fifth Avenue." Midway, a
platform, covered with a canopy of pine boughs, is the
market-place. To this, each day, the rebel commissary
sends our rations, beef and cornmeal. These are apportioned between messes in the ratio of their numbers, the
meat and meal being brought in bulk, and given to the
hands of weighers chosen by ourselves from our own
officers. The cattle have been butchered by selected
men from our own numbers; likewise, these experts enjoy "tit-bits" for themselves, of kidneys, livers, and the
like. To this meat-market comes occasionally some venturous farmer of the neighborhood, allowed to be a sutler
or purveyor, for the nonce. Unfortunate rustic! Victim,

oftentimes, of misplaced confidence! His sugar—held at thirty dollars a pound—is scooped up by a dozen hands before he can identify their owners; his turkeys fly away incontinently; his sacks of flour are passed from hand to hand, and nevermore return to him; and woe, O woe! if the poor man have whiskey! Our Yankee foragers allow no smuggling. Neither commandant nor guards were ever able to protect a sutler's stores. Perhaps they had no interest in them. But we counted "Artful Dodgers" in our motley midst, who would have joyed the heart of venerable Fagin! A rebel officer of the day once had his pistol stolen from him at roll-call, and we were threatened a deprivation of our meat-rations till the article should be restored. The threat was never carried out, however. Another day, a rebel officer was relieved of his pipe, and next morning found it in his pocket, with the "Stars and Stripes" carved on its wooden bowl. Our scamps of Yankee prisoners were forever playing tricks on rebel travellers.

During early prison life here, swine were quite numerous around the precincts of Camp Ford, though bacon-rations seldom visited us within. Our boys, however, in going out, under guards, to cut fire-wood, would take occasion, when accompanied by some "Union" Texan, to kill a fine hog or two, and, cutting the flesh into quarters, "pack" it gracefully under sheltering brush. Shouldering their secreted spoils, our foragers could pass the sentries unsuspected; and, then, ho! for a feast, my masters! One day, the rogues "toted" in a long, hollow log, from which a fine grunter was soon "extracted." Captivity is the mother of "strategy."

See, then, this camp! Besides our officers' quarter, with its street of log-huts, each a small community, every doorway shaded by a broad verandah, thick with evergreens; in some streets these verandahs joining midway, so that the whole space between the houses is protected from the sun, which only strikes our porches in checkered light, at sunset, through latticed leaves; besides this area allotted to the officers, our prison habitations stretch on three sides, densely populated as the tenant-houses of a New York ward. What curious abodes! What odd contrivances for shelter! Here upright sticks sustain a simple thatch of leaves; there poles fixed slant-wise, and overlaid with bark, compose an Indian lodge. Some householders are satisfied with blankets stretched across two saplings; others make a palisaded mansion, eight feet square, with stakes, inserted in the earth, like picket fences, and covered with a roof of twigs. Another's dwelling is of basket-work, wrought out of ashwood peelings; beyond this is a roof, composed of oak-slabs, slanting from a mud-wall six feet high, down to the ground, and plastered with a layer of clay. Hard by the brook are caverns, excavated in the clay bank, with steep earthen stairways entering to their subterrene apartments. Two parallel avenues are thus occupied by troglodytes. All architectural "styles," from Gothic arches, shaped with curved grapevines, down to nondescript contrivances that beavers would reject for domiciles, are here elaborated or improvised, according to the thrift and taste, or lack of both, which may have characterized the squad or individual.

CHAPTER XL.

A DAY AT CAMP FORD.

Long before daybreak the camp begins to stir. There is restlessness among our prison legions—home-sickness, doubtless, in the souls of many sleep-locked hundreds of these ragged citizens. I hear the hum of voices arising out of morning's grey shadows; the crackling of new-lighted bivouac-brands; the matinal twitter of red-birds. Presently the east reddens, and I see the morning star setting over yonder wooded hills outside of our prison-yard.

How royally the sun rises, atmosphered with golden mist, robed in purple haze of woodland exhalations! The camp is alive and vocal. A thousand voices call to other thousands. Tatterdemalions roll out of burrowing places, creep up from caverns, and emerge from hut-openings. Red-capped zouaves, wide-breeched; blue-bloused cavalry men, yellow-trimmed; all hungry-looking; sergeants with service stripes; jack-tars in poly-patched trowsers; wa-goners in broad hats; barefooted cannoniers—rank and file generally—hatless, bootless, shirtless. They swarm out upon the main street; flow into crossways; jostle one another at cooking-fires; pass and repass, laden with fuel, rations, water-vessels. Another day begins.

I mingle in the throng that pours along "Fifth Avenue." I pass the "bakery," where an enterprising New Yorker sells his ten-cent leathery doughnuts and caoutchouc grape-pies for a dollar in greenbacks. I glance a moment at our "jeweller's" window—where a corporal tinkers watches; elbow through the crowd surrounding a lieutenant's turning-lathe, which whirls out chess-men at three dollars per set; peer into a door where sits a captain "editing" our prison-journal, "The Old Flag;"—then reach the "spring," dash head and arms in water, comb tangled locks, and look about me.

"Motley's the only wear!" says Shakspeare, and in Camp Ford we agree with him. Such costumes never were beheld before, outside of Rag Fair or the "Beggars' Opera." I wish our Uncle Abraham, or Sam, could see this "*sans culotte*" procession marching up Pennsylvania Avenue. Such head-gear, from a zouave cap to rimless crowns and crownless rims, and tattered handkerchiefs, and wisps of straw! such effigies of garments! armless shirts and legless trowsers; bits of blankets tied about the loins; such patches, of every size and hue! such scarecrow figures of humanity! Their wives and mothers would not know them from the *chiffoniers* who rake out Northern gutters.

But they are all United States soldiers and sailors; men who have met our foes on land and wave; brave rank and file of fleets and armies sacrificed by stupid commanders, and neglected in their misery by the power which should protect them. God bless them, ragged and rough as they are; for the fire of undying loyalty burns in their bosoms, and they love the "Old Flag," in spite of those who disgrace it!

I sit down at my "shebang" door, to the morning's sumptuous repast. I have corn-meal pan-cakes, with a treacle syrup made of melted sugar at eight dollars per pound in greenbacks. I have a slice of bacon, which cost two dollars per pound. I drink my coffee, made of burnt rye, and am abundantly filled. I watch the mice running over my verandah.

We grow used to both vermin and reptiles. There was a jovial "scare" one night, around the wide-mouthed fire-place of our "Big Mess." Stories and songs were current, with occasional jokes about exchange, while flaming logs roared cheerily; when, suddenly, a monstrous snake-head darted out upon the hearth, and presently a coil shot up amid the smoke and fire, surmounted by the crested neck and forky tongue. Our valiant soldiers of the Union sprang up wildly, and, for a minute's space, the serpent-visiter, a bull snake, five feet long, possessed that battle-field. The bipeds rallied, however, and attacked his reptileship with clubs and chunks of wood, driving him back within the fire-place, where he was soon despatched. This snake had chosen a hollow log for hibernation, where he lay all torpid till revived by scorching heat to crawl out, literally "from the frying pan into the fire."

In laying the floor down in my log hut, we unearthed a serpent of the kind called ground rattle. It burrows under the surface like a mole. One morning, I was awakened by a serpent of the house species, which pursued a little mouse into my hammock. I think the reptile seized the tiny fugitive in his jaws; for presently both fell upon a table under me, the mouse escaping, while the snake lay stunned an instant, and was killed by one of our mess.

Of copperheads, rattlesnakes, and hooded vipers, I saw many in the swampy neighborhoods of Camp Groce, but at Ford prison they seldom showed themselves within the stockade, unless brought in with our firewood. But of venomous pedipalpi and myriapoda we have many specimens. It is a daily chance to find a centipede upon the door-sill or the hearth. Some measure several inches, hard and horny, with a stinger like a rattle snake's tooth. An officer, lying in his bunk of a morning, felt a crawling, stinging sensation on his breast, approaching one of his arm-pits, then descending his shirt sleeve. Lying still and almost breathless, he had the presence of mind to loose his wristband very quietly. A centipede crawled down his arm, out at his wrist, and thence upon the blankets. The officer sprang out to the floor, procured a stick, and killed the animal. It was an old one, and had left its trail upon his breast and arm as legibly as if a line of dots were burned in the skin. The insect's "hundred feet," stung as they moved upon the cuticle, and left a crimson trace of smarting vesicles.

The scorpion, or stinging lizard, as we called it, is another of our insect enemies. Its quick dart from beneath a slab of wood, with curving tail erect, becomes quite familiar to us. I never heard of serious injury from the sting of one, although it is reported to inflict a fatal wound in August or July.

But from another member of the tribe Arachnida we have had positive evidence of noxious capabilities. The horrible spider, the tarantula, is an especial object of hostility, and our boys torment one, when captured, as sailors would a shark. They take good heed, however, to impale it with a pointed stick, before exciting its wrath; for the insect is a plucky one, and can spring upward vertically, to attack. It is a most repulsive object, with its crab-like mandibles and furzy claws, its dorsal hair, und bloated belly. When our prisoners first began to build their log huts at Camp Ford, they suddenly lost a comrade by some strange wound which he discovered on his neck. The surgeon said, it came from a poisonous bite, and tried to arrest the virus, but in vain. The neck swelled tumorously, and the poor man died. A short time afterward, in breaking earth for a new hut, on the ground where he expired, the diggers found an old taran- tula; and no doubt remained that their unfortunate com- rade had been bitten by it.

So much for our more malignant insectivora. As for beetles, bugs and aphides, there is no occasion to men- tion them. Prison-vermin are no respecters of persons in rags and tatters; and our corral-dwellers boast no ex- tensive changes in their sheets or shirts—poor fellows!

While I am still eating my frugal breakfast—corn mush, rye coffee, and a cutting of bacon fat—some one scrapes a salutation on the threshhold. It is "Old Tim," a gunboat man-o'-war's-man.

"Will yez plaze walk out here, sur?" says Tim, with a peculiar wink and head-jerk, in the way of invitation.

"What's the matter, Tim?"

"O, yez never nade ax, if yez just go wan fut wid me, sir! O, begorra! it's the divil's own matther ye'll clap eyes on, sur!"

I rise from my tripod seat, and follow Tim to the main street. A press of blue shirts and blue blouses fills up the area near our meat-block. There is much excitement apparent in the crowd through which Tim makes his way, and I become convinced that "our army can swear ter- ribly," when it finds occasion. I am sure that I hear a variety of expressions, designating persons and places unmentionable in Sabbath reading. Presently, gaining the front of officers, I behold the spectacle which gives rise to general curiosity.

The spot where I stand, with all the throng, is half way up the hill side on which our corral extends. The base of this declivity, as we know, is crossed by our lower stockade posts, and on the other side of those posts rises the eminence whereon head-quarters stand. Thus, while the rebels can look down on us, from the commander's house, we, on our part, can overlook the stockade and observe whatever passes outside. And now an incident is transpiring which possesses a novel interest for Northern men.

Yet it is only a "nigger" wench, receiving customary flagellation.

Such, without doubt, would be the careless observation of a Southern gentleman or a Southern lady, who might cast a casual glance upon the scene. Custom makes all things commonplace. But to me, I must confess, and to rough Jack Tars and private soldiers standing round me, habit has not yet familiarized the sight of woman-whipping. Hence, a very honest vent of expletives, in plain vernacular, gives relief to some among us.

It is a rebel soldier who is doing the whipping duty; whether on a chattel of his own or one belonging to headquarters, we know not. The woman stoops, with lifted arms, holding her single garment, an old calico gown, rolled up above her head, exposing all her person from the shoulders downward, to the flogging. Quite apart from any log building, on an open hill-side, this rebel brute has dragged his helpless victim out into the view of Northern men. Compelling a poor slave to strip the clothing from her limbs, and hold it up at arm's-length, while he whips her, as no Northern man would whip a dog, this cowardly fellow seems to brave the indignation of our gallant boys, who fling out maledictions that, no doubt, are audible to him. We, on our hill, can hear the cracking of his lash as it descends on the back, and hips, and legs, and curls around the body of this shrieking woman! Black she is, and a slave; but she is of the sex that claims our mothers. No wonder that the blood

boils in American veins, and that the hearts of men respond to a woman's cries beneath a Southern sun! I
hear "Old Tim" emit some words that are neither *pater*
nor *ave*; and presently he touches my arm.

"Sur," says Tim, "do yez know what I thought uv the
nagurs whin I kim to Dixie Land?"

"What was it, Tim?"

"Throth an' I thought an' I said, God forgive me, that
slavery was made for the nagur; an' a very good thing it
was, in its place, more be token!"

"You thought that, Tim?"

"Faix, I did, sur! An' do yez know what I think
now, sur?"

"What is it, Tim?"

"I'm bowld to say, sur—as I said before—that slavery
is a good thing in its place, sur; but its place is down
there, sur!—down there, wid the Southern Confederacy,
an' Jeff Davis on top uv it, sur!"

Tim stamps with his foot on the ground, and points his
dexter digits downward, with a significance unmistakable.
And a murmur and swell of hard words all around us, in
response to Old Tim, consigns the Southern Republic, if
words could ever consign it, to the influence of a climate
much hotter than the equator.

Meanwhile, the lash rises and falls with renewed strokes;
the black back, loins, and legs of the slave-woman become
striped with gules; her piercing cries ascend to the heavens, mingled with curses and threats from her rebel
scourger.

I walk back to my cabin, marvelling whether such
things have been daily witnessed on a thousand hill-sides
during seventy years of our mission as a people.

The rebel-drum is beating roll-call.   I hurry to the officers' line, which rests its right upon the western gate and stretches its long ranks within the stockade.   Presently, the rebel adjutant rides in on horseback, followed by a score of guards with muskets, and their officers with lists of prisoners.   The official greybacks then divide, each to a separate detachment of the Yankees.   Then our names are read or spelled out by an intelligent "Southern gentleman," who is given to stammering, and makes hard work of the patronymics.   Meanwhile, we are standing under a broiling sun, which tries the flesh of fat men and the temper of the leanest of us.   But, at length, a welcome drum-roll gives dismissal, and the dress-parade is over. We are our own masters for the day, within the stockade lines.

The sun mounts higher. Everybody seeks a shelter. Our rations must be drawn, for beef comes in daily; but the messmate who is "cook" attends to this.   Time must be killed till dinner hour, and so we look about for weapons to way-lay him with.

The noon heats come, but tempered by a pleasant northern breeze. Our green verandahs cast inviting shade. We gather at our doors, with books often read but still pored over.   I loiter upon Shakspeare; dog-ear a fine-print Plutarch, lent to me by "a good Union man outside." Colonel Burrell comes up and chats; Major Anthony sits down to chess with me.   I write awhile; then study tactics; then beget me to my hammock, swinging just outside of the log-house, under trellised pine-boughs.

A rebel orderly comes in with letters for a few of us. The disappointed listen, wondering why *their* letters never come.   I get a Houston paper, and a crowd surrounds my doorway, waiting for the news.   "Another victory for the South!"   "Ten thousand prisoners cap-

tured by General Lee!"   "Grant totally defeated!"
"Washington to be attacked immediately!"

Cool comfort this in midsummer. It refreshes us. But
nothing yet about "exchange."   "O, bother on the lying
secesh paper!"   "Nothing about exchange!"   "Bosh!"

We eat our dinner. Beef like shoe-leather. A " duff"
or corn pudding, with molasses, at the moderate price of
"thirty dollars in Confederate," per gallon. Rye coffee,
and an after-dinner smoke, in wooden pipes, with Texan
"tabac," at the rate of fifteen dollars per pound, in greenbacks.

Meantime, near my cabin, industry thrives. Next door,
chairs are built on Teutonic pattern, by a German officer.
Here, also, genial Captain Talley, whilom of the City
Belle, with Captain Watts, whom he calls "Uncle John,"
is joining stools and scooping mighty wash-bowls out of
pine slabs, and manufacturing a chess table, whereat I sit,
in roomy-bottomed arm-chair, not long afterwards. In
rear of this *atelier* sundry Western captains play four-
handed chess upon a double board of their own making.

Through our cabin window, latticed with a Venetian
blind—my own sole patent—I can spy that gallant Buck-
eye, Major Berring, with his mess ; busily engaged in
straw-plaiting for summer hats ; while Captain Sowery
times his fingers with a song, and Captain Cochrane trolls
a rousing negro chorus. I bespeak a wide-brimmed *chapeau*, to wear with my new suit of clothes, which our
French tailor is about to fashion from a regulation blanket
of good butternut woollen.

Major Berring and two brave captains challenge to
four-handed chess. We borrow the mammoth board, for
this absorbing game, and presently fall-to. So fly the
hours.

The sun declines, and locomotion recommences. We

visit and make calls. Our youngsters practice at gymnastics in the central square, where turning poles and parallel bars have been erected. Wrestling trials are improvised among the men. A game of quoits goes on. The Kansas boys are playing at ball. More venerable prisoners sit and gossip in their arm-chairs.

We hear the thrum of stringed instruments. Our "fiddler," Captain May, is "entertaining ladies." Motherly Mrs. ALLEN is visiting our corral, with divers rebel dames and demoiselles in her train. They sit in wide arm-chairs of Yankee manufacture, chat with Yankee officers, and hear their Yankee songs, accompanied by Yankee fingers upon banjoes made by Yankee hands. Meantime our Yankee fiddler tunes his catgut, and anon he gives us "Sounds from Home"—which draw the tears from eyes of rebel ladies. So the twilight finds us.

Now the moon rises, silver-orbed, in an unclouded field of blue. Our "secesh" visitors have gone, and Yankee instruments are struck to gayer measures. I hear Cyclopean Johnson, the engineer, out-calling for a dance. "Gentlemen, choose your partners! Forward two' Ladies change! All balancez! Promenade all!"

Dance on, poor prisoners! Cheat your hearts out of loneliness!

CHAPTER XLI.

OPERATIONS IN ARKANSAS.

How different might have been the fate of our Red River campaign, had the veteran Steel, or Blunt, or Canby, been in chief command, instead of such tried generals being subordinated to the whims and passions of arrogant staff-officers, those "powers behind the throne" who really governed military matters in our fine "Department of the Gulf." Steel was a thunderbolt on rebel war-paths, when he led out his frontier-men in earnest. Look at his resistless advance from Helena to Little Rock, in autumn of 1863; when with Gen. Rice and Col. McLean, leading their gallant Western infantry, in two divisions, seven thousand strong, and with Gen Davidson, marshalling his four thousand bold dragoons—the whole force skillfully strengthened by forty pieces of artillery—he drove the rebel masses before him, day after day, in one continuous striding toward victory. First Brownsville fell, under a dash of his cavalry; then the breast-works at Bayou Meteor were carried by assault; then, pushing the foe still harder, he crossed the Arkansas river, on a pontoon bridge; moved up its northern bank to attack the heavy line of fortifications held by rebels; dispatched his cavalry against that of Marmaduke, who kept the suburbs of Little Rock; and, finally, rushing forward impetuously, with all his forces, flanked Confederate General Price completely, and sent him flying across the country. Little Rock became ours, with a loss in the campaign, of scarcely a dozen killed or a hundred hurt, while at least three thousand of the enemy were killed, wounded, and made prisoners. Nor did the doughty Steel stop here. His cavalry hung on Price's rear, harrassing his retreat and chasing him twenty-five miles to Benton, where our bold Missourian dragoons captured his rearmost wagons, destroying the supplies they carried. On followed Steel, with infantry and field-pieces—driving the rebel army into Arkadelphia, and swelling its list of "*hors du combat*" up to five thousand. Then Pine Bluff fell before our cavalry advance, and it was subsequently held by six hundred Kansas boys, against three thousand rebel cavalry, artillery, and infantry, in a bitter fight of half a day, which ended in another rout of Marmaduke. But Steel was active elsewhere all the while; his cavalry, under Clayton, surprising Gen. Dobbin, at Julip, and taking his camp-equipage, and routing Gen. Green's forces at Branchville, with terrible loss to the rebels. This is the style in which Steel conducted that Arkansas campaigning; meantime, re-organizing and disciplining his troops, till they moved and fought like veterans. Six months of such service cleared Central Arkansas of the guerillas who had made the capital their head-quarters; and, when the spring opened, our Federal commander pounced upon Arkadelphia, and thence marched for Camden, to co-operate, thereafter, with the strength of the Gulf, which, under Banks, was threatening Texas. Shelby, the rebel general, made a dash upon our army's trains, at Spoonville, on the road to Washington; but he was beaten off with loss. Again, at Okalona, he attacked the 77th Ohio regiment, but was obliged to sound a brisk retreat. Then Marmaduke swooped down, with reinforcements of his cavalry, but was met by a brigade of Gen. Salomon's division, and a single squadron of horse, at

Elkin's Ford, up on the Little Missouri. Here brave Mc-
Lean, with his infantry, and the Iowa heroes, in their
saddles, met the brunt of battle, and kept the Confederate army at bay, till Rice came up, with his brigade, and
drove off Marmaduke again. The rebels rallied behind
breast-works, but were speedily flanked by our advancing regiments, when they retreated to the Prairie d'Ann,
where other strong defences sheltered them. Steel now
led on, in person, re-inforced by Thayer's five thousand
from Fort Smith, which had lately made a junction with
his little army. Then followed the fight of Prairie d'Ann,
and a rebel retreat, across the prairie, pursued by our
victorious boys till far into the night. Two days elapsed,
and then our army moved in line of battle across that
wide prairie; presenting an unbroken front, with batteries
supporting, and cavalry flanking, and sharpshooters advanced to skirmish with the foe. The march was a consummate piece of soldiership; our line flanking, and ob-
liquing on the angles of rebel works, until, completely
out-generalled, they were forced to evacuate once more,
and fall back, in hot haste, on Washington. Then, Steel,
without pursuing, wheeled upon the Moscow road, which
led to Camden, and thus, abruptly, made the foe aware
of his intentions in that quarter. But their discovery
came too late. They were now in Steel's rear, instead
of front, and their only chance of intercepting the crafty
Federal general was to hasten by the direct highway, to
reach the neighborhood of Camden first. They made
some feints upon our rear, to cover this design, but Steel
was not to be deluded. He only pressed on faster, and
in three days more had entered Camden, driving its
small garrison from their guns without much trouble. In
the meantime, throwing out a force of Clayton's cavalry,

he cut off a rebel brigade, and brought its train, with some three hundred prisoners, before his rear guard.

After such arduous and successful campaigning, whereby Arkansas was nearly recovered from rebel sway, it seems doubly hard that gallant Steel should almost fall a sacrifice to the disasters of our miserably-abortive Red River expedition, under Major-General Banks. That our Arkansas commander-in-chief performed his share of all preliminary fighting and defeating, needs no proof beyond the record of his march from Little Rock to Camden. But arrived there, where was our "Army of the Gulf?" The battle of Mansfield had inaugurated its retreat, and the Red River expedition had degenerated into a disgraceful failure.

Gen. Steel now found himself at Camden; but in his front, and on his flanks, and gathering at his rear, were squadrons of rebels, elated with recent triumphs, and arrogant with future expectations. Already they coveted the capture of Banks, and the annihilation of his fleet and army. Already they looked upon Steel as an easy prey; and nothing less than the permanent expulsion of every Federal from Texas and Arkansas was accepted as the *ultimatum* of rebel conquest. Steel saw himself beset, and marked for destruction.

The first designs of the rebels were directed at our Federal trains. To cut off supplies from Steel, and to encompass Camden with their armies, was thought the safer method of proceeding against one whose prowess and infinite resources of strategy were so well known to his foes. The disaster at "Poison Springs" was a characteristic exploit of Texan warfare.

It was on the 18th of April. Two weeks had elapsed since our primary Red River defeat. A forage train was out on the old military road between Camden and Washington. It was guarded by a few companies of the 18th Iowa infantry, and the 2nd Kansas negro regiment. Within ten miles of camp, this train was attacked by rebel General Maxey, with a division, rebel General Marmaduke, with another division, of cavalry, and rebel General Cobell, with a third division. Maxey's division was composed of Gano's Texas brigade, Walker's brigade of Choctaw Indians, Khrumbaar's battery. There were Missouri regiments, Texan regiments, Arkansas regiments, and aboriginal regiments, with half a dozen Confederate generals to command them. All these were marshalled under Maxey, and marched against half a regiment of infantry, and a few black soldiers, guarding our forage trains, yet the battle was contested stoutly by our devoted boys. Not till two hundred and fifty of its number were killed or wounded, and nearly a hundred captured, did the little band fall back slowly, and yield four guns and about one hundred and seventy wagons to an overwhelming enemy. But very proud, nevertheless, were those rebels of their unusual good fortune against Steel; and Maxey made an official report of the affair which might have served, in details and bombast, for the bulletin of a Waterloo battle.

Another exploit against wagoners and their escorts, soon followed the battle of Poison Springs. On the 23d of April, an empty train of some two hundred wagons, left Camden for Pine Bluffs, to get supplies for our beleaguered troops. This train was placed in charge of the available force of a brigade that Col. McLean commanded, in Salomon's division. There were comprised in it, the 43d Indiana volunteers, in charge of Major Norris, the 36th Iowa regiment, Major Hamilton, and the 77th Ohio infantry, led by Captain McCormick. These regiments had been depleted greatly. With them were dispatched about two hundred of the 1st Indiana and 7th Missouri cavalry, under Majors McCauley and Spellman; the whole commanded by Lieut.-Col. Drake, of the 36th Iowa volunteers. They encamped, after being one day out, on Bayou Mars, and the next morning, as the train advanced, they found the enemy drawn up in line of battle on the road near Mark's Mills, five miles on the Pine Bluff road, and six miles from the Saline River.

Our Indiana boys were in front, and speedily became engaged, assisted by a small detachment of the 5th Kansas volunteers, just coming up from Pine Bluff. Six thousand rebels thundered at our little vanguard, but more than once it drove the enemy's centre; and, reinforced by the 36th Iowa regiment, comprising scarcely four hundred men, which soon dashed up, our brave front withstood unshrinkingly the heavy fire of rifles and cannon concentrated upon it. For more than an hour, this unequal contest, of less than eight hundred against eight times their force, continued undauntedly. Again and again they pierced the serried centre of rebel battle; stubbornly did they dispute every foot of ground; until, at last, after two pieces of Stenge's 2d Missouri artillery had been literally overrun and captured, and retaken by our rallying boys several times, they began to give ground reluctantly before their foes. Not, however, till every horse attached to the battery was killed, and the gunners shot down at their pieces, did those glorious Western soldiers, bleeding and exhausted, give up their portion of the train.

In the meantime, Captain McCormick, who, with the 77th Ohio men, was guarding the rearmost wagons, had been summoned by Col. Drake, to hasten forward with all speed. The captain at once started his regiment on "double-quick," passing impeded trains and a section of artillery, which had become "mired" in the boggy Mars

bottom. For five miles, the Ohio boys advanced at this
rate, but only reached the front in time to see their comrades captured. The whole rebel force was now before
the rear-guard, as it been before the van; but Captain
McCormick, seconded by Captain Whitridge, adjutant-
general of the brigade, brought his little force rapidly in
line, and sought to save the wagons that were yet behind
him. For another hour, the enemy was held in check at
all parts, and twice forced to give way in front. But the
woods were open all around the battle-ground; the rebel
sharp-shooters could screen themselves, on either flank;
heavy lines were massing about the train; and, at length,
to their dismay, the Ohio soldiers found their ammunition
gone. They were compelled to surrender; and thus the
battle of MARK'S MILLS ended, after a most obstinate
struggle by our small force against terrible odds. We
lost two hundred and fifty, in killed and wounded, and
about one thousand in prisoners, with two hundred wagons, and a hundred teamsters. The enemy's loss could not
have been less than a thousand killed and wounded; as
our skirmishers, deployed in the timber, did fearful execution on rebel masses during the protracted engagement.
Beyond mules, wagons, and arms, the enemy obtained
nothing but prisoners; for the train was an empty one.
The needy marauders solaced themselves, however, with
an indiscriminate plundering of Federal soldiers. Money,
watches, and clothing were "appropriated," with cool
effrontery. Tattered head-gear was replaced by Yankee
hats; bare feet rejoiced in Uncle Sam's boots; and the
"sans cullottes" butternuts became speedily transformed
into well-clad "Johnnies," provided with canteens, knapsacks, and comfortable blankets. Our brave Americans,
robbed and maltreated, were then marched to the Red
River, and soon afterwards arrived, weary and worn, at

our populated prison-pen in Camp Ford. Contemplating this new accession of "Steel's men," our soldiers from Mansfield, Pleasant Hill, and other parts, were prepared to appreciate yet more keenly the military foresight whereof they were common victims.

With Steel's soldiers, from "Mark's Mill" battle, and other engagements, arrived many teamsters, traders, and citizens; among the latter a son of John Ross, the Cherokee Chief, whose nephew, D. R. Hicks, I have already mentioned as among the Kansas prisoners. Ross and Hicks were both intelligent and loyal men, and had suffered severely in the cause of Union. Such martyrs as these and their compatriots of the "Nation," deserve well of our Republic in the future. I would gladly, if space permitted, relate the story of their trials and perils. But the rehearsal would involve a national history. I must hasten on with personal narrative.

CHAPTER XLII.

PRISON ASSOCIATIONS.

WITH our privations and hardships there were mingled many consolations in the corral. Friendly converse, mutual good offices, music, sports, and gymnastic exercises, enlivened the monotony of prison life. While the quiet ones re-read or studied a few old books, played chess, or talked; our *athletæ* practised at "parallel bars" and "turning poles"; our "industriels" worked at the lathes and carpenter's bench; our music-lovers met for rehearsal; and our "dancing-men" waltzed or quadrilled. We had base-ball, cricket, and quoits; promenades, wood-chopping, and—sink-digging, moreover, to fight against *ennui* and dyspepsia.

Many good hearts were among us; many kindred spirits became knit together. It would gratify me to dwell upon the traits of better natures developed under the ordeal of captivity; but the compressed limits of my book denies that indulgence. Of a few I may only recall a pleasant memory.

Harry Western, of the "Undaunted Mess," was a type of the generous young sailor. I do not know who claimed him not, some hour in the day, for a friendly helping hand. Like sea-boys, generally, he was expert at a hundred little arts of skill and industry; now shaping out a fancy cap, now fashioning new garments out of rags, now finishing a set of chess-men, now denuding hirsute chins of bristling superfluity, and now exsecting too-redundant locks from polls of fellow-prisoners. Harry was a genius, with notable contempt for land-lubberism, and with more than a dash of poetry in his genial composition. He would give us "Tam O'Shanter," with all its broad Scotch humor, and quote love-lines from Tom Moore with true Catullic fervor. Many a "yarn" was spun when our nautical circle gathered about my hearth-fire; and Harry could twist his thread with the most intricate ; for he had been a sea-wanderer before his teens, and had trodden remotest strands, and passed through many a strange experience, though scarcely yet the beard of manhood fringed his nut-brown cheeks. He had sailed as mate of an ocean clipper ere he turned his twentieth year, and was now, at twenty-two, a veteran naval officer, with a record of service that might compare with many who wore more embroidery on their uniform sleeves.

Harry Western, as before noticed, was latest in command before the surrender of the gunboat Diana, captured on the Atchafalaya by waylaying rebels. Brave Lieutenant Mars, who kept his post in the engine-room till all the steam connections had been shot away by cannon-balls, and clouds of scalding vapor filled the space between decks; gallant infantry Lieutenant Bulkley, who has since found a soldier's grave in the Shenandoah Valley; these and many another choice young officer were wont to gather in our mess-circles, when Harry "spun his yarn."

Captain Dillingham, of the " Morning Light," ever in radiant humor, drew, for our amusement, on his endless fund of anecdote and experience ; Captain Crocker, of the "Clifton,"—dignified and spiritual,—shared with us the treasures of his well-cultured mind ; while the blunt speech and sound judgment of Captain Johnson, of the "Sachem," were relied upon to sever any Gordian knot

of argument. These naval gentlemen, with signal-officer
Dane, whose brilliant spirits defied even fever and ague
to keep them under; and our leading gymnast, Lieut.
Dana, who was a Gabriel Ravel on the "turning bars,"
with Col. Nott, the philosophic and erudite colonel of our
"Ironsides," made up "Fifth Avenue" mess; at which
I took hospitable rations, for a few weeks, till I lapsed
into house-ownership.

The 42nd Massachusetts mess, with brave Colonel
Burrell at the head, maintained domestic *status* in a
"shebang," which boasted a detached cook-house. Around
its bounteous board gathered stout Captain Sherive, who,
with Lieut. Hibbard, of the 23d Connecticut regiment,
performed the onerous duties of volunteer commissaries,
to divide our prison rations; busy Captain Proctor, ever
on the alert to be useful; polite Captain Savage; balmy
Lieut. Newcomb; sweet-singing Lieut. White; sober-
minded Lieut. Stowell; modest Lieut. Humble, of the
Mass. 4th; high-reaching Lieut. Cowdin: and that dashing sworder, Captain King, of N. H. Cavalry.

In my own cabin I received, originally, but a single
mess-mate—Captain Van Tine; whose quiet demeanor
covered sterling qualities of taste and sense. Our family
circle became afterwards enlarged by the admission of
Major Anthony's mess, which gave up its quarters to
some of the poor fellows from Shreveport, who had a
"builders' lien" upon them. Thereafter, having removed
my house—by tearing down and rebuilding—in one day;
so that I dined under its roof some forty rods from the
site on which I had breakfasted within its walls; we
settled down to a mess of six that continued till our
final exodus. Major Anthony became general caterer—
and a provident one; while Lieuts. Morse and Sampson,
and Dr. Brennan, shared in our simple *ménage*.

The "Ironsides" officers were dispersed among various messes. Captain Coe, always cheerful and attractive, with Lieut. Stevenson, were mates of Lt.-Col. Leake and his officers; our studious Lieut. Wellington, and chess-conquering Lieut. Lyons, combined with another circle; while solid Lieut. Babcock migrated to rural districts, near the gate; bright-eyed Lieut. Petrie carried his good heart elsewhere; and that indefatigable "book-collector," Lieut. Robens, built his plank domicile nearly opposite my own verandah. But, I am warned to abbreviate description.

So, therefore, with brief notice of what I would willingly dilate upon, I must pass to the closing chapters of our prison experience. I must advert merely, "*en passant*," as the French say—to kind-hearted Capt. Washburne; quaint engineer Fox, of bird-fancying habits; jovial Major Gray; and thrifty Captain Hammond; to the ingenious Chambers, whose model of the "Morning Light" was a trophy of Yankee naval architecture; to kindly and active Bridges, who, with Lieut. Delemater, devoted his labors to our sick in hospital; and McLaughlin, whose stories of Shreveport prisons might furnish matter for a romance. Nor can I give more than allusion to many incidents and episodes involved in attempts to escape by our comrades; to the punishment of Capt. Reed, who, on recapture, was forced to stand, for eight hours, upon a barrel, at our north-gate—with naked feet and head exposed under the blazing summer-day sun; till his brain became fevered nearly to delirium; or to the brutal treatment of prisoners who sank under sabre-strokes, or were dragged by lariats fastened to their necks, behind mounted rebels; nor to the stories that intersperse my notes, rehearsing the trials and sufferings of loyal Texans—the panics, persecutions, and massacres that marked the first years of Rebellion in Texas. Among the last-mentioned local events, however, was the "Match Plot," which deserves a paragraph:

The breaking out of fires in several stores, at Tyler and other places, awakened a suspicion that two merchants from the Northern States, (who had purchased patent matches, which ignited almost spontaneously,) were incendiaries. The usual senseless hue and cry followed; the traders were thrown into prison; and hundreds of hapless blacks were arrested and tortured—in order to get evidence of the "Yankee Conspiracy." Free negroes and poor white settlers from the North fell under the ban at once. Scores of the latter were hanged by the mob. More than a hundred negroes, free and bond, were executed, as I have been informed, on suspicion alone. Several were burned at the stake. Thirty white men were lynched, in and about Tyler and Palestine; one of the unfortunate merchants who had introduced the matches undergoing this fate—the other escaping by timely flight. Blood flowed in all quarters, till the enlightened "Regulators," finding no more poor whites to kill or banish, decided that "order reigned" again.

Burning men and women at the stake is a popular Southern amusement. A negro was thus executed at Tyler, while our prisoners tarried at Camp Ford. The occasion furnished a gala-day for all the good people of Smith County, our guards included.

I heard one day a story of lynch-law executed in our camp neighborhood; my informant being a friendly guard, who, like many others, was Union at heart, although conforming outwardly to rebel service, as a volunteer.

During the winter, an old lady, living in Van Zandt County, was plundered by a gang of soldiers in Confederate grey, who beat her shamefully, and (as she told the story,) tied her up by her thumbs till she disclosed the place where was concealed her specie (some three hundred dollars) and about two thousand dollars in Confederate currency. It was asserted that Jayhawkers had done this deed, though sober people shook their heads; well knowing that squads of Sibley's men, with some of Richardson's guerillas, and the scattered miscreants of Quantrell's gang, were ranging through these upper counties. But "black flag" rebels charged the crime, as they would any crime, on Union men—of whom hundreds, former citizens, were fugitives in swamps and timber, hiding from conscript hunters. It was easy to accuse such outlawed wanderers; so the chase became set after "Union men." Four individuals were speedily run down: one Reed, a former sheriff of Collin County; an aged citizen, McReynolds, or McRunnells, who had been chief-justice of that district; and two young men, Holcombe and Davis. They were arrested at their homes and dragged to Tyler.

This was in May, when our prison-numbers, at Camp Ford, had been increased some thousands, after the battle of Mansfield. The rebels were exultant everywhere, but with characteristic cowardice the people of these counties feared an outbreak from so large a body of incarcerated Yankees, and affected to discover insurrectionary plots continually. Three noble-hearted Texans, who refused to bow the knee to Davis, were imprisoned in our guardhouse at Camp Ford—two brothers, Whitmore, one of whom had been a prominent member of the Legislature, and Rosenbaum, a former attorney-general of the state. It was the policy of rank Secessionists to fix as many new crimes on the Union men as could be believed, in order that some pretext might be found for general massacre or the enacting of terror laws.

Hence, when Sheriff Reed and Judge McReynolds

were thrown into prison at Tyler, it was decided that they
should never go at large again. So, one May morning,
fifty mounted "Regulators" clattered into Tyler, halted
at the tavern door, and "liquored round;" held confab
with the provost-marshal, galloped up and down the
town awhile, and finally drew rein before the prison, with
a yell:

"Bring out them Jayhawkers!"

The doors were opened, and the men delivered up. A
rope being slung about them, they were dragged behind
the Lynchers to a piece of timber, scarce half a mile out
of Tyler. There, almost within gun-shot of camps, where
fifteen hundred cavalry and infantry were guarding Federal prisoners, these Lynchers began their mockery of a
trial   The first victim pleaded "not guilty."

"You lie, Jim Reed! You're a heap wuss Jayhawker
than Gineral Banks!"

"Silence in the coort!" cries Justice Lynch, a bull-
headed whiskey-still proprietor. "Keep still, you all, .
while I fix his flint. Prisoner, Jim Reed, what have you
got to say why you oughtn't to be black-jacked?"

REED.—I am not guilty. I've been hunted and perse-
cuted for my sentiments ever since the State seceded. I
never fought against the State. My house was burned
over the heads of my family in the town where I lived,
an honest man, and served the country. I had to fly, by
night, with my wife and seven children, to Van Zandt,
and they hounded me out of that. I declare before
Heaven that—

LYNCH, C. J.—Shet up! You know yer an old scoun-
drel, and yer was three ye'rs in Missouri Penitentiary—

REED—I never was in the State of Missouri.

LYNCH, C. J.—Blast yer, then, yer an old deserter

from General McCulloch's army. The papers was found on ye, and yer can't swar 'em down.

REED.—I deny it. I was regularly commissioned by General McCulloch, as an officer. He gave me a position because I preferred to go back to the army rather than be hunted down. I was preparing to join my command when arrested.

LYNCH, C. J.—Yer a skulkin' liar and a thief, Jim Reed, and we've jest had palaver enough out o' yer. I pronounce judgment of the coort. Yer to be hanged at once, till yer dead, dead, dead! and Lord have marcy on yer soul!

Five minutes after, Sheriff Reed was dangling from an oak-limb above his murderers.

Judge McReynolds was then. dragged forward and reviled by the "coort" in like manner. The old man's son, who was one of the rebel soldiers guarding us at Camp Ford, heard about the Lynchers visiting Tyler jail, and, mounting a horse, galloped from his quarters to the town. He there learned that the ruffians had taken their prisoners to the woods. He followed their trail with all the speed he could command, but arrived in time only to find his father swinging on the tree, from which Reed's dead body had been just cut down. This wretched son was forced to beg the remains of his parent from the assassins; and so great was the terror inspired by the boldness and cruelty of these "Regulators," that young McReynolds was unable to hire a wagon to convey the corpse to Kaufman county, where his family lived.

Young Holcombe—like each of the others—stoutly maintained his innocence, and was hanged with the same noose that had strangled his predecessors; for the ruffians had provided only rope enough to hang a single man, and were obliged to wait until one was dead before proceeding to execute another.

This lack of mechanical means to murder was a fortunate circumstance for one of the accused, young Davis. His fellow-prisoners had been hanged before his face, their bodies laid out, stark and still, before him, and the rope was drawn about his own devoted neck, when some one rode up—a passing traveller on horseback, who happened to be an officer in the rebel service. He spoke a word or two with the "coort," and the "coort" ordered stay of proceedings.

"Thar's been a mistake, I reckon!" quoth Judge Lynch. "That yer young chap is a good soldier, and belongs to this yer officer's rigiment—so the coort clar's him."

The rope was taken from the neck of Davis, and he was allowed to depart with his officer for Camp Ford; while the three other victims were left under the shadow of those "black jacks." The Lynchers rode away, about sunset, over the hill-sides of Smith County, with no compunctions for their crime, no fear of punishment or pursuit.

"How long, how long, O Lord!" whispered a Union Texan in my ear, when we listened to a recital of this story, the day following. "When shall WE have our turn?" He compressed his lips, and a dark look came over his face. "There will be a terrible reaction—a bloody retribution—in this State of Texas some day! WE bide our time!"

But I am drawing to the close of my Camp Ford life. I must soon part from comrades in captivity; and I am rejoiced that with none shall I part in unkindness. The little differences inseparable from gregarious habitation are things of a moment, of trifling importance. The arrows of humorous satire, or the darts of friendly badinage, will never rankle in good hearts or clear minds. We, who have been thrown together by common mischances—who have endured common trials—will remember one another, in the future, with more fraternal emotions than can be awakened by a retrospect of mere neighborly relations. The bond of mutual loyalty—the golden link of patriotism—will be brightened when we shall look back upon Camp Ford, by beams of Friendship, Love, Truth—and that "greatest of all" which is CHARITY.

Yet, though my hopes and heart turn northward, I leave regretfully so many friends behind. I feel warm-hand-clasps, I hear fervent good wishes, from men who a few months ago were strangers. I return the strong grasp of stout Western veterans; of men from the loyal South: of gallant comrades out of every Union State, from Maine to Louisiana. Soldiers and sailors! God bless you all! We may never meet again in this world, face to face; but we are all marching to that yet more glorious Union, in a better world, where the Stars never fade, and where there is neither strife nor captivity!

So, good bye, "Undaunteds!" Farewell, "Fifth Avenue!" Adieu, "Big Mess!" and all kindred of good-fellowships! Good bye, honest genial and manly Major Mann, of Kentucky. Good bye, citizens Haley and Clark—Don Quixote and Sancho! Farewell, all! May you speedily leave Camp Ford as desolate as you found it, and may you follow our foot-prints to the homes where your loved ones await you. God bless you all!

CHAPTER XLIII.

CLOSING DAYS.

With the flush tide of prisoners, from Red River and Arkansas, came back that wandering tribe of Federal soldiers, under Lt.-Col. Leake, to whom we had bidden "God speed," on their paroled march, about the first of April. They had been halted· near Marshal, scarcely half-way between Camp Ford and Shreveport, and had remained there till subsequent Red River misunderstandings broke off arrangements for exchange. Meantime, a few newly-arrived prisoners, taken at the battle of Saline River, in Arkansas, brought us the welcome intelligence that Steel had succeeded in baffling the rebels, and withdrawing, without loss, from Camden.

As the month of April drew to a close, we counted more than three thousand captured men within the corral; and the necessary crowding and exposure, as well as personal neglect among some squads, threatened a heavy sick-list for the summer. About this time, a change of rebel commandants took place; Col. Allen being superseded by Col. Anderson, at Tyler, and the charge of prisoners devolving thereafter on a Lieutenant-Colonel, named Borders.

Another *regime* speedily began to make itself felt. Our new rebel ruler was a bitter secessionist, of the demonstrative sort; and he speedily contrived to become obnoxious to many Federal officers and men. Col. Allen and his lady, with their son, the lieutenant, bade us fare-

well, and we were left to the "tender mercies" of un-
sympathizing strangers; a fact which several soon had
reason to regret. For, whatsoever fault might have been
found with Col. Allen, during his administration, he was
always regarded to be conscientious, and was, moreover,
an educated gentleman. Good Mrs. Allen, his wife, was
an especial favorite, and with sufficient cause; for her
acts of kindness to Federal prisoners were neither "few
nor far between."

All are not foes, even in a land of foes; and we had acknowledged this truth in witnessing the kindly ministrations of good and motherly Mrs. Allen. Few forgot that
Col. Allen was a West Point graduate, and so, undoubtedly, many were disposed to judge him harshly on the
score of his ingratitude. But, though his treason to the
government which fostered him had been a hundred-fold,
there was charity enough in kindly Mrs. Allen to have
covered it with a mantle of forgetfulness. We all respected her; a plain, good matron—really "a mother in Israel" to the sick or sorrowful prisoner, whoever he might
be. At morning, after roll-call, we were sure to spy a
little handmaid of this Lady Bountiful slipping into our
corral, with sundry niceties, wrapped in napkins, for some
invalid; a couple of eggs, a little plat of butter, a few
wheaten slices, or a bit of tempting cake. If one of our
sick craved for tea, or "Lincoln coffee," or a cup of
honey, our good "mother," as she liked to have us call
her, never rested till she could procure the treat. I
doubt not this benevolent woman was an angel at her
husband's side, entreating favors for the "Yankee prisoners." Certainly we traced many a needed privilege or
long-petitioned-for amelioration to the influence of Mrs.
Allen. Who so pleased as she, to hurry over with some
scrap of news, which might impart the hope of "an ex-

change?" Who strove to cheer the more despondent—
jested with the merrier ones, and talked on solemn subjects with the serious? When we gathered near the
"quartermaster's grave," on Sabbath days, to hear our
chaplain preach and pray, the wife of Col. Allen always
came and sat among the prisoners, listening to the Word
with them, and singing to Our Father, who has drawn no
line between his love for North and South. When all
of us lie down in our last camping-ground, and when,
awakened by a celestial reveille, we pass in grand review
of souls before our Infinite Commander, there will be no
roll-call of birth-places. I trust, in that dread hour, the
prayers which this good "mother" offered for the soldiers
of both North and South, will have been answered by the
God to whom she prayed; and that the comrades of our
prison-yards will meet dear Mrs. Allen in a clime where
peace shall be proclaimed to all of us forever.

It was though kind Mrs. Allen that many pleasant
Texan ladies came to visit the corral and chat with our
imprisoned officers; loyal Union dames and maidens
among them, too; as we discovered, from time to time.
And once we were descended upon by the Texan Muse,
in the person of sweet, but rebellious, Miss Mollie Moore,
There are "burning Sapphos" in the South, to be
counted by scores; feminine Tyrtæi, whose harps are
constantly jingled with swords and daggers. It is these
whose martial dithyrambics sound like drum-beats and
bugle-calls on the tympani of young Dixie. It is these
who, like mad Cassandras, dance ever in front of rebel
ranks, chanting their fierce denunciations against northern
foes. Had they the power, I verily believe they would
add to their virgin faces and bosoms the talons of harpies,
merely for the satisfaction of having a chance at the eyes

of "hated Yankees." Not a houri of them but would promise immortal bliss in her arms hereafter to any rag-ged Johnny who dies sweetly and decorously for Dixie! Not a lovely Gorgoness of all but would venture "one eye," at least, on an opportunity to petrify some "polluted invader" with a Medusan grimace.

To our prison-corral, under convoy of Mrs. Allen, came the young poetic lioness, though she did not present her-self with many characteristics of a *lioness*. She did not roar nor enter rampant. Her mane was not blood-red nor fire-red, but I must aver that it had a *soupçon* of—in fact, that it was of the peculiar tint which possessors thereof claim to be golden, but which a censorious world will swear to be of a croceous hue. The poetic nose was *retroussé*, rather—that must be confessed—and the white brow and cheeks had been gilded in numerous small spots by the too fierce kisses of Apollo, in spite of all sun-shades. But our Texan Sappho was neither masculine, leonine, rhinocerine, nor elephantine. She was simply a young, sharp, self-possessed, pale-faced, Jane Eyre sort of a little body, who might be taken for a genteel gover-ness or a Yankee "school-ma'am," according to meridian; whose thin lips could curl with bitterness, and whose pale-blue eyes might kindle to white heat under strong provocation; whose temper would be saint-like with a lover and Hecatic with an enemy.

She sat, with her rebel friends, before my cabin door, while our gallant officers sang songs and played on violin and banjo. She kept time, with dancing toe, while Capt. May good-naturedly treated her to "Dixie," but grew fiery and curled her lip when the artful fellow abruptly turned his bowing into "Yankee Doodle." She ex-changed badinage with the wits of our prison-circle, giv-ing and taking some pretty sharp shafts with unruffled composure. And though she was loud in her expression of rebel enthusiasm, and regretted when our musicians had not the notes to accompany her, that she might sing us the "Black Flag Song," I think, on the whole, that Miss Mollie made a favorable impression, though she broke no Yankee hearts. To be sure, our minstrels were so retaliatory as to strike up the "Star-Spangled Banner" when she turned to leave us, and it is a historical fact that at least fifty stentorian voices roared out the national anthem as a parting salute to the lady. But we separated, nevertheless, the most friendly of enemies, and Miss Mollie Moore intimated that she might some time publish her "impressions" of us. Whether she has done so yet I cannot say; but I live in hopes of turning over, at some future day, the leaves of a handsomely-printed volume of this Texan girl's "poems," in the blue and gold of an appreciative Yankee publisher. May we all live to laugh over the little rebel's "Black Flag!"

I had the distinction of provoking another young poetess to the publication of a brace of lyrics in reply to some verses which were contributed to Mr. Cushing's journal at Houston. I regret that lack of space prevents the insertion of these breathings of the Texan muse; but must be content with a couple of rather conflicting stanzas, both addressed, though on different occasions, to my incarcerated Yankee self. The first extract is as follows:

> "As a prisoner you came: as a freeman remain !
> "Desertion from tyrants can ne'er be a stain;
> "Beneath our bright banner we'll proudly enroll
> "The Northern by birth but the Southern in soul !"

This, to be sure, was a tempting invitation; but, as I could not own the "soft impeachment" of being "Southern in soul" the next poetic salutation that I received was not quite so complimentary. "Let him alone!" said the indignant syren:

> "The tyrant in his pride, and in his creed the puritan,
> " Who prays for peace, and lifts the sword to slay his fellow-man;
> " With "South or Hell" upon his brow combined,
> " Behold that Ephraim's to his idols joined!"
>   "Let him alone!"

But the departure of our friendly Allens left the camp without visitors. And indeed the influx of prisoners had deprived our "Old Borough" of the country-village characteristics which formerly distinguished it. We were now a community of comparative strangers to one another. A thousand Federals—the late captures at Marks' Mills—arrived during May, and, with accessions also from Houston and other points, the population soon swelled to more than forty-three hundred men. The check-rein of rebel authority began to gall us. Col. Borders issued arbitrary orders. One morning we discovered posted on the market-place an order, purporting to be from the Confederate general at Shreveport, which ran as follows.

"Hereafter, any Federal prisoner, being detected in trying to make his escape from the prison—either in the act, or after he has made his escape—will be shot by the one capturing him.
             By order of
                        Lt. Col. J. P. Borders,
B. W. McEachan,   Com'd'g Camp Ford Prison.
     Lt. & Acting Adjutant.

This unwarrantable threat created no little excitement. Other events transpired to make us feverish. A man was shot dead by a guard upon the Sabbath. The poor fellow was walking near the gate, but gave no provocation and received no warning. The brutal rebel shot him with a pistol. An effort was made to attribute this assassination to personal revenge. The murderer was said to have recognized the Federal soldier as one who had formerly guarded a Federal prison and treated him (the rebel) with severity. Few credited this story, however, and the bloody deed was probably a wanton act of cowardly hatred. Several sudden deaths, from exposure and latent physical cause, occurred about this time; and a number of guards were killed or wounded by accidental shooting. A poor soldier of the Maine volunteers fell dead before the door of my "shebang." Our sick were now numerous, and it became absolutely necessary to provide hospital accommodations for their treatment. An order from head-quarters, therefore, permitted parties of the prisoners to volunteer in finishing a building outside of our corral, for the reception of sick and convalescent Federals. This structure was one story high, 48 feet long, and 18 feet wide. Squads of our 19th Kentucky boys began the erection of an additional ward, 36 by 8 feet, and one story in height. The task of completing these hospital quarters was entered upon as a "labor of love" by Capt. Wilcox, of the 3d Missouri Cavalry, who assumed charge of the Medical Department, assisted by Maj. Morris, who had been likewise surgically educated. With Capt. Wilcox was associated Capt. Johnson, of the Sachem gunboat, Capt. Talley, Capt. Rider, Lieut. Steinhover of the 60th Indiana volunteers, and Lieut. James Delemater, of the 91st New York volunteers; the latter acting as a hospital steward. These officers, assisted by squads from the 5th, 6th, and 14th Kansas, and 9th Wisconsin regiments, the 19th Kentucky infantry, and others from various commands, were indefatigable in their exertions to fit up the hospital for their suffering fellow-prisoners. Their generous spirit was stimulated by the wants of our sick, who daily increased in numbers, and whose condition, at this period, is described in a letter, written by the Confederate post-surgeon, a copy of which I obtained through one of the assistants. It is as follows:—

TYLER, TEXAS, June 14th, 1864.

Surgeon J. M. HAYDEN,
  Chf. Med. Bureau, T. M. D.

SIR:—In obedience to orders, I reported to the officer in command of the camp of Federal prisoners at this place (Col. Anderson), who immediately placed me on duty, as surgeon in charge. I at once set about examining the sanitary condition of the stockade, and, although, my mind was prepared by representations to meet with abundant materials for disease, it fell far short of the reality. The enclosed ground is entirely too small for the number of men, (over 4500), and it would be impossible to make them healthy in such a crowded condition. The filth and offal have been deposited in the streets and between the quarters from which arises horrible stench. A great number of the enlisted men have no quarter nor shelter, and have to sleep out on the ground, with not even a blanket to cover them. Some of the sick are thus situated, and I am making preparations to provide for their wants and to make them comfortable. We have a hospital in course of erection, and will need bedding very much. The popular prejudice here is so strong against them that I can get no facilities from the people. I have sent to you for approval the requisition which I would have sent directly to the Medical Purveyor, but I thought your signature would be necessary. I am ready to receive into hospital a few, if we had the articles, and they are not to be had here. No regular register of cases or deaths has been kept, up to a recent period, but I visited the grave-yard and counted 25 graves, a much smaller number than I was led to believe.

The names of those surgeons on duty here who have not passed the board, I will send you in a few days. I have not seen them all, but have carried out your directions with regard to their early appearance, as far as I have been able. Very respectfully,
                     your obt. serv't,
                          F. W. MEAGHER.

The hospital, up to the date of the above letter, had received between thirty-five and forty patients, seven of whom died, and two returned to the stockade. The supply of utensils and medicines was very meagre, of course, but the rooms were airy and the beds kept clean. The hospital rations issued were sugar, bacon or beef, flour, meal, salt, and candles.

CHAPTER XLIV.

"EXCHANGED."

AT length the hopes so long cherished, so often damp- ened, drew near realization. Early in May, a Confede- rate officer arrived at Camp Ford, with orders to enroll the names of prisoners preparatory to an immediate ex- change. Enrolled we duly were; but "immediate ex- change" receded into uncertainty. Still, our confidence increased when, in June, the chaplains taken at Mans- field, together with several citizens, were allowed to set out, with their paroles, on a march without escort to our lines. Genial "Father Robb," of the 48th Ohio, a Bap- tist preacher, who had been my guest during his captivity, and who had labored zealously in his vocation, was one of the chosen. With Rev. Mr. McCulloch, a Presbyterian, brother of a gallant captain of that name, who was like- wise a prisoner, "Father Robb" had awakened much interest in religion among the soldiers; so that prayer- meetings were held nightly and several conversions took place under their ministrations., These gentlemen left us about the first of July, and shortly after we welcomed the return of our mustering officer with instructions to parole the "oldest prisoners."

It was a season of mingled rejoicing and disappoint- ment; of joy to us who numbered ourselves among the "earliest settlers," and of "hope deferred" to more than three thousand still left in prison. But, the brave fellows whom we were to leave shared not a little, after all, in the satisfaction; since our "exchange" would be a guaranty for them that the waters of relief were moving and would, in due season, reach their own feet.

It was immediately after our "celebration" of "Independence Day" that we "old prisoners" received the "glad tidings" of coming liberation. That "Fourth of July" will long be remembered. Hogarth ought to have been superincumbent over the corral, to take a sketch on thumb-nail, of our motley multitude. Description would beggar itself in an effort to compute our rags and tatters fluttering on Texan breezes! Fancy might limp in following the *bizarrerie* of looks, motions, and habiliments which, swaying in a dense crowd, made up the "great unwashed" outline of our "fierce democracie" on this immortal day of Independence. But God bless the gallant hearts! They were all loyal American soldiers, though the tongues of many nationalities betrayed their diverse origin; though the "rich Irish. brogue" and "sweet German accent" mingled with New England's nasal idioms and the broad vernacular of Western Prairie Land. God bless them all! They love the "Old Flag," with their honest souls, and their blood has been shed to defend it.

Under the green canopy of our verandahs, united one with another by interlacing foliage, so that the street before my cabin was completely screened from the sun, we raised our platform, and wound about the neighboring posts some blankets of red, white, and blue. Grouped about the rostrum were representative officers from a hundred regiments, embracing colonels, majors, captains, and lieutenants, hailing from every loyal state and from some rebellious ones; bearing the martial monograms of regiments from Maine to Louisiana; wearing on their frontlets the bugles of infantry, the crossed sabres of ca-

valry, the trumpets of sharp-shooters, the turrets and
shields of engineers, the crossed cannon of artillerymen,
and the flaming shells of our ordnance corps. Interspersed with these were gallant sons of Neptune, with gay
gold bands on caps and coat-sleeves. But, to tell the
truth, ponderous majorities of this loyal audience were
not extremely particular regarding costume, as evinced
by the advent of our orator in his shirt-sleeves and our
poet in a butternut coat which bore strong resemblance
to a gipsey's blanket. Squatted on Texan soil, grouped
by log-house corners, and perched upon tripods, they
stretched to left and right, a goodly block of *sui generis*
American timber. And their "hurrahs" were as lusty,
their "Star Spangled Banner" as sonorous, and their
"God Save America" as impressive—albeit the vocal
thunder set their rags all fluttering—as if they had stood,
in pipe-clayed lines, with glittering muskets at an order,
and the Flag of Stars displaying its brilliant folds above
them.

Once, twice, does rebel jealousy threaten to mar our
"celebration." Hardly have the "Declaration's" noble
truths been flung upon Southern air—scarcely has our
orator commenced his exordium—when a tramp is heard
approaching, and the voice of a Confederate captain roars
out :

"Disperse, Yankees! Get into your quarters! Be off!
Quick! Every man of you!"

A file of rebel guards backs the speaker's authority.
We recognize the officer of the day, and some one attempts
an explanation.

"We had permission from Col. Borders to have this
meeting," says our chairman, Col. Burrell, brave defender
of Galveston wharf, who sits on the platform in bran new

glory of blue coat and shoulder-straps, which have hardly been aired by previous wearing.

" I'll see about that," muttered the rebel, turning away toward the guard-house.

Our boys began to steal back again, and our orator lifted his voice for another effort. But before he could launch the American eagle on her wonted flight into the milky way of eloquence, a rebel sergeant was in the midst of us.

"Into your holes with you!" he yelled, with an oath. "Don't let me order you again!"

Thus adjured, our mass meeting began to disintegrate slowly; the boys dispersing toward their cabins, with lowering looks and wrathful objurgations. They knew their own impotence, and that to resist the insulting authority of their jailers could result in no good, and might afford pretext for a general massacre. Nevertheless, free blood asserted itself in the reluctant step, and the "curses not loud but deep," which accompanied the forced degradation of our retreat.

At this juncture, however, the officer of the day returned. He had communicated with Col. Borders and ascertained that our "Yankee celebration" was "legal," and conducted under high sufferance. So our harmless crowds were graciously permitted to congregate under the verandahs once more, our orator again ascended his rostrum, and the rebel guards fell back to the rear. Opposition only gave spice to our enjoyment, and we cheered our orators, pledged our "regular toasts," (with nothing to drink,) and sang our national songs with renewed ardor.

Short leave-takings; full hearts; hurried hand-shakings; and the "old prisoners" are outside the corral, so long their city of bondage. I mount my horse—a Texan pony, hired for the hundred-mile journey to Shreveport, in consideration of some two hundred dollars of Confederate currency. Then, waving our hands, in parting adieus to comrades left behind, we take up our line of march. A dozen others besides myself have bargained for horse-flesh, and bestride their various nags. The rest move on in slow procession. So, the first day, we count twenty miles of traveling, and a like number the day following. On the third evening we reach Marshal, where we bivouac near a railroad track, and have Yankee music and singing at the camp-fire of rebel Major Smith, who commands our escort. Next morning, resigning my saddle to a foot-sore Kentucky officer, I avail myself, with several comrades, of permission to make the day's journey on a twenty-mile section of railroad. Thereafter, with faces and hearts toward Shreveport and "exchange," we march cheerfully on our last twenty-mile stretch to the Red River.

We halt upon our toilsome march—a line of foot-sore prisoners. We have been upon the road since daybreak, and it is now past noon. But here are clumps of forest, and tracks of beaten mud conducting to a spring. The highway forks before us, from this piece of timber, skirting it, and we see two roads, one trending to a hollow at our right, the other branching up a hill in front. A mule-team and a laden wagon, on which sits an ancient negro, with a poll as white as cotton-wool, appear descending to us. "Watermelons!" shout our "boys;" and, quite forgetful of lame joints, they spring up from the shady roadside, and run forward to the sun-parched highway.

"How much, uncle?" "What d'ye ax a-piece, uncle?" "Give us a couple, Sambo!"

"Fifteen dollar fur dis yer, an' ten dollar fur dat dar,

croons the ancient darkey, who has been sent, probably, by his master, from a neighboring farm, to make a profitable market out of passing Yankee prisoners. He points, to large and small specimens of the emerald fruit, heaped up in rich profusion, but is answered by indignant groans.

"Dry up, old cotton-head!"   "Fifteen grannies!" "What's Confed. money worth?"   "Git off that box, old man!" Then there is a movement forward, and by the flanks, and a reconnoissance in force at the wagon-tail.

"Let' dat alone dar!—I sees ye!" The old negro plunges off his box upon the melon-pile. A yell rises from besieging Yankees, as a nimble drummer-boy grips one of the tempting spheroids, ducks suddenly under the wagon, and presently emerges from the press, followed by half a dozen comrades eager to cut into the prize.

"Gorramity! dar's anudder gwine!" screams Uncle Ned, as a burly fellow, ragged and barefoot, seizes one of the largest specimens within his reach, and swings away with it as leisurely as if it had been bought and paid for. At this juncture, a third melon is suddenly whirled up from the heap and finds its way beyond the ring, scrambled after by a dozen scamps with watering mouths.

"Pass round the 'greenbacks,' boys!" yells a *sans culottes*, whose tatters hang about him in a fringe, like Adam's fig-leaves.

"O! de lor-a-massy! 'top dar' 'top t'ief! Free watermelon done gone, an' nary dollar fur massa! G'lang, ole mules! Git out dis yer place!" And, casting himself over the melon-pile, with his long gorilla arms sprawling out to cover it, the superannuated darkey flings his heels across the box, and kicks his mules to start them; but in vain! Twenty hands have laid hold upon the wagon-wheels and pull them back, while shouts and laughter drown the hapless peddler's lamentations.

"'Free watermelon done gone, an' nary'one dollar fur massa! "G'lang, ole mules! Fo' watermelon done gone, an' nary dollar fur massa! G'lang, ye ole fools! Seben watermelon done gone, an' nary dollar fur massa!"

"I say, Uncle Ned! what'll ye take for the balance?" "Drive on, cotton-head: you're lighter than you was!" "Tell your massa to charge 'em to Gineral Banks."

"Free mo' watermelon done gone, an' nary dollar! Fo' mo' watermelon done gone, and nary dollar fur massa!" The ancient darkey bows his white wool in despair, sprawls over the diminished fruit-heap, belabors his wretched mules with both heels, like a drummer with drumsticks beating the roll-call. All the while he glares, rheumy-eyed, upon laughing tormentors, who snatch melon after melon from under his hands, while their comrades hold back the wagon-wheels, stopping all mule-power.

At length, however, a violent effort of the animals, goaded by drubbing heels, succeeds in starting off the wain, and, with a sudden turn, the half-unloaded vehicle is whirled from out the crowd of Yankees, and goes spinning toward the hollow in a cloud of dust. The prisoners toss a portion of their plunder to the rebel guards, and vent a loud hurrah, which adds new speed to the affrighted mules as they plunge down the hill. But backward come the cracked bewailings of poor Uncle Ned:

"Free watermelon done gone! 'leben watermelon gone! seben watermelon! cl'ar gone! done gone! Nary dollar fur massa! Done gone! cl'ar gone—nary——"

Dust, clamor, lamentations! I laugh as I recall that scene. How ludicrously it reminds one of the rebel government and its predicament. This crazy wagon-load of watermelons is no bad symbol of Confederate commonwealths—their mule-power progress stopped by Yankee strength, while, one by one, the watermelon States are lugged off bodily by force of Yankee arms, and cotton-headed Davis is sprawling vainly over all with impotent bemoaning—

"Free mo' watermelon done gone! Fo' mo' watermelon done gone!—cl'ar gone—an' nary dollar fur massa! Done gone—cl'ar gone!

But eager longing for liberty and "home" outstrips the incidents of travel. Fain would I linger, with pleasant roadside halts at farm-houses; fain recal my gossip with whites and blacks; and my confidential chats with loyal Texan guards—eliciting life-histories during short rides in advance of leg-weary pedestrians. But I must hasten over our three-days sojourn at Shreveport; catered for by honest conscript, "Uncle Jack," trusty purveyor for hungry Yankees; with whom I left my last Texan relic in the shape of goat-skin breeches;—I must pass by head-quarters of Kirby Smith, where hang our "Iron-sides" banners, as trophies on rebel walls: I must leap from the levee, and leave behind my long-kept dress-coat, stolen now from rifled knapsack! But what matters the loss of a uniform! What boots it, though I emerge from rebel toils with but aboriginal costume! Here flows the Red River! At its mouth the Mississippi rolls: beyond is—Liberty!

All of our nine hundred will not see the Promised Land of their loyal love—their heart-weary yearnings. This old soldier from Maine—whom we were wont to make merry with, as a half-crazed seer of spirits—this poor dying MOORE! he has made his last march! his comrades bear his body past my bivouac, as we halt on the shores of Red River. And this pale-faced, patient Lieut. Hugg; who has borne suffering so long and bravely; he will never behold the sun-rise again over pine-woods of his native New Jersey. He will pass away, with gallant Captain Adams, under the Stars and Stripes; but the Crescent City moon will look down upon their coffins.

But the STARS AND STRIPES! the "Father of Waters!" the blue Atlantic! the glorious, undivided, indivisible UNION! with all treasures of home; all wealth of responsive hearts! are not these still for us? We have descended, at last, the murky tide of ochreous waters. Far behind us are the ruined mansions and devastated gardens of Alexandria. Yonder lie Federal gun-boats, watchful at Red River gates, like grim mastiffs. Below them, with her prow turned hitherward, moves a Mississippi steamer. Her colors—streaming aloft—flash in meridian sunlight. "Our Flag is still there!"

Presently, we see the small "messenger-boat" passing and repassing. Our Federal Commissioner of Exchange, Col. DWIGHT, has arrived in the river-steamer, bringing Confederate prisoners to exchange for us. Col. Skuymanski, rebel "Commissioner of Exchange," confers with him.... and the assurance comes, at last, that we are— FREE!

It is thirteen months since I unbuckled my sword; eleven months since I heard from home and the beloved who waits for my coming. But now I stand under the "Old Flag" again! I clasp the hilt of a Federal sabre! and, thank heaven! here—at the mouth of Red River—I lift to my lips a well-remembered seal, and trace, with misty eyes, upon a letter-sheet, the dear word—WIFE!

So, with grateful heart—looking forward to our future— I praise the gracious Providence which holds in keep both nations and individuals; and which is mighty forever to save and succor; whether its mercy be invoked from CABINETS and CONGRESSES, or from CAMPS and PRISONS!

THE TENANT HOUSE;

OR,

EMBERS FROM POVERTY'S HEARTHSTONE.

By A. J. H. DUGANNE.

Beautifully Illustrated with Original Designs.

R. M. DEWITT, PUBLISHER, 13 FRANKFORT STREET.

Great truths in all ages have been most powerfully presented to popular apprehension in the form of allegory, or illustrated fiction. That our readers may see the very high estimation in which the book is held by distinguished divines, we subjoin a few of their encomiums, out of more than a hundred letters received:

OPINIONS OF THE WORK.

I am thankful for a voice so touching and earnest.—*Rev. A. S. Stone, D. D.* ——It interested me, it drew me on, till I have read it through.—*Rev. Orville Dewey, D. D.* ——The book commands my respect and my tribute of thanks to the author.—*Rev. W. S. Alger, D. D.* ——It is gold that has passed through the refiner's fire.—*Rev. A. A. Miner.* ——I should feel no hesitation in commending the book.—*Rev. Baron Stow, D. D.* ——It fastens the attention from beginning to end.—*Rev. Rollin H. Neal, D. D.* ——This book is pure as the poems of Cowper. —*Rev. Joel Parker, D. D.* ——The author has achieved the noble task of giving force and impressiveness to facts.—*Rev. Edward Lathrop, D.D.* ——I cannot doubt that it will prove an attractive book, and have a wide circulation.—*Rev. Asa Smith, D.* ——He who begins the reading of this book will find it difficult to lay it down till he reaches the close.—*Rev. John Dowling, D. D.* ——I gratefully confess that, more than any human production I have recently read, "The Tenant House," has taught "me to feel another's woe."—*Rev. A. D. Gillette, D. D.* ——I have read the "Tenant House" with satisfaction, and have risen from its perusal with warmer sympathies.—*Rev. S. D. Burchard, D. D.* ——If the book were less attractive as a literary production, I should still feel that its author had entitled himself to the thanks of the benevolent for his generous effort in the cause of humanity.—*Rev. Francis L. Hawkes, D. D.* ——I have read with interest the volume entitled the "Tenant House."—*Rev. Thomas De Witt, D. D.* ——It treats with great power and pathos the tragic facts of our modern city life.—*Rev. Samuel Osgood, D. D.* ——I read it (in my way) at one sitting, I admired the style, and sympathized with the object of the book.—*Rev. W. S. Hutton, D. D.* —— Drawn in such lights and shades as to move the heart and hand of Christian sympathy.—*Rev. Edwin T. Hatfield, D. D.* ——Very attractive and much commended for its artistic force and beauty.—*Rev. Ralph Hoyt, D. D.* ——I regard the "Tenant House" as an extraordinary book—a good book—one that was much needed.—*R. M. Hartley, Esq., Sec'y N. Y. Association for Improving the Condition of the Poor.*

A

HISTORY of GOVERNMENTS;

SHOWING THE PROGRESS OF CIVIL SOCIETY, AND THE

STRUCTURE OF ANCIENT AND MODERN STATES.

By A. J. H. DUGANNE.

PUBLISHED BY R. M. DEWITT, 13 FRANKFORT ST.

From District-Attorney A. Oakey Hall.

"Its statements of familiar propositions, and its illustrations of political history make this professedly 'pupil' book, a means of interest to the professional teacher. It should belong to the common school department of every state, and be introduced by legislative sanction. A subject usually forbidding has become in these pages interesting from simplicity of statement, yet accuracy in retention of all the important and philosophical principles of government."

From Judge Edwards.

"I have examined this work with care, and am struck with the plain and simple manner in which are treated the essential elements of history as connected with Government. I cannot but think that it must be an excellent school-book. It will be more than that to me, for it is already to me a 'ready reference' to the more important parts of history."

From Rev. A. D. Gillette, D. D.

"I consider the issue of such a work most timely. We need just the information this book gives. Its compactness and comprehensiveness are amazing."

From Wm. Curtis Noyes, L. L. D.

"I like this book on governments exceedingly. It is full to overflowing of what is most valuable, and what all young persons ought to know. The author's power of compressing, as well as of expression, is remarkable."

THE POETICAL WORKS

OF

A. J. H. DUGANNE.

TINTED PAPER. 400 PAGES. WITH PORTRAIT. $6 00.

FROM A REVIEW IN THE "CRITIC AND LONDON LITERARY JOURNAL."

"A volume calculated to arouse many a noble resolve, to excite many a genial smile, to awaken many a blissful sympathy." "His 'Mission of intellect,' is a poem of sterling power, and full of splendid 'poetry.'" "There are such earnestness, vigor and bravery in this poem, that it reads like a new application of old emotions." "In that delightful ballad, 'The Maiden of the Shield,' with what consummate skill the poet has introduced the necessary, and impressive repose which precedes the shock of conflict,—the beautiful before the terrible!" "In his 'Iron Harp,' we find more variety, more tender and beautiful thoughts. Through the stormy chords of this 'Iron Harp' rings ever and anon the melodious tone of a golden lyre." "The satire entitled 'Parnassus in Pillory,' is remarkable for biting sarcasm, for unlicensed banter, for solemn mockery, for crushing antagonism; now tickling an author to death with a feather, and now braining him with a ponderous battle-axe. Its mischief is so delicious, that one hardly wishes the mischief unperpetrated." "Mr. Duganne's intellect searches the depths of suffering, or explores the mazes of injustice, not from the bare surgical relish of amputating some diseased limb of the commonwealth, but lovingly, yet bravely, to soften the sufferings of his human brethren. May he faint not in his generous task, nor weary in his metrical pilgrimage."

FROM A REVIEW BY O. J. VICTOR, ESQ.

Mr. Duganne is one of the Master Spirits of Minstrelsy, whose song has stirred the great heart of man into a grand enthusiasm for the Right, the Free and the Good. His lyrics long have floated over the great sea of the press—like the argonaut Nautili, bearing beauty and hope and a thought of Heaven on their wings. His more elaborate poems stand as monuments of a mind pervaded by the true sublimity of the noblest masters of song. There is, in these elaborate compositions, a wealth of imagery, a boldness of conception, a presence of high thought, that mark Mr. Duganne for one of the most thoughtful and introspective poets of this country. It is with a grateful sense that we turn from them and their mighty thought to the love ballads and lyrical utterances, which give the volume variety and season it with sweets from which all can sip.

FROM A REVIEW IN THE "NATIONAL INTELLIGENCER."

The volume before us is issued in the highest style of typographical art, forming, in every sense of the term, an edition *de luxe*. As to the merits of the poems themselves, a more competent critic than we of the newspaper can presume to think ourselves has said, in that gravest of American quarterlies, the *North American Review*, that they are gems worthy of the casket in which they are so luxuriously enshrined.

FROM A REVIEW BY W. H. BURLEIGH, ESQ,

In his ready sympathy with the popular heart, and his ability to give voice to its thoughts and inspirations, Duganne finds the principal element of his power, and through them he must command a wide popularity. He is recognised as the "Poet of the People."

THE AUTOGRAPH EDITION.

LIMITED TO 75 COPIES.

WITH ILLUSTRATED TITLE PAGE.

Each Volume Containing an Autograph Poem.

NOW READY.

THE TENANT HOUSE.

NOTICES OF THE PRESS.

The following are quoted from editorial notices of the book, in journals throughout every part of the United States and the Canadas:

In descriptive power and touching pathos, the "Tenant House" is not exceeded by anything ever written by Dickens.—*New Haven Daily Register.*——A highly interesting work.—*Providence (R. I.) Advertiser.*——Of startling and strange interest.—*Boston Herald.*——All true to nature, and forcibly drawn.—*Hartford (Ct.) Courant.*——Well sustained.—*Salem (Mass.) Gazette.*——Pure in style.—*Boston Atlas and Bee.*——Only good in its tendencies.—*Springfield (Mass.) Republican.*——To be read with pleasure and profit.—*Manchester (N. H.) Democrat.*——Of thrilling interest.—*Augusta (Me.) Age.*——A good work for humanity.—*Worcester (Mass.) Palladium.*——All will be sure to read it through.—*Lowell Vox Populi.*——Highly recommended.—*Halifax (N. S.) Morning Sun.* An observing eye and earnest spirit.—*Boston Journal.*——Freshly written.—*Portland (Me.) Transcript.*——An absorbing work. *Wilmington (Del.) Gazette.* Food for thought.—*Pittsburgh Daily Dispatch.*——We can testify to its great power.—*Charleston Southern Baptist.*——Portrayed with a master's skill.—*Guide to Holiness.*——Filled with touching scenes.—*Southern Presbyterian.*——Its moral tone is excellent.—*Alton (Ill.) Daily Chronicle.*——A highly interesting volume.—*Ann Arbor (Mich.) Journal.*——A graphic work.—*St. John (N. B.) Colonial Presbyterian.*——Useful and instructive.—*N. Y. Churchman.*——Intensely interesting.—*Canton (N. Y.) Plain Dealer.*——A spirited and earnest writer.—*Norristown (Pa.) National Defender.*——Of most touching interest.—*Pittsburgh (Pa.) Banner and Advocate.*——A work which goes right to the people.—*Newark (N. J.) Daily Advertiser.*——Of a superb and sympathetic style.—*Louisiana Courier.*——It has won high encomiums.—*Iowa City Reporter.*——In an easy, familiar style.—*Laporte (Ind.) Union.*——A masterly production.—*Moline (Ill.) Independent.*——One extract is sufficient to recommend it.—*Greenville (Ala.) Southern Messenger.*——We confess to an agreeable disappointment.—*Washington (D. C.) National Era.*——Has superior merit as a work of art.—*Jacksonville (Ala.) Journal.*——The strangest experiences in a charmed light.—*Fond du Lac (Wis.) Dem. Press.*——Once begun, it will be read through.—*Zion's Herald.* Picturesque and fervid.—*N. Y. Express.*——The language of a warm heart and a poetic brain.—*N. Y. Dispatch.*——By a true romancist as well as a true poet.— *N. Y. Leader.*——Of an intense and thrilling interest.—*Home Journal.*——Let us say it is in Duganne's best style, and we have said enough.—*N. Y. Sunday Times.*——For depth of interest, it ranks with the "Diary of a London Physician."—*Portland Christian Mirror.*——Calculated to do good.—*American Presbyterian.*——A picture of social life in these habitations.—*Philadelphia Ledger.* ——We heartily recommend the book.—*Baltimore Christian Advocate.*——An instructive and sanctifying book.—*Phil. Evening Journal.*——In power to fix the attention we know not its equal.—*Zion's Advocate.*——Artistical, impressive and interesting.—*Phil. Press.*——A work that should be read by all.—*Lawrence (Mass.) American.*——Deeply thrilling pictures.—*N. Y. Daily News.*——It cannot be read without profit.—*Detroit Daily Advertiser.*——Fascinating in its interest as the fabled serpent's eye.—*Burlington (Vt.) Times.*——Appeals to every Christian and philanthropist.—*Toledo Blade.*——A remarkable book.—*Phil. Gazette.*——Truth, vivid actuality.—*Detroit Free Press.*——Full of stirring interest.—*Old Colony (Mass.) Memorial.*——A book of intense interest.—*Leslie's Illustrated Newspaper.*——In a masterly style.—*Richmond Enquirer.*——Deserves a welcome.—*Oswego Times.*——The author has laid the community under obligations.—*N. Y. Tribune.*——By a master hand.—*Avoostook Pioneer.* ——A masterly pen.—*N. Y. Courier and Enquirer.*—For its beauty of sentiment, and chastity of language, pure as the sunbeams.—*Richmond Christian Advocate.*——No ordinary book.—*Colony Canada Star.*——Enchains the reader's attention.—*Life Illustrated.*

Fine Printing in every Style.

John Polhemus

Estner Marburg Wood

37 PARK ROW,
New York

43 Centre Street, N. Y.

UTTERANCES.

ANTE LUCEM.

By A. J. H. DUGANNE.

This collection of poems, on the vital issues of our present war, is printed in elegant style, octavo pages, gilt edged, and bound in rich cloth. PRICE, $2,00.

FROM THE NEW YORK TRIBUNE.

They are suggested by the great struggle with which the country is now convulsed and in which the writer himself has borne an active and honorable part. Ringing with the trumpet notes of liberty, they will touch a chord in every loyal heart. The volume will be equally welcome to the militant friends of freedom, and to the lovers of robust poetry.

FROM THE N. Y. INDEPENDENT.

The poems here collected are outgrowths of the war—all having a true ring for freedom—all earnest, fiery and graphic. This author's style is crisp, twanging, and martial. His verses fall upon the ear like sounds from a brass band. Meaning what he says, he says it with emphasis. Nor is there wanting here and there a strain of tenderness and sympathy, thrown in with true artistic skill, to heighten the effect of his trumpet-notes.

FROM THE N./Y. WEEKLY.

It is perhaps unnecessary for us to say anything in favor of Mr. Duganne as a poet, inasmuch as our readers are already perfectly familiar with his style—as exhibited in the "Ballads of the Bible," and other poems from his pen, which have long since shrined him in their heart of hearts. Still, we cannot help dropping a word in commendation of these "Utterances." Utterances they are, which, while they add a new lustre to the brilliant wreath which decks the poet's brow, do honor, at the same time, to the head and heart of the uncompromising patriot, the ardent lover of liberty, and the cordial hater of wrong and oppression. Utterances which stir the heart like a bugle blast, and which lead the sons of freedom to register anew their vows, that the black banner of secession shall be humbled in the dust, and that the bright standard of the free shall wave over a united and disenthralled country.

BATTLE BALLADS,

By A. J. H. DUGANNE.

A series of poems in the ballad style, rehearsing principal events of the war for our Union.

Splendidly Illustrated With Engravings.

This volume will contain ballads upon the following subjects:

The Fall of Fort Sumter,	Manassas,
The Uprising of a Nation,	The Second Warning,
The March to the Capitol,	Farragut,
The Battle of Bethel,	Sheridan's Harvesting,
The Death of Ellsworth,	The March of Sherman,
The Battle of Bull Run,	The Sun-burst,
The Muster of Pennsylvania,	The Old Flag of Sumter,
Maryland Redeemed,	The Death of Slavery,
The Old Fight,	&c., &c., &c.

The "Battle Ballads" will be issued in the fall of 1865. The volume containing them will constitute an elegant Gift Book for the Holidays; an appropriate patriotic token to pass from friend to friend. Orders must be sent in before November. Specimen numbers, with headings for Subscriptions, and full particulars, can be obtained by agents who desire to canvass for the work.

www.ingramcontent.com/pod-product-compliance
Lightning Source LLC
Chambersburg PA
CBHW030946110726
47900CB00004B/1152